The recipe.

Classic dishes for the home cook from the world's best chefs.

Josh Emett

Photography Kieran E. Scott

RIZZOLI NEW YORK

New York · Paris · London · Milan

Adam Byatt   Al Brown   Alfred Portale   Alice Waters   Alla
Wolf-Tasker   Andoni Luis Aduriz   Andrew McConnell
Angela Hartnett   Anne-Sophie Pic   Annie Smithers
Ben O'Donoghue   Ben Shewry   Bo Songvisava & Dylan
Jones   Bruce Poole   Bruno Loubet   Calum Franklin   Carl
Koppenhagen   Carme Ruscalleda   Casey McDonald
Chantelle Nicholson   Charles Phan   Charmaine Solomon
Cheong Liew   Chris & Jeff Galvin   Christine Manfield
Clare Smyth   Claudia Roden   Colin Fassnidge   Curtis
Stone   Dan Hong   Daniel Boulud   Daniel Humm   Daniel
Puskas   Danielle Alvarez   Darina Allen   Daryle Brantley
Dave Verheul   David Chang   David Kinch   David Lebovitz
Diane Holuigue   Diane Kochilas   Dominique Ansel
Dorie Greenspan   Elena & Juan Mari Arzak   Eric Ripert
Felicity Cloake   Frank Camorra   Gary Lee   Gary Rhodes
Gennaro Contaldo   George Calombaris   Giancarlo &
Katie Caldesi   Giorgio Locatelli   Gordon Ramsay   Grace
Ramirez   Greg & Lucy Malouf   Guy Grossi   Guy Savoy
Harald Wohlfahrt   Harumi Kurihara   Heinz Beck   Hugh
Fearnley-Whittingstall   Ian Kittichai   Jacques Pépin   Jason
Atherton   Jean Michel Raynaud   Jean-André Charial
Jean-Georges Vongerichten   Joan Nathan   Joanne Chang
José Andrés   José Pizarro   Josean Alija   Julien Royer

Kate McDermott Ken Hom Leah Chase Lennox Hastie
Lidia Bastianich Luke Mangan Luke Nguyen Maggie Beer
Makoto Tokuyama Marc Forgione Marc Vetri Marco
Pierre White Marcus Wareing Mark Bittman Mark
Hix Mark Sargeant Markus Glocker Martha Stewart
Massimo Mele Matt Lambert Matt Moran Michael
Caines Michael Meredith Monica Galetti Monique
Fiso Nancy Silverton Natalia Schamroth Natasha
Sideris Nathan Outlaw Nick Nairn Nieves Barragán
Mohacho Nigel Slater Nobu Matsuhisa Norman Musa
Nuno Mendes Olia Hercules Pascal Aussignac Paul
Ainsworth Peter Gilmore Peter Goossens Peter Gordon
Peter Reinhart Philippa Sibley Pierre Hermé Pierre
Koffmann Poh Ling Yeow Rachel Khoo Ray McVinnie
Reuben Riffel Richard Corrigan Rick Stein Rodney
Dunn Ron Paprocki Ruth Reichl Ruth Rogers Sat Bains
Sean Brock Shannon Bennett Sid Sahrawat Simon
Wright Skye Gyngell Stefano Baiocco Stéphane Reynaud
Stephanie Alexander Sylvia Casares Teage Ezard Tetsuya
Wakuda Tom Aikens Tom Kerridge Tom Kitchin Travis
Lett Trine Hahnemann Tyler Florence Vineet Bhatia
Virgilio Martínez Yannick Alléno Yudhika Sujanani

Contents

Introduction

Growing up on a farm in rural New Zealand taught me the importance of making things from scratch. We had a big walk-in pantry with loads of ingredients, but no ready-to-eat foods; if you wanted something to eat, you had to catch it, pick it, or make it. Hunting, fishing, and eating produce from the garden as a child meant I developed a healthy respect for the origin of my food, and the importance of using the whole animal or ingredient. This early farm-to-table experience encouraged me to think about, and embrace, the entire process of preparing, cooking, and most importantly, enjoying food.

After a career spanning twenty-five years cooking in the USA, UK, Australia, and New Zealand, I wanted to create a food 'bible' to celebrate some of the world's great classic dishes; to share what I have learned working with incredible chefs, creating truly outstanding recipes. What follows here is a manual aimed at helping you, the home cook, recreate the very best version of each dish, perfected for enjoyment, based on your own unique interpretation of the recipe's ingredients and flavourings.

I've selected 314 recipes defined, refined, and cooked by the world's best contemporary chefs and cooks. I have sought to include dishes that could be classified as truly 'classic', as well as modern interpretations of traditional dishes, together with a diverse range of regional classics, covering a wide selection from the exceptional chefs in this volume who have tried, tested, and perfected them. These are the recipes that have stood the test of time, and will continue to do so. Some are beautifully simplistic, while others are complex and creative and will challenge you – but they all have one thing in common – they are timeless. These are the dishes that, I believe, everyone needs to cook and experience at least once in their lifetime.

The book is divided into nine recipe sections: Soups, Staples, Salads & Vegetables, Seafood, Poultry, Meat & Offal, Baking, Desserts & Sweets, and Basics. In the process of re-creating the recipes, I have added an at-a-glance guide to each for complexity, prep time, cook time, and servings. I have also provided additional notes where needed, such as preparation, the key element to perfecting a dish, serving suggestions, or tips; and sometimes the chefs' own comments and tips are also included. The Basics section housed at the back of the book features eighty-four of the most essential stocks, sauces, dressings, condiments, pickles, doughs, pastries, fillings and more that a number of recipes throughout the book call for, and that you will likely need to master at some point in your cooking journey.

There is a comprehensive Reference section that includes detailed conversion charts, a glossary of words and terms, and a summary of all the kitchen equipment used in the book. To simplify the navigation process, there are also two indexes to enable you to search by both ingredient and recipe name, together with a complete list of the chefs who have generously donated their recipes, and details of how you can find out more about them and be inspired to create their dishes.

The Recipe is for anyone who loves to cook, and I hope you will treasure it forever. Let it get dog-eared, dusted with flour, and stained with ingredients and cooking splashes (my first tip is that the cover is laminated with a special wipe-clean finish) but most of all loved, and returned to again and again.

– Josh Emett

Borsch, p. 20

Soups

Often stereotyped as simple, it takes skill to carefully marry ingredients, spices, and herbs to achieve a satiating and flavourful soup. The flavour profiles in a bouillabaisse, wonton soup, or laksa, for example, are complex and refined and can take years of practice. Achieving just the right texture and consistency takes precision and care. In the home kitchen, soup can be a nourishing dish that can easily be stored and reheated the next day, or frozen so there is always a nutritious and nourishing meal just minutes away. The key to mastering soup is seasoning which, together with the right garnish, can elevate a soup from great to greatness.

INGREDIENTS

SOUP

1 medium cucumber, peeled, seeded, and chopped

1 green bell pepper/capsicum, seeded and diced roughly

3 lb (1.4 kg) ripe plum tomatoes

2 cloves garlic, peeled

¼ cup (60 ml) sherry vinegar

½ cup (120 ml) Oloroso sherry

¾ cup (180 ml) Spanish extra virgin olive oil

2 cups (480 ml) water

2 tsp kosher/flaky salt

GARNISH

2 thick (1 in/2½ cm) slices rustic bread

¼ cup (60 ml) Spanish extra virgin olive oil

½ cucumber

12 cherry tomatoes, halved

Maldon salt

Tichi's
Gazpacho

José Andrés

COMPLEXITY: EASY | PREP TIME: 20 MINUTES | COOK TIME: 7 MINUTES | SERVES: 4 TO 6

METHOD

Combine the cucumber, bell pepper/capsicum, tomatoes, garlic, vinegar, sherry, olive oil, and 2 cups (480 ml) of water in a food processor or blender. Purée the ingredients until everything is well blended into a thick orange liquid. Pour the gazpacho through a medium strainer into a pitcher. Refrigerate for at least 30 minutes, or until chilled.

Pre-heat the oven to 400°F (200°C). Cut the bread into 1-in (2½-cm) cubes, place in a mixing bowl and toss with 2 tablespoons (30 ml) of the olive oil. Spread the bread over a baking sheet and bake until golden brown, about 7 minutes. Set the croutons aside to cool.

When you are ready to serve, dice the cucumber for the garnish. Put a few croutons, cherry tomato halves, and diced cucumber in each bowl and pour the gazpacho over them. Drizzle each bowl with the remaining olive oil and sprinkle with Maldon salt.

JOSH'S NOTES

Preparation: Ensure the strainer isn't too fine, or the gazpacho will be watery.

Key element: Use the ripest tomatoes, and in season.

Tip: Seasoning is key, season to taste.

French Onion Soup

David Lebovitz

COMPLEXITY: EASY | PREP TIME: 35 MINUTES | COOK TIME: 3 HOURS | SERVES: 6

INGREDIENTS

4 tbsp (55 g) unsalted butter

2½ lb (1.2 kg) yellow or white onions, peeled and very thinly sliced

1 tsp granulated sugar

2 cloves garlic, peeled and minced

2 tsp sea salt or kosher/flaky salt, plus more if needed

1 tsp freshly ground black pepper, plus more if needed

2 tsp all-purpose/plain flour

¾ cup (180 ml) white wine or sherry

2 qt (2 litres) chicken stock (p. 482)

1 to 2 tsp sherry vinegar or balsamic vinegar, plus more if needed

6 thick slices hearty white bread, or about 18 thick-sliced pieces of baguette, well toasted

1 to 2 cloves garlic, peeled and left whole, for rubbing the toast

3 cups (255 g) grated Emmental, Comté, or Gruyère

JOSH'S NOTES

Key element: Most of the flavour comes from the caramelized onions, so take your time over this step.

METHOD

Melt the butter in a large pot or Dutch oven over a medium heat. Add the onions and sugar and cook for 20 minutes, stirring occasionally, until soft and translucent.

Add the garlic, salt, and pepper and continue to cook for 1 hour 30 minutes, stirring less frequently and lowering the heat to avoid burning as the onions continue to cook down. (You may wish to use a flame diffuser if your cooktop doesn't allow a low enough heat.) As the onions cook, if they brown on the bottom of the pan in places, use a spatula to scrape those appetizing brown bits into the onions because they'll add flavour. The onions are done when they have collapsed into a thick, amber-brown paste.

Stir in the flour and cook, stirring constantly, for 1 minute. Add the wine and use a flat utensil to loosen any remaining brown bits from the bottom and sides of the pan, stirring them into the onions. Add the stock, bring to the boil, then lower the heat and simmer slowly for 45 minutes. Turn off the heat and add the vinegar, tasting it to get the balance right, adding a touch more vinegar, salt, and pepper, if desired.

Pre-heat the oven to 400°F (200°C). Set six ovenproof bowls on a baking sheet lined with parchment paper or tinfoil. Divide the hot soup between the bowls. Rub both sides of the toasted bread with the garlic. Put the toasts on the soup, then sprinkle the tops with the cheese.

Bake the soup on the upper rack of the oven until the cheese is deeply browned, about 20 minutes. Alternatively, if your bowls can withstand the heat, you can set the cheese-topped soups under a hot grill, cooking them until the cheese is melted and starting to brown. Serve immediately.

"Beef stock is thought to be traditional in this soup, but it's heavier, and I rarely have beef stock on hand, so I use chicken stock."

– DAVID LEBOVITZ

Chicken Soup

Joan Nathan

COMPLEXITY: EASY | PREP TIME: 30 MINUTES | COOK TIME: 2 HOURS 30 MINUTES
SERVES: 10

INGREDIENTS

4 qt (4 litres) water

1 large chicken,
preferably stewing or
a large roaster, cut into
about 6 pieces

2 onions, unpeeled

4 parsnips, peeled and
left whole

2 sticks celery

½ cup (30 g) chopped
celery leaves

6 carrots, peeled and
left whole

6 tbsp chopped fresh
flat-leaf parsley

6 tbsp snipped fresh dill

1 tbsp salt

¼ tsp freshly ground
black pepper

matzo balls
(optional, see below)

MATZO BALLS

4 large eggs

2 tbsp (30 ml) chicken
fat or vegetable oil

6 tbsp (90 ml) chicken
stock (p. 482) or water

1 cup (100 g) matzo
meal

1 tbsp grated fresh
ginger

½ tsp grated nutmeg

2 tbsp chopped fresh
dill (or flat-leaf parsley)

2 tsp salt

METHOD

Put the water and chicken in a large pot and bring the water to the boil. Skim off the froth. Add the onions, parsnips, celery and leaves, 4 of the carrots, the parsley, 4 tablespoons of the dill, and the salt and pepper. Cover and simmer for 2 hours 30 minutes, adjusting the seasoning to taste near the end of the cooking time.

Strain the liquid into a bowl. Remove the chicken, discard the vegetables, and refrigerate the liquid until the fat rises to the top and solidifies, at least 2 to 3 hours or preferably overnight. Remove the skin and bones from the chicken and cut the meat into bite-sized chunks. Refrigerate. When the fat on the refrigerated, jellied liquid is solid, remove the fat with a large spoon.

When ready to serve, bring the liquid to the boil in a large pot. Slice the remaining 2 carrots into thin rounds and add to the pot along with several pieces of chicken. Simmer until the carrots are cooked but still firm, about 15 minutes. Serve with the remaining dill and with matzo balls, if desired.

Matzo Balls

COMPLEXITY: EASY | PREP TIME: 10 MINUTES | COOLING TIME: A FEW HOURS
COOK TIME: 20 MINUTES | MAKES: 12 BALLS

Break the eggs into a bowl. Using a fork, stir in the chicken fat, stock, matzo meal, ginger, nutmeg, dill, and 1 teaspoon of the salt, mixing very well. Cover and put into the refrigerator for a few hours or overnight.

Bring a pot of water to a boil and add the remaining salt. While the water is heating, fill another bowl with cold water. Dip your hands into the cold water and form the matzo mix into 12 balls. Drop them into the boiling water, cover, and simmer for about 20 minutes for al dente matzo balls and longer for really soft ones.

Minestrone

Josh Emett

COMPLEXITY: EASY | PREP TIME: 20 MINUTES | COOK TIME: 40 MINUTES | SERVES: 4

INGREDIENTS

5 tsp olive oil

4 cloves garlic, sliced

1 onion, diced

2 carrots, peeled and diced

2 sticks celery, diced

1 zucchini/courgette, diced

½ leek, diced

2 plum tomatoes, diced

14 oz (400 g) can borlotti or cannelloni beans, drained

2 cups plus 1¼ tbsp (500 ml) vegetable or chicken (p. 482) stock

sea salt and freshly ground black pepper

basil pesto, to serve (p. 437)

METHOD

Start with a large pot set over a medium heat. Add the olive oil, then the garlic and onion, and sweat down without colouring until transparent. Add the carrot and celery, and cook until they have softened. Add the zucchini/courgette and leek, and cook for 2 more minutes, then add the tomatoes, beans, and stock. Season with salt and pepper and simmer for 30 minutes until all the flavour has come out of the vegetables.

Taste and adjust the seasoning. Serve with a large spoonful of the basil pesto in the centre.

"Served with fresh, crusty bread, this is a hearty meal in itself."

– JOSH EMETT

JOSH'S NOTES

Key element: Cut the vegetables the same size so that they cook evenly.

Tip: Rice or pasta is classically used in this dish, so substitute the beans if you prefer.

Borsch

Olia Hercules

COMPLEXITY: EASY | PREP TIME: 35 MINUTES | COOK TIME: 1 HOUR 20 MINUTES
SERVES: 6

INGREDIENTS

STOCK

1 organic chicken or cockerel, whole

1 onion, peeled and halved

2 carrots, scrubbed and roughly chopped

2 sticks celery, roughly chopped

½ small celery root/celeriac, peeled and roughly chopped

1 parsley root, peeled and roughly chopped (or a few parsley stalks)

2 bay leaves

JOSH'S NOTES

Preparation: Allow adequate time to cook the chicken and stock.

Key element: Maintain an even, low temperature when slow-poaching the chicken.

Tip: Use a mortar and pestle to combine the pork *lardo* and garlic.

Comment: This is a hearty winter soup; the beets/beetroot brings a lovely sweetness complemented by the fresh dill.

METHOD

To make the stock, put all of the stock ingredients into 5 quarts (5 litres) of cold water in a stockpot, season lightly with salt and bring to the boil. Now lower the heat to its lowest setting and skim the foam off the top of the stock. Cook slowly for about 45 minutes, then check whether the chicken is done by pulling at the leg – it should come off the carcass easily. You can now reserve the stock and the meat and discard the vegetables, or leave the vegetables in if they don't seem too overcooked for you.

Add the potatoes to the stockpot and boil for about 7 minutes before adding the ingredients prepared as below.

Skim off a bit of the chicken fat from the top of the stock with a ladle, and pour it into a large frying pan set over a medium heat. When it sizzles, add the onion and cook over a lowish heat, stirring occasionally, until the onion softens, then add the carrot and cook for another 5 minutes or so. If it becomes too dry, skim more fat off the stock and add it to the frying pan. You are looking to slightly caramelize the onions and carrots, to draw the sugars out – as borsch is all about the perfect sweet, sour, and salty flavour.

Add the beets/beetroot and cook for another 2 minutes, and finally add the chopped tomatoes. Season this with some salt and let it boil off rapidly for a few minutes. Then pour all of this into your stockpot, along with the chopped cabbage, and cook for 3 to 4 minutes. The potatoes should be cooked through, but the beets/beetroot and the cabbage should remain al dente.

Mash the cured pork fat with the garlic and a handful of salt, and stir it through the borsch for the last minute of cooking. Add the flaked chicken, then heat through. Taste the soup – it should be sour, sweet, well-seasoned and have a spicy, garlicky hit.

Serve with dill and some thick crème fraîche if you wish.

SUMMER VARIATION

In the summer, we use fresh, ripe, grated tomatoes and also we would leave out the celery root/celeriac. Sliced sweet red peppers/capsicums would be added along with the beets/beetroot. I love adding a whole bruised chilli at that stage as well, instead of the *lardo* and garlic. In terms of protein, you can use anything – pork or beef ribs or oxtail are fantastic, and so is duck. Just collect some duck carcasses and use them to make the stock. Some regions of Ukraine use fish bones to make the stock and fry small fish to serve in the soup.

_____

"Whatever the country or region, borsch includes beetroot roots or tops, depending on the season. This is a hearty cold-season version. If you can get hold of some fermented vegetable brine (beets, tomatoes, or sauerkraut), add a dash of that in as well."

– OLIA HERCULES

INGREDIENTS CONT.

BORSCH

2 potatoes, peeled and chopped into 1¼-in (3-cm) chunks

1 onion, peeled and finely diced

1 large carrot, scrubbed and roughly grated

2 pink or regular beets/beetroot, peeled and julienned

14 oz (400 g) canned chopped tomatoes

½ small white or savoy cabbage, chopped

1¾ oz (50 g) *salo* or *lardo* (cured pork fat)

2 cloves garlic, peeled and roughly chopped

handful of chopped dill

crème fraîche (optional), to serve

Image on p. 10

INGREDIENTS

SOUP BASE

½ cup (120 ml) olive oil

7 oz (200 g) carrots, peeled and finely sliced

5 oz (150 g) leeks, trimmed and finely sliced

9 oz (250 g) onions, finely sliced

5 cloves garlic, chopped

1 star anise

½ tsp coriander seeds, toasted and crushed

5 cardamom pods, crushed

½ fresh chilli, chopped

zest of ¼ orange

18 oz (500 g) whiting bones, heads, and trimmings

25 oz (700 g) gurnard bones, heads, and trimmings

18 oz (500 g) sea bream bones, heads, and trimmings

21½ oz (600 g) sole or plaice bones

¾ cup plus 4 tsp (200 ml) white wine

14 oz (400 g) can good-quality chopped tomatoes

2 tbsp tomato purée/ paste

1 tsp dried Provençal herbs

salt and black pepper

Sustainable Bouillabaisse with Rouille

Bruno Loubet

COMPLEXITY: MODERATE | PREP TIME: 45 MINUTES | COOK TIME: 2 HOURS | SERVES: 8

METHOD

Start by making the soup base. Pre-heat the oven to 400°F (200°C) fan-bake. Put half the olive oil in a large pan and sweat the carrots, leeks, onions, garlic, star anise, coriander seeds, cardamom, chilli, and orange zest over a medium heat, stirring from time to time to avoid colouration.

Meanwhile, place all the fish bones, heads, and trimmings in a roasting tray with the remaining olive oil and place in the oven for 6 to 8 minutes to set the proteins.

Add the white wine to the vegetables, bring to a vigorous boil and boil for 30 seconds, then add the chopped tomatoes and tomato purée/paste and stir well. Add the cooked fish bones, then cover them with 2 in (5 cm) of cold water. Increase the heat and bring to the boil, then lower the heat and skim the surface. Now you can add the Provençal herbs. Leave to simmer uncovered for an hour, stirring from time to time and making sure you scrape the bottom of the pan, otherwise the vegetables could catch. Check the liquid level in the pan and add more water if necessary. After an hour, the fish bones should be very soft and beginning to break down.

Pass the soup liquid through a colander set over another pan. Using a potato masher, mash the vegetables and bones as much as you can, then pour the cooking liquid back into the first pan. Pass the mixture through a fine sieve or colander, then pass it a second time through a fine sieve, pressing down with a small ladle or large spoon to extract as much liquid as possible.

Put the soup in a clean pan to use as a base for cooking the rest of the dish. Add the fennel and bring the liquid to the boil, then lower the heat and simmer for 10 minutes. Add the leeks, potatoes, and saffron, return to a simmer and cook for another 10 minutes, then lower the heat and leave to simmer gently for another 10 minutes. The soup is now ready to receive the pieces of fish.

About 20 minutes before serving, add the gurnard and leave to simmer slowly for 3 minutes, then add the sea bream, mackerel, mussels, and shrimp/prawns, and leave to simmer for another

3 minutes. Add the diced tomatoes and scatter over the basil leaves, if using. Check the seasoning.

Remove from the heat and serve within the next 10 to 15 minutes, with the rouille sauce and toasted baguette.

TIP

When buying the fish for the soup, ask your fishmonger to fillet it for you and keep all the bones and heads so that you can use them for the soup base. Ask the fishmonger to give you some extra sole or plaice bones.

....

Rouille

COMPLEXITY: EASY | PREP TIME: 20 MINUTES | COOK TIME: 15 MINUTES
MAKES: 1⅓ CUPS PLUS 2 TBSP (350 ML)

Place the potatoes in a large pan, cover with cold water, bring to the boil, and simmer for 12 to 15 minutes or until tender. Drain and mash well with a potato masher.

Soak the saffron in the lemon juice and 2 teaspoons of water, for about 10 minutes.

Place the egg yolks in a medium-sized bowl together with the mustard and whisk well. While whisking continuously, slowly pour in the olive oil in a thin stream. Add the mashed potato, the saffron and its soaking liquid, the harissa, chilli, garlic, and seasoning, and whisk well to combine.

_____

"Overfishing, wastage, and a disregard for seasonality all mean that we are in danger of losing some of our fish species altogether. If you're not already a sustainable fish supporter, I'd urge you, please, to make it your mission to buy conscientiously."

– BRUNO LOUBET

INGREDIENTS CONT.

BOUILLABAISSE

1 bulb fennel, sliced

9 oz (250 g) leeks, sliced

16 new potatoes, peeled and boiled

2 pinches saffron threads

21½ oz (600 g) gurnard, cut into large chunks

18 oz (500 g) sea bream

18 oz (500 g) mackerel fillets

28½ oz (800 g) mussels, cleaned and de-bearded

8 raw shrimp/tiger prawns, peeled but with heads and tails still on

3½ oz (100 g) tomatoes, diced

handful of small basil leaves (optional)

TO SERVE

rouille sauce (see below)

40 slices of baguette, toasted

ROUILLE

3½ oz (100 g) Desiree potatoes, peeled and cut into large chunks

pinch of saffron

1 tbsp (15 ml) lemon juice

2 egg yolks

1 tsp Dijon mustard

½ cup plus 2 tbsp (150 ml) olive oil

1 tsp harissa paste

⅓ red chilli, de-seeded and very finely chopped

4 cloves garlic, very finely chopped

salt and freshly ground black pepper

Chestnut Soup

Alla Wolf-Tasker

COMPLEXITY: EASY | PREP TIME: 45 MINUTES | COOK TIME: 30 MINUTES
SERVES: 3 TO 4

INGREDIENTS

2¼ lb (1 kg) fresh chestnuts

5¼ to 7 tbsp (75 to 100 g) butter

3 shallots, finely chopped

⅓ cup (7 g) porcini powder

1 tbsp (15 ml) balsamic vinegar

2 tbsp (30 ml) dry sherry

2 tbsp (30 ml) cognac

1 qt (1 litre) water

1⅔ cups (400 ml) cream

salt and pepper to taste

1 tbsp fresh black truffle trimmings, evenly chopped

JOSH'S NOTES

Preparation: Peel the chestnuts ahead of time.

Key element: Use chestnuts when they are in peak season – they are easier to peel and fuller in flavour.

Tip: Add a touch more liquid if necessary; this will depend on the size of your pot and how quickly the chestnuts soften.

METHOD

Pre-heat the oven to 325°F (170°C). Cut a cross in the rounded side of the chestnuts. Place them on a baking tray and roast until browned and the skins begin to burst, 7 to 8 minutes. Alternatively, they can be boiled. Remove from the oven, or drain.

When cooled just sufficiently to handle, peel the nuts and also discard the inner skins.

Melt the butter in a pot. Add the shallots and cook, stirring, until soft. Add the chestnuts, increase the heat and cook, stirring, until the chestnuts are golden.

Stir in the porcini powder, vinegar, sherry, and cognac. Continue to cook for a few minutes to drive off the alcohol. Add the water. Add the cream and stir, scraping up any residue from the bottom. Lower the heat and simmer for 20 to 25 minutes, or until the chestnuts are completely soft.

Transfer to a blender and blend the soup to a purée. Return to the pot to reheat to the desired temperature. Preferably do not bring to the boil. Season with salt and pepper as necessary.

Before serving, blitz with an immersion blender to create a more aerated texture if desired. Stir in the fresh truffle just before serving.

Pea & Ham Soup
London Particular

Mark Hix

COMPLEXITY: EASY | PREP TIME: 10 MINUTES, PLUS OVERNIGHT SOAKING
COOK TIME: 3 HOURS | SERVES: 4 TO 6

INGREDIENTS

1 ham hock, soaked overnight in cold water, 21½ oz (600 g)

1¾ tbsp (25 g) butter

1 onion, finely chopped

few sprigs of thyme

9 oz (250 g) green split peas, soaked overnight in cold water or according to packet instructions

freshly ground black pepper

METHOD

Rinse ham hock, place in a large, heavy-based saucepan and cover with cold water. Bring to the boil, then turn heat down and simmer gently for 1 hour 30 minutes to 2 hours, until tender, skimming the top occasionally and topping up with more water if necessary. Remove hock to a plate to cool, then separate out the meat and set aside. Reserve the stock.

Melt butter in a heavy-based saucepan over a medium heat, add onion and cook gently for a few minutes until soft, without allowing it to colour. Add thyme, drained soaked peas, and 6¼ cups (1½ litres) of ham stock. Bring to the boil and skim the surface, then add some black pepper (not salt) and simmer for 1 hour. The peas should be soft and beginning to fall apart; if not, just simmer for a little longer (you may have to top up with more stock or water as necessary). Cooking times can vary, depending on how old the peas are.

Once the peas are cooked, blend about a quarter of the soup in a blender or with a stick blender, as coarsely or as smoothly as you wish, and return it to the pan. Check the seasoning and add a little salt and more pepper if necessary.

Shred some of the cooked ham trimmings, add to the soup and simmer for a few more minutes before serving.

"This thick and warming soup was given its name by Charles Dickens, referring to the fog that once formed a blanket around London: a 'pea-souper'."

– MARK HIX

JOSH'S NOTES

Key element: Ensure the peas are cooked nicely, and aren't crunchy.

Tips: Try variations of blending the peas slightly coarse, or until silky smooth, depending on your preference – it tastes great both ways.

INGREDIENTS

about 1¼ cups
(300 ml) light chicken
stock (p. 482)

pinch of salt

5 peeled Thai shallots
(about 1½ oz/45 g)

6 bird's-eye chillies
(about ¾ oz/20 g)

10 (about ¼ oz/5 g)
mouse shit chillies
(see glossary)

2 stalks lemongrass
(about 1 oz/30 g)

5 lime leaves, torn and
crumpled

3½ oz (100 g) market-
fresh fish, ideally white-
fleshed and not too oily

2 to 3 tbsp (30 to 45 ml)
good-quality fish sauce

pinch of unpolished
sugar

½ cup (10 to 15 g)
picked holy basil

1 small dried
bird's-eye chilli

fresh lime juice to
taste (roughly 2 limes,
depending on the
variety and season)

Hot & Sour Fish Soup
Dtom Yum Pla

Bo Songvisava & Dylan Jones

COMPLEXITY: EASY | PREP TIME: 20 MINUTES | COOK TIME: 20 MINUTES | SERVES: 1

METHOD

Bring the stock to the boil and add the pinch of salt.

Using a stone mortar and pestle, bruise the shallots, chillies, and lemongrass separately. Add the bruised vegetables and lime leaves to the stock and simmer until fragrant, about 10 minutes.

Add the sliced fish and leave to poach gently, seasoning with some fish sauce and the smallest pinch of sugar. When the fish is almost cooked, about 3 to 4 minutes, add the holy basil and remove from the heat. Ladle into a bowl and season with lime juice and dried bird's-eye chilli.

Taste before serving and adjust the seasoning accordingly.
It should be hot, sour, and salty.

JOSH'S NOTES

Key element: Adjust the
seasoning to achieve
the right ratio of sweet,
sour, and salty.

Tip: The recipe calls for
sliced fish, but I have
served it whole here.
Strain the soup if you
prefer a clean broth.

Complements: Great
with deep-fried chilli
as a garnish.

INGREDIENTS

9 oz (250 g) wonton skins

FILLING

9 oz (250 g) peeled uncooked shrimp/ prawns, de-veined and chopped coarsely

9 oz (250 g) ground/ minced pork

1 tsp salt

½ tsp freshly ground white pepper

1½ tbsp (22½ ml) light soy sauce

2 tbsp green onion/ spring onion, finely chopped

1 tbsp (15 ml) Shaoxing rice wine or dry sherry

1 tsp sugar

2 tsp sesame oil

1 egg white, beaten lightly

SOUP

2 pints (1 litre) chicken stock (p. 482)

1 tbsp (15 ml) light soy sauce

1 tsp sesame oil

GARNISH

green onion/spring onion, chopped

Wonton Soup

Ken Hom

COMPLEXITY: MODERATE | PREP TIME: 1 HOUR | COOK TIME: 10 MINUTES
SERVES: 4 TO 6

METHOD

Put shrimp/prawns and pork in a large bowl, add salt and pepper and mix well, either by kneading with your hand or by stirring with a wooden spoon. Add all the other filling ingredients and stir them well into the shrimp/prawn and pork mixture. Cover the bowl with plastic wrap and chill for at least 20 minutes.

When you are ready to stuff the wontons, put 1 tablespoon of filling in the centre of the first wonton skin. Dampen the edges with a little water and bring up the sides of the skin around the filling. Pinch the edges together at the top so that the wonton is sealed; it should look like a small filled bag. Repeat to stuff all the wontons.

When the wontons are ready, put stock, soy sauce, and sesame oil in a large pot and bring to a simmer over a medium heat.

In another large pot, bring lightly salted water to the boil and poach the wontons, in batches if necessary, for 1 minute or until they float to the top. Remove them immediately and transfer them to the pot with the stock. This procedure will result in a cleaner-tasting broth. Continue to simmer the wontons in the stock for 2 minutes. Transfer to either a large soup bowl or individual bowls. Garnish with green onion/spring onion and serve immediately.

JOSH'S NOTES

Preparation: Buy good-quality wonton skins from your local Asian food store.

Momofuku
Ramen

David Chang

COMPLEXITY: EASY | PREP TIME: 15 MINUTES | COOK TIME: 10 MINUTES | SERVES: 1

INGREDIENTS

2 cups (480 ml) ramen broth (see overleaf)

taré (see overleaf), kosher/flaky salt, and/or mirin if needed, to taste

5 to 6 oz (150 to 175 g) fresh ramen noodles (store-bought is fine)

2 to 3 slices pork belly (p. 32)

½ cup (about 125 g) pork shoulder for ramen (p. 33)

2 3-in x 3-in (7½-cm x 7½-cm) sheets nori (cut from larger sheets)

¼ cup (25 g) thinly sliced green onions/ spring onions (greens and whites)

2 thin slices store-bought fish cake

4 or 5 pieces bamboo shoots

¼ cup (about 40 g) seasonal vegetables, such as carrots, onions, and turnips

1 slow-poached egg (optional)

Ingredients continued overleaf

METHOD

First, get everything ready. The broth should be hot, just shy of boiling. Taste it one last time and make any adjustments (*taré* for depth? Salt for roundness? Mirin for sweetness? Water to dilute it?). The large pot of boiling water for the noodles should be well salted. Any meat you are adding should be hot. Nori should be cut into squares, onions and fish cakes sliced, bamboo shoots stewed, seasonal vegetables prepared, eggs cooked. Have a strainer (or colander, something to drain the noodles in), ladle, chopsticks, spoon or measuring cup at the ready. Bonus points for heating up your ramen bowls (which should comfortably hold about 3 cups/ 720 ml) in a low oven. If you're attempting to make more than a few portions at a time, you may want to enlist a helper.

Next, boil the noodles according to the recipe you've used or according to the manufacturer's instructions. Portion them out into your ramen bowls. Top with hot broth.

Dress the soup: Arrange the meat (shoulder and belly) and other garnishes (sliced onion, bamboo shoots, fish cake, vegetables) around the edges of each bowl. Plop the egg, if using, into the middle of the bowl. Finish by tucking a couple of pieces of nori about one-third of the way into one side of the soup, so they lean against the side of the bowl and stand up above the rim. Serve hot.

"Ramen = broth + noodles + meat + toppings and garnishes. It's that simple and that complex, because the variations are endless. Here's how we put together a bowl of our Momofuku ramen. Scale this up – double or triple or more – as desired to feed the number in your crew."

– DAVID CHANG

Continued overleaf

RAMEN BROTH

2 3-in x 6-in (7½ cm x 15-cm) pieces *konbu*

6 qt (6 litres) water

2 cups (about 200 g) dried shiitakes, rinsed

4 lb (1.8 kg) chicken, either a whole bird or legs

5 lb (2.3 kg) meaty pork bones

1 lb (450 g) smoky bacon

1 bunch green onions/ spring onions

1 medium-sized onion, cut in half

2 large carrots, peeled and roughly chopped

taré (p. 31) preferably, or kosher/flaky salt, soy sauce, and mirin, to taste

TARÉ

2 to 3 chicken backs, or the bones and their immediately attendant flesh and skin reserved from butchering

1 chicken

1 cup (240 ml) sake

1 cup (240 ml) mirin

2 cups (480 ml) *usukuchi* (light soy sauce)

freshly ground black pepper

Ingredients continued overleaf

Momofuku Ramen cont.

....

Ramen Broth

COMPLEXITY: EASY | PREP TIME: 20 MINUTES | COOK TIME: 10 HOURS
MAKES: 5 QUARTS (5 LITRES)

Rinse the *konbu* under running water, then place it with the water in an 8-quart (8-litre) stockpot. Bring the water to a simmer over a high heat and turn off the heat. Leave to steep for 10 minutes.

Remove the *konbu* from the pot and add the shiitakes. Turn the heat back up to high and bring the water to the boil, then turn the heat down so that the liquid simmers gently. Simmer uncovered for 30 minutes, until the mushrooms are plumped and rehydrated and have lent the broth their colour and aroma.

Heat the oven to 400°F (200°C).

Remove the mushrooms from the pot with a spider or slotted spoon. Add the chicken to the pot. Keep the liquid at a gentle simmer, with bubbles lazily and occasionally breaking the surface. Skim off and discard any froth, foam, or fat that rises to the surface of the broth while the chicken is simmering, and replenish the water as necessary to keep the chicken covered. After about 1 hour, test the chicken; the meat should pull away from the bones easily. If it doesn't, simmer until that's the case and then remove the chicken from the pot with a spider or slotted spoon.

While the chicken is simmering, put the pork bones on a baking sheet or in a roasting pan and slide them into the oven to brown for an hour; turn them over after about 30 minutes to ensure even browning.

After removing the chicken from the pot, add the roasted bones to the broth, along with the bacon. Adjust the heat as necessary to keep the broth at a steady simmer; skim off the scum and replenish the water as needed. After 45 minutes, fish out the bacon and discard it. Then gently simmer the pork bones for 6 to 7 hours – as much time as your schedule allows. Stop adding water to replenish the pot after hour 5 or so.

Add the green onions/spring onions, onion, and carrots to the pot and simmer for the final 45 minutes.

Remove and discard the spent bones and vegetables. Pass the broth through a strainer lined with cheesecloth. You can use the broth at this point, or, if you're making it in advance and want to save on storage space, you can do what we do: Return it to the pot, and reduce it by half over a high heat, then portion out the concentrated broth into containers. It keeps for a couple of days in the refrigerator and up to a few months in the freezer. When you want to use it, dilute it with an equal measure of water and reheat it on the stove.

In either case, finish the broth by seasoning it to taste with *taré*. Some days the salt of the bacon, or the seaweed, or whatever, comes out more than others. Only your taste buds can guide you as to the right amount of seasoning; start with 2 or 3 tablespoons per quart (litre). Taste it and get it right. I like it so that it's not quite too salty, but almost. Very seasoned. Under-seasoned broth is a crime.

"This makes enough broth for about 10 portions of ramen, more than you'll need for one sitting. But it freezes nicely. Making less seems like a waste of time when you've got a pot on the stove."
– DAVID CHANG

Taré

COMPLEXITY: EASY | PREP TIME: 10 MINUTES | COOK TIME: 2 HOURS
MAKES: ABOUT 2½ CUPS (600 ML)

Pre-heat the oven to 450°F (230°C).

Cut the chicken back into three pieces, split the rib cages in half, and separate thigh from leg bones. (More surface area = more browning area = deeper, better flavour, as long as you don't burn the bones.)

Spread the bones out in a wide (12 to 14 in/30 to 35 cm) ovenproof frying pan and put it in the oven for 45 minutes to 1 hour: Check on the bones after about 40 minutes to make sure they're just browning, not burning. You want deeply browned bones, and you want the fond – the fatty liquid caramelizing on the bottom of the pan – to be very dark but not blackened. (A fleck of black here and there, or at the edges of the pool, is fine, but charred fond is useless; it will only add bitterness and should be discarded.) Watch as the bones colour, and pull them out when they're perfectly browned.

When the bones are browned, remove the pan from the oven and put it on the stovetop. Pour a splash of the sake onto the pan, and put the pan over a burner and turn the heat to medium-high.

Continued overleaf

PORK BELLY

3-lb (1.4-kg) slab
skinless pork belly

¼ cup (60 g) kosher/
flaky salt

¼ cup (50 g) sugar

PORK SHOULDER

3-lb (1.4-kg) piece
boneless pork shoulder

¼ cup (60 g) kosher/
flaky salt

¼ cup (50 g) sugar

Momofuku Ramen cont.

Once the sake starts to bubble, scrape the fond up off the bottom of the pan. Once the fond is free of the bottom of the pan, add the remaining sake, mirin, and soy to the pan and turn the heat under it to high. Bring the liquid to the boil, then lower the heat so that it barely simmers. Cook for 1 hour. It will reduce somewhat, the flavours will meld, and the *taré* will thicken ever so slightly.

Strain the bones out of the *taré* and season the liquid with 5 or 6 turns of black pepper. The *taré* can be used right away or cooled and then stored, covered, in the refrigerator for 3 or 4 days.

―――――――

"The meaning of the term *taré* isn't consistent up and down Japan, but in Tokyo, where I learned about it, it is essentially Japanese barbecue sauce. *Taré* is the main seasoning – the primary 'salt' component – in ramen shops, at least in Tokyo."
– DAVID CHANG

Pork Belly

COMPLEXITY: EASY | PREP TIME: 10 MINUTES | MARINATE TIME: 6 TO 24 HOURS
COOK TIME: 2 HOURS | MAKES: ENOUGH FOR 6 TO 8 BOWLS OF RAMEN

Nestle the belly in a roasting pan or other oven-safe vessel that holds it snugly. Mix together the salt and sugar in a small bowl and rub the mix all over the meat; discard any excess salt-and-sugar mixture. Cover the container with plastic wrap and put it in the fridge for at least 6 hours, but no longer than 24.

Heat the oven to 450°F (230°C).

Discard any liquid that has accumulated in the container. Put the belly in the oven, fat side up, and cook for 1 hour, basting it with the rendered fat at the halfway point, until it's an appetizing golden brown.

Turn the oven temperature down to 250°F (120°C) and cook for another 1 hour to 1 hour 15 minutes, until the belly is tender – it shouldn't be falling apart, but it should have a down-pillow-like yield to a firm finger poke. Remove the pan from the oven and transfer the belly to a plate. Allow the belly to cool slightly.

When it's cool enough to handle, wrap the belly in plastic wrap or tinfoil and put it in the fridge until it's thoroughly chilled and firm, about 3 hours. (You can skip this step if you're pressed for time, but the only way to get neat, nice-looking slices is to chill the belly thoroughly before slicing it.)

Cut the pork belly into slices ½ in (1 cm) thick and about 2 in (5 cm) long. Warm them, for serving, in a pan over a medium heat, just for a minute or two, until they are jiggly soft and heated through. Use at once.

———————

"We get pork belly without the skin. If you can only find skin-on belly, don't fret. If the meat is cold and your knife is sharp, the skin is a cinch to slice off. "

– DAVID CHANG

....

Pork Shoulder

COMPLEXITY: EASY | PREP TIME: 10 MINUTES | MARINATE TIME: 6 TO 24 HOURS
COOK TIME: 6 HOURS 30 MINUTES | MAKES: ABOUT 3 CUPS (720 ML),
ENOUGH FOR ABOUT 6 BOWLS OF RAMEN

Put the pork shoulder in a roasting pan or other oven-safe vessel that holds it snugly. Mix together the salt and sugar in a small bowl and rub the mix all over the meat; discard any excess salt-and-sugar mixture. Cover the container with plastic wrap and put it in the fridge for at least 6 hours, but no longer than 24.

Heat the oven to 250°F (120°C).

Discard any liquid that has accumulated in the container. Put the shoulder in the oven and cook for 6 hours, basting it with the rendered fat and pan juices every hour. Take it out of the oven and let it rest for 30 minutes.

Shred the meat, pulling it into ropy strands using two forks, as you would pulled pork. If you need to hold the pork for a day or so, add some of the rendered fat from the pan to the shredded meat to keep it moist and store it, tightly covered, in the refrigerator.

Reheat it in a low oven (250 or 300°F/120 or 150°C) before using.

———————

"Multiply this recipe as needed. A 10-lb (4.5-kg) shoulder – a whole shoulder, the size we typically cook – takes three times as much seasoning as a 3-lb (1.4-kg) one, but the same amount of time to cook."

– DAVID CHANG

Beef Noodle Soup
Pho Bo

Charles Phan

COMPLEXITY: EASY | PREP TIME: 20 MINUTES | COOK TIME: 1 HOUR | SERVES: 6

INGREDIENTS

1 lb (450 g) beef brisket

3 qt (3 litres) beef stock (p. 484)

fish sauce for seasoning

1 lb (450 g) packet dried wide rice noodles, cooked according to packet directions

12 oz (340 g) beef top round, thinly sliced

1 bunch green onions/ spring onions, trimmed and thinly sliced (about 1 cup/100 g)

GARNISHES

½ cup (about 12½ g) Thai basil sprigs

1 cup (100 g) mung bean sprouts

1 lime, cut into wedges

2 jalapeño chillies, stemmed and thinly sliced into rings

3 tbsp plus 1 tsp (50 ml) Sriracha sauce

3 tbsp plus 1 tsp (50 ml) hoisin sauce

JOSH'S NOTES

Preparation: Prepare the other ingredients while the brisket cooks.

Tip: Find which way the grain goes on the brisket in order to slice it correctly.

METHOD

Place the brisket in a large pot and add the stock. Bring to the boil over a high heat, then lower the heat until the liquid is at a vigorous simmer. Cook the brisket for 30 to 45 minutes, until cooked through. To check for doneness, remove the brisket from the pot to a plate and poke with the tip of a chopstick; the juices should run clear.

Just before the brisket is ready, prepare an ice-water bath. When the brisket is done, remove it from the pot, reserving the cooking liquid, and immediately submerge it in the ice-water bath, which will stop the cooking and give the meat a firmer texture. When the brisket is completely cool, remove from the water, pat dry, and thinly slice against the grain. Set aside.

Return the stock to the boil over a high heat. Taste for seasoning and add fish sauce if needed.

To ready the garnishes, arrange the basil, bean sprouts, lime wedges, and jalapeño on a platter and place on the table. Put the Sriracha and hoisin sauces alongside.

Divide the cooked rice noodles evenly between warmed soup bowls. Top with the brisket slices and then with the raw beef slices, dividing them evenly. Ladle the hot stock over the top, dividing it evenly, and top with the green onions/spring onions. Serve immediately, together with the platter of garnishes.

"In Vietnam, bowls of noodle soup are built from the bowl up – first the noodles, then the meat, with hot stock ladled over at the last minute and garnishes served alongside. This is especially important with pho bo because the beef is added to the bowl raw and the heat from the stock cooks it just enough."

– CHARLES PHAN

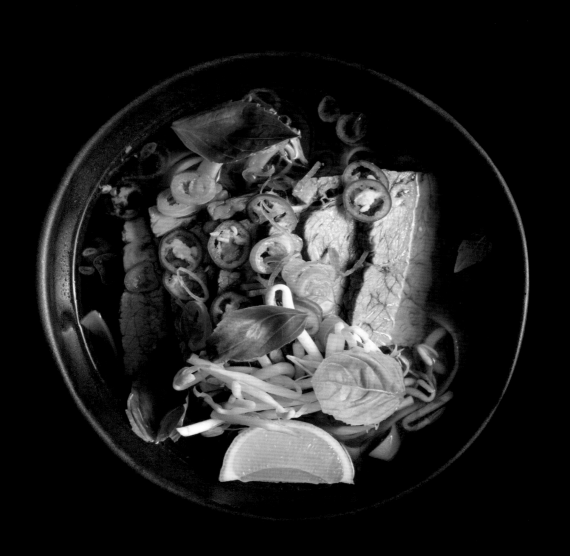

INGREDIENTS

2 tbsp (30 ml) vegetable oil

6¼ cups (1½ litres) chicken stock (p. 482)

18 oz (500 g) boneless, skinless chicken thigh, cut into ¼-in (3-cm) chunks

1 tbsp (15 ml) liquid palm sugar or shaved palm sugar

2 cups plus 1¼ tbsp (500 ml) coconut milk

18 oz (500 g) raw shrimp/ tiger prawns, peeled and de-veined, leaving the tails intact

3½ oz (100 g) fried tofu puffs

juice of ½ lime

LAKSA PASTE

8 dried red chillies, soaked in hot water for 15 minutes, then drained

2 tbsp dried shrimp, soaked in hot water for 15 minutes, then drained

5 red Asian shallots, chopped

4 cloves garlic, chopped

1½-in (4-cm) piece galangal, peeled and chopped

2 stalks lemongrass, white part only, finely diced

¾-in (2-cm) piece turmeric, peeled and chopped

4 candlenuts or cashew nuts

1½ tbsp *mam ruoc* (Vietnamese fermented shrimp paste)

2 tsp ground coriander

1 tsp ground cumin

1 tsp ground chilli powder

3 tbsp (45 ml) groundnut/ peanut oil

Chicken & Prawn Curry Laksa

Luke Nguyen

COMPLEXITY: MODERATE | PREP TIME: 45 MINUTES | COOK TIME: 25 MINUTES | SERVES: 4

METHOD

To make the laksa paste, place all the ingredients except the groundnut/peanut oil in a food processor. Pulse together, gradually adding the groundnut/peanut oil, until a fine paste forms. Set aside.

Heat the vegetable oil in a large saucepan or stockpot over a medium heat, add the laksa paste and sauté for 4 minutes until fragrant. Add the chicken stock and bring to the boil, then add the chicken pieces and palm sugar, reduce the heat and simmer for 5 minutes. Pour in the coconut milk and simmer for another 5 minutes, then add the shrimp/prawns, tofu puffs, and lime juice and cook for a further 5 minutes, until the shrimp/prawns are pink and cooked through.

To serve, divide the noodles between four soup bowls and ladle over the curry broth, dividing the shrimp/prawns, chicken, and tofu pieces evenly. Top with the bean sprouts, cilantro/coriander, fried shallots, and cracked black pepper and serve with lime wedges and sambal *oelek* on the side.

TO SERVE

14 oz (400 g) rice vermicelli noodles, cooked according to packet instructions

5¼ oz (150 g) bean sprouts

4 sprigs cilantro/ coriander

2 tbsp fried red Asian shallots

pinch of cracked black pepper

1 lime, cut into wedges

4 tbsp sambal *oelek* chilli paste, store-bought or made (p. 441)

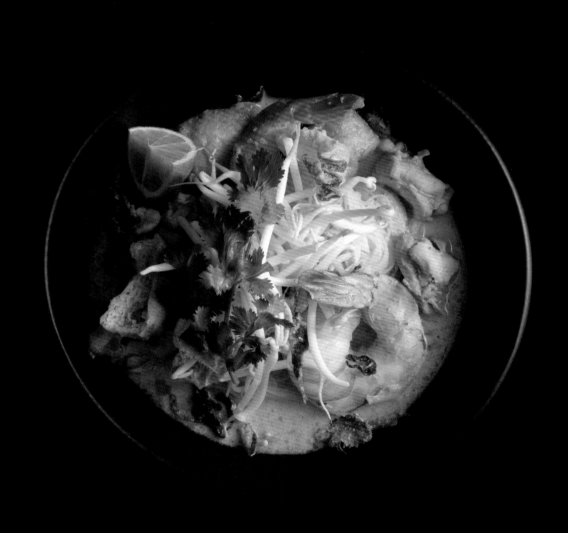

Spaghetti with Peperoncino and Garlic, p. 54

Staples

Pasta, rice, noodles, corn, legumes, and eggs are an integral part of cuisines around the world. And for good reason. They're affordable, easy to cook, nutritious, and filling. Mastering key staple dishes is a great place to start for anyone learning to cook or wanting to experiment with their culinary repertoire. They provide a strong basis for any meal, and their versatility means they can be served as accompaniments to other dishes or as part of a larger menu, as well as being meals in their own right. You'll find yourself returning to them again and again.

Pappardelle with Prawns, Peas & Parmesan

Massimo Mele

COMPLEXITY: EASY | PREP TIME: 15 MINUTES | COOK TIME: 25 MINUTES | SERVES: 4

INGREDIENTS

4 tbsp (60 ml) extra virgin olive oil

1 medium-sized white onion, finely chopped

3 cups (450 g) freshly shucked peas

sea salt and freshly ground black pepper

4 tbsp (55 g) unsalted butter

10½ oz (300 g) peeled and de-veined shrimp/prawns, chopped

18 oz (500 g) fresh homemade pappardelle

1 cup (100 g) freshly grated Parmigiano Reggiano

½ cup (15 g) packed fresh mint leaves, torn in half

JOSH'S NOTES

Preparation: Make your pasta in advance or buy good quality dried pappardelle.

Key element: Ensure the correct amount of pasta cooking water is stirred through the sauce to get the desired consistency.

Tip: Be organized – the elements of the dish all come together at the last minute.

METHOD

In a large frying pan, heat oil over a medium-high heat until it is just smoking. Add onion and 2 cups (300 g) of the peas, and sauté until softened and cooked through, about 10 to 12 minutes. Transfer to a food processor and pulse until coarsely puréed, season generously with salt and pepper and set aside.

Melt butter in the frying pan, add remaining peas and the shrimp/prawns, and cook slowly until just softened, 4 to 5 minutes. Add pea purée to whole peas and set aside.

Bring a large pot of water to the boil and add 2 tablespoons of salt. Add pappardelle, bring back to the boil and simmer until almost cooked.

Just before the pasta is done, pour a ladle of the starchy cooking water into the pan with the pea purée and stir to loosen the sauce. Continue to cook pasta until al dente (tender but still with a slight 'bite'), then drain well, reserving the pasta water. Immediately toss pasta into the pan with the pea mixture and place over a medium heat. Stir gently to mix well, adding a little pasta water to achieve the correct texture, not too dry and not too wet – the noodles should be dressed like the greens of a salad.

Add Parmigiano Reggiano and mint leaves, and toss to combine. Serve immediately.

Spaghetti with Clams
Spaghetti alle Vongole

Danielle Alvarez

COMPLEXITY: EASY I PREP TIME: 15 MINUTES I COOK TIME: 20 MINUTES I SERVES: 2

INGREDIENTS

extra virgin olive oil

6 cloves garlic, finely minced

10 to 12 stems parsley, leaves picked and finely chopped, stalks reserved

12½ oz (350 g) vongole (or other small clam)

¾ cup plus 1¼ tbsp (200 ml) white wine

10½ oz (300 g) dried spaghetti

½ to 1 tsp (to your taste) finely chopped fresh red chilli, or substitute dried chilli flakes

1 lemon

2 tbsp (30 g) butter

JOSH'S NOTES

Preparation: Make sure everything is ready to go. Once you start, everything happens very quickly.

Key element: Add the chopped parsley at the very end to keep it nice and fresh.

Tip: I prefer using diamond shell clams, as they are sweeter.

METHOD

To a large, wide pan (with lid nearby) set over a medium heat, add about 2 tablespoons (30 ml) of extra virgin olive oil and sauté half of the minced garlic for 20 seconds. Add the parsley stalks and quickly drop the vongole into the pan, pour over the white wine, and quickly turn the heat to high and put the lid on. Allow the clams to steam for 1 to 2 minutes.

Take the lid off and remove any of the clams that have opened, leaving the broth in the pan. If any haven't opened, place the lid back on and keep cooking, checking them every couple of seconds (if some don't open at all, discard them).

Once all the clams are out, reduce the heat to medium and taste the liquor that the clams have released. If it still tastes like there is some alcohol remaining in the wine, let it cook out a bit more. It will probably be a bit salty, but that's good. Strain this liquid through a fine sieve and set aside.

Set a large pot of water to boil and season very well with salt. Add your spaghetti and cook until al dente, or just before al dente as I prefer to do.

Return the same wide pan you cooked the clams in to a medium heat and add another 2 tablespoons (30 ml) of extra virgin olive oil. Add the remaining garlic along with the chilli, and sauté until they are soft and fragrant. Add your wine and clam liquor back in (it should be about ⅔ to 1 cup/150 to 200 ml). Let this come to a simmer.

When the pasta is done, lift it out of the water using tongs and drop it straight into the wide pan. Add approximately ¾ cup (180 ml) of pasta water. Toss this together (this is why you want a big, wide pan) for a couple of minutes or until the liquid is almost cooked out and the pasta looks nicely coated. Now add your clams back in, along with 3 to 4 tablespoons of chopped parsley, a couple of microplane scrapings of lemon zest, the juice of half the lemon (maybe a little less if you don't like much acidity), and about 2 tablespoons (20 g) of butter. Toss everything together and taste. Feel free to adjust the salt, lemon juice, or add more butter for a richer taste, whatever you think! Finally, divide between your bowls and serve.

Fideua

Nigel Slater

COMPLEXITY: MODERATE | PREP TIME: 25 MINUTES | COOK TIME: 25 MINUTES | SERVES: 6

INGREDIENTS

1 medium-sized onion

2 squid, cleaned

3 tbsp (45 ml) olive oil

4 cloves garlic

1⅓ lb (600 g) tomatoes

2 level tbsp sweet smoked paprika

generous pinch of saffron (optional)

18 oz (500 g) pasta, such as stortini bucati

1 qt (1 litre) chicken (p. 482) or fish (p. 483) stock

salt

12 large shrimp/prawns, uncooked

9 oz (250 g) clams

12 mussels

JOSH'S NOTES

Preparation: Have everything ready before you start.

Key element: Allow the base to crust over to create the *socarrar*.

Tip: Use a trusted paella or non-stick pan, and ensure you have control over the heat.

Comment: Toasting instead of cooking the pasta gives this dish a delicious nutty flavour.

METHOD

Peel the onion and cut it into small dice. Remove the tentacles from one of the squid and cut the body sac into small dice. Cut the second squid into wide strips, removing the tentacles as you go, and set aside.

Place a shallow paella pan over a medium heat and pour in 2 tablespoons (30 ml) of the olive oil. When the oil is hot, add the diced squid and cook quickly, letting it sizzle and colour lightly on both sides.

Peel the garlic and slice each clove very finely, then add to the pan, still set over a medium heat, together with a little more oil if needed. Chop the tomatoes, fairly finely, add them and all their juice to the pan, and cook, stirring, for 2 minutes. Stir in the paprika, saffron (if using), and pasta.

Let the pasta toast for a minute, then pour on the stock, season with salt, bring to the boil and leave to cook for 8 minutes, or until two-thirds of the liquid has evaporated. At this point do not stir again until a fine crust has formed on the base.

While the pasta cooks, warm the remaining tablespoon (15 ml) of oil in a shallow pan, add the reserved strips of raw squid and the shrimp/prawns, and cook for 2 minutes, until lightly browned. Remove immediately.

Place the clams and mussels, and the squid and shrimp/prawns, over the surface of the pasta, then make a loose dome of kitchen foil over the pan and leave everything to steam for 2 or 3 minutes, till the mussels and clams have opened. Serve immediately.

"Fideua is a Valencian pasta dish cooked in the style of a paella, using tiny macaroni-style pasta instead of rice. The crust that forms on the base of this dish is known by various terms including *socarrar*, to singe – this will only form if you leave the dish alone to get on with things itself. It should stick to the pan, as with paella, firm enough to be scraped off, but caught before it burns. This is not something to cook by the clock, or by the book, but something you get to know by making it over and over again, learning to trust your pan, your ingredients and your skill."

– NIGEL SLATER

Spaghetti with Tomato Sauce & Ricotta Cheese with Herbs

Heinz Beck

COMPLEXITY: EASY | PREP TIME: 15 MINUTES | COOK TIME: 30 MINUTES | SERVES: 4

INGREDIENTS

TOMATO SAUCE

8¾ oz (250 g) cherry tomatoes (I use Ciliegini)

1 tbsp (15 ml) extra virgin olive oil

2 cloves garlic

dried chilli pepper

1 sprig basil, picked

salt

RICOTTA CHEESE WITH HERBS

1 tsp chopped marjoram leaves

1 tsp chopped tarragon leaves

1 tsp chopped basil leaves

1 tsp chopped chervil leaves

3½ oz (100 g) buffalo's milk ricotta

2 tbsp grated Grana Padano

salt

PASTA & GARNISH

10 oz (280 g) spaghetti (I use De Cecco, no. 12)

a few sprigs marjoram

METHOD

Wash the tomatoes. Heat the oil in a frying pan over a medium heat, add the tomatoes, garlic, and chilli pepper, and sauté for 15 minutes before adding the well-washed basil leaves. Remove the garlic and the basil, and pass the sauce through a chinois. Season with salt.

Add the chopped aromatic herbs to the ricotta together with the Grana Padano and mix well. Season with salt.

Cook the spaghetti in plenty of salted boiling water. Drain the pasta a few minutes before the end of cooking, add to the pan of tomato sauce and stir to coat the pasta. Season with salt and chilli pepper, and serve. Decorate the dish with 2 tablespoons of the ricotta cheese with herbs, and some marjoram leaves.

Ragù Bolognese

Gennaro Contaldo

COMPLEXITY: EASY | PREP TIME: 20 MINUTES | COOK TIME: 2 HOURS 30 MINUTES
SERVES: 4

INGREDIENTS

3 tbsp (45 ml) extra
virgin olive oil

2 tbsp (30 g) butter

1 onion, finely chopped

1 stalk celery, finely
chopped

1 carrot, finely chopped

5½ oz (150 g) pancetta,
cubed

7 oz (200 g) ground/
minced beef

7 oz (200 g) ground/
minced pork

¾ cup plus 1¼ tbsp
(200 ml) red wine

1½ tbsp tomato purée/
paste

¾ cup plus 4 tsp
(200 ml) beef stock
(p. 484) – or use a
bouillon/stock cube

6¾ tbsp (100 ml)
full-fat milk

METHOD

Heat the olive oil and butter in a large saucepan, add the onion, celery, carrot, and pancetta, and sweat on a gentle heat for about 10 minutes, until the onion has softened.

Add the meat and brown all over. Increase the heat, add the wine and allow to evaporate. Stir often. Dilute the tomato purée/paste in a little of the stock and stir into the meat. Reduce the heat to low, cover with a lid and cook on a gentle heat for 2 hours, checking and adding a little extra stock from time to time to prevent the sauce from drying out.

About 10 minutes before the end of cooking time, stir in the milk.

Serve with freshly cooked tagliatelle.

FOR A SLOW COOKER

Sweat the vegetables and pancetta and brown the meat as above. Add the wine and allow to evaporate, then dilute the tomato purée/paste in 1⅓ cups plus 2 tablespoons (350 ml) of stock, bring to the boil and transfer to a medium-sized slow-cooker pot. Cover and cook on low for 8 to 9 hours. Stir in the milk and cook for 10 minutes. Serve as above. For a large slow-cooker pot, make double the quantity; cooking times remain the same.

"Although one of the most popular pasta sauces worldwide, the Bolognese is so often made badly outside of Italy: too much tomato, not cooked for long enough, and usually served with spaghetti, hence the term 'spag bol' – unheard of in Italy! Because of all these differences and others, the Bolognese association of the Accademia Italiana della Cucina decided in 1982 to declare an official recipe."

– GENNARO CONTALDO

JOSH'S NOTES

Key element: Make sure the grind of the beef and pork is not too fine.

Tip: The correct size and depth of pan will ensure that the sauce reduces at an optimum rate.

Pappardelle with Rabbit Ragù & Peaches

Marc Vetri

COMPLEXITY: MODERATE | PREP TIME: 35 MINUTES | COOK TIME: 2 HOURS | SERVES: 4

INGREDIENTS

1 rabbit (about 3 lb/ 1.4 kg)

kosher/flaky salt and freshly ground black pepper

3 tbsp (45 ml) grapeseed or canola oil

⅓ cup (40 g) peeled and chopped carrot

⅓ cup (35 g) chopped celery

⅓ cup (55 g) chopped red onion

⅓ cup (80 ml) dry white wine

¾ cup (135 g) cherry tomatoes, halved

8 oz (227 g) egg yolk pasta dough (p. 504), rolled into sheets about ⅛ in (3 mm) thick

¼ cup (60 ml) extra virgin olive oil

3 oz/¾ stick (85 g) unsalted butter

⅓ cup (25 g) grated Parmesan cheese, plus some for garnish

2 ripe peaches, halved, pitted, and thinly sliced

METHOD

Pre-heat the oven to 350°F (175°C).

Rinse the rabbit and remove the innards and excess fat deposits. Reserve the innards for another use. Remove the hind legs and forelegs by driving your knife straight through the hip and shoulder joints. Cut each leg in half through the centre joint. Snip through the breastbone with kitchen shears, and then cut the rabbit crosswise into 6 to 8 pieces. Season the rabbit pieces all over with salt and pepper.

Heat the gapeseed or canola oil in a Dutch oven or casserole over a medium-high heat. When the oil is hot, add the rabbit pieces, in batches if necessary to prevent crowding, and sear them, turning them once, until they are golden brown on both sides, about 5 minutes per side. Transfer the pieces to a platter as they are done.

Add the carrot, celery, and onion to the same pan and cook over a medium heat until the vegetables are lightly browned, about 4 minutes. Pour in the wine and simmer, scraping up any browned bits on the pan bottom, until the liquid evaporates, 2 to 3 minutes. Return the rabbit to the pan along with the tomatoes. Pour in enough water to come three-quarters of the way up the sides of the ingredients. Cover the pan and braise the rabbit in the oven until it is tender and the meat pulls easily away from the bone, 1 to 1½ hours.

Let the rabbit cool slightly in the pan, then shred the meat and discard the skin and bones. Pass the vegetables and braising liquid through a food mill fitted with a medium die, or pulse them briefly in a food processor just until the vegetables are finely chopped but not puréed. Return the ragù to the pan. If it is thin and watery, boil it over a medium heat until it has reduced to a thick consistency similar to that of tomato sauce.

Return the shredded meat to the ragù. Taste it, adding salt and pepper until it tastes good to you. Use it immediately, or transfer it to an airtight container and refrigerate it for up to 3 days or freeze it for up to 2 months. Reheat the ragù before proceeding with the recipe.

Lay a pasta sheet on a lightly floured work surface and trim the edges square. Cut the sheet crosswise into strips a little less than 1 in (2½ cm) wide, preferably with a fluted cutter. Repeat with the second sheet. Dust the strips with flour, cover them and use them within 1 hour or refrigerate them for up to 4 hours. You can also freeze them in a single layer, transfer them to a zip-lock bag, and freeze them for up to 1 month. Take the pasta straight from the freezer to the boiling pasta water.

Bring a large pot of salted water to the boil. Drop in the pappardelle and cover the pot to quickly return the water to the boil. Cook the pasta until it is tender but still a little chewy when bitten, about 2 minutes. Using a spider strainer or tongs, drain the pasta by transferring it to the pan of ragù. Reserve the pasta water.

Add the oil and butter to the pan and cook over a medium-high heat, tossing and stirring vigorously, until the sauce reduces slightly, becomes creamy, and coats the pasta, about 1 minute. Add a little pasta water if necessary to create a creamy sauce. Remove the pan from the heat and stir in the Parmesan. Keep the pasta moving until pasta and sauce become one thing in the pan. Taste it, adding salt and pepper until it tastes good to you. Stir in the peaches.

Dish out the pasta into warmed plates and garnish each serving with some Parmesan.

"When we started making this rabbit ragù, it needed a little pop but adding vinegar or lemon juice wasn't enough. Fruit gave it so much more – acid, sugar, aroma, and something to bite into."

– MARC VETRI

Spaghetti alla Carbonara

Giorgio Locatelli

COMPLEXITY: EASY | PREP TIME: 10 MINUTES | COOK TIME: 15 MINUTES | SERVES: 6

INGREDIENTS

18 oz (500 g) good-quality dried spaghetti

salt as needed

small knob butter

10 slices guanciale or pancetta, chopped into dice, about ½ in (1 cm)

1 tsp black peppercorns, plus extra if wished

5 egg yolks

1 whole egg

5 tbsp grated young pecorino Romano

METHOD

In a large pot, bring plenty of well-salted water to the boil, add spaghetti and start it cooking.

Meanwhile, melt butter in a frying pan over a medium heat, add guanciale or pancetta and fry until golden and crispy, about 8 minutes. Using a slotted spoon, transfer to a warm plate, so that it stays crunchy.

Put black peppercorns in the pan and crush with a meat hammer or the end of a rolling pin, then add a couple of spoons of cooking water from the pasta. Stir it around to lift up all the bits of guanciale or pancetta which may have stuck to the bottom of the pan.

In a large, warm bowl, beat egg yolks and whole egg with 3 tablespoons of grated pecorino Romano until combined. One minute before the spaghetti is ready, start to mix in a ladleful of cooking water at a time until the eggs and cheese become creamy. Drain the pasta, reserving the cooking water, and toss it in the pan of pepper together with the guanciale or pancetta. Add a little more cooking water if the pasta seems too dry, then transfer it to the bowl of eggs and cheese and toss well, until coated in the silky mixture. The heat of the spaghetti will cook the eggs without scrambling them. Add a little extra cracked black pepper, if you like.

Serve with remaining pecorino Romano sprinkled over.

"Spaghetti alla carbonara, as you may know, is a classic dish of Roman cuisine. We stick to the original recipe by using guanciale (cured pork cheek) not bacon, and pecorino Romano – these two ingredients are key to a successful carbonara."

– GIORGIO LOCATELLI

JOSH'S NOTES

Key element: It's worth taking the time to source guanciale if you can get it.

Tip: Work quickly with the pasta once it's drained so that it retains the heat and cooks the egg.

Spaghetti with Olives, Anchovies & Capers
Spaghetti alla Puttanesca

Ray McVinnie

COMPLEXITY: EASY | PREP TIME: 10 MINUTES | COOK TIME: 20 MINUTES | SERVES: 4 TO 6

INGREDIENTS

4 tbsp (60 ml) extra virgin olive oil

4 cloves garlic, finely chopped

¾ cup (130 g) pitted Kalamata olives, halved

8 anchovy fillets, halved

4 tbsp drained capers

large pinch of red pepper/chilli flakes

2 tbsp tomato purée/paste

2 x 14 oz (400 g) cans chopped tomatoes in juice

salt and freshly ground black pepper

16 oz (450 g) spaghetti

METHOD

Heat the oil over a moderate heat in a large frying pan and add the garlic. Let it fry for 10 seconds, then add the olives, anchovies, capers, red pepper/chilli flakes, tomato purée/paste, and tomatoes. Bring to the boil and simmer, stirring frequently, for 15 minutes or until thick and jammy. Taste and season with salt and freshly ground black pepper.

Drop the spaghetti into a very large, well-salted saucepan of boiling water. Stir until it comes back to the boil, and boil until al dente or tender to the bite.

Drain the spaghetti and place in a large, warm serving bowl. Add the tomato mixture and mix well. Serve immediately.

"Everything you need for this is found in the pantry. It is a great pasta dish from the Naples area (also popular in Rome). Sometimes drained canned tuna in oil is added."

– RAY MCVINNIE

JOSH'S NOTES

Key element: Use good quality dried spaghetti, or make your own fresh.

Tip: Adjust the taste to your liking: if you want more chilli or anchovies, for instance, just increase the quantity slightly.

Spaghetti with Peperoncino & Garlic
Spaghetti Aglio Olio e Peperoncino

Angela Hartnett

COMPLEXITY: EASY | PREP TIME: 5 MINUTES | COOK TIME: 10 MINUTES | SERVES: 2

INGREDIENTS

8½ oz (240 g) dried spaghetti

2 to 3 tbsp (30 to 45 ml) olive oil

1 clove garlic, finely sliced

2 peperoncino (dried red chillies), crushed

1 to 2 tbsp chopped fresh flat-leaf parsley

salt and freshly ground black pepper

freshly grated Parmesan to serve

METHOD

Bring a large pan of salted water to the boil. Add the spaghetti and stir as it starts to cook. Boil for 7 to 8 minutes, or according to packet instructions, until the pasta is al dente.

Meanwhile, heat the olive oil in a large, deep frying pan, add the garlic and peperoncino and cook for 30 seconds, until soft, but without colouring. Remove from the heat and set aside.

Drain the cooked spaghetti and toss with the peperoncino and garlic mixture. Stir in the chopped parsley, season to taste and scatter with Parmesan before serving immediately.

_____

"This is a very simple Italian standby dish. It can be quickly put together after a busy day at work because it uses just store-cupboard basics. Beware: the peperoncino can be very spicy."
– ANGELA HARTNETT

JOSH'S NOTES

Key element: Chop the parsley very finely; everything needs to be well prepared for this deliciously simple dish.

Tip: Sweat the garlic *very* gently.

Complements: Although this is great as it is, it also goes very well with shellfish.

Comment: I love this type of purity in cooking, where simplicity reigns.

Image on p. 38

Bavette with Cheese & Pepper
Bavette Cacio e Pepe

Nancy Silverton

COMPLEXITY: EASY | PREP TIME: 5 MINUTES | COOK TIME: 10 MINUTES | SERVES: 4

INGREDIENTS

kosher (flaky) salt

12 oz (340 g) bavette (or linguine fine)

½ cup (120 ml) extra virgin olive oil

1 tbsp plus 1 tsp fresh coarsely ground black pepper, plus more to serve (optional)

¼ cup (25 g) freshly grated Parmigiano Reggiano

¼ cup (25 g) freshly grated pecorino Romano

4 tsp finishing-quality extra virgin olive oil

METHOD

Fill a pasta pot or a large stockpot with 6 quarts (6 litres) of water, add 6 tablespoons (100 g) of salt, and bring the water to the boil over a high heat. If you are not using a pasta pot, put a colander in the sink or have a wire strainer handy to lift the pasta out of the pot. Drop the pasta into the boiling water, stir to prevent the strands from sticking together, partially cover the pot so that the water returns to a boil quickly and continues boiling, and cook until it's al dente, using the time indicated on the package as a guide.

While the pasta is cooking, combine the olive oil, pepper and ½ cup (120 ml) of the pasta cooking water in a large frying pan. About 1 minute before the pasta is done, place this sauce over a high heat. Lift the pasta out of the cooking water, or reserve 1 cup (240 ml) of the water and drain the pasta, and immediately add the pasta to the pan with the sauce. Cook the pasta with the sauce for 2 minutes, stirring with a rubber spatula or tongs to stain the pasta with the sauce, adding some of the reserved pasta water if the pasta is dry and sticky instead of slippery and glistening.

Turn off the heat and let the pasta rest in the pan for 1 minute. (Letting the pasta rest before you add the cheese prevents it from melting and becoming stringy.) Add the grated Parmigiano Reggiano and pecorino Romano, stirring vigorously and shaking the pan until the oil and cheese form a homogenous, emulsified sauce. Drizzle the finishing-quality olive oil over the pasta and stir quickly to combine.

Use tongs to lift the pasta out of the pan and onto the centre of four plates, dividing it evenly, and twirling it as it falls onto the plate to form a tight mound. Spoon any sauce left in the pan over the pasta. Coarsely grind black pepper over the pasta, if desired, and serve.

"This is a very simple Roman pasta dish made with nothing but black pepper and pecorino Romano cheese. The pepper for this dish must be coarsely ground."

– NANCY SILVERTON

INGREDIENTS

GOAT CHEESE RAVIOLI

12 oz (340 g) fresh goat cheese

1 large egg plus 1 egg yolk

coarse salt and freshly ground white pepper

semolina pasta dough (p. 506)

egg wash (1 large egg beaten with 1 tbsp/ 15 ml water)

½ cup (60 g) unbleached flour, to cover work surface

PANCETTA & SHALLOT SAUCE

4 cups (960 ml) white chicken stock (p. 482)

2 tsp olive oil

8 oz (225 g) pancetta, ⅛ in (3 mm) thick, cut into ½-in (1-cm) squares

1 cup (100 g) thinly sliced shallots

coarse salt and freshly ground white pepper

ASSEMBLY

3 tbsp (40 g) herbed garlic butter (p. 437), cut into 3 pieces

3 ripe plum tomatoes, peeled, seeded, and cut into ¼-in (5-mm) dice

2 tsp finely minced fresh chives

4 large basil leaves, cut into chiffonade

Goat Cheese Ravioli in Pancetta & Shallot Sauce

Alfred Portale

COMPLEXITY: MODERATE | PREP TIME: 1 HOUR | COOK TIME: 30 MINUTES | SERVES: 6

METHOD

FOR THE RAVIOLI

In a bowl, beat the goat cheese, egg, and egg yolk until smooth. Season with salt and pepper. Transfer to a pastry bag fitted with a number 5 plain tip.

Roll out a quarter of the dough at a time. Place the pasta dough sheet on a lightly floured work surface. Brush off excess flour from the dough. Cut off any irregularly shaped ends, making a long rectangle, then cut the sheet in half to make two equal-sized rectangles.

About 1 in (2½ cm) from the top of one sheet of dough, pipe out mounds of the filling about 1½ in (4 cm) apart. The mounds should be about ¾ in (2 cm) wide. Pipe out another row of mounds parallel to the first, about 1 in (2½ cm) from the bottom of the dough. Brush the second sheet lightly with the egg wash.

Place the egg-washed sheet, brushed side down, over the piped sheet. Using your fingers, gently press around each mound of cheese filling to seal. Using a fluted pastry wheel, cut out ravioli about 1½ in (4 cm) square, trimming away the excess dough as necessary. Place the ravioli on a semolina-dusted baking sheet. Repeat the procedure with the remaining dough and filling, placing the ravioli on more baking sheets as needed. Refrigerate until ready to use.

FOR THE SAUCE

In a medium-sized saucepan, bring the stock to a boil over a high heat. Cook until the stock has reduced to 3 cups and the flavour concentrates, 10 to 15 minutes.

Heat a large frying pan over a medium-low heat. Add the oil, then the pancetta. Cook, stirring occasionally, until the pancetta begins to release some of its fat, about 3 minutes. Add the shallots and cook, stirring often and without browning, until softened, about 3 minutes. Stir the pancetta mixture into the reduced stock. Season with salt and pepper. Set aside.

TO ASSEMBLE

Bring the pancetta and shallot sauce to the boil over a high heat.
Reduce the temperature to low and whisk in the herbed garlic
butter, one piece at a time. Stir in the diced tomatoes. Keep the
sauce warm.

Meanwhile, bring a large pot of salted water to the boil over a
high heat. Add the prepared ravioli and cook until tender, about
3 minutes. Carefully drain the ravioli in a colander.

Place the ravioli in warmed soup plates. Ladle the sauce over them,
then garnish with the chives and basil.

VARIATION

As a vegetarian option, you can omit the pancetta and shallot sauce
and drizzle the ravioli with extra virgin olive oil and a healthy dash of
freshly ground black pepper. Sprinkle this dish with chives, basil, and
grated Parmigiano Reggiano.

"The ravioli may be prepared up to one day in advance, covered,
and refrigerated. They may also be frozen for up to two months.
Freeze the ravioli on flour- or cornmeal-dusted baking sheets just
until hard, then transfer them to plastic freezer bags."

– ALFRED PORTALE

Mushroom & Prosciutto Vincisgrassi

Giorgio Locatelli

COMPLEXITY: EASY | PREP TIME: 40 MINUTES | COOK TIME: 45 MINUTES | SERVES: 8

INGREDIENTS

1⅔ cups (400 ml) good-quality chicken stock (p. 482)

1 oz (30 g) dried porcini mushrooms

3½ tbsp (50 g) unsalted butter

2 cloves garlic, lightly crushed

5 oz (150 g) sliced prosciutto, chopped

14 oz (400 g) mixed wild mushrooms, sliced

1 glass (¼ cup plus 2 tsp/70 ml) white wine

7 oz (200 g) grated Parmesan

about 20 sheets dried lasagne

BÉCHAMEL

2 qt (2 litres) milk

sea salt and freshly ground black pepper

10 tbsp/1¼ sticks (140 g) unsalted butter

1 cup plus 2 tbsp (140 g) all-purpose/plain flour

JOSH'S NOTES

Preparation: You can make the béchamel in advance, and you can prepare the dish in advance with a bit of pre-planning to bake later.

Key element: To maximize the mushroom flavour, I use a mixture of mushrooms, such as enoki, woodear, shiitake, and field.

METHOD

In a large pan, bring the chicken stock to the boil. Add the dried mushrooms, remove from the heat straight away and leave to infuse for 1 hour.

For the béchamel, place the milk in a pan, bring to the boil over a medium heat, and season with salt and pepper. In a separate pan, melt the butter, whisk in the flour, and cook gently for 3 minutes over a low heat. Gradually whisk the milk into the butter/flour mixture, and continue to whisk over a low heat for 2 minutes, until you have a thick sauce. Remove from the heat and keep warm.

Lift the dried mushrooms from the stock (but retain this) and chop them finely.

Melt the butter in a large pan, add the garlic, prosciutto, and chopped dried mushrooms, and cook, stirring gently, for 2 minutes, taking care not to burn the garlic. Add the sliced mixed mushrooms and cook, stirring gently, for another 3 minutes to release their liquid, then add the white wine and let it bubble up to evaporate the alcohol.

Pour in the reserved chicken stock, bring to the boil, then stir in three-quarters of the béchamel sauce and remove the pan from the heat. Keep the rest of the béchamel to one side.

Pre-heat the oven to 350°F (180°C). Ladle about a quarter of the béchamel, mushroom, and ham mixture over the base of a large ovenproof dish and cover with 4 to 5 pasta sheets, overlapping them a little if necessary so that there are no gaps.

Ladle in another layer of the béchamel mixture, followed by about 2 tablespoons of grated Parmesan and another layer of pasta. Repeat these layers twice more. Finally, ladle in the reserved plain béchamel for the final layer and top with plenty of Parmesan. Bake for 20 to 25 minutes, until golden and crispy on top.

"Vincisgrassi is a family dish from the region of Marche in the centre of Italy [and] is very easy to make."

– GIORGIO LOCATELLI

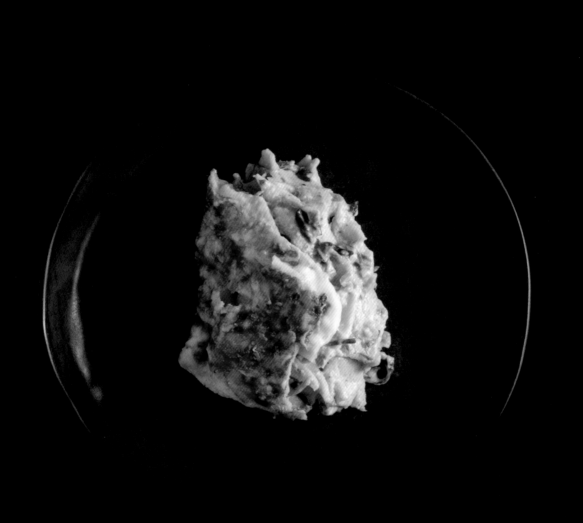

Lasagne

Guy Grossi

COMPLEXITY: MODERATE | PREP TIME: 1 HOUR | COOK TIME: 2 HOURS | SERVES: 6 TO 8

INGREDIENTS

PASTA DOUGH
(MAKES ABOUT 1¾ LB/800 G)

4 oz (115 g) whole eggs

8 oz (225 g) egg yolks

18 oz (500 g) durum
flour

olive oil, for drizzling

BÉCHAMEL SAUCE

1 qt (1 litre) milk

½ small onion

1 bay leaf

1 clove

6 tbsp (80 g) unsalted
butter

½ cup plus 2¼ tbsp
(80 g) all-purpose/plain
flour

salt and white pepper

nutmeg

JOSH'S NOTES

Preparation: Season
each layer to taste as
you go.

Key element: Put as
many layers as you
can in your baking tray.

Tip: Don't make the
béchamel too thick – it
needs to be pourable.

METHOD

LASAGNE SHEETS

Place all the ingredients except the olive oil in a mixing bowl fitted with the dough hook attachment and mix on slow speed until a dough has formed. Wrap in plastic wrap and leave to rest in the fridge for 2 hours before laminating.

Divide the chilled dough into 2 or 3 pieces so that it is easier to work with. Roll out each piece by running it through a pasta machine on the highest setting. Fold the dough and run it through the machine a number of times. This process is called laminating. You need to laminate the pasta until it is silky and smooth. Adjust the setting on the pasta machine down each time until it is about ¹⁄₁₆ in (2 mm) thick.

Cut the pasta into the shape of the tray to be used for baking the lasagne. Place the sheets of pasta onto a floured tray. Bring a pot of salted water to the boil and cook the pasta sheets for 4 minutes. Remove the pasta sheets and refresh in a bowl of cold water. Remove from the cold water, drizzle with olive oil and set aside.

BÉCHAMEL SAUCE

Put the milk, onion, bay leaf, and clove in a pot. Warm over a moderate heat until simmering. Remove from the heat and rest for 15 minutes to allow the flavours to infuse.

Melt the butter in a heavy-based saucepan, then add the flour and stir with a wooden spoon until the mixture forms a smooth paste (roux). Cook, stirring continuously, for 2 to 3 minutes, taking care not to colour the roux. Strain the milk, discarding the solids, and stir the milk into the roux. Bring to the boil, beating vigorously to avoid lumps forming, then reduce the heat, season with salt, white pepper, and nutmeg, and simmer gently for 2 minutes, while stirring. Remove from the heat and cover the surface of the béchamel with a piece of greaseproof paper to prevent a skin forming.

BOLOGNESE SAUCE

Heat the olive oil in a large pot over a medium heat, add the onion and garlic, and sauté for 4 to 5 minutes, until soft and golden. Add all the meat and sauté, stirring continuously, until golden brown. Mix in the herbs and spices and season with salt and black pepper. Add the tomato purée/paste and cook, stirring, for 2 minutes. Pour in the wine and simmer to reduce by half. Add the water and mix well. Bring to the boil, then reduce the heat and simmer gently uncovered for 60 minutes until rich in consistency.

LASAGNE

Pre-heat the oven to 325°F (170°C) fan-bake.

Ladle a small amount of both sauces into an ovenproof tray. Cover with a layer of pasta. Ladle some more Bolognese over the pasta and a ladle of béchamel, and sprinkle with Parmigiano Reggiano. Continue to layer in this way until you reach the top of the tray, finishing with the Bolognese and béchamel and sprinkling of Parmigiano. Bake for 35 minutes.

Serve with a little extra bolognese sauce if necessary, and grated Parmigiano.

INGREDIENTS CONT.

BOLOGNESE SAUCE

6¾ tbsp (100 ml) olive oil

1 large onion, finely chopped

2 cloves garlic, finely chopped

1¾ lb (800 g) ground/ minced beef

3½ oz (100 g) ground/ minced pork

3½ oz (100 g) ground / minced chicken

1 tsp fresh sage, finely chopped

1 tsp chopped chilli

¼ bunch flat-leaf parsley, chopped

1 bay leaf

2 cloves, ground

½ nutmeg, grated

sea salt and freshly ground black pepper

10½ oz (300 g) tomato purée/paste

¾ cup plus 4 tsp (200 ml) red wine

1 qt (1 litre) water

TO ASSEMBLE

9 oz (250 g) Parmigiano Reggiano, grated

INGREDIENTS

3 cups (720 ml) hot chicken stock (see overleaf) or mixed meat stock, or as needed

1 oz (30 g) dried porcini mushrooms

2 lb (900 g) fresh (not smoked) boneless pork butt or shoulder

2 large carrots, peeled and cut into thick slices (about 3 cups)

2 stalks celery, trimmed and cut into thick slices (about 2¼ cups)

1 onion, peeled and quartered

3 sprigs fresh rosemary, leaves removed from the branches

salt

5 tbsp (75 ml) extra virgin olive oil

1 cup (240 ml) dry white wine

4 oz (115 g) mortadella, in one piece

4 cloves garlic, peeled

2 lb (900 g) spinach, stems removed, leaves washed and spun dry in a salad spinner, or two 10-oz (285-g) packets spinach leaves

freshly ground black pepper

béchamel sauce (p. 470)

1¼ cups (125 g) grated Parmigiano Reggiano, plus more for serving if you like

ground nutmeg, preferably freshly grated

2 large eggs, beaten

cooked pasta squares (see overleaf)

Ingredients continued overleaf

Meat & Spinach Cannelloni
Cannelloni Ripieni di Carne e Spinaci

Lidia Bastianich

COMPLEXITY: MODERATE | PREP TIME: 6 HOURS | COOK TIME: 4 HOURS | SERVES: 6

METHOD

Pour the hot stock over the porcini in a small heatproof bowl. Let stand until softened, about 20 minutes. Drain the porcini, reserving the liquid. Rinse the porcini to remove sand and grit, and strain the soaking liquid through a coffee filter or a double thickness of cheesecloth. Reserve the mushrooms and liquid separately.

Pre-heat the oven to 400°F (200°C). Cut the pork into 2-in (5-cm) pieces and place them in a roasting pan large enough to hold them comfortably. Add the carrot, celery, onion, rosemary leaves, and the reserved porcini. Season lightly with salt, drizzle 3 tablespoons (45 ml) of the olive oil over all, and toss well. Pour in the wine. Roast until the wine has evaporated and the meat begins to brown, about 25 minutes.

Continue roasting, adding a handful of the reserved mushroom-soaking liquid every 15 minutes or so, until the meat and vegetables are well browned and the meat is tender, about 2 hours. At the end of the roasting, there should be about 1½ cups (360 ml) of liquid in the roasting pan. Drain the meat and vegetables, reserving the liquid. Toss the mortadella in with the meats and vegetables and cool to room temperature.

Meanwhile, in a wide frying pan, heat the remaining 2 tablespoons (30 ml) oil over a medium heat. Whack the garlic with the flat side of a knife, add it to the oil, and cook until lightly browned, about 2 minutes. Add as much spinach as will fit comfortably into the pan. Continue cooking, stirring and adding the remaining spinach, a large handful at a time, until all the spinach is added. Season lightly with salt and pepper and cook until all the spinach is wilted and tender. Remove from the heat.

Make the béchamel sauce, p. 470.

Pass the meat-and-vegetable mixture through a meat grinder fitted with a disc with holes about ¼ in (5 mm) in diameter. Stir in ¼ cup (25 g) of the grated cheese and ½ cup (120 ml) of the béchamel sauce, blending the filling well as you do. Season to taste with salt, pepper, and nutmeg. Beat the eggs until foamy, then stir them into the ground-meat mixture.

Continued overleaf

INGREDIENTS CONT.

CHICKEN STOCK

3 lb (1.4 kg) chicken and/or capon wings, backs, necks, and giblets (not including the liver)

1 lb (450 g) turkey wings

5 qt (5 litres) water

1 large onion (about ½ lb/225 g), cut in half

3 medium-sized carrots, trimmed, peeled, and cut into 3-in (7½-cm) lengths

2 large ripe tomatoes, quartered, or 1 tbsp tomato purée/paste

8 cloves garlic, unpeeled

10 sprigs fresh Italian parsley

12 black peppercorns

salt

COOKED PASTA SQUARES

fresh egg yolk pasta dough (p. 504)

salt

2 tbsp (30 ml) olive oil

JOSH'S NOTES

Preparation: Allow a few hours to cook the pork.

Key element: Squeeze the spinach dry once cooked so it doesn't release too much moisture.

Tip: If you don't have a meat grinder, chop by hand or pulse in a food processor.

Meat & Spinach Cannelloni cont.

Preheat the oven to 375°F (190°C). Ladle about ¾ cup (180 ml) of the béchamel sauce in an even layer over the bottom of each of two 13 x 9 in (33 x 23 cm) baking dishes. Spoon ⅓ cup (about 80 g) of the filling in a more or less even mound along one edge of one of the pasta squares. Roll up into a tube, pressing and evening out the tube as you roll. Arrange the cannelloni into the prepared baking dish, side by side and seam side down. Divide the remaining béchamel evenly between the two baking dishes, smoothing it into an even layer over the cannelloni. Drizzle about three-quarters of the reserved meat-cooking liquid over the cannelloni, dividing it evenly. Sprinkle the tops with 1 cup (100 g) of the grated cheese.

Cover the dishes with tinfoil and bake for 20 minutes. Uncover the baking dishes and continue baking until the tops are golden brown and bubbling, about 20 minutes. If the tops are browning unevenly, rotate the baking dishes from side to side and shelf to shelf, then continue baking.

Let stand 5 minutes before serving. Lift the cannelloni to warm plates with a spatula, and spoon some of the sauce over each serving. Pass round additional grated cheese if you like.

"I always roast meats by adding some liquid to the roasting pan first, then allowing it to cook away and the meat to brown. The aromatic steam penetrates the meat before the surface of the meat is seared by the heat."

– LIDIA BASTIANICH

Chicken Stock

COMPLEXITY: EASY | PREP TIME: 20 MINUTES | COOK TIME: 4 HOURS
MAKES: ABOUT 4 QUARTS (4 LITRES)

Rinse the poultry pieces in a colander under cold running water and drain them well. Place them in an 8- to 10-quart (8- to 10-litre) stockpot. Pour in the cold water and bring to the boil over a high heat. Boil for a minute or two and you will see foam rising to the surface. Skim off and discard the foam, lower the heat to a strong simmer, and cook for 1 hour, occasionally skimming the foam and fat from the surface.

Add the remaining ingredients except the salt to the pot. Bring to the boil, then adjust the heat to simmering. Cook, partially covered, for 2 to 3 hours, skimming the foam and fat from the surface occasionally.

Strain the broth through a very fine sieve, or a colander lined with a double thickness of cheesecloth or a clean kitchen towel. Season lightly with salt. To use the stock right away, wait a minute or two and spoon off the fat that rises to the surface. The last little traces of fat can be 'swept' off the surface with a folded piece of paper towel. It is much easier, however, to remove the fat from chilled stock — the fat will rise to the top and solidify, where it can be easily removed.

VARIATION: MIXED MEAT STOCK

For a rich meat stock, simply substitute 3 lb (1.4 kg) meaty veal and beef bones — like beef shin, veal shank bones, and/or short ribs — for 2 lb (900 g) of the chicken/capon bones and all the turkey bones. Continue as described above.

....

Cooked Pasta Squares

COMPLEXITY: MODERATE | PREP TIME: 25 MINUTES | COOK TIME: 2 TO 3 MINUTES
MAKES: 18 TO 24 SQUARES LARGE ENOUGH FOR CANNELLONI)

Prepare the pasta dough and let it rest for at least 1 hour.

To form the pasta squares by machine, cut the dough into six equal pieces and roll them out, following the directions on p. 504, to strips 6 in (15 cm) wide and approximately 24 in (60 cm) long. Cut each strip crosswise into four 6-in (15-cm) squares.

To form the pasta by hand, cut the rested dough into four equal pieces. Following the directions on p. 504, roll each piece out to a rectangle approximately 18 x 12 in (45 x 30 cm). Cut each rectangle lengthwise into two strips 6 in (15 cm) wide, and cut each strip crosswise into three 6-in (15-cm) squares.

Bring 6 quarts (6 litres) of salted water and the olive oil to the boil in an 8-quart (8-litre) pot set over a high heat. Set a large bowl of iced water next to the stove. Stir about half the pasta squares into the boiling water. Return to the boil, stirring gently. Cook the pasta, semi-covered, stirring occasionally, until the pasta squares float to the top, 1 to 2 minutes.

Remove the pasta squares with a wire skimmer and transfer them to the iced water. Let them stand until completely chilled. Repeat the cooking and cooling with the remaining pasta squares. When the cooked squares are chilled, remove them from the ice bath and stack them on a baking sheet, separating the layers with clean, damp kitchen towels.

INGREDIENTS

1-lb (450-g) chunk butternut squash/pumpkin (about half a medium-sized squash/pumpkin)

1 tbsp (15 ml) extra virgin olive oil

2 medium-sized russet potatoes (about 12 oz/340 g)

¼ cup (25 g) freshly grated Grana Padano

1 large egg

1 tsp kosher/flaky salt

¼ tsp freshly grated nutmeg

1½ cups (210 g) all-purpose/plain flour, plus more as needed

butter and sage sauce (p. 464)

JOSH'S NOTES

Preparation: Roast the squash/pumpkin ahead of time to allow it to cool. Take time making the gnocchi.

Key element: Don't overwork the dough, and season well to begin with.

Tip: Make sure all the elements are ready before beginning the butter and sage sauce.

Butternut Squash Gnocchi
Gnocchi di Zucca

Lidia Bastianich

COMPLEXITY: MODERATE | PREP TIME: 1 HOUR, PLUS DRAINING TIME OVERNIGHT
COOK TIME: 1 HOUR | SERVES: 4 TO 6

METHOD

Pre-heat the oven to 400°F (200°C). Scoop the seeds from the squash/pumpkin, and place the squash/pumpkin in a baking pan, cut side up. Drizzle with the olive oil. Bake until tender throughout, about 45 minutes to 1 hour. Let cool slightly. When it is cool enough to handle, scrape the flesh from the squash/pumpkin, set in a cheesecloth, and let hang or set in a strainer in the refrigerator overnight to drain. You should have about ¾ cup (150 g) of squash/pumpkin.

Cook the potatoes in a medium-sized saucepan with water to cover until tender, 20 to 25 minutes. Drain, let cool until you can peel them, then peel and press through a ricer into an even layer on a shallow baking tray. Let cool completely. You should have 2 cups (450 g) of potatoes. Pass the drained squash/pumpkin through the ricer as well.

In a large bowl, place the squash/pumpkin, potatoes, grated cheese, egg, salt, and nutmeg, and mix until smooth. Sprinkle in 1¼ cups (175 g) the flour and mix to combine. Dump the dough onto your work surface and knead until it comes together. If the dough is still sticky, add the remaining ¼ cup (35 g) flour, and knead just until smooth. Do not over-knead the dough: It will require more flour, and the gnocchi will be heavier.

When you are ready to make the gnocchi, bring a large pot of salted water to the boil. Divide the dough into eight equal pieces. Line two large rimmed baking sheets with baking paper and sprinkle the paper lightly with flour. Working with one dough piece at a time, roll the dough out on a floured surface to a rope about ½ in (1 cm) thick. Cut the rope crosswise into ¾-in (2-cm) pieces. Working with one piece at a time, roll the gnocchi along the back of fork tines dipped in flour, making ridges on one side and a dimple on the other. Transfer the gnocchi to the floured baking sheets. Repeat with the remaining dough.

Cook the gnocchi in two batches in the boiling water, giving them just a couple of minutes more after they all float to the surface. Remove with a spider, and transfer to the waiting sauce.

Serve with butter and sage sauce.

Layered Lamb Breyani

Yudhika Sujanani

COMPLEXITY: MODERATE | PREP TIME: 45 MINUTES | COOK TIME: 3 HOURS | SERVES: 4 TO 6

INGREDIENTS

18 oz (500 g) basmati rice

4 medium-sized potatoes

8⅔ tbsp (130 ml) sunflower oil, plus extra for frying

3 onions

1 large stick cinnamon

2 bay leaves

4 cardamom pods

1 tsp cumin seeds

1½ tsp coarse salt

1 tbsp crushed garlic

4 tsp crushed ginger

2 tbsp red chilli powder

2⅔ lb (1.2 kg) lamb knuckles

2 tsp ground coriander

2 tsp ground cumin

1½ tsp garam masala

½ tsp turmeric powder

boiling water as needed

6¾ tbsp (100 ml) fresh cream

2 x 14 oz (400 g) cans brown lentils, drained

4¼ tbsp (60 g) unsalted butter, chopped

few drops of egg-yellow food colouring

fresh cilantro/coriander, to garnish

METHOD

For the rice: Cook in rapidly boiling water with salt and ⅔ tablespoon (10 ml) sunflower oil. Use a fork to gently stir the rice, separating the grains. Cook for half the time stipulated on the packaging instructions. Test the rice by pressing a grain between your fingertips – it should be slightly hard in the centre. Pour rice into a strainer and pour a cup of cold water over to stop the cooking process and to rinse off the excess starch. Leave to cool completely.

Peel the potatoes and slice into thick rounds. Heat 4 tablespoons (60 ml) sunflower oil in a pan and fry until tender, about 20 minutes. Remove from the oil and leave to drain. Gently remove excess oil with a paper towel.

Finely slice two of the onions, and finely chop the third, keeping them separate. In the same oil, fry the onion slices until light golden brown. Remove and spread over an absorbent paper towel.

Heat 4 tablespoons (60 ml) sunflower oil over a medium heat in a large thick bottomed pot with a tight-fitting lid. Fry the cinnamon stick and bay leaves for a few minutes until fragrant. Add the cardamom pods and cumin seeds. When the cumin seeds start to sizzle, add the chopped onion and salt. Sauté, stirring, until the onion is light golden brown, about 15 minutes.

Add crushed garlic and ginger. Stir for a few seconds then add the chilli powder. Stir well and add the lamb knuckles. Mix the knuckles in the chilli paste and continue stirring until the meat begins to stick. Lower the heat, and scrape the bottom of the pot with a wooden spoon. Add the ground coriander, cumin, garam masala and turmeric, and continue stirring. When the spices start to brown, pour in boiling water to cover the knuckles. Simmer uncovered on a low heat, adding more water if necessary until the knuckles are tender and the sauce has reduced, about 1 to 1½ hours.

Layer the fried potatoes over the lamb. Pour in the fresh cream, layering half the lentils over the potatoes. Layer the half-cooked rice over the lentils and scatter the remaining lentils on top. Dot the rice with butter. Pour ¾ cup plus 1¼ tablespoons (200 ml) of boiling water into the pot and scatter a few drops of egg-yellow food colouring over the rice. Sprinkle the fried onion slices over the rice and cover the pot with a tight fitting lid. Simmer the breyani on the lowest heat setting until the rice has steamed through and puffed up. Gently toss the breyani, and garnish with fresh cilantro/coriander before serving.

Risotto with Pecorino, Olive Oil & Balsamic Vinegar

Risotto con Pecorino, Olio e Aceto Balsamico

Gennaro Contaldo

COMPLEXITY: EASY | PREP TIME: 10 MINUTES | COOK TIME: 25 MINUTES | SERVES: 4

INGREDIENTS

6¼ cups (1½ litres) vegetable stock

4 tbsp (60 ml) extra virgin olive oil

½ small onion, very finely chopped

12⅓ oz (350 g) Arborio rice

3 tbsp plus 1 tsp (50 ml) white wine

2¾ oz (80 g) pecorino, freshly grated, plus extra to serve

balsamic vinegar, for drizzling

METHOD

Put the stock in a saucepan and bring to a gentle simmer. Leave over a low heat.

Heat 2 tablespoons (30 ml) of the olive oil in a medium-sized saucepan, add the onion and sweat until soft. Add the rice and stir until all the grains are coated with oil, then add the white wine and keep stirring until it evaporates. Add a couple of ladlefuls of the stock and cook, stirring all the time, until it has been absorbed. Repeat with more stock. Continue adding the stock in this way until the rice is cooked al dente, which usually takes about 20 minutes. Check for seasoning and adjust if necessary.

Remove from the heat, and beat in the pecorino and the remaining olive oil with a wooden spoon. Leave to rest for a minute, then divide between four plates. Drizzle with some balsamic vinegar, sprinkle with some more pecorino, and serve.

———————

"A plain risotto with some butter or olive oil and cheese is great comfort food as well as being quick to make. I made this risotto when I had nothing in the house but a chunk of Sardinian pecorino cheese, some risotto rice, and extra virgin olive oil."

– GENNARO CONTALDO

JOSH'S NOTES

Key element: Cook the rice so it is just done (al dente).

Tip: Add the stock slowly, and use a good aged balsamic.

Comment: The pecorino adds a nice sharpness, and the balsamic finishes it off beautifully.

Risotto with Saffron
Risotto con Zafferano

Giancarlo & Katie Caldesi

COMPLEXITY: EASY | PREP TIME: 15 MINUTES | COOK TIME: 30 MINUTES | SERVES: 6

INGREDIENTS

5½ to 6¼ cups (1.3 to 1½ litres) beef (p. 484), chicken (p. 482), or vegetable stock

pinch of good-quality saffron

3 tbsp (45 ml) olive oil

4½ oz (120 g) shallots or red onion, finely chopped

2 cloves garlic, finely chopped

14 oz (400 g) risotto rice (Arborio or Carnaroli)

¾ cup plus 1¼ tbsp (200 ml) white wine

good pinch of salt and freshly ground black pepper

7 tbsp (100 g) unsalted butter

1¾ oz (50 g) freshly grated Parmesan

JOSH'S NOTES

Key elements: Good-quality saffron and stock, and toasting the rice.

Complements: This is traditionally served with osso bucco, but is also excellent on its own.

Tip: The key to any risotto is the right liquid ratio. Add more stock at the end if necessary.

METHOD

Pour the stock into a large saucepan and place over a medium heat. When hot, measure 3 tablespoons (45 ml) into a small bowl, add the saffron and set aside to infuse (if not using saffron, omit this step).

Heat the olive oil in another large pan over a medium heat. When hot, add the onion and garlic and fry, stirring, for 7 to 10 minutes, until softened but not coloured. Add the rice and 'toast' it for a few minutes so that it absorbs the flavours of the other ingredients and starts to become translucent. Keep stirring with a large wooden spoon so that it doesn't burn.

When the rice is toasted, stir in the wine and allow it to evaporate for a few minutes while continuing to stir.

Add the saffron-infused stock, if using, and stir in. Add a ladleful of hot stock. Hold the pan with one hand and stir the rice with a folding action, as if making a cake. As the rice cooks, this stirring will break down the outer shell of the rice grains and create a creamy risotto. Make sure you scrape any rice grains on the sides of the pan down into the risotto, or you will have the odd hard, uncooked grain in your finished risotto.

When most of the stock has been absorbed, you will see a crescent-moon shape appearing at the bottom of the pan as you stir; this indicates that you need to add more hot stock, a ladleful at a time.

Repeat this process until you think the rice is done. It will take between 20 and 25 minutes; you may or may not need to add all the stock. When the rice grains have only a hint of crunch in the centre, it is time to stop adding stock.

Remove from the heat, add butter and Parmesan and stir well. Season with salt and pepper. Cover the pan for no more than 3 minutes while you prepare warmed bowls. Serve straight away.

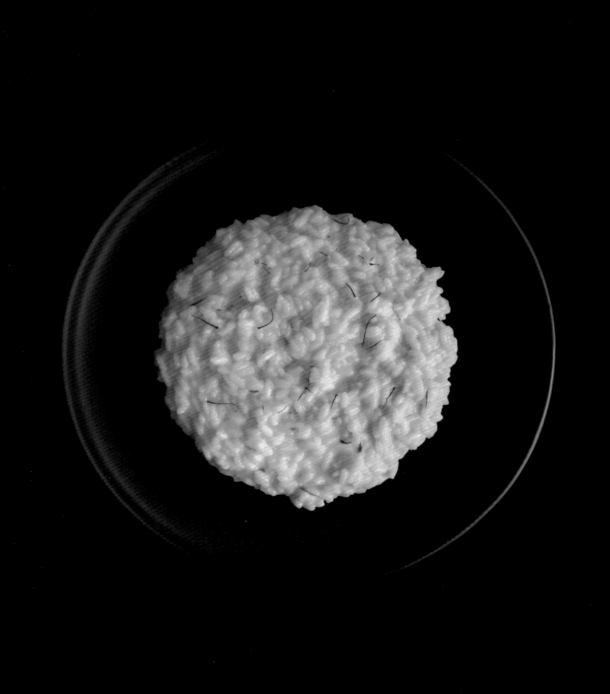

Squid Ink Risotto
Risotto Nero

Ruth Rogers

COMPLEXITY: EASY | PREP TIME: 10 MINUTES | COOK TIME: 25 MINUTES | SERVES: 6

INGREDIENTS

1 qt (1 litre) fish stock (p. 483)

sea salt and freshly ground black pepper

2⅔ oz / ⅔ stick (75 g) butter

4 cloves garlic, peeled and finely chopped

10½ oz (300 g) risotto rice

½ cup (120 ml) white wine

3 sachets (3 tbsp) squid or cuttlefish ink

2 tbsp flat-leaf parsley, finely chopped

METHOD

Heat the fish stock, and check for seasoning.

Melt the butter in a saucepan, add the garlic and fry for 1 minute. Add the rice and continue to cook gently, stirring, for a further minute. Pour in the white wine and cook until it has been absorbed by the rice. Add a ladle of hot fish stock, stirring continually until it too has been absorbed. Continue to add more fish stock until the rice is al dente, then add the squid ink. When there is only one ladle of stock left, turn off the heat and add this remaining stock. Stir in the parsley and season with salt and pepper.

VARIATION

Add about 1 lb (450 g) small squid, hand size. Clean and cut the body sacs into thin tagliatelle-type strips, and separate the tentacles. Heat 1 tablespoon (15 ml) olive oil until very hot, throw in the squid pieces and stir-fry for no more than 30 seconds. Remove and season. Make the risotto as above, using an extra clove of garlic. Add the squid to the risotto as you stir in the squid ink.

Fried Rice with Crab

Andrew McConnell

COMPLEXITY: EASY | PREP TIME: 15 MINUTES | COOK TIME: 25 MINUTES | SERVES: 2

INGREDIENTS

1 cup (200 g) short-grain Japanese rice, rinsed and drained

2 tbsp (30 ml) grapeseed oil

2 green onions/spring onions, thinly sliced into rings

½ clove garlic, finely chopped

1 egg plus 1 egg white, lightly beaten together

2 tsp light soy sauce

1 tbsp picked mustard greens, finely chopped

pinch of superfine/caster sugar

5¼ to 7 oz (150 to 200 g) picked, cooked spanner crab meat

pinch of toasted sesame seeds

few drops sesame oil

pinch of ground white pepper

METHOD

Place the rice in a stainless steel saucepan and cover with 1½ cups (360 ml) of cold water. Bring to a simmer over a medium-high heat, stirring occasionally, then reduce the heat to low, cover the saucepan, and cook until just tender, 10 to 12 minutes. Turn the heat off under the saucepan, remove the lid and cover the pot with a tea towel. Let the rice stand for 5 minutes before spreading it out over a tray to cool. At this stage the rice should be cooked and loose. If it seems gluey and wet, discard and start again.

Heat the oil in a large wok or non-stick frying pan over a medium-high heat. Add the green onion/spring onion and garlic, stirring and cooking until the garlic is fragrant. Add the egg mix and swirl it around the pan as if making a crêpe. Working quickly, scatter the cooled rice over the egg and mix with a wooden spoon, breaking up the egg as you do so. Add the soy sauce, mustard greens, and sugar. Stir the rice continuously until it's coated with soy sauce and egg.

Gently toss the crab through the rice just before serving, and finish with a pinch of sesame seeds, a few drops of sesame oil, and some white pepper.

———————

"I like to serve this with a small bowl of XO Sauce [p. 443] on the side."

– ANDREW MCCONNELL

JOSH'S NOTES

Preparation: Source good-quality crab meat; it makes all the difference.

Key element: Ensure the rice grains are separated and loose after cooking.

Tip: Check the seasoning before serving.

Hainanese Chicken Rice

Poh Ling Yeow

COMPLEXITY: MODERATE | PREP TIME: 45 MINUTES | COOK TIME: 2 HOURS 30 MINUTES
SERVES: 2 TO 4

INGREDIENTS

CHICKEN

3⅓ lb (1½ kg) whole chicken

1 clove garlic, crushed

1¼ in (3 cm) piece ginger, sliced and crushed

5 green onions/spring onions, knotted together

2 tbsp (30 ml) Shaoxing rice wine

2 tbsp (30 ml) light soy sauce

1 tsp sesame oil

1 tsp salt

RUB

1 tbsp (15 ml) light soy sauce

3 tsp sesame oil

RICE

2 tbsp (30 ml) vegetable oil or groundnut/peanut oil

2 cloves garlic, peeled and finely chopped

2 slices ginger, ¼ in (5 mm) thick, crushed

3 cups (600 g) jasmine rice, washed and drained in a sieve

1 tsp salt

1 pandan leaf, fresh or frozen

4½ cups (1 litre) chicken stock, from poaching the chicken

METHOD

Cut the fat surrounding the inner part of the chicken cavity away and reserve for the rice. Stuff all the other chicken ingredients into the cavity of the chicken and secure the opening with a short skewer. Lower the chicken into a stockpot that fits it snugly around the sides but is tall enough to allow the chicken to be covered with water. Pour in the water, bring to the boil, cover, and reduce the heat to poach the chicken very gently for 1 hour, so that there is only a slow, steady stream of bubbles. Skim any frothy impurities and oil off the surface of the stock as it cooks.

Meanwhile, prepare the rub by mixing the soy and sesame oil in a small bowl. To test whether the chicken is cooked, lift it by one of the legs; if it pulls away easily where the thigh joins the body, it is done. Transfer the bird to a plate and massage with the rub. Cover and set aside, then bring the stock back to the boil. Boil for 1 hour, or until you have reduced the stock by one-third (you'll need at least 2⅔ quarts/2½ litres left).

To cook the rice, heat the oil and reserved chicken fat in a large non-stick saucepan over a medium heat. When the pieces of fat have shrunk considerably, add the garlic and ginger and sauté until fragrant and slightly golden. Add the rice and stir for a few seconds to toast the grains. Add the salt, pandan leaf, and chicken stock, stir and bring to the boil. Reduce to a simmer, cover and cook for about 10 minutes, until the surface is dotted with pits and no liquid is visible. Reduce to the lowest heat and cook for another 10 minutes, then turn the heat off and rest for 15 minutes before uncovering and fluffing with a fork. Cover and set aside.

Blitz all the red sauce ingredients with a blender or stick blender until smooth. If using a mortar and pestle, pound the chilli and garlic in small amounts, then mix with the vinegar, sugar, and salt. Refrigerate until needed. Mix all the green sauce ingredients together and set aside until needed.

To serve, debone the chicken and slice into ¾-in (2-cm) pieces, then divide the chicken and cucumber between 4 dinner plates. Pour about 1 cup (240 ml) of broth into 4 individual bowls and garnish with the sliced green onions/spring onions and deep-fried shallots. Press about 1 cup of rice into a small rice bowl, then invert onto individual dinner plates. Divide the sauces and the *kecap manis* into small dishes so that everyone has their own. Don't hold back on the sauces when you are eating this meal. Because the chicken is subtly flavoured, all the seasoning comes in the form of the sauces. Make sure you put a little of each in every spoonful.

_____

"If you are a lover of chicken and comfort food, I doubt you will find another dish that celebrates both quite so thoroughly. As well as the traditional ginger and green onion (spring onion) sauce, Malaysians also serve it with a garlic chilli sauce and *kecap manis*, a sweet, sticky soy. It's such a simple meal to make, and if you don't count the poaching time, it only takes 20 minutes to put together."

– POH LING YEOW

INGREDIENTS CONT.

RED SAUCE

3 to 4 long red chillies, roughly sliced

3 cloves garlic, peeled and roughly sliced

⅓ cup (80 ml) white vinegar

⅓ cup (80 g) superfine/caster sugar

½ tsp salt

GREEN SAUCE

8 green onions/spring onions, finely sliced

2¼ to 2¾ in (6 to 7 cm) ginger, peeled and finely grated

2 tsp salt

⅓ cup (80 ml) vegetable oil or groundnut/peanut oil

TO SERVE

sliced cucumber

1 green onion/spring onion, finely sliced

1 tbsp deep-fried shallots

¼ cup (60 ml) *kecap manis* (sweet soy sauce)

Pearl Barley Kedgeree

Nigel Slater

COMPLEXITY: EASY | PREP TIME: 10 MINUTES | COOK TIME: 30 MINUTES | SERVES: 2 TO 4

INGREDIENTS

7 oz (200 g) pearl barley

2 cups plus 1¼ tbsp (500 ml) vegetable stock

2 eggs

3½ tbsp (50 g) butter

3 tsp curry powder

5¼ oz (150 g) cooked peas

8¾ oz (250 g) smoked mackerel

METHOD

Put the pearl barley in a saucepan together with the vegetable stock and bring to the boil. Lower the heat to an enthusiastic simmer and leave to cook uncovered for about 20 minutes, until almost all the stock has been absorbed.

Put the eggs on to boil, about 9 minutes. Warm the butter in a shallow pan and add the curry powder. Sizzle the spices for a minute or two, then add the cooked peas. (Frozen peas, cooked for 2 minutes then drained, are perfect for this.)

As soon as the peas are hot and coated in the spiced butter, stir them through the cooked pearl barley. Tear the smoked mackerel into large shards and fold gently through the barley. Shell the eggs and cut into quarters, then tuck them into the barley and serve.

TIPS

Take care cooking the barley. It is worth keeping an eye on the liquid levels, topping up with a little more hot stock if needed. Ideally there should be a thin film left in the bottom of the pan at the end. Note that 'pot' barley still has its husk and will take a lot longer to cook than pearl.

You could happily swap the mackerel for poached smoked haddock and use rice instead of pearl barley. My own temptation would be to include some wild rice, for the textural contrast.

INGREDIENTS

4 hard-shelled crabs, cleaned and cracked

8 oz (230 g) Creole hot sausage, cut into bite-sized pieces

8 oz (230 g) smoked sausage, cut into bite-sized pieces

8 oz (230 g) boneless veal stew meat

8 oz (230 g) chicken gizzards

½ cup (120 ml) vegetable oil

¼ cup (30 g) all-purpose/plain flour

1 cup (120 g) chopped yellow onion

4 qt (4 litres) water

6 chicken wings, cut in half

8 oz (230 g) chicken necks, skinned and cut into bite-sized pieces

8 oz (230 g) smoked ham, cubed

1 lb (450 g) shrimp, peeled and de-veined

1 tbsp paprika

1 tsp salt

3 cloves garlic, finely chopped

½ oz (15 g) chopped fresh flat-leaf parsley, plus extra for garnish

1 tsp ground dried thyme

24 oysters, shucked and liquor reserved

1 tbsp filé powder

steamed rice (about ½ cup/65 g per person), to serve

Creole Gumbo

Leah Chase

COMPLEXITY: MODERATE | PREP TIME: 1 HOUR | COOK TIME: 2 HOURS | SERVES: 8 TO 10

METHOD

Put the crabs, sausage, veal, and gizzards in a 6-quart (6-litre) pot over a medium heat. Cover and let the mixture cook in its own fat for 30 minutes (it will produce enough fat, but continue to watch the pot).

Heat the vegetable oil in a frying pan and stir in the flour to make a roux. Stir constantly until brown, 15 to 20 minutes. Lower the heat, add the onion, and cook over low heat until the onion wilts.

Pour the onion mixture over the ingredients in the large pot. Slowly add the water, stirring constantly. Bring to the boil. Add the chicken wings and necks, ham, shrimp, paprika, salt, garlic, parsley, and thyme. Let simmer, covered, for 30 minutes. Add the oysters and their liquor. Cook for 10 minutes longer. Remove from the heat and add the filé powder, stirring well. Serve over steamed rice.

Seafood Paella

José Pizarro

COMPLEXITY: MODERATE | PREP TIME: 30 MINUTES | COOK TIME: 30 MINUTES | SERVES: 6

INGREDIENTS

6 tbsp (90 ml) extra virgin olive oil

1 lb (450 g) locally sourced monkfish, cubed

2 small onions, diced

2 cloves garlic, sliced

3 ripe tomatoes, chopped (or 14 oz/ 400 g can chopped tomatoes)

½ cup plus 1 tsp (125 ml) white wine (mild)

1 tsp paprika

salt and freshly ground black pepper

10 oz (285 g) squid, ready cleaned and sliced

3⅔ to 4⅛ cups plus 2 tsp (875 ml to 1 litre) chicken (p. 482) or fish (p. 483) stock, warmed

pinch of saffron, about 30 threads, soaked in 2 tbsp hot water

2 cups (400 g) paella rice, such as Calasparra

12 raw shrimp

1 cup (150 g) peas, fresh or frozen

10 oz (285 g) mussels

12 oz (340 g) clams

5 sprigs flat-leaf parsley, chopped

6 slices lemon

METHOD

Heat the olive oil in a very large frying pan, or, ideally, a paella pan that's roughly 18 in (45 cm) in diameter. Add the monkfish and cook over a medium heat until browned – this will take about 3 minutes. Remove and set aside in a warm place while you prepare the sofrito (onion and garlic mixture) in the same pan.

Cook the onion and garlic for 5 minutes until soft, then add the tomatoes and wine; allow to simmer and reduce a little for another 5 minutes, then stir in the paprika. Season with salt and pepper.

Add the squid and give everything a good stir. Stir in 3⅔ cups (875 ml) stock and the saffron water, turn the heat up to high, and bring the liquid to the boil. Pour in the rice, give it another good stir, then add the monkfish and stir once. Cook, uncovered, over a high heat for 10 minutes. Do not stir again – this is not a risotto.

Add the shrimp, followed by the peas, and lastly the shellfish. Cover with foil, reduce the heat to low, and cook for another 8 minutes. Remember that the shellfish will release their own juices so you probably won't need to add extra stock towards the end, but if you think the rice is looking dry, then add a ladle more.

Remove from the heat, remove the foil, and replace with some paper towels or a kitchen towel; let sit for 5 minutes to allow the paella to breathe.

Scatter the parsley over the paella, arrange the lemon slices, then put the paella in the middle of the table and let everyone help themselves. You may find there is some crusty, slightly caramelized rice on the base of the pan; this is called the socarrat and is the sign of a well-cooked paella.

JOSH'S NOTES

Tip: Avoid stirring during the final cooking stage – this will ensure you end up with that delicious crust.

INGREDIENTS

3½ oz (100 g) rice stick noodles

5 tsp sesame oil

DRESSING

6¾ tbsp (100 ml) rice wine vinegar

¾ oz (25 g) palm sugar

3 tbsp plus 1 tsp (50 ml) fish sauce

4 tbsp (60 ml) tamarind concentrate

1 stalk lemongrass, microplaned

⅓ oz (10 g) peeled and microplaned fresh ginger

1 clove garlic, peeled and microplaned

1 green chilli, seeds removed

zest and juice of 1 lime

TO FINISH

2 tbsp (30 ml) vegetable oil

2 eggs

½ tsp table salt

7 oz (200 g) shrimp/prawns, de-veined

3½ oz (100 g) bean sprouts

4 tbsp cilantro/coriander leaves, roughly chopped

¾ oz (25 g) white sesame seeds, toasted

1¾ oz (50 g) blanched groundnuts/peanuts, roasted and finely chopped

JOSH'S NOTES

Preparation: Use a wok instead of a frying pan if you have one.

Key elements: Use the dressing as you would seasoning, to taste.

Prawn, Sesame & Peanut Pad Thai

Chantelle Nicholson

COMPLEXITY: EASY | PREP TIME: 20 MINUTES | COOK TIME: 10 MINUTES | SERVES: 2

METHOD

Soak the noodles in cold water for 15 minutes, strain off the water, then add the sesame oil, mixing well to coat the noodles and ensure that they do not stick together.

For the dressing, place everything in a blender and blitz until a smooth dressing is formed.

Heat 1 tablespoon (15 ml) of oil in a non-stick frying pan set over a medium heat. Beat the eggs together, season with salt and add to the pan to form an omelette. Move the egg around for a minute, then allow to cook through. Tip out onto a plate and allow to cool before slicing into strips ½ in (1 cm) thick.

Place the remaining oil in a large frying pan over a high heat. Coat the shrimp/prawns in one-quarter of the dressing and cook over a very high heat until cooked through. Remove from the pan and set aside. To the hot pan add half of the noodles, bean sprouts, egg strips, and another quarter of the dressing, and toss quickly to heat through. Transfer to a serving platter and repeat.

Top the noodle mix with the shrimp/prawns, remaining dressing, cilantro/coriander, sesame seeds, and groundnuts/peanuts.

———————

"Pad thai is a noodle dish traditionally made with eggs and rice noodles. Prawns have been added to this recipe, along with a little sesame oil. While not traditional, it adds a lovely nuttiness to the overall dish."

– CHANTELLE NICHOLSON

INGREDIENTS

2 tbsp (30 ml) light
soy sauce

1 tbsp (15 ml) thick
dark soy sauce

2 tbsp (30 ml)
vegetable oil

2 cloves garlic,
finely chopped

1 lap cheong (Chinese
sausage), thinly sliced

6 raw shrimp/prawns,
peeled and de-veined

3½ oz (100 g) fish cake,
sliced (see recipe tip)

14 oz (400 g) fresh flat
rice noodles

1 tsp ground white
pepper

1 tsp vinegared chilli
sauce (optional)

1 tbsp pork lard crisps
(see below)

1 egg

handful of bean sprouts

handful of garlic chives,
cut into 2-in (5-cm)
lengths

PORK LARD CRISPS

7 oz (200 g) pork fat

⅔ cup (150 ml)
rapeseed/canola oil

Stir-fried Rice Noodles
Char Kway Teow

Cheong Liew

COMPLEXITY: EASY | PREP TIME: 15 MINUTES | COOK TIME: 5 MINUTES | SERVES: 2 TO 3

METHOD

To make the pork lard crisps, dice the pork fat into ½ in x ½ in
(1 cm x 1 cm) cubes. Heat the oil to 320°F (160°C). Gently add the
pork fat and cook until golden brown and crispy. Remove from the
heat and allow to cool. These keep for a long time in the fridge.

Combine the light soy and thick dark soy sauces with 2 tablespoons
(30 ml) of water, mixing well.

In a wok, heat the vegetable oil over a high heat, then add the
garlic and lap cheong and stir-fry for 1 minute. Add the shrimp/
prawns and fish cake slices and stir-fry for a further minute until the
shrimp/prawns are cooked.

Add the rice noodles, season with the soy sauce mixture, white
pepper, and chilli sauce, if using, and stir-fry until the noodles are
charred and well coated in the sauce.

Push the rice noodles to one side to make a clear space in the wok,
then add the lard crisps and crack the egg into the resulting oil.
Breaking up the egg, stir to cover it with noodles and let it cook for
10 to 15 seconds before you start stir-frying again. Lastly, add the
bean sprouts and garlic chives, turn the heat off, give everything
in the wok a toss to combine, and tip out onto a serving plate.
Serve immediately.

TIP

Fish cake is available ready-made from most Asian grocery stores.
It is a traditional ingredient in Chinese cooking, made by blending
fish meat into a paste before being steamed.

JOSH'S NOTES

Tip: Keep all the
ingredients close to
hand; once you start
to cook it all happens
very fast.

INGREDIENTS

10½ oz (300 g) dried egg noodles

3 tbsp (45 ml) vegetable oil, plus extra for scrambling eggs

5 cloves of garlic, finely chopped

10½ oz (300 g) boneless chicken breasts, thinly sliced

7 oz (200 g) squid, scored and cut into pieces

3 tbsp chilli paste, ready-made from a jar or homemade (p. 441)

4 tbsp (60 ml) dark soy sauce

4 tbsp (60 ml) light soy sauce

2 tbsp tomato ketchup

1½ tbsp (22½ ml) white vinegar

2⅔ oz (75 g) sweet potato, boiled and puréed with a dash of water

2 eggs

7 oz (200 g) bean sprouts

5¼ oz (150 g) potatoes, boiled and cut into chunks

3½ oz (100 g) spinach, cut into 4-in (10-cm) strips

6 savoury mamak fritters (see below), cut into small chunks

1 lime, cut into 4 wedges

SAVOURY MAMAK FRITTERS

6½ tbsp (50 g) all-purpose/ plain flour

5 tbsp (50 g) rice flour

3½ tbsp (25 g) cornstarch/ cornflour

½ tsp dried yeast

½ tsp granulated sugar

½ tsp fine sea salt

2 cups plus 1¼ tbsp (500 ml) vegetable oil, for frying

Malaysian Fried Noodles
Mee Goreng Mamak

Norman Musa

COMPLEXITY: EASY | PREP TIME: 20 MINUTES | COOK TIME: 15 MINUTES | SERVES: 4

METHOD

Bring 2½ quarts (2½ litres) of water to the boil in a large, deep saucepan. Add the noodles and cook for 10 minutes, until soft, then drain and set aside.

Heat a large wok or frying pan over a high heat, then add the oil and garlic, and sauté until fragrant. Add the chicken and squid and cook, stirring regularly, for 2 minutes.

Now add the chilli paste and fry for 1 minute, then add the noodles, both soy sauces, tomato ketchup, vinegar, and sweet potato purée and fry, stirring, for another 2 minutes.

Scoop the noodles to one side of the pan. Drizzle in a little oil, crack the eggs into the pan, let them scramble, stirring gently, then mix them with the noodles. Add the bean sprouts, potatoes, spinach, and the cooked fritters. Fry until the vegetables wilt, then transfer to a platter and serve immediately, with the lime wedges.

....

Savoury Mamak Fritters

COMPLEXITY: EASY | PREP TIME: 5 MINUTES | COOK TIME: 5 MINUTES | MAKES: 6

Place all the ingredients except the frying oil into a bowl, add ½ cup plus 2 tablespoons (150 ml) of water and mix well. Set aside for at least 30 minutes.

Heat the oil over a medium heat. Drop in the batter one spoonful at a time and fry for few minutes, until crisp and golden brown.

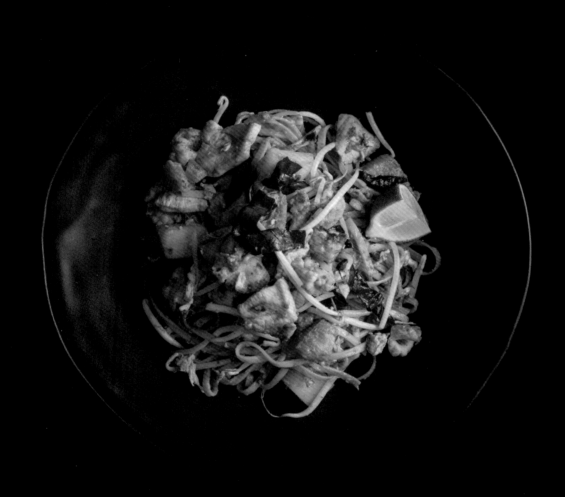

Yellow Dal with Spinach
Dal Palak

Christine Manfield

COMPLEXITY: EASY | PREP TIME: 10 MINUTES | COOK TIME: 20 MINUTES | SERVES: 4

INGREDIENTS

ghee, for frying

2 tsp cumin seeds

1 red onion, finely diced

1 tsp minced garlic

1 tsp minced green chilli

½ tsp ground turmeric

½ tsp salt

3½ oz (100 g) chana dal

2 tbsp chopped spinach

½ tsp chilli powder

METHOD

Heat 1 tablespoon of ghee in a saucepan over a medium heat and fry half of the cumin seeds until they start to crackle. Add the onion and cook, stirring occasionally, until softened and pink, then add the garlic, green chilli, turmeric, and salt. Stir to combine, then add the chana dal and stir until thoroughly coated. Add 1½ cups (375 ml) water and stir, then cover and simmer for 15 minutes until the dal is soft and most of the water has been absorbed without the mixture being dry.

Meanwhile, fry the spinach in a little ghee until wilted. Add to the dal and stir to combine.

In a separate small frying pan, heat 1 tablespoon of ghee, add the remaining cumin seeds and the chilli powder and fry, stirring, until fragrant. Pour over the spinach dal and serve.

JOSH'S NOTES

Key element: Frying the cumin seeds to the right degree is essential to the flavour of this dish.

Tip: Choose the right size pot – if it's too wide in diameter, the liquid may evaporate too fast.

Complements: Steamed rice and/or roti.

French-style Lentils
Lentils à la Française

Michael Caines

COMPLEXITY: EASY | PREP TIME: 5 MINUTES | COOK TIME: 10 MINUTES | SERVES: 2

INGREDIENTS

2 oz (60 g) smoked
bacon lardons, finely
sliced

18 oz (500 g) braised
lentils, drained (juices
reserved)

⅓ cup (80 ml) lentil
cooking juices (see
above)

1¾ oz/3½ tbsp (50 g)
unsalted butter

1 tbsp chopped fresh
parsley

salt and freshly ground
black pepper

METHOD

Put the bacon lardons into a pan and cover them with cold water.
Bring to the boil, then drain and refresh under running cold water –
this removes some of the salt.

Put the drained lentils into a heavy-based pan and add the blanched
lardons and the lentil cooking juices. Bring to the boil, add the
butter, then reduce to a simmer and cook for 5 minutes, until the
starch in the lentils starts to bind with the butter. Add the chopped
parsley and cook for 1 minute more, then season with salt and
pepper and serve.

For a vegetarian option, omit the lardons.

PLANNING AHEAD

Cook the braised lentils first by boiling in water for approximately
30 minutes or until just cooked. Leave them to rest before
starting this dish.

Falafel

Mark Bittman

COMPLEXITY: EASY | PREP TIME: 24 HOURS SOAKING | COOK TIME: 1 HOUR
SERVES: 6 TO 8

INGREDIENTS

1¾ cups (350 g) dried garbanzo beans/chickpeas (or 1 cup/200 g dried garbanzo beans/chickpeas and ¾ cup/90 g dried split fava beans), rinsed and picked over

1 cup (about 30 g) chopped fresh parsley or cilantro/coriander

2 cloves garlic, lightly crushed

1 small onion, quartered

1 tbsp (15 ml) fresh lemon juice

1 tbsp ground cumin

1 tsp ground coriander

about 1 scant tsp cayenne (or 2 tsp mild chilli powder)

1 tsp salt

½ tsp pepper

½ tsp baking soda

good-quality vegetable oil, for frying

METHOD

Put the garbanzo beans/chickpeas in a large bowl and cover with water by 3 to 4 in (1¼ to 1½ cm). (They will triple in volume as they soak.) Soak for 24 hours, checking once or twice to see if you need to add more water to keep the garbanzo beans/chickpeas submerged.

Drain the garbanzo beans/chickpeas well and transfer to a food processor with the herb, garlic, onion, lemon juice, cumin, ground coriander, cayenne, salt, pepper, and baking soda. Pulse until almost smooth, scraping down the side of the bowl as necessary. Add 1 or 2 tablespoons (15 or 30 ml) of water if necessary to allow the machine to do its work, but keep the mixture as dry as possible. Taste and adjust the seasoning, adding more salt, pepper, cayenne, or lemon juice as needed.

Pour oil into a large, deep pot to a depth of at least 2 in (5 cm). More is better; the narrower the pot, the less oil you need, but the more oil you use, the more patties you can cook at the same time. Turn the heat to medium-high and heat the oil to about 350°F (180°C); a pinch of the batter should sizzle immediately.

Scoop out heaped tablespoons of batter and shape into balls or small patties. Fry in batches, without crowding, until nicely browned, turning as necessary; total cooking time will be less than 5 minutes per batch. Use a slotted spoon to transfer to paper towels to drain (they can be kept warm in a low oven, if you like, until they are all cooked). Serve hot or at room temperature.

Store leftovers in an airtight container in the refrigerator; reheat in a 350°F (180°C) oven until hot and crisp, about 15 minutes.

"One of the things that makes falafel different from other bean fritters is that it's made from uncooked chickpeas. It's best when these are soaked for a full day in plenty of water; the result is a wonderfully textured and moist interior with a crisp, browned exterior."

– MARK BITTMAN

INGREDIENTS

2 oz (60 g) double-smoked bacon, cut into strips 2 in x ¼ in (5 cm x ½ cm) in size

8 oz (225 g) fresh chorizo, cut into slices ½ in (1 cm) thick

3 poblano peppers, seeded and finely chopped

3 cloves garlic, peeled and chopped

1 large white onion, peeled and sliced

1 tbsp cumin seeds

1 tsp crushed red pepper flakes

2 qt (2 litres) water

2 lb (900 g) dried black beans, picked over and rinsed

1 lb (450 g) baby back pork ribs, cut into individual servings

8 oz (225 g) blood sausage (such as morcilla), cut into slices ½ in (1 cm) thick

8 oz (225 g) boneless beef sirloin, cut into 16 pieces

8 oz (225 g) smoked beef tongue, peeled and sliced

2 bay leaves

finely grated zest of 1 orange

coarse sea salt or kosher/flaky salt, and freshly ground black pepper

8 oz (225 g) kale, stems removed, leaves roughly chopped

3 tbsp chopped fresh flat-leaf parsley leaves

3 tbsp chopped fresh cilantro/coriander leaves

Brazilian Black Bean Stew
Feijoada

Daniel Boulud

COMPLEXITY: MODERATE | PREP TIME: 1 HOUR, PLUS SOAKING OVERNIGHT
COOK TIME: 3 HOURS 30 MINUTES | SERVES: 6 TO 8

METHOD

The day before you want to serve the dish, put the beans in a large bowl, cover with water by at least 2 in (5 cm), and refrigerate. The next day, drain before using.

Centre a rack in the oven and pre-heat the oven to 275°F (140°C).

In a large cast-iron pot or Dutch oven set over a medium-high heat, cook the bacon and fresh chorizo until they render their fat and colour lightly, about 10 minutes. Add the poblano peppers, garlic, onion, cumin seeds, and red pepper flakes and cook, stirring, for another 10 minutes. Add 2 quarts (2 litres) water, the drained black beans, pork ribs, blood sausage, sirloin, beef tongue, bay leaves, orange zest, and salt and pepper to taste.

Bring to a simmer, cover, and transfer to the oven. Braise for 2½ hours. Stir in the kale, parsley, and cilantro/coriander, and continue to braise, covered, for 30 minutes more.

––––––––––

"Feijoada, the national dish of Brazil, is one of my favourite things about the country ... It's a rustic, hearty stew of black beans flavoured with all kinds of meat, including bacon, pork sausage, ribs, blood sausage, beef sirloin, and tongue."

– DANIEL BOULUD

Sweetcorn Pancakes
Cachapas

Grace Ramirez

COMPLEXITY: EASY | PREP TIME: 15 MINUTES | COOK TIME: 15 MINUTES | MAKES: 8

INGREDIENTS

3 cups (500 g) corn/
sweetcorn kernels
(cut off raw fresh cobs,
or thawed frozen, or
canned and drained)

1 tbsp sugar

1½ tbsp salt

⅔ cup plus 2 tsp
(170 ml) milk

1 egg

5 tbsp pre-cooked
white maize meal/
cornmeal

oil for frying

4 balls fresh buffalo
mozzarella, sliced

JOSH'S NOTES

Preparation: Make sure
you source the correct
type of maize meal/
cornmeal, to ensure the
right consistency.

Key element: When
frying, wipe the pan with
oil, as you would when
making pancakes.

Complements: Excellent
with good-quality
mozzarella, cured meat
and ham.

Tip: Fold the cachapas
when warm so they
keep their shape.

Comment: These can
be filled with almost
anything, and are best
eaten straight out of
the pan.

METHOD

Place corn/sweetcorn kernels, sugar, salt, milk, egg, and maize meal/
cornmeal in a blender and pulse until just combined. Make sure you
don't purée the mix.

Lightly oil a griddle or a heavy-based frying pan and place over a
medium-high heat. Use a ladle to add cachapas mixture to the pan,
shaping each cachapa like a pancake about 4 in (10 cm) across.
When bubbles start to form on top, lower the heat and continue
to cook for about 2 minutes. Flip each cachapa over and cook for
another 2 to 3 minutes, until cooked through. Place mozzarella
slices on one half of each cachapa and fold the other half over.

Serve immediately.

_____

"You can stuff a cachapa with whatever you like, but they are
traditionally served with some *crema agria* (sour cream) or butter
inside and on top, and Venezuelan cheese or a ham and cheese
combo inside."

– GRACE RAMIREZ

Scrambled Eggs

Josh Emett

COMPLEXITY: EASY | PREP TIME: 2 MINUTES | COOK TIME: 3 MINUTES | SERVES: 1

INGREDIENTS

3 eggs

pinch of salt

5 tsp cream

1 tbsp (15 g) butter

METHOD

Crack the eggs into a bowl and add the cream and a pinch of salt. Beat until just combined.

Melt the butter in a non-stick frying pan over a medium heat until it starts to bubble gently, then pour in the egg mixture. Fold carefully with a spatula every 10 seconds or so, to cook the eggs slowly without colouring them. Remove just before they are cooked and check the seasoning.

"Eggs don't need to be confined to breakfast. Serve them with your favourite toasted or grilled bread, tomatoes, avocado, smoked bacon, smoked salmon or a crisp green salad, for a more substantial brunch, or light lunch."

– JOSH EMETT

JOSH'S NOTES

Key element: Free-range, organic eggs really make a difference.

Tip: Fold the eggs gently so you achive a nice, light texture.

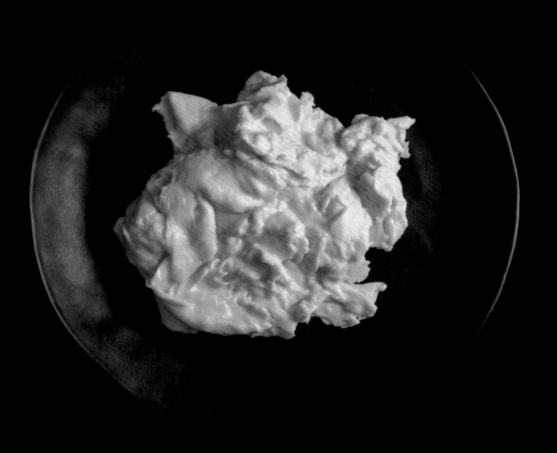

Bacon, Pea & Goat Cheese Frittata

Gordon Ramsay

COMPLEXITY: EASY | PREP TIME: 10 MINUTES | COOK TIME: 20 MINUTES | SERVES: 4 TO 6

INGREDIENTS

olive oil, for frying

8 slices/rashers smoked streaky bacon, chopped into bite-sized pieces

1 red bell pepper/capsicum, deseeded and sliced

3 green onions/spring onions, trimmed and sliced diagonally

5¼ oz (150 g) frozen peas

handful of basil, leaves roughly chopped

2 goat's cheese crottins (about 4¼ oz/120 g in total)

8 eggs, beaten

3 to 4 tbsp grated Parmesan

freshly ground black pepper

METHOD

Pre-heat the oven to 350°F (180°C).

Heat a glug of oil in a 10½-in (27-cm) non-stick ovenproof frying pan and fry the bacon for 2 to 3 minutes. Add the bell pepper/capsicum and continue to cook for another few minutes until the bacon is golden brown and crisp.

Add the green onions/spring onions and sweat for 4 to 5 minutes until everything is tender. Stir in the peas, and heat through. Sprinkle in the basil, roughly mixing it through the vegetables. Cut one of the goat's cheeses into chunks and scatter on top.

Heat the grill on its highest setting.

Put the beaten eggs in a bowl, add the Parmesan and season generously with pepper. Pour into the pan over the vegetables and gently shake over a medium heat. As the egg begins to set at the bottom, grate the remaining goat's cheese on top and season with pepper.

Place the pan under the hot grill in the hot oven for 4 to 5 minutes, until cooked through and golden on top. Slide the frittata out of the pan and cut into wedges to serve.

JOSH'S NOTES

Key element: Fry the bacon until it's as crispy as possible.

Tip: A non-stick pan is essential to a successful frittata.

Potato Tortilla
Tortilla de Patatas

Frank Camorra

COMPLEXITY: EASY | PREP TIME: 20 MINUTES | COOK TIME: 25 MINUTES | SERVES: 8

INGREDIENTS

12 large free-range eggs

1 tsp cooking salt

2½ lb (1.2 kg) royal
blue potatoes

1 qt (1 litre) olive oil

1 large brown onion,
diced (you need
7¾ oz/220 g)

sea salt to taste

METHOD

Place eggs in a bowl and beat well, then add salt and stir in.
Set aside.

Peel potatoes and cut into ½-in (1-cm) cubes. Pour olive oil into a
deep, wide pan, heat over a medium heat until just warm, then add
potato and onion. Cook on low to medium for 20 minutes, without
colouring – the oil should be just gently bubbling away.

Remove potato and onion, and drain well, then place in a mixing
bowl and season with sea salt. Once potato has cooled a little,
add beaten egg and mix well.

Using a large non-stick frying pan heat ¼ cup (60 ml) of olive oil over
a high heat. When very hot, pour in potato and egg mixture and stir
well with a spatula for 30 seconds.

Turn the heat down to medium, and break up the potatoes a little
with the end of the spatula. Every so often run the spatula around
the edges of the tortilla. Do this for 3 to 4 minutes.

Turn the tortilla over using a large plate that covers the pan totally
– place the plate upside down over the pan, and holding the edges
with tea towels over your hands, flip plate and pan over together.
Place the pan back on the heat and slide the tortilla back in,
uncooked side down. Cover with the plate and cook for a further
3 to 4 minutes over medium heat. The tortilla should be only lightly
browned, but cooked almost through. A little eggy softness in the
centre is ideal. Once cooked, replace the plate with a clean serving
plate that fits generously over the pan. Once again, flip plate and
pan to turn the tortilla out onto the plate. Cover with plastic wrap
for 15 minutes before serving.

JOSH'S NOTES

Tip: Make sure the eggs
are cooked enough so it
holds together the first
time you flip it.

Old-fashioned Omelette

David Kinch

COMPLEXITY: EASY | PREP TIME: 5 MINUTES, PLUS 3 HOURS TO INFUSE TRUFFLE
COOK TIME: 5 MINUTES | SERVES: 1

INGREDIENTS

5 farm-fresh eggs

1 egg yolk

1 black truffle

3½ tbsp (50 g) salted butter

fleur de sel

METHOD

Crack the eggs into a bowl and add the yolk. Peel the truffle and save the peelings for another use. Working with a small sharp paring knife over the egg bowl, whittle down the truffle into little shavings as thin as possible and in small pieces. Take your time to create these fragments, as this technique does wonders to preserve the texture and the aroma of the truffle that can be lost chopping them with a knife. Use as much truffle as you can afford; I like to use a lot myself.

Occasionally stir the eggs with a fork to push the truffles below the surface. Do not beat the eggs at this time, as it is important to maintain the integrity of the curds. After this is finished, cover the bowl with plastic wrap and allow to sit at room temperature for 3 hours to infuse the aroma throughout the eggs. Do not salt the eggs and do not stir!

You will make the omelette without salt, which is the beauty of this recipe. The lack of salt mixed with the eggs will guarantee a soft custard-like curd, a treasure compared with the hard-curd scrambled-egg texture of most omelettes.

Heat an 8-in (20-cm) non-stick pan, or the pan you have reserved for egg cookery. Now lightly beat the eggs with fork. You just want to mix the eggs and not incorporate any kind of air into them. Drop a nugget of half the salted butter into a pan. The pan will be the correct temperature if the butter sizzles right away and melts fast without browning. Add the eggs quickly and stir with the tines of the fork until the eggs have formed the curds, shiny and soft. Do not overcook.

Turn the eggs out onto a plate, rolling it to approximate the shape of an omelette. You can shape it perfectly by covering it with a kitchen towel and gently pressing it into shape. The magic now is to rub the exterior surface of the eggs with a COLD piece of salted butter to make it shiny and then shower the surface with the *fleur de sel*. You will have a perfectly seasoned omelette with the soft curd of a just-made cheese.

Enjoy immediately with a great glass of Burgundy and some buttered sourdough toast.

"This might be one of the most satisfying recipes for me, one of my favourite dishes to eat ever. I love omelettes. An omelette has always been about eggs and butter, salt, and sometimes, if you are blessed, a truffle."

– DAVID KINCH

Green Shakshuka

Greg & Lucy Malouf

COMPLEXITY: EASY | PREP TIME: 20 MINUTES | COOK TIME: 15 MINUTES | SERVES: 4

INGREDIENTS

2 tbsp (30 ml) extra virgin olive oil

2 green onions/spring onions, finely sliced

2 long green chillies, finely shredded

1 heaped tsp ground cumin

1 heaped tsp ground coriander

2 cloves garlic, finely chopped

1 medium-sized zucchini/courgette, coarsely grated

4 loosely packed cups (120 g) of spinach (thoroughly washed)

2 cups (60 g) kale, torn into bite-sized pieces

2 ripe plum tomatoes, grated

½ cup (90 g) yellow plum tomatoes, thickly sliced

juice of ½ lemon

½ tsp sea salt

8 free-range eggs

2 tbsp finely shredded parsley

toasted sourdough bread, to serve

METHOD

Heat an overhead grill to its maximum setting, or heat the oven to 400°F (200°C).

Heat a small paella pan (10 to 11 in/25 to 28 cm diameter) over a medium heat and add the oil. Fry the green onions/spring onions, chilli, spices, and garlic until fragrant, then add the zucchini/courgette and fry for a minute. Add the spinach, kale, and the grated tomatoes and cut yellow plum tomatoes; season with lemon and sea salt, mix, and cover until the leaves are just wilted and the tomatoes soften slightly.

Make 8 indents in the vegetables and crack an egg into each. Cook for about 2 minutes on the stovetop and then transfer to the grill or oven for a further 2 minutes, until the tops of the eggs are set but they are still runny in the centre.

Sprinkle with parsley and serve with toasted sourdough bread.

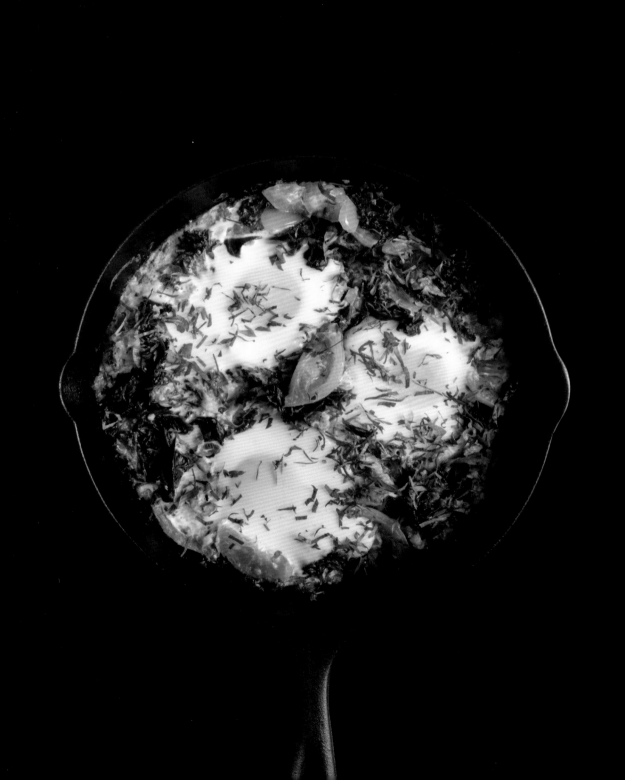

Pumpkin Seed Coleslaw, p. 115

Salads & Vegetables

The role of the vegetable has recently come full circle with a growing return to an emphasis on plant-based, organic, and seasonal food. More and more we're interested in the provenance of our produce and the soil in which it is grown. The dishes you will find here hark from a time when vegetables could only be sourced in season and were celebrated for a limited while each year. Fresh asparagus, dripping in butter, heralds the welcome arrival of spring; Spanish *pan con tomate*, a joyful flavour explosion of juicy, summer-ripened tomatoes; St George's mushrooms, freshly picked from their woodland hiding places and served in a rich, creamy sauce is a perfect addition as the weather starts to cool; and the humble potato, a versatile and comforting accompaniment to any winter meal. Source and cook with the seasons, and you'll be rewarded with enjoying these tried and true classics at their best.

Waldorf Salad

Martha Stewart

COMPLEXITY: EASY | PREP TIME: 20 MINUTES | COOK TIME: 15 MINUTES | SERVES: 6 TO 8

INGREDIENTS

4 oz (115 g) pecans

1 bulb fennel, trimmed (1 lb/450 g)

2 tbsp (30 ml) plus 1 tsp freshly squeezed lemon juice (about 1 lemon)

1 Granny Smith apple

1 bunch seedless red grapes, halved (about 1½ cup)

4 stalks celery, thinly sliced crosswise

6 to 8 escarole leaves, stacked, cut crosswise into thin strips

¼ cup (5 g) chopped fresh dill

¼ cup (60 ml) plain yoghurt

2 tbsp (30 ml) extra virgin olive oil

coarse salt and freshly ground black pepper

METHOD

Pre-heat the oven to 350°F (180°C). Spread the pecans in a single layer over a rimmed baking tray; toast in the oven until golden and fragrant, 10 to 15 minutes. Let cool, then halve the pecans and set aside.

Very thinly slice the fennel using a mandolin or sharp knife. Transfer to a large bowl; add 1 teaspoon of lemon juice, and toss to coat.

Slice the apple into thin wedges; add to the bowl with the fennel, and toss to coat with the juice. Add the grapes, celery, escarole, and half the dill to the bowl. Toss to combine. The salad may be made up to this point 4 hours ahead, and refrigerated, covered.

In a small bowl, combine the remaining 2 tablespoons (30 ml) of lemon juice with the yoghurt and oil; season with salt and pepper. Toss the salad with just enough vinaigrette to lightly coat it. Transfer to a serving bowl, and garnish with the remaining dill and the reserved pecan halves. Serve the salad with the remaining vinaigrette on the side.

Caesar Salad with Potato Croutons

Tyler Florence

COMPLEXITY: EASY | PREP TIME: 20 MINUTES | COOK TIME: 35 MINUTES | SERVES: 6

INGREDIENTS

8 oz (225 g) new potatoes (approximately 8 to 10 golf-ball-sized potatoes)

½ cup plus 1 tbsp (135 ml) extra virgin olive oil

1 tsp sea salt, plus more to taste

4 bay leaves

2 anchovy fillets, drained, patted dry, and oil reserved

1 clove garlic

6 tbsp freshly grated Parmesan, plus more for garnish

freshly ground black pepper

1 lb (450 g) mixed lettuces (romaine/cos, gem, and butter)

Caesar dressing (p. 475) as desired

shavings of Parmesan, to taste

JOSH'S NOTES

Preparation: Make the dressing in advance.

Key element: Good quality of the Parmesan and anchovies.

Tip: Be careful not to over-dress, or the salad becomes heavy.

METHOD

Pre-heat the oven to 425°F (220°C).

Rinse the potatoes and slice in half. Place on a roasting tray and toss with ¼ cup (60 ml) of the oil, the sea salt, and the bay leaves. Make sure the potatoes are skin side down on the pan. Roast for 25 minutes, until nice and crisp. Discard the bay leaves.

Finely chop together the anchovies, garlic, and a pinch of sea salt, then mash with the side of your knife until it's a paste. Transfer to a large bowl and add ¼ cup (60 ml) of the oil, 4 tablespoons of the Parmesan, and a drop of the reserved anchovy oil. Whisk together, and season with pepper.

Fill a large bowl with cold water, and place the lettuces in the water. Gently agitate the leaves to loosen any dirt, which will sink to the bottom while the leaves float on top. Transfer the leaves to towels and gently pat dry. (Salad spinners tend to bruise lettuce.) Keep small leaves whole, and tear large leaves into generous-sized pieces.

Toss the potatoes in the anchovy-cheese paste, then put them back in the oven for another 5 to 7 minutes, until the cheese melts. Toss with the remaining 2 tablespoons of Parmesan.

Smear a generous layer of dressing on the inside of a large mixing bowl – this helps to incorporate the dressing evenly. Add the lettuce leaves to the bowl, and toss to coat the leaves with dressing. Toss in more dressing, if desired. Add a few shavings of Parmesan cheese, a sprinkling of black pepper, and the remaining 1 tablespoon (15 ml) of oil. Place the dressed leaves on a platter, and top with the potato croutons and a final shower of grated Parmesan. Serve immediately.

"What makes a Caesar salad special? To me it's about striking the perfect balance between fresh romaine (cos) and flavourful dressing, with croutons for crunch. We substituted crispy potatoes for the croutons."

– TYLER FLORENCE

Image on p. 121

Fingerling Potato Salad

Markus Glocker

COMPLEXITY: EASY | PREP TIME: 10 MINUTES | COOK TIME: 20 MINUTES | SERVES: 2

INGREDIENTS

8 oz (225 g) fingerling potatoes

salt and freshly ground black pepper

small bunch of chives

2 banana shallots

1 tbsp (15 ml) Champagne vinegar

1 tbsp whole-grain Dijon mustard

1½ tbsp (22½ ml) chicken demi-glace

This recipe accompanies Markus Glocker's Chicken Schnitzel with Potato Salad & Lingonberry Jam recipe, p. 200.

METHOD

Wash the potatoes and place in a medium-sized pot, cover with cold water and add a big pinch of salt. Bring to the boil over a high heat, then boil gently for 14 to 16 minutes, or until tender when pierced with a fork. Drain thoroughly. When cool enough to handle, use your fingers and a paring knife to remove the skins. Slice the potatoes into rounds ¼ in (5 mm) thick, place in a bowl and set aside. Rinse and dry the pot.

While the potatoes cook, wash and dry the chives, then mince finely and set aside. Peel and mince the shallots to get 2 tablespoons of minced shallot; place in a bowl with the vinegar.

In the pot used to cook the potatoes, combine the mustard, demi-glace, and shallot-vinegar mixture; season with salt and pepper. Cook over a medium-high heat, stirring occasionally, for 1 to 2 minutes, or until thoroughly combined and warmed through. Transfer to the bowl of sliced potatoes. Add half the chives and season with salt and pepper to taste. Stir to thoroughly combine. Set aside to marinate, stirring occasionally, for 10 minutes.

INGREDIENTS

TUNA STEAKS

4 x 5-oz (150 g) tuna steaks (ask your fishmonger to cut you 2-in x 2-in/5-cm x 5-cm centre-cut fillets)

4 tbsp olive tapenade (p. 434)

½ cup (10 g) chopped fresh curly parsley

3 tbsp chopped fresh chives

3 tbsp chopped fresh tarragon

3 tbsp chopped fresh chervil

extra virgin olive oil

rapeseed/canola oil

WAX BEAN SALAD

1 cup (125 g) yellow wax beans

1 cup (125 g) haricots verts or green beans

¼ cup (50 g) pickled red onion (p. 454)

3 tbsp minced preserved lemon (p. 453; I use Meyer lemons)

1 tbsp chopped fresh curly parsley

1 cup (240 ml) extra virgin olive oil

⅓ cup (80 ml) fresh lemon juice

1 tsp *piment d'espelette* or hot paprika

kosher/flaky salt

Ingredients continued overleaf

Niçoise Salad
Salade Niçoise

Marc Forgione

COMPLEXITY: DIFFICULT | PREP TIME: 1 HOUR | COOK TIME: 1 HOUR 30 MINUTES | SERVES: 4

METHOD

TUNA STEAKS

Rinse the fish and pat it dry. Make a 1-in (½-cm) slit in the centre of each tuna fillet and stuff about 1 tablespoon of olive tapenade into each cavity. In a medium-sized bowl, mix together the parsley, chives, tarragon, and chervil. Brush the tuna with olive oil and coat it in the herb mixture on both sides. Set aside.

When ready to serve, add enough rapeseed/canola oil to a large frying pan to cover the bottom of the pan and set it over a high heat. Just before the oil starts to smoke, add the tuna and sear for 20 seconds on each side. Transfer to a tray lined with parchment paper.

WAX BEAN SALAD

Trim the wax beans and haricots verts, and bring a pot of salted water to the boil. Set up a bowl of iced water. Blanch the beans in the boiling water for 1 minute and immediately transfer to the ice bath. Let cool to room temperature.

Cut the beans in half lengthwise and toss with the pickled red onions, preserved Meyer lemon, and parsley. In a small bowl, stir together the olive oil, lemon juice, and *piment d'espelette*. Drizzle the dressing over the vegetables and toss to combine. Season to taste with salt and set aside.

SILVER DOLLAR POTATOES

Pre-heat the oven to 400°F (200°C); position the rack in the middle.

Cut the potatoes in half widthwise, and use a 2-in (5-cm) ring mould to punch out uniform cylinders; you should wind up with 6 cylinders. Using an adjustable mandolin, slice the cylinders into slices ⅛ in (3 mm) thick.

Bring a pot of salted water to the boil. Blanch the potato slices in the boiling water for 1 minute, then transfer to a baking tray and brush generously with clarified butter. Line six 4-oz (115-g) ramekins with foil and fill each ramekin with potato slices.

Continued overleaf

SILVER DOLLAR POTATOES

3 large Yukon Gold
potatoes (1½ lb/680 g)

8 oz (225 g) clarified
butter or melted
unsalted butter

TO SERVE

4 oil-cured white
anchovy fillets, halved
lengthwise

4 tbsp olive tapenade
(p. 434)

upland cress (optional)

flaky sea salt, such as
Maldon

12 baby radishes
or French breakfast
radishes

Niçoise Salad cont.

Pour in enough of the clarified butter to come to ¼ in (5 mm) from
the top of each ramekin. Bake the potatoes for about 1 hour, or until
the edges are crispy. Turn the potatoes out of the ramekins and set
aside. Reserve any remaining clarified butter for another use.

ASSEMBLE THE DISH

Divide the wax bean salad between 4 plates, and scatter the silver
dollar potatoes around. Slice the tuna steaks and place them on top
of the bean salad. Top with the halved anchovies. Drizzle some of the
bean salad dressing from the bottom of the bowl around the plate,
dot with bits of olive tapenade, and finish with some upland cress,
if using, and flaky sea salt. Serve with the radishes.

MAKE IT FASTER

Instead of making the silver dollar potatoes, go a bit more of a
traditional route – boil some fingerling potatoes in salted water and
serve alongside the salad.

"Niçoise salad, made famous in the United States by the late,
great, Julia Child, is a traditional French mixed vegetable salad
topped with tuna and anchovies. In keeping with tradition, the
salad components are arranged on a bed of lettuce set on a large
plate. The tuna typically used in a Niçoise salad is a quality tuna
packed in oil."

– MARC FORGIONE

JOSH'S NOTES

Preparation: Make the
tapenade, pickled red
onion, and preserved
lemons in advance.

Key element: Extremely
fresh tuna, and precise
cooking time.

Comment: This is a
complex dish, but the
reward is superb flavour
combinations.

Pumpkin Seed Coleslaw

Ben Shewry

COMPLEXITY: EASY | PREP TIME: 15 MINUTES | COOK TIME: 10 MINUTES | SERVES: 4

INGREDIENTS

- 19 oz (550 g) organic cabbage, finely shredded
- 2½ oz (75 g) organic red onion, thinly sliced
- 7 oz (200 g) organic squash/pumpkin seeds, lightly toasted and half of them crushed
- ¼ cup plus 2 tsp (70 ml) organic cold-pressed squash/pumpkin seed oil
- 3 tbsp plus 1 tsp (50 ml) sweet Chardonnay vinegar
- salt and pepper to taste
- juice of 1 large lemon
- 1 bunch organic chives, thinly sliced
- 1½ oz (40 g) organic flat-leaf parsley leaves, shredded
- 6 free-range, organic eggs, hard-boiled and coarsely grated

Combine the cabbage, onion, squash/pumpkin seeds, squash/pumpkin seed oil, and vinegar with a large pinch of salt. Toss well in a large bowl.

Add the lemon juice, chives, parsley, and grated eggs and toss gently to combine. Season to taste.

Image on p. 106

Tabbouleh

Image on p. 121

Claudia Roden

COMPLEXITY: EASY | PREP TIME: 15 MINUTES | COOK TIME: 15 MINUTES | SERVES: 8

INGREDIENTS

- 2⅛ oz (60 g) medium-ground bulgur
- large bunch of flat-leaf parsley (about 6⅓ oz/180 g)
- bunch of mint (about 1 oz/30 g)
- 6 green onions/spring onions, trimmed and finely sliced
- 4 tbsp (60 ml) lemon juice
- ½ cup (120 ml) extra virgin olive oil
- salt and black pepper
- 2 large firm ripe tomatoes, diced

Rinse the bulgur in a strainer under the cold water tap, then put it in a bowl and pour plenty of boiling water over it. Leave for 10 to 15 minutes, until tender, then drain and press the excess water out.

Hold the parsley in small bunches and shred the leaves finely, or pick the leaves off the stems and chop them with a sharp knife. Pick the mint leaves and shred or chop them.

Just before serving, mix all the ingredients gently together.

"A traditional way of eating tabbouleh is to scoop it up with romaine (cos) lettuce leaves cut in half, or the leaves of Little Gem lettuces."

– CLAUDIA RODEN

Pumpkin Kibbeh Stuffed with Feta & Spinach

Greg & Lucy Malouf

COMPLEXITY: EASY | PREP TIME: 30 MINUTES, PLUS COOLING TIME | COOK TIME: 1 HOUR
MAKES: 12

INGREDIENTS

KIBBEH SHELL

1 lb (450 g) butternut squash/pumpkin

salt and freshly ground black pepper

olive oil

3½ oz (100 g) fine bulgur

½ small onion, finely chopped

1 tbsp tahini, well stirred

1 tbsp all-purpose/plain flour

¼ tsp ground allspice

¼ tsp ground cinnamon

FETA & SPINACH FILLING

1 tbsp (15 ml) olive oil

1 tbsp (15 g) butter

1 small onion, finely diced

3½ oz (100 g) spinach leaves, stalks removed

salt and freshly ground black pepper

feta, or your choice of melting white cheese or savoury butter

TO FINISH

vegetable oil, for cooking

Greek-style yoghurt, to serve

extra virgin olive oil, to serve

METHOD

Make the kibbeh shell first. Pre-heat the oven to 350°F (180°C). Cut the butternut squash/pumpkin into chunks and arrange in a small roasting tray. Toss with salt, pepper, and a generous splash of olive oil. Cover with foil and roast for 25 to 30 minutes, or until very tender. Remove from the oven and leave to cool.

While the butternut squash/pumpkin is cooling, soak the bulgur in warm water for 5 minutes. Tip into a sieve and, using your hands, squeeze out as much water as you can. Then tip into a tea towel and twist to extract even more water. When it's as dry as you can manage, tip it into a large mixing bowl.

Slice away the skin from the butternut squash/pumpkin and weigh out 9 oz (250 g) of flesh. Add this to the bowl with the bulgur and mash the two together to form a smooth purée. Add the onion, tahini, flour, and spices, and season generously with salt and pepper. Knead with your hands until the mixture is thoroughly blended. Chill for at least 30 minutes, which will make the paste easier to work with.

To make the filling, heat the oil and butter in a medium-sized frying pan over a medium heat and add the onion. Sweat, stirring occasionally, for 5 to 10 minutes, until soft and translucent. Add the spinach leaves and stir over the heat, turning it around frequently until it wilts. Remove from the heat and leave to cool. Season with salt and pepper, then chop finely.

When you are ready to make the kibbeh, divide the shell mixture into 12 even portions. Take one portion in the palm of your left hand and roll it smooth with the other hand. Using the forefinger of your right hand, make an indentation in the ball and start to shape it carefully into a hollow shell. Try to make the shell as thin and even as you can. Wet your finger from time to time, to make it easier.

Continued overleaf

Pumpkin Kibbeh Stuffed with Feta & Spinach cont.

Fill the shell with a scant teaspoon of the spinach filling, together with a small cube of feta or your choice of flavoured butter. Add another pinch of spinach, then wet the edges of the opening and carefully pinch it closed. Make sure you don't trap any air inside. You are aiming to form a small torpedo-shaped dumpling, with slightly tapered ends. Repeat with the remaining mixture and filling.

Leave the stuffed kibbeh on a tray in the fridge, covered, for at least 30 minutes, or up to 4 hours, until you are ready to cook them.

When ready to cook, pour vegetable oil into a medium-sized, heavy-based saucepan to a depth of about 2½ in (6 cm) and heat to 350°F (180°C). Fry the kibbeh, a few at a time, for 4 to 5 minutes, or until they turn a deep golden brown. Turn them around in the oil to ensure that they colour evenly all over. Drain them on paper towel and serve piping hot with a dollop of yoghurt and a drizzle of extra virgin olive oil.

JOSH'S NOTES

Preparation: A small amount of vegetable prep, and some cooling time to set the mixture.

Key element: Deep-fry at the right temperature. Use a probe if you have one.

Tip: Make the end shape of the kibbeh before hollowing it out, to help ensure the correct final shape.

Classic Ratatouille

Jacques Pépin

COMPLEXITY: EASY | PREP TIME: 30 MINUTES | COOK TIME: 1 HOUR 30 MINUTES | SERVES: 6

INGREDIENTS

about ½ cup (120 ml) olive oil

1 aubergine/eggplant (1¼ lb/570 g), trimmed but not peeled, and cut into 1-in (2½-cm) cubes

3 medium-sized zucchini/courgettes (about 1¼ lb/570 g), trimmed and cut into 1-in (2½-cm) cubes

12 oz (340 g) onions (2 to 3), cut into 1-in (2½-cm) cubes

1 lb (450 g) green bell peppers/capsicums (2 to 3), cored, seeded, and cut into 1-in (2½ cm) squares

4 to 5 ripe tomatoes, peeled, halved, de-seeded, and coarsely cubed

5 to 6 cloves garlic, crushed and very finely chopped

½ cup (120 ml) water

2 tsp salt

½ tsp freshly ground black pepper

METHOD

Heat ¼ cup (60 ml) of the oil in one, or better, two, large frying pans. First sauté the aubergine/eggplant cubes until browned, about 8 minutes; remove with a slotted spoon and transfer to a large, heavy flameproof casserole. (The aubergine/eggplant will absorb more oil while cooking than the other vegetables.) Then sauté the zucchini/courgette cubes until browned, about 8 minutes. Transfer to the casserole.

Add about ¼ cup (60 ml) more oil to the pan(s) and sauté the onions and peppers/capsicums together for about 6 minutes. Add them to the casserole.

Add the tomatoes, garlic, water, salt, and pepper to the casserole and bring to the boil over a medium heat. Reduce the heat to low, cover, and cook for 1 hour.

Remove the cover, increase the heat to medium, and cook for another 20 minutes to reduce the liquid, stirring once in a while to prevent scorching. Let the ratatouille rest off the heat for at least 30 minutes before serving.

Carrots Vichy, p. 124

Celeriac Remoulade, p. 125

Cauliflower Cheese, p. 132

Mustard Greens, p. 122

Creamed Spinach, p. 123

Tabbouleh, p. 115

Caesar Salad, p. 110

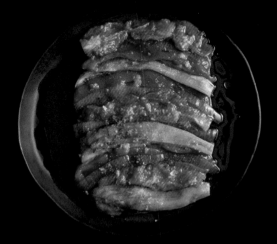

Roasted Vegetables, p. 130

Mustard Greens

Daryle Brantley

COMPLEXITY: EASY | PREP TIME: 15 MINUTES | COOK TIME: 1 HOUR | SERVES: 6 TO 12

INGREDIENTS

2 bunches turnip greens

3 bunches mustard greens

2 to 3 pieces of bacon, salt pork, short rib, ham hock (or any other meat of your choice)

1 small onion

salt and pepper, to taste

1 tsp crushed red pepper flakes (optional)

METHOD

Wash the greens in cold water, rinsing each leaf front and back, then pull apart, discarding any large stems. Rinse again for good measure.

Fry the bacon (or your choice of meat) just until brown in the pot you will use for the greens.

Cut the onion into small dice, then add to the pot with the bacon and cook, stirring occasionally, until tender.

Fill the pot one-third full with water. Add seasoning to the pot, including the red pepper flakes, if using, then bring to the boil. Add the greens to the pot, a few at a time. The hot water allows the greens to cook down faster. Cook, uncovered, until all the greens have cooked down into the liquid. You may need to add a little more water. Now cover the pot and cook over a medium-high heat for 15 minutes, stirring as needed.

Adjust the seasoning if necessary, cover the pot, lower the heat to medium and simmer for 45 minutes or until the greens have the desired consistency.

JOSH'S NOTES

Key element: Cook until the leaves are tender.

Tip: Cooking the bacon over a medium heat renders out the fat and maximizes the flavour.

Comment: Good-quality smoky bacon will deliver the best flavour, but do experiment with other meats, such as leftover ham hock or short rib.

Image on p. 120

Creamed Spinach

Josh Emett

COMPLEXITY: EASY | PREP TIME: 15 MINUTES | COOK TIME: 10 MINUTES | SERVES: 4

INGREDIENTS

1 lb (450 g) spinach, washed and trimmed

2 tbsp (30 g) butter

½ onion, finely chopped (brunoise)

2 cloves garlic, microplaned

1½ cups (360 ml) cream, plus extra if needed

½ whole nutmeg, grated

sea salt to taste

METHOD

Bring a large pot of water to the boil, add the spinach and blanch for 30 seconds. Tip into a colander and chill under cold running water, then squeeze thoroughly to get rid of all moisture. Once dry, chop roughly.

Melt the butter in a pot over a medium heat, add the onion and garlic and sweat down until soft but not coloured, about 3 minutes. Add the cream, bring to a simmer and reduce until thick, 2 to 3 minutes. Finally, add the spinach and cook, stirring, until completely bound together.

Finish by seasoning with grated nutmeg and sea salt. Stir in a little more cream if the consistency needs adjusting.

───────────

"This delicious winter side-dish will perfectly complement any meat dish, but is particularly good when paired with steak."

– JOSH EMETT

JOSH'S NOTES

Key element: Dry the spinach well.

Tip: A clean tea towel or cloth is the most effective way to wring the spinach.

Image on p. 121

Carrots Vichy

Josh Emett

COMPLEXITY: EASY | PREP TIME: 10 MINUTES | COOK TIME: 25 MINUTES | SERVES: 3 TO 4

Trim the carrots, then cut on an angle into rounds 1 in (2½ cm) long. Place all the ingredients except the chives in a pot together. Set over a medium heat and cook for about 25 minutes, stirring occasionally, until most of the liquid has evaporated and the carrots are glazed and shiny.

Finish the seasoning with sea salt, garnish with the chives, and serve.

Image on p. 120

INGREDIENTS

6 medium-sized carrots (1 lb/450 g)

few sprigs of thyme

5¼ tbsp (75 g) butter

¾ cup plus 3 tbsp (225 ml) water

3¼ tsp sugar

pinch of sea salt

½ bunch chives, finely chopped

JOSH'S NOTES

Key element: Cook the carrots evenly so they are uniformly glazed.

Tip: Start with similar-sized carrots so that you have equal-sized pieces that will cook evenly.

Flemish-style Asparagus

Peter Goossens

COMPLEXITY: EASY | PREP TIME: 10 MINUTES | COOK TIME: 10 MINUTES | SERVES: 4

Boil the eggs for 5 minutes, then allow to cool. Peel the eggs and place in a bowl. Add the melted butter and heat slightly. Season to taste with salt, pepper, nutmeg, and the chopped parsley.

Wash and peel the asparagus. Boil the peel in salted water for 5 minutes, then remove. Add the peeled asparagus to the same water and boil gently for 5 minutes. Allow to cool.

Cut each asparagus spear on an angle into 3 pieces, and heat in the butter until warmed through. Season to taste with salt, pepper, and nutmeg.

To serve, arrange the asparagus neatly on a plate, then place the egg mixture over the top.

INGREDIENTS

EGGS

4 eggs

3 oz/¾ stick (90 g) unsalted butter, melted

salt and freshly ground black pepper

freshly ground nutmeg

4 tsp chopped parsley

ASPARAGUS

16 white asparagus stalks

¾ tbsp (10 g) unsalted butter

salt and freshly ground black pepper

freshly ground nutmeg

Celeriac Remoulade

Josh Emett

COMPLEXITY: EASY | PREP TIME: 5 MINUTES | SERVES: 4

INGREDIENTS

1 large celery root/celeriac, peeled and julienned

sea salt

¼ cup (50 g) mayonnaise (p. 474)

¼ cup (50 g) sour cream

2½ tbsp whole-grain mustard

1½ tbsp Dijon mustard

1 tsp celery salt

¼ cup (7 g) chopped parsley

JOSH'S NOTES

Tip: Celery roots/celeriac vary in size, so add the dressing gradually – you may not need to use all of it.

Place the julienned celery root/celeriac in a bowl and lightly salt. Leave for about an hour, then wash off the salt and lightly squeeze the celery root/celeriac to remove excess moisture.

In a bowl, mix the mayonnaise, sour cream, and mustards, and season lightly with celery salt. Fold this mix through the celery root/celeriac, then add the chopped parsley and fold through.

Image on p. 120

Bread with Tomato
Pan con Tomate

Nieves Barragán Mohacho

COMPLEXITY: EASY | PREP TIME: 5 MINUTES | SERVES: 4

INGREDIENTS

4 slices white sourdough bread, each ¾ in (2 cm) thick

1 clove garlic, peeled and halved

8 to 12 plum tomatoes, halved

4 tbsp (60 ml) extra virgin olive oil

Maldon salt and freshly ground black pepper

1 tbsp chopped fresh flat-leaf parsley

Lightly toast the bread on both sides and rub each slice with the cut side of the garlic. Using your hands, squeeze 2 or 3 tomatoes over each slice so that the juice and pips fall on to the toasted bread.

Drizzle a tablespoon of olive oil over each slice. Season well with salt and pepper and sprinkle with a little chopped parsley before serving.

"It's all about the ingredients here – good tomatoes, good extra virgin olive oil, and good bread."
– NIEVES BARRAGÁN MOHACHO

St George's Mushrooms, Garlic & Parsley on Sourdough Toast

Tom Kerridge

COMPLEXITY: EASY | PREP TIME: 15 MINUTES | COOK TIME: 15 MINUTES | SERVES: 4

INGREDIENTS

5¼ tbsp (75 g) butter

2 tbsp (30 ml) rapeseed/canola oil

4 cloves garlic, crushed

1 banana shallot, finely chopped

14 oz (400 g) St George's mushrooms, wiped and trimmed – nice small ones are best, but if you can only get large ones, halve them

truffle oil, to taste

6¼ tbsp (100 ml) heavy/double cream

3½ oz (100 g) wild garlic leaves

3 tbsp parsley leaves, very finely chopped

2 tbsp chives, finely chopped

lemon juice, to taste

salt and pepper, to taste

4 slices sourdough bread, toasted, to serve

3½ oz (100 g) Parmesan, to serve

METHOD

Melt the butter with the rapeseed/canola oil in a large frying pan set over a medium heat. Add the garlic and shallot and fry, stirring, for 2 to 3 minutes until the shallot is just softened. Add the mushrooms, increase the heat to high and fry, stirring, for 3 to 4 minutes until they are just tender. Add the cream and a splash of truffle oil, and leave the cream to bubble until the mushrooms are glazed and creamy, 3 to 4 minutes.

Stir in the wild garlic leaves, parsley, and chives. Season and add lemon juice to taste. Spoon the mushroom mix on top of the hot pieces of toast. Grate the Parmesan over the top and serve immediately.

"Mushrooms on toast is a real favourite of mine. It was one of the first 'dishes' that I learnt to cook at home with my mum. This version is right in time for the spring season, using St George's mushrooms and wild garlic, but you can vary the ingredients depending on the season's available wild mushrooms."

– TOM KERRIDGE

JOSH'S NOTES

Preparation: Get a nice golden colour on the mushrooms to add flavour.

French-style Peas
Petit Pois à la Française

Josh Emett

COMPLEXITY: EASY | PREP TIME: 15 MINUTES | COOK TIME: 10 MINUTES | SERVES: 2

INGREDIENTS

3 slices/rashers bacon

2 tbsp (30 g) unsalted butter

½ onion, finely diced

2 cloves garlic, microplaned

10½ oz (300 g) peas, fresh or defrosted

1 oz (30 g) baby gem lettuce, roughly chopped

¼ cup plus 2 tsp (70 ml) cream

handful of parsley, chopped

sea salt to taste

METHOD

Pre-heat the oven to 350°F (180°C). Lay the bacon in an oven tray and bake for about 15 minutes, until crispy. Allow to cool, chop, and set aside.

Put a wide-based pot over a medium heat, add the butter and gently melt, without colouring. Add the onion and garlic, and sweat down for a few minutes, without colouring. Add the peas and lettuce, wilt the lettuce slightly and then add the cream. Bring to the boil, and simmer to reduce until the cream thickens and coats everything. Stir through the bacon and parsley, season to taste with sea salt and serve.

Roasted Vegetables Catalan-style
Escalivada Catalana

José Andrés

COMPLEXITY: EASY | PREP TIME: 15 MINUTES | COOK TIME: 1 HOUR | SERVES: 4

INGREDIENTS

1 medium-sized aubergine/eggplant

1 red bell pepper/capsicum

3 large ripe tomatoes

2 Spanish onions

olive oil, for roasting

¼ cup (60 ml) Spanish extra virgin olive oil

½ tbsp (7½ ml) sherry vinegar

salt and white pepper to taste

METHOD

Heat the oven to 400°F (200°C).

Take all the vegetables and, using a brush, coat them with a thin film of olive oil. Place them in a baking tray or a terracotta casserole, and roast the vegetables for 40 minutes. Remove the aubergine/eggplant, pepper/capsicum, and tomatoes, and set aside. Leave the onion in the oven for another 15 minutes until it, too, is soft. Remove and set aside.

By now the skins of the vegetables will be soft and loose. When cool enough to handle, peel the skins off the vegetables. De-seed the pepper/capsicum and remove the top. Remove the top of the tomato and the aubergine/eggplant with a knife.

Using your hands, tear the pepper/capsicum into strips and the tomato into three or four pieces. Do the same to the aubergine/eggplant. With a knife, slice the onion into rings. Mix the vegetables together and place them in a serving dish. Cover them with the extra virgin olive oil and sherry vinegar. Sprinkle with salt and pepper and serve.

TIP

If you have a barbecue, the ideal way to do this dish is on charcoal outdoors. In any case, this is a dish you can prepare days ahead and store in your refrigerator. It's wonderful served hot or cold.

JOSH'S NOTES

Key element: Take time to roast the vegetables properly, until nice and soft.

Tip: You'll need a very sharp knife to cut the roasted onions.

Complements: Great with Bread with Tomato (*Pan con Tomate*), p. 125, and Spanish sardines or anchovies.

"*Escalivada* comes from the Catalan verb *escalivar*, which is the process of cooking food slowly very close to the embers of a barbecue. The smokiness of the charcoal enriches the food and gives it an earthy quality. This recipe is for oven-roasting, but its soul comes from the open fire."

– JOSÉ ANDRÉS

Image on p. 121

Caponata

Rodney Dunn

COMPLEXITY: EASY | PREP TIME: 25 MINUTES | COOK TIME: 1 HOUR | SERVES: 6

INGREDIENTS

10½ oz (300 g) aubergine/eggplant, cut into ½-in (1-cm) dice

sea salt and freshly ground black pepper

6¾ tbsp (100 ml) extra virgin olive oil

1 stalk celery, finely diced

1 small red bell pepper/capsicum, seeds removed and flesh finely diced

1 onion, finely chopped

3 cloves garlic, finely chopped

¾ cup (150 ml) tomato passata

1 tbsp (15 ml) red wine vinegar

1 tsp sugar

¼ cup/1¼ oz (50 g) small salted capers, rinsed under warm water

2 tsp currants

1 tbsp pine nuts, toasted

This recipe accompanies Rodney Dunn's Beef Carpaccio with Caponata recipe, p. 244.

METHOD

Place the aubergine/eggplant in a colander, sprinkle with a little salt and toss to combine. Leave for 30 minutes, then rinse well and pat dry.

Heat 2 tablespoons (30 ml) of olive oil in a frying pan, add the celery and cook, stirring occasionally, over a medium heat for 5 to 7 minutes, or until soft, then remove from the pan and drain on paper towel. Add the bell pepper/capsicum to the pan and cook, stirring occasionally, for 5 to 7 minutes, or until soft, then remove from the pan and drain on paper towel.

Add the remaining olive oil to the pan, add the aubergine/eggplant and cook, stirring, for 5 minutes, or until soft, then remove from the pan and drain on paper towel. Add the onion and garlic to the pan and cook, stirring occasionally, for 5 minutes, or until soft. Stir in the tomato passata, celery, bell pepper/capsicum, aubergine/eggplant, vinegar, and sugar, and season to taste. Cook, stirring frequently, for 10 minutes, then reduce the heat to low and simmer for 15 minutes. Add the capers, currants, and pine nuts, and stir to combine. Taste and adjust the seasoning, if required.

Cauliflower Cheese

Josh Emett

COMPLEXITY: EASY | PREP TIME: 15 MINUTES | COOK TIME: 45 MINUTES | SERVES: 4

INGREDIENTS

sea salt to taste

1 large head cauliflower, cut into golfball-sized pieces

1¼ cups plus 2 tbsp (450 ml) milk

3 tbsp (40 g) unsalted butter

⅓ cup (40 g) all-purpose/plain flour

3½ oz (100 g) grated Cheddar

1 tsp Dijon mustard

TO FINISH

2 tbsp grated Cheddar

2 tbsp grated Parmesan

METHOD

Preheat oven to 375°F/190°C.

Bring a large pot of salted water to the boil, add the cauliflower and blanch for about 1 minute. Drain, and transfer the cauliflower to a large ovenproof dish, spreading it out evenly.

Pour the milk into a pot and bring close to the boil over a medium to low heat. In a separate pot, melt the butter and stir the flour in to make a roux, cooking out for 4 to 5 minutes without colouring. Remove from the heat and start to slowly add the hot milk, ladle by ladle, stirring until completely combined and smooth before adding more. Add the Cheddar cheese and Dijon mustard and stir until thoroughly combined. Season with sea salt.

Pour the sauce over the cauliflower, then sprinkle with Cheddar and Parmesan to finish. Bake for about 30 minutes, until golden brown all over. Serve immediately.

JOSH'S NOTES

Key element: Take time to make sure the cheese is well combined.

Tip: If it isn't golden brown and caramelized after 30 minutes, leave it longer in the oven.

Comment: Use a whisk to make my sauce extra-smooth.

Image on p. 120

Potato Gratin

Julien Royer

COMPLEXITY: EASY | PREP TIME: 15 MINUTES | COOK TIME: 35 MINUTES | SERVES: 8

INGREDIENTS

1¼ cups (300 ml) cream

1¼ cups (300 ml) milk

1 oz (5 cloves) garlic, peeled. Save 1 clove for end of recipe.

4 tbsp plus ½ tsp fresh thyme leaves

2 dried bay leaves

⅛ nutmeg

salt and pepper to taste

4½ lb (2 kg) Belle de Fontenay (or Charlotte) potatoes

3½ tbsp (50 g) butter

14 oz (400 g) young Comté cheese, aged 12 months

METHOD

Pre-heat the oven to 350°F (180°C).

Place the milk and cream in a saucepan and bring to the boil. Reduce the heat to a simmer, add ¾ oz (4 cloves) garlic, the thyme and bay leaves, and grated nutmeg, and leave, gently simmering, to infuse for 10 minutes. Remove the garlic and herbs. Season the milk and cream mixture with salt and pepper.

Peel and slice the potatoes to a thickness of ¹⁄₁₆ in (2 mm) using a Japanese mandoline. Add the potatoes to the simmering milk and cream mixture and continue to simmer until the potatoes are nearly fully cooked, and still holding their shape.

Remove the potatoes from the liquid, turn up the heat a little and reduce the liquid by half.

Meanwhile, grate 1 clove of fresh garlic and butter onto an oven-safe serving tray. Layer the potato slices in the serving tray for baking. Pour the reduced milk and cream mixture into the tray to cover the potatoes. Using a microplane, grate the Comté over the top of the potatoes. Bake for 20 to 25 minutes. And serve straight away.

Colcannon

Darina Allen

COMPLEXITY: EASY | PREP TIME: 15 MINUTES | COOK TIME: 35 MINUTES | SERVES: 8

INGREDIENTS

2 to 3 lb (900 g to
1.4 kg) 'old' potatoes,
e.g. Golden Wonders
or Kerr's Pinks

salt and freshly ground
black pepper

1 lb (450 g) savoy or
spring cabbage, or kale

about 3½ tbsp
(50 g) Irish butter
(I use Kerrygold)

about ¾ cup plus 3 tbsp
(225 ml) milk

4 oz (115 g) green
onions/spring onions,
finely chopped

METHOD

Scrub the potatoes, put them in a saucepan of cold water, add a good pinch of salt and bring to the boil. When the potatoes are about half-cooked, after about 15 minutes at a gentle boil, strain off two-thirds of the water, then replace the lid on the saucepan, put over a gentle heat and allow the potatoes to steam until just tender.

Remove the dark outer leaves from the cabbage. Wash the rest and cut into quarters, remove the core and cut finely across the grain. Boil in a little boiling water until soft, about 5 minutes. Drain, season with salt and pepper and add a little butter.

When the potatoes are cooked, put the milk and onion in a clean saucepan and bring to the boil. Meanwhile, pull the peel off the potatoes and discard. Mash the potatoes quickly while they are still warm, and beat in enough boiling milk to make a fluffy purée. (If you are making a large quantity, put the potatoes in the bowl of a food mixer and beat with the paddle.)

Stir in the cooked cabbage, taste and adjust seasoning. For perfection, serve immediately in a hot dish with a lump of butter melting in the centre.

Colcannon may be prepared ahead and left to cool without topping with butter. Re-heat in a moderate oven (350°F/180°C) for 20 to 25 minutes, keeping it covered so it doesn't get too crusty on top.

JOSH'S NOTES

Preparation: Slice cabbage ahead of time.

Key elements: Good-quality potatoes and nice, rich salted butter.

Complements: Very good with almost anything – roast lamb in particular.

Tip: Season the water well when boiling the potatoes, to ensure the flavour works through.

"Songs have been sung and poems have been written about colcannon. This comfort food at its very best has now been 'discovered' and is often a feature on smart restaurant menus in London and New York."
– DARINA ALLEN

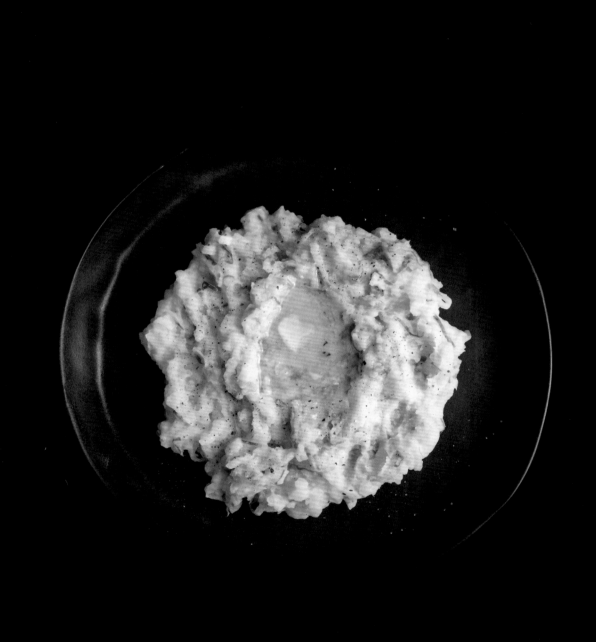

Potato Purée
Pommes Mousseline

Shannon Bennett

COMPLEXITY: EASY | PREP TIME: 10 MINUTES | COOK TIME: 35 MINUTES | SERVES: 6

INGREDIENTS

18 oz (500 g) potatoes

8¼ oz/2¼ sticks (250 g) butter, chopped into fine dice

1 to 2 tbsp (15 to 30 ml) warm milk

2 tbsp sea salt

METHOD

Cook the potatoes for 25 minutes in boiling salted water. Test with a knife – if it slides in without resistance, they are cooked. Immediately mash with 3 oz/¾ stick (90 g) of the butter. Mix any visible butter into the purée with a wooden spoon.

Place the purée in a saucepan, add 1 tablespoon (15 ml) of the milk and whisk on a low heat for 3 to 4 minutes. Add the remaining butter, a quarter at a time, whisking rapidly. If the butter starts to separate, the purée is too hot. Remove it from the heat, beat in 1 tablespoon (15 ml) of milk, then whisk like mad to bring it together. When all the butter is incorporated, check the seasoning, add salt if necessary, and serve.

"Marco Pierre White's head chef, Robert Reid, showed me this technique."

– SHANNON BENNETT

JOSH'S NOTES

Tip: Pass the potato through the finest sieve you have, to ensure a silky mash.

Key element: Process the mash very quickly; if it cools, the texture changes dramatically.

Comment: This is a very indulgent dish, but exactly what a great potato purée should taste like.

Potato Puffs
Pommes Dauphine
Anne-Sophie Pic

COMPLEXITY: MODERATE | PREP TIME: 30 MINUTES | COOK TIME: 45 MINUTES | SERVES: 4

INGREDIENTS

18 oz (500 g) potatoes

2 cups plus 1¼ tbsp
(500 ml) water

fine salt and freshly
ground black pepper

4½ tbsp (65 g) butter

1 cup (125 g) all-
purpose/plain flour,
plus extra for rolling

4 egg yolks, lightly
beaten

pinch of freshly grated
nutmeg

2 qt (2 litres) groundnut/
peanut oil for deep-
frying

JOSH'S NOTES

Preparation: Coordinate
the potato and choux
so they are the same
temperature when
combining.

Key element: Dry
potatoes – after
draining, pop them back
on the heat briefly to
remove excess moisture.

Tip: Test the
temperature of the oil
with one puff first.

METHOD

Cook the potatoes, unpeeled, in boiling water. Once cooked, peel and then mash them using a potato ricer or Mouli. Put the potato flesh in a bowl and keep to one side.

For the choux pastry, bring the water to the boil in a saucepan, then add the butter and a pinch of fine salt. When the butter has melted, with the pan still on the heat, add the flour all in one go and mix well with a spatula. Cook, stirring constantly, for about 10 minutes over a medium heat until the mixture is dry and starting to come away from the sides of the pan.

Remove from the heat and tip into a large bowl, then slowly work in the beaten egg yolks. Add the potato flesh and the nutmeg, season with salt and pepper, and mix well. With lightly floured hands, form the mixture into balls. Put them on a lightly floured work surface.

Heat the oil in a large saucepan or deep-fryer to 350°F (180°C), then immerse the balls in the hot oil and fry until they are a lovely golden colour. Remove with a slotted spoon, drain on kitchen paper and season with a little fine salt. Transfer to a dish and serve immediately.

"Though these potato puffs might seem like a cheffy invention, they actually date from the nineteenth century and are typical of the sort of side dishes found on bistro menus. A perfect combination of choux pastry and nutmeg-scented mashed potatoes formed into balls and then quick-fried, they are loved by children."

– ANNE-SOPHIE PIC

Potato Rösti

Josh Emett

COMPLEXITY: MODERATE   I   PREP TIME: 25 MINUTES   I   COOK TIME: 20 MINUTES   I   SERVES: 4

INGREDIENTS

3 medium-sized Agria
potatoes

½ tsp sea salt, plus extra
as needed

4¼ tbsp (60 g) unsalted
butter, melted

METHOD

Peel the potatoes, then grate or julienne into a bowl. Season
with sea salt and leave for 20 minutes, until the moisture has
been released.

Drain, then transfer to a clean tea towel or similar and wring out
until completely dry. Tip into a clean bowl, add the butter and
mix well, seasoning to taste with extra sea salt.

Place a small frying pan over a medium heat. Tip the potato mix
into the centre and press it out to the sides, flattening it neatly.
Continue to cook while closely monitoring the temperature and
watching for colour on the potato around the outside of the pan,
about 6 to 8 minutes.

Once the potato is completely coloured and crispy, use a palette
knife to gently release it from the pan, then flip it over to colour
on the other side. Press gently down with the palette knife, and
cook the underside until golden as well, about 6 to 8 minutes.

Serve once crispy and the potato is cooked through.

_____

"This is not only a great accompaniment to more hearty fare,
my kids also love this for breakfast with bacon and eggs."

– JOSH EMETT

JOSH'S NOTES

Preparation: Make your
prep quicker by using a
grating attachment on a
food processor.

Key element: Use good
quality potatoes, then
wring them out well,
after salting, with a
tea towel.

Tip: Take your time
cooking the rösti –
super-crispy on the
outside and a little soft
on the inside is perfect.

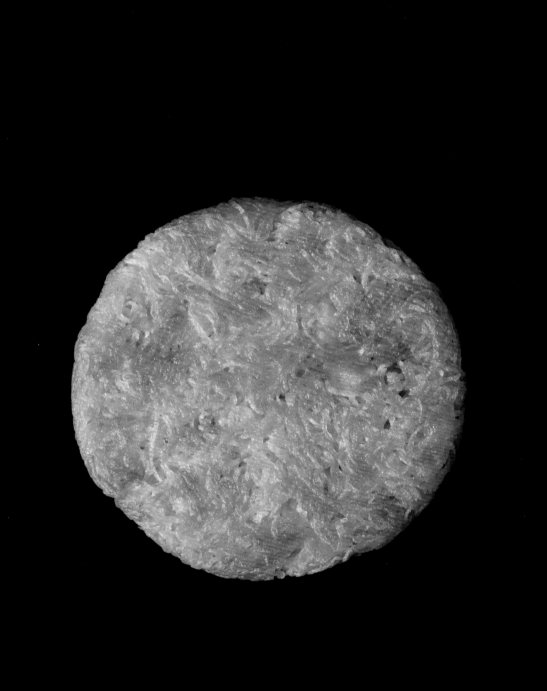

Potatoes Anna
Pommes Anna

Josh Emett

COMPLEXITY: MODERATE | PREP TIME: 10 MINUTES | COOK TIME: 1 HOUR 30 MINUTES
SERVES: 6 TO 8

INGREDIENTS

6 medium-sized
potatoes, Agria or
similar (3⅓ lb/1½ kg)

½ cup plus 2 tbsp
(150 g) clarified butter

1 tsp salt

METHOD

Preheat oven to 350°F (180°C).

Peel the potatoes, then use a mandolin to slice finely into a large
bowl. Pat dry with paper towel, then pour clarified butter over the
top. Season with sea salt and gently toss to coat evenly.

Take an ovenproof frying pan, and begin to layer potato slices
around the side and the base. Do this neatly, as it will form the
pattern of the Pommes Anna once cooked and turned out.

When the base is covered, continue to layer potato into the pan,
finishing with an even layer. Drain off any excess water that may
have come off the potato.

Place the pan over a medium heat and begin to cook – you are
essentially cooking blind to get the colour, so heat until you can see
the butter sizzling and the potatoes starting to turn golden around
the outside. Transfer to the oven and bake for 1 hour 15 minutes,
until golden all over. Halfway through, remove from the oven and
gently press to make sure the layering is tight.

Once cooked, remove from the oven and rest for at least 30 minutes
to allow to set. You can then either turn out and reheat on a baking
tray, or cut and reheat in the oven to serve (20 minutes if whole,
8 to 10 minutes if cut). To turn out, place a flat plate over the pan,
holding the sides with a tea towel, then flip over and allow to
release from the pan.

JOSH'S NOTES

Preparation: Allow time
to cool if you'd like to
cut to serve; it's difficult
to cut when just cooked.

Key element: Start
cooking over a medium
heat – if you get it right,
it won't burn.

Tip: Take your time
over layering the
potato – it will result
in an impressive effect
when serving.

"Perfect with a beautiful steak and accompanying sauce to
soak up the flavours."
– JOSH EMETT

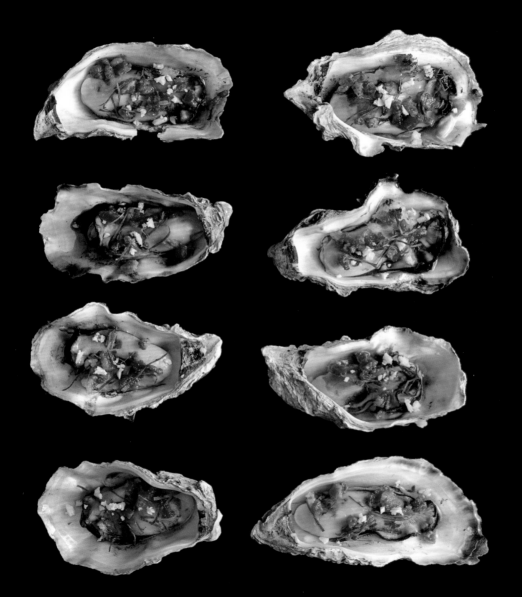

Oysters Kilpatrick, p. 148

Seafood

The bounty of the ocean provides a generous and diverse offering, and its largesse is transformed into an equally wide array of dishes favoured by any cuisine within a day's travel of a sea, lake, or river. The simplicity of steamed or grilled fillets served with a squeeze of lemon; the rich umami flavours of a classic Basque *marmitako*; the complex depth of cured, confit, or marinated fish; and the delicacy of freshly harvested shellfish, imparting the very essence of the depths from which it comes. There is only one essential requirement to creating a superb seafood dish – freshness. The minimum amount of time possible between hooking or harvesting your catch and cooking it will ensure you create a dish fit for Poseidon himself. And if you can't catch your own, be sure to source sustainably so that future generations can continue to enjoy *les fruits de mer*.

Iced Poached Oysters

Guy Savoy

COMPLEXITY: MODERATE | PREP TIME: 1 HOUR 30 MINUTES | COOK TIME: 10 MINUTES
MAKES: 15

INGREDIENTS

15 raw oysters
(I use Prat Ar Coum
spéciales no. 2)

¾ cup plus 1¼ tbsp
(200 ml) cream

5 gelatine leaves,
softened in cold water
and squeezed out

salt and freshly ground
black pepper

1 carrot

4 spinach leaves

18 oz (500 g) seaweed

juice of 1 lemon

8 oyster leaves

JOSH'S NOTES

Preparation: Set the
oyster cream and oyster
jelly in advance.

Key element: Use good-
quality fresh oysters,
and set the cream to the
correct consistency.

Tip: Be very gentle
when opening the
oyster shells so as not
to cut into the oyster.

METHOD

Open the oysters, setting aside the water contained within the shell
for later. Remove the oysters from their shells with the point of a knife,
being careful not to damage the flesh, and set the shells aside. Wash
the oysters one by one under cold running water to remove any residual
sand, then place on absorbent paper and keep cool. Scrub the shells to
remove any remaining sand and unreleased oyster flesh, then dry.

In a small saucepan, bring half of the cream to the boil and mix in
2 leaves of softened gelatine until fully dissolved. Remove from the heat.

Place the remaining cream in a blender, add 3 oysters and blend until
smooth. Mix the two cream mixtures together, then pass through a
chinois and season to taste with salt and pepper if necessary. Place
1 tablespoon of oyster cream in the base of each shell and place in
the refrigerator to set.

Strain the reserved oyster juice through a fine cloth to remove any
remaining sand. If the juice is over-seasoned, add a small amount
of water. Decant 10½ oz (300 g) of the juice into a bowl. In a small
saucepan, warm a small amount of this juice, add the remaining
3 leaves of softened gelatine, stir until dissolved, then stir this mixture
into the juice in the bowl. Cover and place in the refrigerator to set.

Peel and cannele the carrot (i.e. cut grooves at regular intervals along
the length of the carrot), then slice into discs $1/24$ in (1 mm) thick.
Set up a bowl of iced water and bring a pot of water to the boil.
Cook the carrot slices in the boiling water for 4 to 5 minutes, until
just cooked, then refresh in the iced water. Cut the spinach leaves
into juliennes $1/16$ in (2 mm) thick.

Set up another bowl of iced water. Bring a large pan of water to the
boil, blanch the seaweed for 1 to 2 minutes, and refresh in the iced
water to fix the colour. Rinse and set aside. Place a slice of carrot on top
of each oyster and finish with a stalk of spinach to resemble a flower.

In a mixing bowl, whisk the lemon juice into the oyster jelly. Lay the
oysters within their shells, on top of the set cream. Cover each oyster
with the oyster jelly. Place the shells on a bed of blanched seaweed.
Finish with a twist of pepper and place the oyster leaves on top of
the oyster shells.

Cushion of Oyster with Ossetra Caviar Grains

Yannick Alléno

COMPLEXITY: MODERATE | PREP TIME: 30 MINUTES | COOK TIME: 45 MINUTES | SERVES: 4

INGREDIENTS

SOLE VELOUTÉ

1 oz (30 g) shallot, sliced

1 oz (30 g) white onion, sliced

1 oz (30 g) leek (white part only), sliced

⅓ oz (10 g) button mushrooms, sliced

3 oz/¼ stick (80 g) butter

1 clove garlic, crushed

sprig of thyme

white pepper to taste

10½ oz (300 g) sole bones

6½ oz (100 g) Noilly Prat

2 cups plus 1¼ tbsp oz (500 g) still mineral water

4 tsp cream

1½ tsp cornstarch/cornflour

1 tsp gelatine, rehydrated in cold water

½ oz (15 g) Savora mustard

OYSTER CUSHIONS

4 Belon oysters (I use no. 000)

8 slices sandwich bread

3½ oz (100 g) creamed butter

TO SERVE

3 oz (80 g) Ossetra caviar

METHOD

For the sole velouté, sweat the aromatic garnish (the shallot, onion, leek, and mushrooms) in the butter, along with the garlic, thyme, and white pepper, over a medium-low heat until soft but not coloured. Add the fish bones and deglaze with the Noilly Prat. Simmer to reduce by half, add the mineral water, and leave to cook for 20 minutes. Remove from the heat to rest for 15 minutes, then strain without pressing down on the solids.

Measure 6¾ tablespoons (100 ml) of fish stock into a small saucepan, add the cream and cornstarch/cornflour and stir until smooth. Warm over a low heat to thicken. Remove from the heat, add the gelatine and Savora and stir until the gelatine is fully dissolved. Lay a piece of plastic wrap on the surface of the velouté and place in the refrigerator to cool rapidly.

For the oyster cushions, open the oysters, remove the nerve and keep the oysters in their water. Dab the centre of 2 slices of sandwich bread with sole velouté and sandwich an oyster in the middle. Butter both sides well, then press the sandwich between two plates before vacuum-packing. Keep in the refrigerator.

To finish and assemble, place a frying pan over a medium heat, carefully remove each cushion from its mould, then trim it and brown on both sides while maintaining the temperature at medium. Place each cushion on a plate and add ¾ oz (20 g) of caviar per cushion.

JOSH'S NOTES

Key element: Use very fresh oysters; if they are small, you could use two.

Tip: When pan frying, watch for hot spots in the pan and keep the temperature even.

Oysters Kilpatrick

Michael Meredith

COMPLEXITY: EASY | PREP TIME: 15 MINUTES | COOK TIME: 7 MINUTES | MAKES: 24

INGREDIENTS

3 cups plus 2¾ tbsp (840 g) rock salt

24 Pacific rock oysters, freshly shucked (see p. 144 for method)

3 tbsp Worcestershire sauce

7 oz (200 g) rindless smoked shoulder bacon, diced

½ cup (15 g) flat-leaf parsley, roughly chopped

fresh horseradish

lemon wedges

Pre-heat the grill on a medium-high heat. Place the rock salt on a baking tray. Arrange the shucked oysters in the half-shell on the rock salt.

Sprinkle the Worcestershire sauce over the oysters and top with the bacon. Grill for 5 to 7 minutes, or until the bacon is crisp. Sprinkle with parsley and freshly grated horseradish, and serve with lemon wedges on the side.

JOSH'S NOTES

Preparation: Make sure you dislodge the oysters from the shell for ease of eating.

Key element: Be careful to clean off any grit when shucking the oysters.

Image on p. 142

Clam Bruschetta with Roasted Vegetables

Heinz Beck

COMPLEXITY: EASY | PREP TIME: 25 MINUTES | COOK TIME: 10 MINUTES | SERVES: 4

INGREDIENTS

CLAMS

14 oz (400 g) clams

1 tbsp (15 ml) extra virgin olive oil

1 clove garlic

1 sprig thyme

6¾ tbsp (100 ml) white wine

1 sprig parsley, leaves chopped

ROASTED VEGETABLES

2 carrots

2 stalks celery

1 small fennel bulb

1 small onion

1 tbsp (15 ml) extra virgin olive oil

salt and black pepper

BRUSCHETTA

8 slices Tuscan bread

few sprigs parsley

METHOD

Bleed the clams in salted water for a couple of hours, renewing the water often. Drain before using.

Heat a little oil in a large pan, with the garlic and thyme. Add the drained clams, sprinkle with the white wine, put on the lid and keep the heat high until the clams are all open (a few minutes). Discard any that do not open. Remove the clams from the shells and set aside.

Add the chopped parsley to the clam cooking liquid, stir in, then filter the liquid through a few thicknesses of muslin cloth placed over a colander.

Clean, wash, and peel the carrot, celery, and fennel, and cut them into brunoise. Chop the onion into brunoise.

Heat a little extra virgin olive oil in a frying pan over a medium heat and fry the onion for 3 minutes, without colouring. Add the vegetables and cook until tender, then sprinkle with the clam liquid. Allow the liquid to absorb for a few minutes, then adjust the seasoning with salt and pepper.

To serve, grill the slices of bread until golden. Place the roasted vegetables on top, then the clams. Garnish with a few tufts of parsley.

JOSH'S NOTES

Preparation: Rinse the clams of any excess sand and saltiness.

Tip: This is a very subtle dish; sweat the vegetables gently to allow their sweetness to come through.

Image on p. 192

Mussels in White Wine
Moules Marinière

Rick Stein

COMPLEXITY: EASY | PREP TIME: 10 MINUTES | COOK TIME: 5 MINUTES | SERVES: 4

INGREDIENTS

4 lb (1¾ kg) mussels, scrubbed, rinsed, and beards removed

3½ tbsp (50 g) unsalted butter

1 medium-sized onion, finely chopped

3 tbsp plus 1 tsp (50 ml) dry white wine

1 tbsp coarsely chopped parsley

METHOD

Put the mussels, butter, onion, and white wine into a very large pan. Cover and cook over a high heat for 3 to 4 minutes, shaking the pan every now and then, until the mussels have opened. Discard any that do not open.

Spoon the mussels into bowls. Add the parsley to the remaining juices, then pour all but the last tablespoon or two, which might contain some grit, back over the mussels.

_____

"There was a time, when a bowl of moules marinière, was to me simply the most exotic thing. You couldn't get mussels in Britain unless you picked them yourself off the rocks."

– RICK STEIN

JOSH'S NOTES

Tip: Clean and de-beard the mussels before cooking.

INGREDIENTS

**TIGER'S MILK BASE
(MAKES 7¾ OZ/220 G)**

3½ oz (100 g) celery, roughly chopped

3½ oz (100 g) onion, roughly chopped

2 cloves garlic, peeled but left whole

1¼ in (3 cm) piece fresh root ginger, peeled

2 tbsp fine sea salt

1 tsp sugar

3½ oz (100 g) cilantro/coriander stems

CEVICHE

9 oz (250 g) cherry tomatoes

1 recipe freshly made tiger's milk (see below)

fine sea salt

10½ oz (300 g) very fresh scallops, shelled and cleaned

cilantro/coriander flowers (if available) or leaves, to garnish

**TIGER'S MILK
(MAKES 14 OZ/400 G)**

½ cup (120 ml) lime juice (from about 2 lb/900 g limes)

2 tbsp (30 ml) tiger's milk base (see above)

1 oz (30 g) very fresh, skinless white fish fillet

7 oz (200 g) ice cubes

fine sea salt

TO SERVE

1 tsp ají limon chilli or pickled jalapeño, deseeded and finely chopped

Scallop & Tomato Ceviche

Ceviche de Conchas y Tomates

Virgilio Martínez

COMPLEXITY: MODERATE | PREP TIME: 30 MINUTES, PLUS REFRIGERATION TIME | SERVES: 4

METHOD

For the tiger's milk base, place all the ingredients except the cilantro/coriander stems in a blender and blend until puréed. Add the cilantro/coriander stems to the purée, then leave to marinate in the refrigerator for 1 hour before removing and discarding the cilantro/coriander. Cover tightly and refrigerate until ready to use.

To skin the tomatoes, bring a saucepan of water to the boil. Put some cold water and ice in a bowl. Score a small cross in one end of each cherry tomato. Add the tomatoes to the boiling water and leave for 10 seconds, then transfer to the iced water but remove almost immediately. Using a paring knife, remove the skin.

Put half the tomatoes in a blender and blend for 2 minutes, then strain the juice through a fine-meshed sieve. Add 5 tablespoons (75 ml) of the tomato juice to the blender with freshly made tiger's milk and blend for 3 minutes. Pass through a fine-meshed sieve and adjust the seasoning, adding more salt if necessary. Cover and set aside in the refrigerator.

For the tiger's milk, place the lime juice, tiger's milk base, fish, and ice cubes in a blender and blend for 1 minute. Strain through a fine-meshed sieve into a non-reactive bowl. Adjust the seasoning with salt and add the chilli. Cover and refrigerate for 5 minutes (no longer) before using.

Cut the scallops in half. Mix the reserved tomatoes with the tiger's milk mixture, then spoon into a serving dish and arrange the scallops on top. Garnish with cilantro/coriander flowers, if available, or leaves, and serve immediately.

TIP

The limes should be freshly juiced whenever you prepare tiger's milk, never in advance. Also, never squeeze the limes with a machine but by hand. The complete recipe for tiger's milk should always be made fresh and used immediately.

Grilled Scallops with Sweet Chilli Sauce & Crème Fraîche

Peter Gordon

COMPLEXITY: EASY | PREP TIME: 10 MINUTES | COOK TIME: 3 MINUTES | SERVES: 4

INGREDIENTS

12 large diver-caught scallops, cleaned, coral left attached

1 tsp sesame oil

salt and freshly ground black pepper

picked watercress or wild arugula/rocket leaves

3 tbsp plus 1 tsp (50 ml) sweet chilli sauce (p. 459)

1¾ oz (50 g) crème fraîche

METHOD

Drizzle the scallops with the sesame oil and lightly season them with salt and pepper. Heat a chargrill or heavy-based frying pan until very hot, then cook the scallops for around 1 minute on each side, until golden. Avoid overcooking them, as they will become tough.

Place the watercress on each plate and sit 3 scallops on top. Dollop on the sweet chilli sauce, then the crème fraîche.

JOSH'S NOTES

Preparation: Make the sweet chilli sauce in advance; you will have leftovers and it keeps well.

Tip: The bigger the scallops are, the easier it is to control the cooking time.

INGREDIENTS

16 raw king shrimp/prawns, peeled and de-veined, tails left intact

sea salt and freshly ground black pepper

extra virgin olive oil, for drizzling

¼ iceberg lettuce, thinly sliced

1 avocado, diced

Vietnamese mint leaves, to garnish

MANGO SALSA

2 ripe mangoes

¼ red onion, very finely diced

1 red chilli, seeded and finely chopped

2 tbsp roughly chopped Vietnamese mint

2 tbsp roughly chopped cilantro/coriander leaves

1½ tbsp (22½ ml) Chardonnay vinegar or white wine vinegar

1 tbsp (15 ml) extra virgin olive oil

sea salt and freshly ground black pepper

Barbecued Prawns with Avocado & Mango Salsa

Luke Mangan

COMPLEXITY: EASY | PREP TIME: 20 MINUTES | COOK TIME: 5 MINUTES | SERVES: 4

METHOD

For the mango salsa, peel the mangoes, then cut off the cheeks and as much flesh off the stones as possible. Dice the mango flesh and place in a mixing bowl. Add the remaining salsa ingredients, seasoning to taste with sea salt and freshly ground black pepper, and mix lightly. Set aside.

For the shrimp/prawns, pre-heat a barbecue or heavy-based frying pan until hot. Place the shrimp/prawns on a tray. Season and drizzle with just enough olive oil to coat them. Transfer the shrimp/prawns to the barbecue or frying pan and cook for 2 minutes on one side. Turn over and cook for a further 2 minutes. Remove and rest on a plate for another 2 minutes.

To serve, add the lettuce to the mango salsa and place on a platter or four individual serving plates. Scatter the shrimp/prawns and avocado on top. Garnish with Vietnamese mint, drizzle with a little more olive oil and serve.

JOSH'S NOTES

Preparation: Make the salsa in advance to allow the flavours to develop.

Key element: A perfectly ripe mango, but not too soft.

Tip: Make sure your barbecue or pan is nice and hot; only season the shrimp/prawns seconds before you put them on to cook.

Image on p. 192

INGREDIENTS

1¾ oz (50 g) piece cucumber

2¾ oz (80 g) cooked peeled shrimp/prawns

handful of shredded gem or iceberg lettuce

1 or 2 green onions/ spring onions, finely sliced on an angle

¼ cup (60 ml) cocktail sauce (recipe below)

cayenne pepper, to taste

1 wedge lemon

COCKTAIL SAUCE
(MAKES 2 CUPS + 4 TSP
/500 ML)

1¼ cups (300 g) mayonnaise (p. 474)

¾ cup plus 1¼ tbsp (200 g) tomato ketchup

1½ tbsp horseradish sauce

½ tbsp (7½ ml) Worcestershire sauce

½ tsp Tabasco, or to taste

lemon juice, to taste

Prawn Cocktail

Mark Hix

COMPLEXITY: EASY | PREP TIME: 15 MINUTES | SERVES: 1

METHOD

Mix all of the sauce ingredients together, and adjust according to taste. Set aside.

Cut the cucumber in half lengthways and remove the seeds. Finely julienne the skin and flesh, keeping them separate. Set aside.

Using a nice serving bowl, place 2 shrimp/prawns in the bottom with a small amount of cocktail sauce.

Mix the lettuce, cucumber flesh, and green onions/spring onions together, and place in the bowl. Add remaining shrimp/prawns and coat with remaining cocktail sauce. Finish with a shake of cayenne and the cucumber skin. Serve with the wedge of lemon. The cocktail sauce will keep in the refrigerator for a few days.

JOSH'S NOTES

Preparation: Make the sauce in advance; slice the salad ingredients at the last minute so they're nice and crisp.

Tip: Poach the shrimps/ prawns gently in salted water so they remain plump and full of flavour.

Pan-fried Squid with Broad Beans & Chorizo

Rodney Dunn

COMPLEXITY: EASY | PREP TIME: 15 MINUTES | COOK TIME: 3 TO 4 MINUTES | SERVES: 4

INGREDIENTS

10½ oz (300 g) young fava/broad beans (from about 28½ oz/ 800 g pods)

17½ oz (500 g) squid, cleaned, tentacles reserved

⅓ cup (80 ml) olive oil

6 cloves garlic, thinly sliced

3½ oz (100 g) chorizo, cut into ½-in (1-cm) pieces

3 strips lemon rind

sea salt and freshly ground black pepper

large handful of mint leaves

coarsely torn lemon wedges, to serve

METHOD

Bring a large saucepan of salted water to the boil over a high heat. Add the fava/broad beans and cook for 1 minute, then drain in a sieve and refresh under cold running water.

Using a sharp knife, thinly slice the squid tubes into strips about 2 in (5 cm) long. Cut the tentacles to separate each leg.

Heat the olive oil in a large frying pan over a medium-high heat, add the garlic and sauté until fragrant, about 1 minute. Add the squid and chorizo, and sauté until the squid is just cooked and beginning to colour. Add the fava/broad beans and lemon rind, then season with salt and pepper and cook until the beans are just warmed through. Stir through the mint leaves and serve immediately, with lemon wedges for squeezing over.

"Broad [fava] beans usually divide the crowd – people seem to either love them or hate them. On closer investigation, those who hate them have usually suffered through mealy and starchy broad beans that have been picked too late. To add insult to injury, the beans have then been boiled until they are grey and watery. Broad beans need to be picked young and sweet, like peas. At this size they can be eaten raw or just lightly blanched – and come with a proud track-record of converting every hater I've come across into a lover. Well, let's say a liker . . ."

– RODNEY DUNN

JOSH'S NOTES

Key element: Use fresh squid if you can source it, and good-quality chorizo.

Octopus Fairground-style
Pulpo a la Feria

Rick Stein

COMPLEXITY: EASY | PREP TIME: 15 MINUTES | COOK TIME: 1 HOUR | SERVES: 4

INGREDIENTS

1 octopus, about 1⅔ lb (750 g)

1 onion, peeled

4 bay leaves

salt

½ tsp pimento picante (smoked hot Spanish paprika)

3 tbsp plus 1 tsp (50 ml) good olive oil

½ to 1 tsp sea salt flakes

METHOD

Clean the octopus by rinsing thoroughly, for about 5 minutes. Bring a large pan of water to the boil along with the onion, bay leaves, and salt at the ratio of 1 teaspoon per 3⅛ cups (750 ml). Add the octopus and simmer for at least 45 minutes. Test, then cook for a further 15 to 20 minutes if it is still a little tough.

Lift the octopus out of the pan and drain away all the excess water. Put it on a board, cut off the tentacles and slice each one on the diagonal into pieces about ¼ in (5 mm) thick. Cut the body into similar-sized pieces. Sprinkle with the pimento picante.

Warm the olive oil in a small pan and drizzle it over the octopus, then sprinkle with the sea salt and serve.

———————

"Translated as 'Octopus, fairground style', this is the classic Galician way of serving it. Buy octopus with two rows of suckers on each tentacle, called the common octopus (*Octopus vulgaris*); it is noticeably more tender than any others."

– RICK STEIN

JOSH'S NOTES

Key element: Cook the *pulpo* perfectly; test it as you go.

Tip: Be very gentle when trimming the octopus; the pulpo could also be finished on a barbecue if you like.

Image on p. 192

INGREDIENTS

1 green chilli, sliced thinly on an angle

1 red chilli, sliced thinly on an angle

12 cherry tomatoes, sliced in half

7 oz (200 g) white crab meat (picked)

salt and freshly ground black pepper

zest and juice of 1 lemon

1 tbsp sliced basil

1 green onion/spring onion, sliced thinly on an angle

1 tbsp chopped coriander

olive oil

2 large slices good-quality sourdough

1 clove garlic

zest and juice of 1 lime

COLD PICKLE

1¼ cups (300 ml) water

⅓ cup (75 ml) white wine vinegar

¾ cup (175 ml) superfine/caster sugar

5 tsp olive oil

1 tsp salt

1 red onion, thinly sliced

CEVICHE DRESSING

3 tbsp plus 1 tsp (50 ml) white wine vinegar

3 tbsp plus 1 tsp (50 ml) rice wine vinegar

sea salt to taste

1 cup plus 2 tsp (250 g) olive oil

½ tbsp (7½ ml) sesame seed oil

Padstow Crab on Toast

Paul Ainsworth

COMPLEXITY: MODERATE | PREP TIME: 35 MINUTES | COOK TIME: 5 MINUTES | SERVES: 4

METHOD

For the cold pickle, place all the ingredients except the onion in a saucepan and warm to a tepid temperature to dissolve the sugar. Then cool. Add the sliced red onion, cover with plastic wrap and leave in the fridge overnight.

For the ceviche dressing, place both vinegars in a large bowl and season lightly with salt, then add the olive oil and sesame oil and use a hand blender to emulsify the dressing together. Set aside.

Have two small pans of boiling-hot, lightly salted water and two bowls of iced water ready. Place the green chilli in one pan of boiling water and the red chilli in the other, blanch for 30 seconds and immediately refresh in the ice-cold water. Repeat three times in total. This takes the hotness of the chillies to a milder flavour.

Liberally douse the cherry tomatoes with the ceviche dressing, reserving some for later, and warm gently in a small saucepan.

Place the crab meat in a bowl, and season well with salt and pepper, a good squeeze of fresh lemon and some microplaned lemon zest, and a pinch of basil. Mix gently and taste to correct the seasoning.

Remove the red onion from the pickling liquid and place in a bowl. Add the green and red chilli, green onion/spring onion, chopped coriander, and remaining sliced basil, to make a salsa.

Drizzle olive oil over the sourdough, and toast or chargrill until nice and golden brown, then rub with the garlic clove.

When the cherry tomatoes are warmed, blow-torch them until beautifully charred and bursting as the skin tightens. Add the tomatoes to the salsa mix, season, and add a little more ceviche dressing along with a squeeze each of lime and lemon juice.

Dress the salad onto the chargrilled sourdough, then spoon the white crab mix over the top. Sprinkle a little lemon and lime zest over, and finish with a little more of the ceviche dressing.

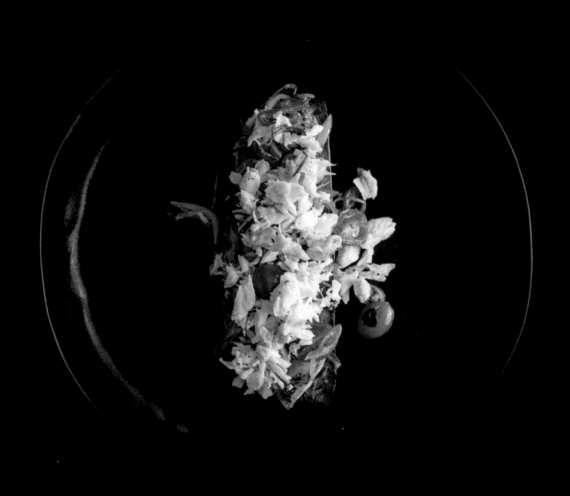

INGREDIENTS

1 carrot, chopped

1 onion, chopped

1 stalk celery, chopped

1 sprig of thyme

1 small bunch of parsley

20 white peppercorns, crushed

2 cups plus 1¼ tbsp (500 ml) white wine

2 cups plus 1¼ tbsp (500 ml) white wine vinegar

1 bay leaf

10 qt (10 litres) water

salt

6 x 18 oz (500 g) live native lobsters

8¾ oz/2¼ sticks (250 g) unsalted butter, softened

THERMIDOR SAUCE

¾ cup plus 1¼ tbsp (200 ml) fish velouté (p. 465)

1 to 2 tbsp Colman's English mustard

¾ cup plus 1¼ tbsp (200 ml) hollandaise sauce (p. 473)

2 tbsp whipped cream

4 egg yolks

salt and freshly ground white pepper

TO FINISH

3½ oz (100 g) Gruyère cheese, grated

few sprigs of picked chervil, to garnish

Lobster Thermidor

Marco Pierre White

COMPLEXITY: MODERATE | PREP TIME: 45 MINUTES | COOK TIME: 45 MINUTES | SERVES: 6

METHOD

Make the stock first. Put the carrot, onion, celery, thyme, parsley, peppercorns, wine, vinegar, bay leaf, and water in a large pot. Bring to the boil, turn down the heat and simmer until all of the vegetables are cooked, about 15 minutes. Turn off the heat and leave to infuse for 1 hour. Strain into a clean pot and season with salt to taste.

Bring the stock to just below boiling point. Carefully remove the bands from the lobster claws, and plunge the lobsters into the pan for 4 minutes. Remove them, wrap them in plastic wrap and set them to one side for 5 minutes to relax.

Remove the claws from the bodies, crack them open with the back of a heavy cook's knife and take out the meat. Also remove the meat from the knuckles and set aside. With a large, sharp knife, cut the lobsters in half lengthways and remove the meat, discarding the brain sac. Clean out the lobster shells.

Place the softened butter in a piping bag and pipe a small amount of butter into the cavity of both shells, from end to end. Cut the body meat into three or four pieces, and place them back in the opposite side of the shell so that the red meat shows. Put the knuckle meat and claw into the brain cavity. Pipe a little more butter over the top to cover.

Pre-heat the oven to 400°F (200°C).

To make the sauce, heat the velouté to room temperature and whisk in the mustard. The hotter you like it, the more you add. Carefully fold in the hollandaise sauce, whipped cream, and egg yolks. Adjust the seasoning as required.

Heat a roasting dish in the oven, put the lobsters on it and bake them for 3 to 4 minutes. Don't let the butter burn. Take the lobsters out of the oven and turn the oven to grill. Spoon the sauce over the top of the lobsters and sprinkle with the cheese. Flash them under the hot grill until the sauce begins to turn golden brown. Arrange on a plate and decorate with the chervil.

"I like to think that our juicy, sweet British lobsters make our version of Lobster Thermidor the best in the world."
– MARCO PIERRE WHITE

Tuna Tataki Salad

Harumi Kurihara

COMPLEXITY: EASY | PREP TIME: 15 MINUTES | COOK TIME: 10 MINUTES | SERVES: 4

INGREDIENTS

BANNO SOY SAUCE

6¾ tbsp (100 ml) mirin

1¼ cups (300 ml) soy sauce

4-in (10-cm) piece *konbu* seaweed, wiped of any salty deposits

SALAD

9 oz (250 g) daikon (mooli or Japanese white radish)

10 basil or shiso leaves, roughly shredded

2 tbsp (30 ml) sunflower or vegetable oil

16 oz (450 g) sashimi-quality tuna

salt and pepper to season

⅓ oz (10 g) garlic, finely sliced

wasabi, and *banno* soy sauce (see above) or ponzu sauce (p. 479), to serve

JOSH'S NOTES

Key element: Once the crispy garlic is removed from the pan, make sure it is nice and hot for searing the tuna.

Tip: Be confident and slice the tuna with purpose; if you hesitate, it can tear.

METHOD

To make the *banno* soy sauce, bring the mirin to the boil in a small saucepan set over a medium heat, then reduce the heat and cook on low for a further 2 to 3 minutes to burn off the alcohol. Remove from the heat and add the soy sauce and *konbu*. Cool and refrigerate.

Peel the daikon and chop into fine julienne strips 2 in (5 cm) long. Place in iced water for 10 minutes to crisp up. Drain and dry. Mix the daikon and basil together.

Place the oil in a frying pan and heat. Meanwhile, season the tuna with salt and pepper. When the pan is hot, add the sliced garlic and fry until slightly crispy, taking care as it can burn easily. The garlic gives the oil a wonderful aroma. When cooked, remove the garlic with a slotted spoon and set aside.

Put the tuna into the hot, garlic-infused oil in the frying pan. Cook quickly, 2 to 3 minutes, crisping both sides but taking care not to overcook – the inside of the tuna should stay rare.

Using a very sharp knife, cut the tuna into ¾-in (2-cm) slices and place on a serving plate. Dress with a mix of the julienned daikon, basil leaves, and cooked garlic chips.

Prepare a small plate per person with a dab of wasabi and a little *banno* soy sauce or *ponzu* sauce for dipping.

"The term *tataki* is used to describe a method of cooking tuna and beef that involves searing the outside, leaving the inside rare. I think this is the best way to ensure that you taste the real flavour of the ingredient. This recipe also works well with beef."

– HARUMI KURIHARA

Image on p. 193

Whitebait Japanese Custard
Whitebait Chawanmushi

Makoto Tokuyama

COMPLEXITY: MODERATE | PREP TIME: 5 MINUTES | COOK TIME: 20 MINUTES | SERVES: 4

INGREDIENTS

5 oz (150 g) whitebait

3 eggs

2 cups plus 1¼ tbsp
(500 ml) cool *ichiban*
dashi stock (p. 478)

1 tsp light soy sauce

½ tsp salt

1 tsp mirin

1 tsp sake

1 tbsp (15 ml) neutral oil

few sprigs cilantro/
coriander

METHOD

Heat 1 cup of water in a small pot until boiling, then add 2 teaspoons of salt and 1 tablespoon of sake. Turn the heat off and immediately put 3½ oz (100 g) of the whitebait into the pot, stirring for about 5 seconds, then immediately strain and spread out over a large, flat plate. Place this in the refrigerator for a few minutes, to cool the whitebait down as quickly as possible.

Lightly beat the eggs in a large bowl. Try not to aerate the eggs. In a separate bowl, mix the *ichiban* dashi stock, light soy sauce, salt, sake, and mirin together. Add the dashi mixture gradually to the egg mixture, stirring to combine. Strain the egg mixture.

Divide the strained whitebait between 4 *chawanmushi* cups. Fill each cup to three-quarters full with the egg mixture. Cover the cups with foil.

Pre-heat a steamer over a high heat. Turn the heat down to low and carefully place the *chawanmushi* cups in the steamer. Steam for a few minutes over a high heat, then turn the heat down to low and continue to steam for 10 to 15 minutes (15 minutes at 180°F/82°C), or until done. Poke a bamboo stick into the *chawanmushi*; if clear soup comes out, it's done.

While the *chawanmushi* are steaming, heat the oil in a small frying pan over a medium heat, add the reserved whitebait and fry until crispy. Garnish the tops of the *chawanmushi* with the fried whitebait and some fresh cilantro/coriander, and serve.

———————

"*Chawanmushi* is a Japanese custard steamed in a cup. In Japanese, *chawan* means tea cups or rice bowls, and *mushi* means steaming. You can replace the whitebait with other favourite items, such as chicken or mushrooms."

– MAKOTO TOKUYAMA

Fish Congee

Luke Nguyen

COMPLEXITY: EASY | PREP TIME: 10 MINUTES | COOK TIME: 30 MINUTES | SERVES: 4 TO 6

INGREDIENTS

¾ cup (150 g) long-grain rice

1½ qt (1½ litres) chicken stock (p. 482)

10½ oz (300 g) ling fillets, sliced into bite-sized pieces

1 tbsp (15 ml) fish sauce

1 tbsp (15 ml) light soy sauce

1 tbsp sliced green onion/spring onion

1 tbsp sliced cilantro/coriander leaves

freshly ground black pepper

In a large frying pan, dry-roast the rice over a low heat until fragrant, but not brown. Transfer to a large saucepan, then pour in the chicken stock and bring to the boil. Add the fish pieces to the pan and cook for 2 minutes, then remove the fish with a slotted spoon and set aside.

Reduce the heat to a simmer and cook the rice, stirring regularly, for 25 minutes, then add the fish sauce and soy sauce and stir through.

Transfer the congee to a serving bowl, place the fish on top and garnish with the green onion/spring onion and cilantro/coriander. Sprinkle each serving with a pinch of freshly ground black pepper.

JOSH'S NOTES

Key element: The rice should be very soft and split – this thickens the dish.

Tip: If the pieces of fish are small, add them towards the end of cooking.

Complements: I like to add boiled egg, crispy fried shallots, and fried anchovies or toasted groundnuts/peanuts.

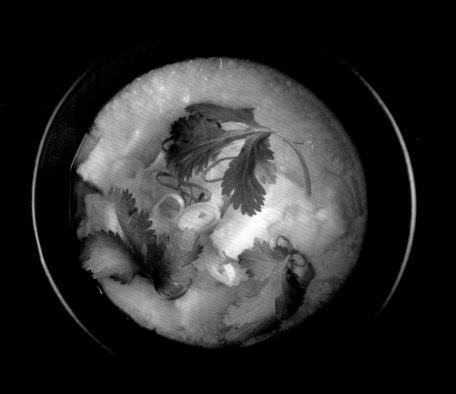

Cured Salmon

Matt Lambert

COMPLEXITY: EASY | PREP TIME: 20 MINUTES, PLUS CURING TIME | COOK TIME: 2 MINUTES
SERVES: 10 OR MORE

INGREDIENTS

1 whole salmon, filleted, skinned and pin-bones removed (approx. 2½ lb/1.2 kg)

CURE MIX

zest of 2 oranges

zest of 1 lemon

zest of 1 lime

½ cup (145 g) kosher/ flaky salt

⅓ cup (75 g) superfine/ caster sugar

1 tsp Himalayan pink salt

ice, for refreshing

METHOD

Line a large tray with baking paper. In a bowl, combine the cure mix ingredients together. Gently cover the flesh of the salmon with the cure mix, using about 5 oz (150 g) on each side of each fillet.

Place the salmon on the lined tray, cover and place in the fridge for 36 hours. Every 12 hours, line a clean tray with baking paper and carefully turn the fish over onto the clean tray, discarding the liquid from the previous tray. Air flow is important to help with the curing process.

After 36 hours, the flesh should have firmed up greatly. You can serve in this form as thinly sliced cured salmon.

Alternatively, wash off the cure and place the salmon in a zip lock bag, removing as much air as possible. Heat water to 140°F (60°C) and fill a deep roasting dish two-thirds full. Fill another deep roasting dish with ice and water. Submerge in the hot water for 2 minutes, then refresh in the icy water to cool quickly. This will poach the fish and make it incredibly soft. Portion into thick slices and set aside.

JOSH'S NOTES

Preparation: Curing anything takes time, so this is a dish to plan ahead for.

Key element: Source a good-quality large salmon and make sure it is expertly filleted – any tears or breaks will make it harder to carve.

Tip: If the salmon turns out a little too salty, soak it in chilled water to remove some of the saltiness.

Complements: Serve with pickles, capers, or a Japanese-style dressing.

Image on p. 193

Gravad Lax with Honey Mustard Sauce

Trine Hahnemann

COMPLEXITY: EASY | PREP TIME: 20 MINUTES, PLUS CURING TIME
CURE TIME: 48 HOURS | SERVES: 10

INGREDIENTS

1 side of salmon
(about 4 lb/1.8 kg)

2 tbsp whole
peppercorns

1 tbsp coriander seeds

⅓ cup plus 1½ tbsp
(120 g) coarse salt

¾ cup (170 g) superfine/
caster sugar

7 oz (200 g) dill, very
finely chopped, plus
6 sprigs extra

sliced white or spelt
bread, to serve

SAUCE

3 tbsp dark brown sugar

3 tbsp Dijon mustard

3 tbsp (30 ml) white
wine vinegar

3 tbsp honey

2 tbsp (45 ml)
vegetable oil

7 oz (100 g) dill,
chopped

METHOD

Remove any pin-bones from the salmon and trim the outer edges of the fillet. Wipe off any scales with a paper towel and lay the salmon, skin side down, on a sheet of plastic wrap.

Crush the peppercorns and coriander seeds using a mortar and pestle, and mix with the salt and sugar. Spread the finely chopped dill evenly over the salmon, then cover with the spiced sugar mixture. Cut the salmon into two equal portions. Lay three of the dill sprigs over one piece, then cover with the other piece of fish, laying it flesh side down. Wrap in plastic wrap and leave in the refrigerator for 2 days.

To make the sauce, place all the ingredients in a blender or food processor and whizz until the mixture is smooth.

To serve, unwrap the salmon and wipe off all the salt and sugar mixture with a paper towel. The traditional cut starts diagonally at one corner of the salmon, and then works back towards the centre of the fillet. Place the gravad lax on a serving dish and garnish with the remaining dill sprigs. Serve with the honey mustard sauce and white or spelt bread.

"I love salmon, and this is the perfect way to eat it: served with this sauce (called fox sauce) and fresh dill, with an ice-cold beer alongside."

– TRINE HAHNEMANN

Pacific-Island-style Cured Fish

Monica Galetti

COMPLEXITY: EASY | PREP TIME: 15 MINUTES | COOK TIME: 1 MINUTE | SERVES: 6

INGREDIENTS

1½ lb (650 g) very fresh stone bass fillets, or similar

sea salt

finely grated zest and juice of 2 lemons

5 medium-sized tomatoes

3 stalks celery, de-stringed with a peeler

3 green onions/spring onions, trimmed

1⅔ cup (400 ml) coconut milk

Tabasco sauce, to finish

lime leaves, to garnish (optional)

METHOD

Remove the skin from the fish fillets, trim if necessary and check for pin-bones, removing any with kitchen tweezers. Dice the fish into small cubes, about ½-in (1-cm), and place in a bowl. Season with 3 generous pinches of salt. Add the lemon zest and the juice of 1 lemon. Toss well, then cover and place in the fridge to cure for 10 minutes.

Meanwhile, immerse the tomatoes in a bowl of hot water for 30 seconds or so to loosen the skins, then drain and peel. Halve and de-seed the tomatoes, then cut the flesh into ¼-in (5-mm) dice. Cut the celery into similar-sized dice. Slice the green onions/spring onions thinly on the diagonal.

Fold the tomato, celery, and onion through the cured fish, then fold in the coconut milk. Taste and adjust the seasoning with the remaining lemon juice and a pinch of salt as required. Add a few drops of Tabasco sauce according to taste. Leave to stand for 5 minutes before serving, garnished with lime leaves if available.

"This is truly one of my earliest memories of Samoan cuisine, and to this day it is still one of my favourites. If you are unable to buy stone bass, opt for sea bass or bream instead. Freshness is the key."

– MONICA GALETTI

Image on p. 193

INGREDIENTS

12½ oz (350 g) ocean trout (I use Petuna), filleted

6½ tbsp (100 ml) grapeseed oil

⅓ cup (80 ml) olive oil

½ tbsp ground coriander

½ tsp white pepper

10 whole leaves basil

3 stalks thyme

¼ tsp garlic, finely chopped

2 stalks celery, finely chopped

2 small carrots, finely chopped

PARSLEY OIL

leaves from ¼ bunch flat-leaf parsley

6¾ tbsp (100 ml) olive oil or grapeseed oil

½ tbsp salted capers, rinsed and drained

FENNEL SALAD

¼ bulb fennel

1 tsp lemon juice

salt and pepper

½ tsp lemon-scented oil or lemon zest

TO SERVE

3 tbsp chopped chives

4 tbsp *konbu*, finely chopped

½ tsp sea salt

2 tbsp ocean trout caviar

JOSH'S NOTES

Tip: If you can't source ocean trout, substitute it with salmon.

Confit of Ocean Trout with Fennel Salad

Tetsuya Wakuda

COMPLEXITY: MODERATE | PREP TIME: 30 MINUTES, PLUS MARINATING TIME
COOK TIME: 10 MINUTES | SERVES: 4

METHOD

Skin the ocean trout and cut crosswise into about 2½ to 2¾ oz (70 to 80 g) pieces – they should weigh no more than 3½ oz (100 g). In a little tray, immerse the ocean trout in the grapeseed oil and olive oil together with the coriander, white pepper, basil, thyme, and garlic. Cover and allow to marinate for a few hours in the fridge. If you do not want to use too much oil, paint the surface of the fish with oil and press on the herbs.

To cook the fish, pre-heat the oven to the absolutely lowest setting possible.

Take the fish out of the oil and allow it to come to room temperature. Spread the celery and carrots over the base of a baking tray. Put the ocean trout on top and place in the oven. Cook with the door open so that the fish cooks gently. Paint the surface every few minutes with the marinade.

Depending on the size and thickness of the fish, cooking takes 7 to 8 minutes (no more than 10 minutes). When you touch the end part, your finger should just go through the flesh. The flesh should not have changed colour at all, but remain a brilliant orangey-red and feel lukewarm to the touch.

Remove the fish from the oven and allow to cool down immediately. Lift out of the tray and allow to come to room temperature.

To make the parsley oil, purée the parsley with the olive oil or grapeseed oil in a blender. Add the capers and blend until smooth.

To make the fennel salad, finely shave the fennel using a mandoline. Toss the fennel with the lemon juice, salt and pepper to taste, and some lemon-scented oil or lemon zest.

To serve, sprinkle the top of the fish with finely chopped chives, *konbu*, and a little sea salt. Place some fennel salad on the base of each plate. Put the ocean trout on top and drizzle a little parsley oil all around. Dot the ocean trout caviar around at regular intervals and serve.

Image on p. 192

Snapper Escabeche

Josh Emett

COMPLEXITY: EASY | PREP TIME: 20 MINUTES | COOK TIME: 5 MINUTES | SERVES: 2 TO 4

INGREDIENTS

2 large fillets (each
7 oz/200 g) red snapper
(or similar fish), skin on

2 carrots, peeled

1 red bell pepper/
capsicum, cored and
de-seeded

2 cloves garlic

½ onion, cut into
quarters

2 tsp coriander seeds

½ cup plus 2 tbsp
(150 ml) olive oil

pinch of saffron threads

3½ tbsp (50 ml) white
wine vinegar

6½ tbsp (100 ml) white
wine

salt and freshly ground
black pepper

handful of chopped
fresh cilantro/coriander

METHOD

Remove the pin-bones from the snapper fillets, then cut into neat
strips 1¼ in (3 cm) wide. Put aside.

Finely slice the carrots, garlic, bell pepper/capsicum, and onion,
cutting across the onion layers. Crush the coriander seeds to a
medium grind, not too fine, using a mortar and pestle.

Heat the olive oil in a frying pan over a medium heat and sweat
off the onion, carrot, garlic, coriander seeds, and saffron until soft,
without browning the onion. Add the vinegar and wine and cook
out for a couple of minutes. Adjust the seasoning with salt and
pepper, then remove from the heat.

Put a separate frying pan over a medium heat for a few minutes.
Put the snapper in, skin side down, and leave for 2 to 3 minutes,
without moving it, to seal the skin. Remove from the heat when
fish is only 50 per cent cooked. Transfer snapper pieces to a shallow
tray, skin side up, and pour sauce over. The fish will finish cooking in
the hot sauce.

Serve at room temperature, scattered with chopped
coriander/cilantro.

JOSH'S NOTES

Preparation: Prepare the
sauce before you seal
the fish.

Key elements: Searing
the fish properly; pour
the sauce over the fish
at the right temperature
so it doesn't overcook.

Tip: Take time to sweat
off the vegetables;
that is where all
the sweetness will
come from.

Pan-fried Crispy Skate with Ponzu Sauce

Al Brown

COMPLEXITY: EASY | PREP TIME: 10 MINUTES | COOK TIME: 15 MINUTES | SERVES: 3

INGREDIENTS

1 large fresh skate fillet
(boneless), cut into 3

seasoned flour

clarified butter
(or regular butter)

1½ cups plus 1 tbsp
(375 ml) ponzu sauce
(p. 479)

lime wedges

METHOD

Bring a frying pan up to a medium-high heat. Pre-heat the oven to 210°F (100°C).

Lightly dust the skate fillets in the seasoned flour. Pat off any excess.

Once the pan is hot, add a liberal amount of butter. Cook the skate fillets one or two at a time for a couple of minutes on either side, until golden and crisp on the outside. Keep the cooked skate warm by placing on a cake rack in the oven while you cook the other fillets.

To serve, place the skate fillets on pre-heated plates with a little dish of ponzu sauce next to each fillet. A wedge of fresh lime, and you're good to go.

"This recipe came from a restaurant called Duane Park Cafe in New York City where I worked nearly thirty years ago. The dish was one of the chef's (Japanese) signature dishes. With just two components on the plate, crisp skate wing and ponzu sauce on the side, it was simplicity personified."

– AL BROWN

JOSH'S NOTES

Preparation: You can make the ponzu sauce well in advance.

Key element: Cook the fish 80 per cent on the presentation side and just turn to finish off.

Complements: Serve with rice.

Tip: Don't forget to season the flour well, so that the dish in turn is well-seasoned.

INGREDIENTS

NOBU-STYLE *SAIKYO* MISO

½ cup plus 2 tbsp (150 ml) sake

½ cup plus 2 tbsp (150 ml) mirin

2 cups (450 g) white miso paste

1¼ cups (225 g) granulated sugar

AMA-ZU (SWEET VINEGAR)

½ cup (120 ml) rice vinegar

6 tbsp granulated sugar

2½ tsp sea salt

COD

4 black cod fillets, about ½ lb (230 g) each

3 cups (800 g) Nobu-style *saikyo* miso (see above)

PICKLED *HAJIKAMI* GINGER

4 stalks *hajikami* ginger (available at Japanese/ Asian supermarkets)

1 qt (1 litre) water

1 tbsp (15 ml) rice vinegar

sea salt

6¾ tbsp (100 ml) *ama-zu* (see above) mixed with 6¾ tbsp (100 ml) water

JOSH'S NOTES

Preparation: Allow time for the fish to be steeped for 2 to 3 days, and the ginger for 12 hours.

Key element: Good-quality miso paste, and the best black cod you can source.

Tip: Bake until you achieve a good colour, and the fish is cooked through.

Black Cod with Miso

Nobu Matsuhisa

COMPLEXITY: EASY | PREP TIME: 20 MINUTES, PLUS MARINATING TIME
COOK TIME: 45 MINUTES | SERVES: 4

METHOD

For the Nobu-style *saikyo* miso, bring the sake and mirin to the boil in a medium-sized saucepan over a high heat. Boil for 20 seconds to evaporate the alcohol. Turn the heat down to low and add the miso paste, mixing with a wooden spoon. When the miso has dissolved completely, turn the heat up to high again and add the sugar, stirring constantly with the wooden spoon to ensure that the bottom of the pan doesn't burn. Remove from the heat once the sugar is fully dissolved. Cool to room temperature.

For the *ama-zu*, heat the vinegar, sugar, and salt in a small saucepan over a medium heat until fully dissolved. Remove from the heat immediately – do not leave on the heat any longer, as the acidity of the rice vinegar will boil off. Cool to room temperature.

Pat the fillets thoroughly dry with paper towels. Slather the fish with Nobu-style *saikyo* miso and place in a non-reactive dish or bowl. Cover tightly with plastic wrap and leave to steep in the refrigerator for 2 to 3 days.

For the pickled *hajikami* ginger, remove any sand and debris from the ginger and cut it into 6-in (15-cm) lengths. Bring the water to the boil, add the rice vinegar and plunge the ginger into the boiling water for 20 seconds. Drain and sprinkle thoroughly with sea salt. Let cool to room temperature. Pour the diluted *ama-zu* over the ginger, cover, and leave in the refrigerator to pickle for 12 hours.

On the day of serving, pre-heat the oven to 400°F (200°C). Pre-heat a grill or broiler to hot. Lightly wipe off any excess miso clinging to the fillets, but don't rinse it off. Place the fish on the grill, or in a broiler pan, and grill or broil until the surface of the fish turns brown, 2 to 3 minutes. Then bake for 10 to 15 minutes.

Arrange the black cod fillets on individual plates and garnish with the pickled *hajikami*. Add a few extra drops of Nobu-style *saikyo* miso to each plate.

───────

"Black cod is steeped in sweet miso before being baked in the oven. The sweetness of the Nobu-style *saikyo* miso is an excellent match with the plumpness of the fish. "

– NOBU MATSUHISA

INGREDIENTS

1 (1½ lb/680 g) whole white fish (such as sea bass, branzino, or flounder), cleaned with head and tail intact

kosher/flaky salt and freshly ground black pepper

2 x ½-in (1-cm) piece of fresh ginger, peeled and finely julienned

¼ cup plus 1 tsp (65 ml) light soy sauce

1 tbsp (15 ml) rice wine

1 green onion/spring onion, white and light green parts only, julienned

4 sprigs cilantro/coriander

½ cup plus 1 tsp (125 ml) rapeseed/canola oil

JOSH'S NOTES

Key element: Handle the fish gently once it is cooked.

Tip: Open the cavity to check if it is cooked through, or check up by the head, which is the thicker part of the fish.

Comment: A clean-tasting dish, seasoned by the accompanying soy.

Complements: Serve with steamed jasmine rice.

Steamed Whole Fish with Ginger, Scallions & Soy

Charles Phan

COMPLEXITY: EASY | PREP TIME: 10 MINUTES | COOK TIME: 10 MINUTES | SERVES: 2 TO 4

METHOD

Rinse the fish in cold water and pat dry with paper towels. Season the fish inside and out with salt and pepper. Place the fish on a heatproof plate that is both large enough to accommodate it (a glass pie plate works well) and will also fit inside your steamer, bending the fish slightly if it is too long. Stuff half of the ginger inside the cavity of the fish and spread the remaining ginger on top of the fish.

Pour water into a wok or stockpot, and set a steamer basket in the wok or on the rim of the stockpot. Make sure that the water does not touch the bottom of the steamer. Bring the water to the boil over a high heat. Place the plate holding the fish in the steamer, cover, and steam for about 8 minutes, until the fish flakes easily when tested with the tip of a knife.

While the fish is steaming, place the soy sauce, wine, and 1 tablespoon of water in a small bowl and stir together. Set aside.

When the fish is ready, carefully remove the plate from the steamer and pour off any accumulated liquid. Lay the green onion/spring onion and cilantro/coriander along the top of the fish. In a small frying pan, heat the oil over a high heat until it is hot but not smoking. Remove the oil from the heat and pour it directly over the onion and herb to 'cook' them. Drizzle the soy mixture over the fish and serve immediately.

HOW TO PREPARE A WHOLE FISH

Most markets sell fish that have already been scaled and gutted. If a fish has not been cleaned, you can ask the fishmonger to clean it for you. When we serve a whole fish at the restaurants, we also trim off the fins because the fish is easier to serve without them. With a pair of scissors, cut off the fins from both sides of the fish, from the belly, and then the dorsal fins (the ones running along the back). Finally, trim the tail by cutting it into a V shape and score the fish.

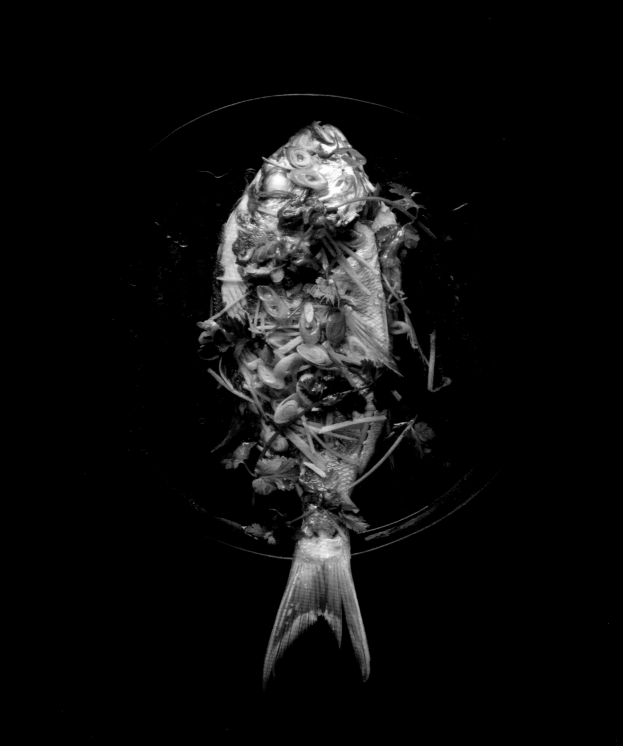

Whole Flounder with Capers, Lemon & Butter

Josh Emett

COMPLEXITY: MODERATE | PREP TIME: 15 MINUTES | COOK TIME: 10 MINUTES | SERVES: 1

INGREDIENTS

1 whole flounder, cleaned and gutted

seasoned flour for dusting

5 tsp olive oil

3½ tbsp (50 g) butter

2 lemons

1 shallot, finely diced

1¾ oz (50 g) capers

handful of parsley, chopped

sea salt

METHOD

Trim the tail and wings of the flounder and dust the fish in the seasoned flour. Over a medium heat, heat a pan large enough to fit the fish, and place the fish in, skin side down first, and fry for 4 to 5 minutes, until the skin is well coloured. Gently flip the fish over, add the butter and cook for another 4 to 5 minutes until the fish is cooked through. Remove the fish and place on a serving plate, leaving all the liquid in the pan.

While the fish cooks, peel 1 lemon, separate the segments and dice. Slice the other lemon and set aside for the garnish.

Place the pan back on the heat, add the shallot, and fry, stirring, for 1 minute. Now add the capers, diced lemon, and parsley. Swirl in the pan until it comes together as a sauce, then season with sea salt before pouring over the fish.

Serve with a slice of lemon on the side.

JOSH'S NOTES

Preparation: Dice the shallot in advance.

Key element: The right size pan will help you cook the fish without breaking the skin, and turn without damaging it.

Tip: Be confident with the heat when cooking the fish – crispy skin is essential for flavour, and helps hold the fish together.

Hake with Clams in Green Sauce

Elena & Juan Mari Arzak

COMPLEXITY: EASY | PREP TIME: 15 MINUTES | COOK TIME: 10 MINUTES | SERVES: 4

INGREDIENTS

4 hake loins (7 oz/200 g each), skin on

¾ cup (180 ml) olive oil

4 cloves garlic

2 tbsp chopped parsley

pinch of flour (optional)

9 oz (250 g) clams

½ cup plus 1 tsp (125 ml) cold water

salt

METHOD

Clean the loins, salt them and set them aside. Take a big, shallow casserole dish – so that the loins are not crowded – add the olive oil, garlic, and chopped parsley (setting some aside for serving) and cook over a low heat (without a lid). Before the cloves of garlic start to brown, add the pinch of flour (if using) and mix in well. Then add the clams and the hake loins with the skin facing up. Add the water and keep cooking for about 3 minutes (the time depends on how thick the loins are), shaking the dish so that the sauce will thicken.

Turn the loins over and cook for another 3 minutes. By then the clams will be open. (Discard any that aren't.) Cover with the lid and leave for 3 to 4 minutes. Check that the sauce has thickened; if it hasn't, remove the loins, remove the dish from the heat and shake until the sauce thickens.

Plate one loin per person, place the clams around the fish and pour the sauce over. Sprinkle some of the remaining parsley over each loin and decorate with some more parsley.

TIP

Some people prefer to substitute the water for stock or white wine, but water allows for the subtle flavour of the hake to come through. Just a question of taste.

JOSH'S NOTES

Preparation: Salt the fish a little ahead.

Key element: Use a heavy, shallow casserole dish and a consistent cooking temperature.

Tip: Be very gentle with the fish when turning the loins over, as they can be fragile.

Cod Kokotxas in Pilpil Sauce

Josean Alija

COMPLEXITY: EASY | PREP TIME: 10 MINUTES | COOK TIME: 20 MINUTES | SERVES: 4

INGREDIENTS

2 oz (60 g) peeled garlic

1⅔ cups (400 ml) olive oil

3 dried cayenne chillies, chopped

19½ oz (550 g) cod *kokotxas* (the flesh under a fish's jaw; 1 oz/25 g each)

sea salt

METHOD

Remove the germ from the garlic, then slice the outer part of the garlic very finely and place it in a saucepan with the olive oil and chillies. Heat over a low heat until the garlic is golden brown, about 8 minutes. Remove from the heat, allow to stand for 30 minutes, then strain.

In a saucepan, heat the garlic and chilli oil to 160°F (70°C). The amount of oil should be enough to cover the *kokotxas* almost completely. Put the *kokotxas*, skin upwards, in the oil and cook at 150°F (65°C) for 5 minutes, the time necessary to cook them and allow them to release their gelatine.

Remove from the heat, turn them over carefully and let the oil cool down. At this point remove half of the oil from the saucepan, trying to leave all the gelatine in the pot. With a circular movement, bind the sauce; if necessary, when the sauce becomes thicker, add a little bit of oil back in.

Add salt to taste and heat the *kokotxas* in the sauce just before serving.

Basque Fish Stew
Marmitako

Nieves Barragán Mohacho

COMPLEXITY: EASY | PREP TIME: 25 MINUTES | COOK TIME: 40 MINUTES | SERVES: 6

INGREDIENTS

¾ cup (175 ml) extra virgin olive oil

2 cloves garlic, crushed

1 onion, finely diced

1 large red bell pepper/capsicum, finely diced

7 oz (200 g) Padrón peppers, finely diced

sea salt and freshly ground black pepper

1 bay leaf

2 dried *choricero* peppers, soaked in water overnight and flesh scooped out

1 fresh red chilli, de-seeded and finely chopped

3 or 4 fresh ripe plum tomatoes, grated

¾ cup plus 1¼ tbsp (200 ml) Txakoli (sparkling Basque wine), or sherry, or a crisp white wine

2 to 3 medium-sized potatoes, peeled and cut into rough chunks

2 qt (2 litres) fish stock (p. 483)

4½ lb (2 kg) bonito (or 2¼ lb/1 kg fresh tuna)

1 bunch fresh flat-leaf parsley, roughly chopped

crusty bread, to serve

METHOD

Put 6¾ tablespoons (100 ml) of olive oil into a large pan set over a medium-low heat. Add the garlic and stir for 30 seconds, then add the onion, bell pepper/capsicum, Padrón peppers, and a pinch of salt, and cook gently, stirring occasionally, for 12 to 15 minutes.

Add the bay leaf, *choricero* peppers, chilli, and grated tomatoes, and cook, stirring occasionally, until paste-like. Pour in the wine and cook until the alcohol has evaporated. Add the potatoes and stir together with the paste to coat them. Add the fish stock – the potatoes should be more or less covered. Cook for 15 to 20 minutes on a medium-low heat, until the potatoes are really nice and soft but not broken up.

When the potatoes are cooked, cut the bonito into 1¼-in (3-cm) chunks and season with a little salt and pepper. Put the remaining ¼ cup plus 1 tablespoon (75 ml) of olive oil into another pan over a medium-high heat and sear the bonito very quickly – you don't want to cook it through, just seal it so that it doesn't break up.

Add the bonito to the stew, take off the heat and mix everything together. Put the lid on the pan and leave for 5 minutes. Sprinkle over the chopped parsley and serve with bread to scoop up the juices.

———

"This is one of the most typical of Basque dishes. If you don't have bonito, you can use tuna, which is very similar, or mackerel – an oily fish is basically what you're looking for. A marmita is a big pot. It's what the fishermen use to cook with when they're out at sea and need something hot to keep them going – everything gets put in the one pot with the freshly caught fish."

– NIEVES BARRAGÁN MOHACHO

Fishcakes

Bruce Poole

COMPLEXITY: MODERATE | PREP TIME: 35 MINUTES, PLUS REFRIGERATION TIME
COOK TIME: 45 MINUTES | SERVES: 4

INGREDIENTS

12½ oz (350 g) passed cooked floury potato (weight after peeling, cooking and passing through a sieve/Mouli)

18 oz (500 g) firm, boned fish, ideally in 1 piece and skin-on (salmon, turbot, cod, hake, monkfish, etc.)

3½ oz/7 tbsp (100 g) unsalted butter

4 banana shallots, very finely chopped or minced

1 clove garlic, very finely chopped or minced

6¾ tbsp (100 ml) dry white vermouth such as Noilly Prat, or white port

sea salt, ground black pepper, and cayenne pepper

zest and juice of 1 lemon

1 cup plus 1 tbsp (140 g) all-purpose/plain flour

1 egg, beaten

2 cups plus 2 tbsp (100 g) fresh white breadcrumbs, or simply extra all-purpose/plain flour, to coat

neutral oil, or butter, for cooking

METHOD

First peel, cook, and pass the potatoes through a sieve or Mouli. Keep warmish.

In a saucepan not much wider than the piece of fish, melt the butter over a low heat and sweat the finely chopped shallots and garlic gently in the melted butter until softened – do not fry them! Add the vermouth and simmer to reduce the alcohol by about two-thirds.

Season the fish really well with salt and lay on top of the shallot reduction. Turn the flame/heat to its lowest setting, put a lid on the pan and steam the fish very gently until just cooked. The time will depend on the thickness and cut of the fish, say 10 minutes for a thickish fillet of salmon. If the reduction is too dry, add a splash (only) of water – there needs to be enough steam just to cook the fish, but it must not be overly wet. Remove the pan from the heat and leave the lid on the pan for 10 or so minutes. The idea is to just cook the fish – gentle heat is the way to go.

Remove the fish from the pan and remove the skin. Gently flake or break up the fish, trying to preserve nice chunks, and add these back to the pan with all the buttery, fishy, shallot juices etc. Add the lemon zest and a generous squeeze of juice. Add the passed potato but do not yet mix together. Season the lot with sea salt, ground pepper, and a good pinch of cayenne. You could add freshly chopped herbs at this point, but I prefer to keep herbs out and use these in the accompanying sauce/garnish if desired.

Using your hands, bring the whole lot together. Do not over-mix or beat, as the fish will fragment and the texture of the fishcake will be too smooth – a chunky, fishy cake is what we're after. Check for seasoning – it should be well seasoned and zingy from the lemon and cayenne. As soon as the mixture has come together, stop mixing.

Wash and dry your hands before forming the mixture into patties about 2¼ in (6 cm) in diameter and about ¾ in (2 cm) deep. Dust very lightly in flour and refrigerate on greaseproof paper/parchment.

If deep-frying, coat in more flour, then beaten whole egg, then fresh white breadcrumbs. Bring the oil to 350°F (180°) in a heavy-based pot or deep-fryer. Drop small batches of fishcakes into the hot oil and fry until golden and crisp. They can also be shallow-fried in a frying pan in gently sizzling butter, turning as they cook. Alternatively, they can simply be dusted in flour and pan-fried as they are, in a pan with plenty of butter. It is important that the fishcakes are chilled down and have firmed up before progressing to the finishing-off stage.

Serve with whatever you fancy: Lemon wedges, tartare sauce, herb mayonnaise, aïoli, beurre blanc, hollandaise, green salad, shellfish sauce, an Asian dipping sauce, etc., etc.

JOSH'S NOTES

Preparation: You can make the mix a day ahead, but crumb the cakes just before cooking.

Key element: Chill the mix before shaping and crumbing.

Tip: Use a floury dry potato.

Complements: Great with lemon and mayonnaise.

Image on p. 193

Spanish Mackerel with Artichokes & Prunes

Colin Fassnidge

COMPLEXITY: EASY | PREP TIME: 30 MINUTES | COOK TIME: 1 HOUR | SERVES: 4

INGREDIENTS

1 cup (500 g) rock salt

18 oz (500 g) Jerusalem artichokes

6¾ tbsp (100 ml) extra virgin olive oil, plus extra as needed

sea salt

½ x 13-oz (375-g) can prunes, pitted

6¾ tbsp (100 ml) Pedro Ximenez sherry

juice of 1 lemon, plus extra to taste

freshly ground black pepper

vegetable oil, for deep-frying

splash of olive oil

1½ lb (720 g) Spanish mackerel, cut into 4 pieces

1½ tbsp (20 g) butter

1 clove garlic, crushed

1 sprig of thyme

JOSH'S NOTES

Preparation: Roast the artichokes ahead of time.

Key element: Don't let the crispy artichokes get too dark, or they become bitter; watch the artichokes when cooking, as cook times may change according to season.

METHOD

Pre-heat the oven to 300°F (150°C). Cover a baking tray with the rock salt and place the artichokes on top. Bake for 45 minutes, or until tender when pierced with a skewer. Cool, then cut in half and scrape out the flesh, keeping the skins separate and in large pieces.

Increase the oven temperature to 400°F (200°C). Drizzle the skins with a little oil and sea salt, place them back in the oven and roast until golden, about 15 minutes. Remove and place on one side.

Heat the prunes, prune liquid, and sherry in a saucepan. Stir in the 6¾ tablespoons (100 ml) of extra virgin olive oil and half the lemon juice. Season with salt and black pepper and set aside.

Half-fill an ovenproof frying pan with vegetable oil and place over a high heat. When hot, add the mackerel and cook until golden on each side, 2 to 3 minutes. Place the pan in the oven and cook for 2 minutes on each side; if your fish is smaller and thinner it may not need oven time at all. Working quickly, add the butter, garlic, thyme, and remaining lemon juice to the pan with the fish. Baste twice, and remove the fish from the pan.

Reheat the soft artichokes in a small pot and season with salt, pepper, a splash of extra virgin olive oil, and lemon juice. Slice the fish and serve with the soft and crisp artichokes, and the drained prunes.

Classic Fish Pie

Josh Emett

COMPLEXITY: EASY | PREP TIME: 40 MINUTES | COOK TIME: 45 MINUTES | SERVES: 4

INGREDIENTS

1¼ cups (300 ml) milk

1¼ cups (300 ml) fish stock (p. 483)

few sprigs thyme

5 oz (150 g) shrimp/ prawns, cut in half horizontally

5 oz (150 g) salmon, cut into 1¼-in (3-cm) dice

5 oz (150 g) cod or similar white fish, cut into 1¼-in (3-cm) dice

5 oz (150 g) smoked fish, in a whole piece

4½ tbsp (65 g) butter

½ cup (65 g) all-purpose/plain flour

2 tbsp chopped dill

2 tbsp chopped chives

2 tbsp chopped tarragon

sea salt and freshly cracked pepper

MASH

18 oz (500 g) peeled and diced potato

sea salt

2¾ tbsp (40 ml) cream

1 egg yolk

METHOD

Place the milk, fish stock, and thyme in a wide pan, season with salt and bring to a simmer over a medium heat. Add the shrimp/prawns, salmon and cod, then the smoked fish. Simmer for about 1 minute until the fish is two-thirds cooked.

Gently strain through a colander placed over a bowl. Discard the thyme and reserve the liquid. Lay the fish in an ovenproof baking dish, and gently flake the smoked fish through the rest.

Make a roux: Place the butter in a medium-sized pot and melt it over a medium heat, then add the flour and cook the roux out, stirring, for a few minutes. Start to slowly add the reserved milk and stock while constantly stirring, until all the liquid is added and you have a nice smooth mixture.

Add the herbs to this and season again with salt and cracked pepper. Leave to cool for a few minutes, then pour over the fish until it is completely covering it and mixed through. Set aside.

Pre-heat the oven to 350°F (180°C).

Place the potatoes in a small pot, cover with water and season with salt. Bring to the boil and boil gently until cooked through, then drain and pass through a fine sieve or ricer. Place back in the pot and add the cream, stir well, then remove from the heat and add the egg yolk and beat well until combined and smooth. Allow to cool for a few minutes, then spread or pipe over the top of the fish until completely covered.

Bake for 30 minutes until cooked through and bubbling at the sides. If it needs more colour on the top, switch to the oven grill for a few minutes until golden brown and crispy.

JOSH'S NOTES

Tip: If your roux starts to get lumpy, add the liquid more slowly and whisk until smooth.

Barbecued Prawns, p. 156

Confit of Ocean Trout, p. 171

Clam Bruschetta, p. 149

Octopus Fairground-style, p. 159

Fishcakes, p. 186

Tuna Tataki Salad, p. 163

Pacific-Island-style Cured Fish, p. 170

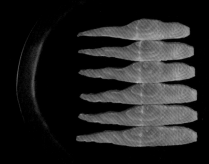

Cured Salmon, p. 168

Poultry

Hunting, plucking, and preparing poultry is not for everyone, but it has instilled chefs and cooks throughout history with a respect for utilizing the whole animal in their cooking. Today, most butchers and supermarkets offer a variety of free-range offerings and aside from being a more ethical way of eating, most of us would agree free-range, and where possible, organic, poultry makes for better eating. Different types of birds require different levels of attention to detail and here some of the world's best chefs share how they handle theirs. Trust them, even if a recipe seems particularly complex – these dishes are worth it.

Chicken in Wine
Coq au Vin

Josh Emett

COMPLEXITY: EASY | PREP TIME: 25 MINUTES, PLUS MARINATING OVERNIGHT
COOK TIME: 1 HOUR | SERVES: 4

INGREDIENTS

8 chicken legs, skin on

2 cups plus 1¼ tbsp (500 ml) red wine, or just enough to cover the thighs

⅔ cup plus 2 tsp (150 ml) port

rapeseed/canola oil for cooking

9 oz (250 g) smoked bacon, diced

10 baby onions, peeled and quartered

9 oz (250 g) button mushrooms, halved

5 whole cloves garlic

2 cups plus 1¼ tbsp (500 ml) beef stock (p. 484)

¼ bunch of thyme

handful of parsley, to garnish

METHOD

Split the chicken into thighs and drumsticks, place in a plastic container and just cover with the red wine and port. Cover and refrigerate overnight, but mix a few times in the first few hours to ensure that the chicken is properly coated.

Next day, pre-heat the oven to 320°F (160°C).

Drain the chicken in a colander placed over a bowl, reserving the liquid for later. Pat the chicken dry with paper towels.

Heat some oil in a large ovenproof frying pan over a medium heat, add the chicken, in batches if necessary, and fry until golden brown on all sides. Remove and set aside. Add the bacon and onions to the same pan and fry for about 10 minutes, until golden, then add the mushrooms and garlic and continue to fry until golden and the moisture has gone, about 5 minutes.

Pour in the reserved wine and port, bring to a light boil and reduce by half. Add the chicken back in at this stage, then add enough beef stock to cover. Bring back to the boil, then skim the surface. Add the thyme, and cover with a cartouche then a lid. Bake in the oven for about 45 minutes.

Serve straight away, garnished with parsley, or leave to cool and gently reheat when ready to serve.

JOSH'S NOTES

Preparation: Marinate the chicken the day before; mix well when marinating so that the chicken is covered and not patchy.

Key element: Pat the marinated chicken dry, and ensure a good colour all over the skin for the best flavour.

"This is a traditional French dish, which literally translates as 'rooster in wine'. You can serve it straight away, or make it ahead of time and reheat. Serve it with steamed or mashed potatoes to help soak up all the juices. It also goes well with rice, or even pasta."
– JOSH EMETT

Chicken Cordon Bleu

Annie Smithers

COMPLEXITY: MODERATE | PREP TIME: 30 MINUTES | COOK TIME: 30 MINUTES | SERVES: 4

INGREDIENTS

a little butter, for greasing

4 boneless, skinless chicken breasts, 7 to 9 oz (200 to 250 g) each

2 tsp Dijon mustard

4 tsp chopped fresh chives

4 very thin slices lean cooked leg ham

4 very thin slices Swiss cheese, or 3 oz (85 g) grated Gruyère

½ cup plus 1 tsp (75 g) all-purpose/plain flour

salt and freshly ground black pepper

1 egg

1 tbsp (15 ml) milk

¼ cup (40 g) fine breadcrumbs

¼ tsp paprika

METHOD

Pre-heat the oven to 375°F (190°C). Grease an 8-in (20-cm) square baking dish with butter. Split the chicken fillets horizontally to give two flatter pieces. Place each between two sheets of plastic wrap or waxed paper, and a meat mallet or rolling pin to flatten each chicken breast to a thickness of ¼ in (5 mm).

Spread each chicken breast with ½ teaspoon mustard and sprinkle each with 1 teaspoon chives. Cut the ham and cheese slices to fit the chicken. Top each chicken breast with a ham and a cheese slice. Roll up, tucking the ends inside.

Place the flour in a shallow dish, and season with salt and pepper. In a shallow bowl, combine the egg and milk, beating slightly.

Place the breadcrumbs in another shallow dish. Coat chicken rolls in turn with flour, then egg mixture, then roll in crumbs. Place in the baking dish and sprinkle with paprika.

Bake for 25 to 30 minutes, or until chicken is no longer pink in the middle.

JOSH'S NOTES

Key elements: Flatten the chicken evenly, and then roll, and wrap tightly in plastic wrap. Refrigerate for approximately 30 minutes to set the shape.

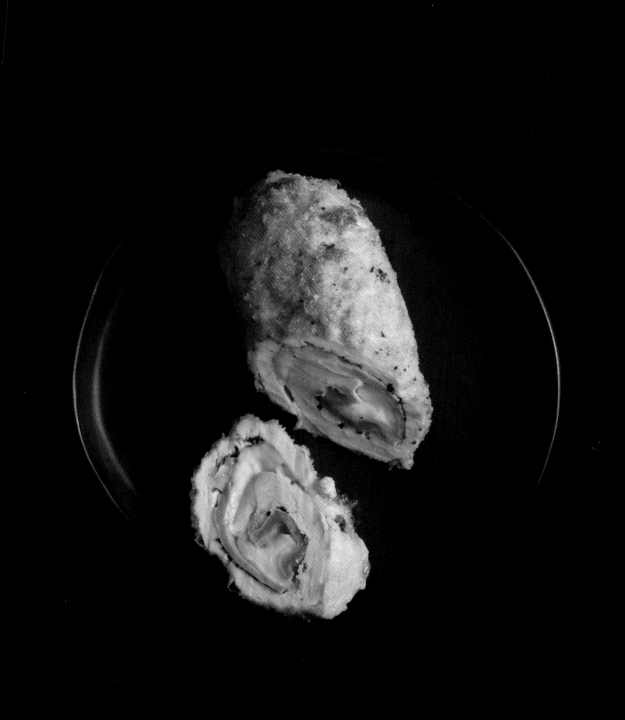

Chicken Schnitzel with Potato Salad & Lingonberry Jam

Markus Glocker

COMPLEXITY: MODERATE | PREP TIME: 10 MINUTES
COOK TIME: 35 TO 45 MINUTES | SERVES: 2

INGREDIENTS

8 oz (225 g) fingerling potatoes

salt as needed

1 bunch of chives

2 banana shallots

1 tbsp (15 ml) Champagne vinegar

2 boneless, skinless chicken breasts, about 6 oz (175 g) each, thinly sliced

1 tbsp wholegrain Dijon mustard

1½ tbsp (22 ml) chicken demi-glace, or ¾ cup plus 4 tsp (200 ml) chicken stock (p. 482) reduced to a glaze

salt and freshly ground black pepper

3 tbsp all-purpose/ plain flour

½ cup (75 g) plain breadcrumbs

1 free-range egg

oil, for frying

fingerling potato salad (p. 111)

2 tbsp lingonberry jelly/ jam (or use cranberry jelly)

METHOD

Wash the potatoes and place in a medium-sized pot, cover with cold water, and add a big pinch of salt. Heat to boiling on high and boil gently for 14 to 16 minutes, or until tender when pierced with a fork. Drain thoroughly. When cool enough to handle, use your fingers and a paring knife to remove the skins. Slice potatoes into rounds ¼ in (5 mm) thick, place in a bowl and set aside. Rinse and dry the pot.

While the potatoes cook, wash and dry the chives, then mince finely and set aside. Peel and mince the shallots to get 2 tablespoons of minced shallot; place in a bowl with the vinegar.

Pat the chicken dry with paper towels, and place on a sturdy surface between two pieces of plastic wrap. Using a heavy pan or pot, pound the chicken to a thickness of ¼ in (5 mm). Set aside.

In the pot used to cook the potatoes, combine the mustard, demi-glace, and shallot–vinegar mixture; season with salt and pepper. Cook over a medium-high heat, stirring occasionally, for 1 to 2 minutes, or until thoroughly combined and warmed through. Add to the bowl of sliced potatoes. Add half the chives and season with salt and pepper to taste. Stir to combine thoroughly. Set aside to marinate, stirring occasionally, for 10 minutes.

While the potato salad marinates, place the flour and breadcrumbs in two separate, shallow, medium-sized bowls or deep plates; season each with salt and pepper. Crack the egg into a shallow, medium-sized bowl and beat until smooth. Pat the pounded chicken dry with paper towels and season with salt and pepper on both sides. Working with one piece at a time, thoroughly coat the seasoned chicken in the seasoned flour (tapping off any excess), then the beaten egg (letting the excess drip off), then the seasoned breadcrumbs (pressing to adhere). Place the breaded chicken on a plate.

While the potato salad continues to marinate, heat a thin layer of oil in a medium-sized frying pan (non-stick, if you have one) over a medium-high heat until hot. Once the oil is hot enough that a few breadcrumbs sizzle immediately when added to the pan, add the breaded chicken. Cook for 3 to 5 minutes per side, or until golden brown and cooked through. Transfer to a plate lined with paper towel, and immediately season with salt and pepper.

To serve, divide the finished chicken and potato salad between two dishes. Top with the lingonberry jam. Garnish with the remaining chives. Enjoy!

JOSH'S NOTES

Preparation: Pound and crumb the chicken evenly, which ensures even colouring when cooked.

Image on p. 230

INGREDIENTS

BRINE

4 qt (4 litres) water

38 regular tea-bags, or
4 oz (115 g) loose tea

1 cup (240 g) kosher/
flaky salt

1 cup (200 g) sugar

CHICKEN

1 chicken
(about 3 lb/1.4 kg)

2 qt (2 litres) whole-milk
buttermilk

3 tbsp Husk Hot Sauce
(or similar hot sauce)

1 tbsp plus 1 tsp freshly
ground black pepper

1½ lb (680 g) chicken
skins, cut into ½-in
(1-cm) squares

6 cups (720 g) all-
purpose/plain flour

1 cup (150 g) fine maize
meal/cornmeal

2 tbsp cornstarch/
cornflour

1½ tsp garlic powder

1½ tsp onion powder

½ tsp cayenne pepper

½ tsp smoked paprika

1 cup (205 g) rendered
fresh lard

1 cup (240 ml)
rapeseed/canola oil

2 oz (60 g) slab bacon

2 oz (60 g) smoked ham,
diced

2 tbsp (30 g) unsalted
butter

sea salt

gravy, to serve
(see overleaf)

Ingredients continued
overleaf

Fried Chicken & Gravy

Sean Brock

COMPLEXITY: EASY | PREP TIME: 30 MINUTES, PLUS BRINING OVERNIGHT
COOK TIME: 20 MINUTES | SERVES: 2

METHOD

For the brine, put the water in a pot and bring to the boil over a high heat. Remove from the heat, add the tea, and let it steep for 8 minutes.

Remove the tea bags, or strain the liquid if you used loose tea. Add the salt and sugar to the hot water and stir to dissolve them. Pour the brine into a heatproof container and cool it to room temperature, then refrigerate until completely cold.

Cut the chicken into 8 pieces: 2 legs, 2 thighs, 2 wings, and 2 breast pieces. Rinse with cold water. Place in the brine, cover, and refrigerate for 12 hours.

After the chicken has spent 12 hours in the brine, make an ice bath in a large bowl with equal amounts of ice and water. Place the chicken in the ice bath for 5 minutes. (The ice will rinse away any impurities.) Remove the chicken and pat it dry.

Combine the buttermilk, hot sauce, and 1 tablespoon of the black pepper in a large container. Add the chicken to the buttermilk mixture, cover, and let marinate for 1 hour at room temperature.

While the chicken is marinating, put the chicken skins in a small saucepan over a very low heat, adding a small amount of water to prevent the skins from sticking and burning. Cook the skins, stirring frequently so that they don't burn, until their fat is rendered. Strain the fat; you need 1 cup.

Drain the chicken, quickly rinse under cold water, and pat dry.

Combine the flour, maize meal/cornmeal, cornstarch/cornflour, garlic powder, onion powder, the remaining 1 teaspoon black pepper, the cayenne pepper, and smoked paprika in a large bowl and mix well. Add the chicken and toss to coat thoroughly. Allow it to sit for 15 minutes, then shake off any excess, transfer the chicken to a wire rack, and let sit for 15 minutes.

Meanwhile, put the chicken fat, lard, and rapeseed/canola oil in a large, deep cast-iron skillet. Add the bacon and ham and heat the fats to 275°F (140°C). Turn the heat off and allow the bacon and ham to infuse the fats and oil for 10 minutes.

Continued overleaf

Fried Chicken & Gravy cont.

INGREDIENTS CONT.

GRAVY

¾ cup plus 1 tbsp
(165 g) cooking fat
from the fried chicken

¾ cup (90 g) all-purpose/plain flour

2 cups (480 ml) whole
milk

1 tbsp kosher/flaky salt

1 tbsp freshly ground
black pepper

1 tbsp (15 ml) soy sauce

With a skimmer or slotted spoon, remove the bacon and ham from the skillet (discard them or eat as a snack), and heat the oil to 300°F (150°C). Add the breasts and thighs and cook for 3 minutes. Add the legs and wings and cook for 5 minutes. (Remove the fat needed for the gravy at this point and start the gravy.)

Turn the chicken over, cover the skillet, and cook until the pieces of chicken are the colour of hay, about another 5 minutes. Remove the lid, turn the pieces again, cover, and cook the chicken until golden brown, another 3 minutes. Add the butter and continue cooking, turning the pieces once, for another 2 minutes or so on each side. The chicken should be crispy and golden brown. Let the chicken rest and drain on wire racks or on a plate covered with paper towels for about 8 minutes, but no longer.

Sprinkle with sea salt and serve with the gravy.

Gravy

COMPLEXITY: EASY | COOK TIME: 20 MINUTES | MAKES: 2½ CUPS

After the chicken has fried for 8 minutes and is ready to turn, carefully remove the fat needed to make the gravy from the skillet. Put ¾ cup (155 g) of the fat in a medium-sized saucepan over a medium heat, stir in the flour to make a roux, and cook for 2 minutes, stirring constantly. Gradually whisk in the milk. Reduce the heat to medium-low and cook the gravy, stirring occasionally to be sure that you don't have any lumps, for 15 minutes to cook out the taste of the raw flour.

Add the salt, pepper, and soy sauce, then whisk in the remaining tablespoon of cooking fat to make the gravy glossy. The gravy can be kept warm, covered, over the lowest heat for up to 20 minutes.

JOSH'S NOTES

Preparation: Brine
the chicken a day in
advance.

Key element: Correct
butchery of the chicken
to even sized pieces.

"To do the chicken right, you need an old black cast-iron skillet (frying pan) with a lid. Sure, you can make it in a deep-fryer, but I prefer the old-fashioned way. This is the way grandmas cook fried chicken in the South, and it's the way everyone should be making fried chicken at home."

– SEAN BROCK

INGREDIENTS

MARINADE

1¼ cups (300 ml)
  Shaoxing wine
3 tbsp salt
1 tbsp sugar
2 cloves garlic,
  finely grated
1 tsp finely grated
  fresh ginger

SPATCHCOCKS

2 whole spatchcocks
  (poussin), cut up into
  wings, breasts, thighs
  and drumsticks
vegetable oil, for
  deep-frying
2 tbsp spicy salt
  (see below)

KIMCHI MAYO

3½ oz (100 g) kimchi
  (store-bought)
10½ oz (300 g)
  Japanese mayonnaise

COATING MIXTURE

3½ oz (100 g) wheat
  starch
¾ cup plus 2½ tsp
  (100 g) all-purpose/
  plain flour
¾ cup (100 g)
  cornstarch/cornflour
½ cup plus 2 tbsp
  (100 g) rice flour
3 tbsp onion powder
3 tbsp garlic powder

SPICY SALT

1 tbsp Sichuan
  peppercorns
3 tbsp coriander seeds
1 cinnamon stick
1 tsp cloves
2 tsp chilli flakes
6 tbsp (110 g) sea salt
  flakes
1 tbsp Iranian sumac
1 tbsp sugar
4 star anise
½ teaspoon white
  peppercorns

Fried Baby Chicken with Kimchi Mayonnaise

Dan Hong

COMPLEXITY: MODERATE | PREP TIME: 35 MINUTES, PLUS MARINATING TIME
COOK TIME: 5 TO 6 MINUTES | SERVES: 2 TO 3

METHOD

Whisk all the marinade ingredients together in a bowl until the sugar and salt dissolve. Put the spatchcock pieces in a bowl, add the marinade and toss to coat. Cover with plastic wrap and leave to marinate for at least 4 hours. Overnight in the fridge is even better.

To make the kimchi mayo, purée the kimchi in a food processor until smooth. Transfer to a bowl, add the mayonnaise and whisk to combine. Set aside.

Mix all the coating ingredients together in a bowl until combined.

Fill a deep-fryer or large, heavy-based saucepan one-third full with oil and heat to 325°F (170°C), or until a cube of bread dropped into the oil turns golden in 20 seconds. Remove the spatchcock pieces from the marinade and cover each piece in the coating mixture until it feels dry. Deep-fry in batches in the hot oil for 5 to 6 minutes, or until the skin is golden and crispy. Remove with a slotted spoon, drain on paper towels and sprinkle with spicy salt. Serve immediately with the kimchi mayo.

Spicy Salt

In a dry frypan over a medium heat, toast the Sichuan peppercorns, coriander seeds, cinnamon stick and cloves until fragrant and lightly coloured. Mix with the rest of the ingredients and blitz in a spice grinder to a fine powder. This mixture will keep in an airtight container for up to 2 months.

"This is a simple dish, but really pleasing. I really like Korean fried chicken and will visit any place in Chinatown if there's the slightest possibility it could be good. Korean Fried Chicken (KFC) influenced this recipe."

– DAN HONG

INGREDIENTS

1 large (3⅓ to 4½ lb/ 1½ to 2 kg) free-range chicken

1 onion, peeled and quartered

2 stalks celery, cut into ¾-in (2-cm) pieces

1 leek, cut into ¾-in (2-cm) pieces

1 large peeled carrot, cut into ¾-in (2-cm) pieces

2 cloves garlic, peeled and squashed with the side of a heavy knife blade

1 bunch of thyme

2 bay leaves

1 punnet (9 oz/ 250 g) button (Paris) mushrooms

salt and freshly ground black pepper

12 button onions

5¼ tbsp (75 g) butter, plus 2 knobs

⅔ cup (75 g) all-purpose/plain flour

3 tbsp plus 1 tsp (50 ml) heavy/double cream

freshly grated nutmeg (optional)

1 tsp Dijon mustard (optional)

squeeze of lemon juice (optional)

18 oz (500 g) all-butter puff pastry

2 tbsp chopped flat-leaf parsley

1 tbsp chopped tarragon

egg yolk to glaze (3 or 4 egg yolks)

Chicken Pot Pie

Bruce Poole

COMPLEXITY: MODERATE | PREP TIME: 40 MINUTES, PLUS OVERNIGHT REFRIGERATION
COOK TIME: 1 HOUR 30 MINUTES | SERVES: 4 TO 6

METHOD

Start the day before the pie is to be eaten. Put the whole chicken in a roomy stockpot or pan together with the onion, celery, leek, carrot, garlic, thyme, and bay leaves. Cover generously with cold water. Bring to the boil, skimming the surface frequently, and as soon as the water comes to the boil, turn the heat down to the merest simmer and poach the chicken very gently for 30 minutes or until the legs are just cooked. Turn off the heat and leave the chicken to cool in the broth.

After a couple of hours or so, lift out the chicken and set aside. Pass the stock through a fine sieve into a clean pan, discarding the solids. Bring back to the boil, ensuring that you skim well as the broth comes to the boil, as fat will rise to the top and this must be removed. Boil gently to reduce by about three-quarters – you should end up with about 3⅛ to 4 cups (750 ml to 1 litre) of really well flavoured chicken stock. Pass again through the fine sieve and set aside.

Remove all the chicken meat from the bone. Try to take the breast and leg meat cleanly and avoid shredding it. Make sure that all the delicious meat from the underside of the chicken is also taken. The carcass should be 'clean' when finished and can be discarded with the skin. Cover and refrigerate the stock and cooked chicken.

The following day, shallow-fry the button onions in a generous knob of butter, with seasoning. Cook very gently until slightly softened, 10 minutes or so; no colour is needed. Set aside, then cook the button mushrooms the same way.

Make a velouté sauce using a roux and 3⅛ cups (750 ml) of the chicken stock. Melt the butter in a saucepan over a medium heat, add the flour and whisk until smooth. Cook, whisking constantly, for 3 to 4 minutes until the flour mixture changes colour, then pour in the stock in a steady stream, whisking constantly. Cook, while whisking, until the sauce has thickened, about 3 minutes.

Continued overleaf

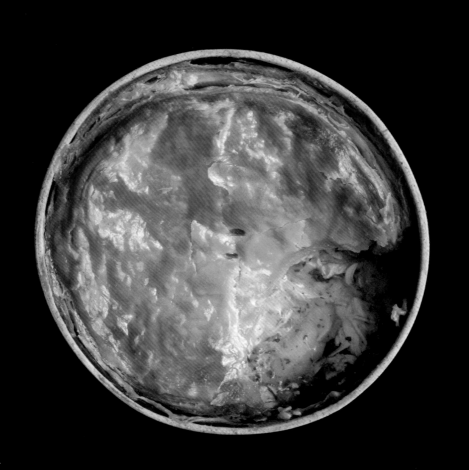

Chicken Pot Pie cont.

Add the double cream and season well with salt, pepper, and a little grated nutmeg if liked. The sauce should be slightly thicker than heavy/double cream. You can always whisk in a little additional roux to thicken it slightly, or add a little milk or stock to thin it. A teaspoon of Dijon mustard (no more) and a squeeze of lemon juice would also be nice. If the sauce has been correctly made, it will not need passing, but if not completely smooth then pass through a fine sieve. Keep the sauce warm, as it will not combine properly with the meat if cold.

Roll out the puff pastry to a thickness of about ⅛ in (3 mm). Set the oven to 325°F (170°C).

Dice the cooked chicken into large (¾ in/2 cm, say) neat pieces and place in a large mixing bowl. Add the sauce, the button onions and mushrooms, and the chopped parsley and tarragon. Combine the whole lot together and check the seasoning.

With a slotted spoon, fill a large pie dish with the mixture. Ideally the mixture should come to within ½ in (1 cm) or so of the top of the dish. Add enough sauce to make the whole pleasantly 'sloppy' – it should be neither too thick nor too runny! You may not need all the sauce.

Cut the rolled-out pastry so that it is slightly bigger than the pie dish. Cover the pie with the pastry and crimp firmly around the edge. Brush any excess flour off with a pastry brush. Brush the lid with egg yolk and make half a dozen incisions with the point of a knife to enable steam to escape. Bake the pie for 35 to 40 minutes until the top is nicely bronzed and the filling is completely heated through.

Buttered peas, braised gem lettuce, and boiled potatoes would be nice with this. It must be served straight from the oven and piping hot.

JOSH'S NOTES

Preparation: Start a day in advance.

Key element: When removing the chicken from the carcass, keep the pieces similar in size to the onions and mushrooms.

Tip: Use plenty of herbs.

Complements: Buttered peas, braised gem lettuce, and boiled potatoes.

INGREDIENTS

1 to 2 tbsp all purpose/plain flour

salt and freshly ground black pepper

3½ lb (1.6 kg) free-range, corn-fed chicken, cut into 12 pieces

¾ cup plus 2 tsp (190 ml) olive oil

3 brown onions, finely diced

4 bay leaves

5 cloves garlic, sliced

2 pinches of saffron threads

3⅛ cups (750 ml) Spanish Fino sherry

1 cup plus 2 tsp (250 ml) dry white wine

6 juniper berries

about 3 cups (700 ml) chicken stock (p. 482)

yolks of 4 hard-boiled eggs

⅔ cup (100 g) toasted almonds

large handful of flat-leaf parsley, roughly chopped

PICADA

yolks of 6 hard boiled eggs

⅔ cup (100 g) toasted almonds

pinch of saffron threads

salt as needed

JOSH'S NOTES

Preparation: Ask your butcher to cut the chicken into pieces if you aren't familiar with doing so for a casserole.

Chicken in Pepitoria Sauce
Pollo en Pepitoria

Frank Camorra

COMPLEXITY: MODERATE | PREP TIME: 30 MINUTES | COOK TIME: 1 HOUR | SERVES: 4

METHOD

Preheat the oven to 350°F (180°C).

Season the flour with salt and pepper, and lightly coat the chicken pieces with the flour.

Heat ½ cup plus 1 teaspoon (125 ml) of olive oil in a large, ovenproof, heavy-based frying pan (that has a lid) over a high heat and add 6 pieces of chicken. After 30 seconds, reduce the heat to medium. Season with a pinch of salt. After 4 minutes, turn the chicken over, season the other side, and cook for a further 4 minutes, until lightly browned. Remove from the pan and repeat the process with the remaining chicken pieces.

Discard the oil, scrape the pot clean, and heat the remaining oil in the pan over a medium heat. Add the onion, bay leaves, and garlic, and sauté, stirring occasionally, for about 10 minutes until the onion is soft and beginning to brown. Add the saffron and cook, stirring, for 1 minute. Add the Fino and wine and stir, scraping the bottom of the pan with a wooden spoon to deglaze it. Allow to boil for a few minutes, then reduce to a simmer and cook, uncovered, for 10 minutes.

Add the chicken and juniper berries, and enough stock to just cover the chicken pieces. Increase the heat to high and bring to the boil, then reduce to a slow simmer. Cover and cook in the oven for 1 hour. After 30 minutes, check the seasoning and add salt if necessary.

Meanwhile, make the *picada*. Using a mortar and pestle, pound toasted almonds until broken up like fine breadcrumbs. Add cooked egg yolks and pound until well mashed together. Gently toast saffron threads in a small, dry, non-stick pan set over a medium heat until you can just detect the aroma coming from the pan. This should only take a minute or so. Transfer saffron to a small dish, add 1 tablespoon (15 ml) of water, then add this to the almond mix and stir in. Season with a pinch of salt.

When the meat is ready, it should be beginning to separate and come away from the bone. Just before serving, stir through the *picada* and simmer for 1 minute to thicken the sauce.

Spicy Chicken with Peanuts
Gongbao Chicken

Ken Hom

COMPLEXITY: EASY | PREP TIME: 20 MINUTES | COOK TIME: 5 MINUTES | SERVES: 4

INGREDIENTS

8 oz (225 g) boneless
chicken breasts

1 dried red chilli, split
lengthways

1½ tbsp (22½ ml)
groundnut/peanut or
vegetable oil

3 oz (75 g) raw
groundnuts/peanuts,
shelled

SAUCE

1 tbsp (15 ml) chicken
stock (p. 482) or water

1 tbsp (15 ml) Shaoxing
rice wine or dry sherry

2 tsp dark soy sauce

1 tsp sugar

1 tsp garlic,
finely chopped

2 tsp green onion/spring
onion, finely chopped

½ tsp fresh ginger,
finely chopped

1 tsp Chinese white rice
vinegar or cider vinegar

½ tsp salt

1 tsp sesame oil

METHOD

Cut chicken into 1-in (2½-cm) cubes. Heat a wok or large frying-pan over a high heat until hot, add oil and chilli and stir-fry for a few seconds. (You may remove it when it turns black, or leave it in.) Next add the chicken cubes, groundnuts/peanuts, and vegetables and stir-fry for 1 minute. Remove from the pan.

Put all the sauce ingredients except the sesame oil in the pan. Bring to the boil, then turn the heat down. Return chicken and groundnuts/peanuts to the pan and cook for about 2 minutes in the sauce, mixing well all the while. Finally, add sesame oil, give the mixture a good stir, remove the chilli and serve immediately.

JOSH'S NOTES

Key element: Cut the
chicken cubes exactly
the same size, so they
cook evenly.

Image on p. 230

Chicken Korma

Yudhika Sujanani

COMPLEXITY: EASY | PREP TIME: 25 MINUTES | COOK TIME: 20 MINUTES | SERVES: 4 TO 6

INGREDIENTS

½ cup cashew nuts

6¾ tbsp (100 ml) boiling water

4 tbsp (60 ml) sunflower oil

2 onions, finely sliced

4 tbsp (60 ml) boiling water

1 bay leaf

2 tbsp shredded/desiccated coconut

2 tsp crushed ginger

2 tsp crushed garlic

1 tsp red chilli powder

1 tsp ground coriander

1 tsp garam masala

28½ oz (800 g) chicken fillet, sliced

1½ tsp coarse salt

1 cup plus 2 tsp (250 ml) coconut milk

pinch of sugar

chopped fresh cilantro/coriander

METHOD

In a heatproof bowl, soak the cashew nuts in the boiling water for 10 minutes.

Heat 2 tablespoons (30 ml) oil in a frying pan over a medium heat, add the onion slices and sauté for 5 to 10 minutes, until golden brown. Remove from the oil and drain on absorbent paper towel. Pour the 4 tablespoons (60 ml) of boiling water into a blender together with the cooked onion and process until smooth. Pour the onion paste into a bowl and set aside.

Rinse the blender. Using a slotted spoon, transfer the cashew nuts to the blender. Add a little of the soaking liquid and process until smooth. Set aside.

Heat the remaining 2 tablespoons (30 ml) of oil in a large pot over a medium heat. Add the bay leaf and fry for a few minutes, until fragrant. Add the coconut and sauté for a few minutes until light golden in colour. Add the crushed ginger and garlic and stir for a few seconds. Pour the onion paste into the pan and sauté, stirring, until the excess moisture evaporates. Add the chilli, coriander, and garam masala, stir for a few seconds, then add the chicken. Stir to coat the chicken with the spices, then fry until the chicken pieces are sealed on all sides. Season with salt.

Add the cashew paste and stir-fry until the mixture begins to thicken, then pour in the coconut milk and sprinkle over the sugar. Simmer for 2 to 3 minutes, until the chicken is cooked through; if the sauce seems a little thick, thin with a couple of tablespoons of water.

Garnish with cilantro/coriander before serving.

JOSH'S NOTES

Preparation: Prepare the onions and cashew nuts in advance.

Tip: Cooking a few hours before serving allows the flavours to develop more fully.

INGREDIENTS

¾ oz (20 g) tandoori
chicken spice

1¾ oz (50 g) chilli
powder

¾ oz (20 g) cilantro/
coriander powder

¾ oz (20 g) cumin
powder

3½ oz (100 g) plain
unsweetened yoghurt

1¼ oz (35 g) salt

5 tsp oil

2¼ lb (1 kg) skinless
chicken thighs

Chicken Tikka

Sid Sahrawat

COMPLEXITY: EASY | PREP TIME: 15 MINUTES, PLUS MARINATING OVERNIGHT
COOK TIME: 25 MINUTES | SERVES: 4

Mix the spices, yoghurt, salt, and oil together in a non-metallic bowl.
Add the chicken, mix well to coat with the marinade, cover and
leave in the refrigerator for 24 hours.

Pre-heat the oven to 480°F (250°C) and bake the chicken for
10 minutes. Check to see if it's cooked through, and if not, cook
for a few minutes longer. Remove from the oven, cover loosely
with tinfoil and rest for 10 to 15 minutes before serving.

INGREDIENTS

1 pigeon, top quality

7 oz (200 g) fresh thyme

1 fresh bay leaf

2 cloves garlic,
unpeeled and crushed

7 tbsp (100 g) unsalted
butter

3 tbsp plus 1 tsp (50 ml)
olive oil

salt and freshly ground
black pepper

JOSH'S NOTES

Key element: Regular
basting while roasting,
to achieve a perfect
colour.

Roasted Pigeon

Julien Royer

COMPLEXITY: MODERATE | PREP TIME: 10 MINUTES | COOK TIME: 20 MINUTES | SERVES: 1

Pre-heat the oven to 350°F (180°C).

With a blow torch, lightly torch the skin of the pigeon to remove
any fur. Remove the head and wing tips. Remove all innards from
the pigeon, then rinse it thoroughly with water. Pat dry with a cloth.
Set aside the liver and heart for other dishes.

Stuff the thyme, bay leaf, and garlic cloves into the pigeon. Rub the
outside of the pigeon thoroughly with butter. Roast in the oven for
10 to 12 minutes, basting every 5 minutes with the melted butter.
Remove from the oven, cover loosely with foil and leave to rest
for 10 minutes before serving.

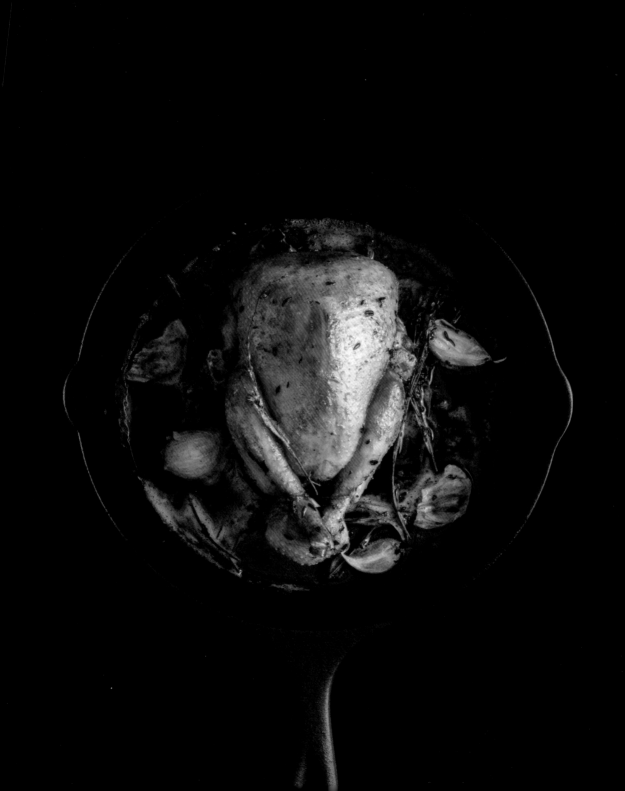

Roast Grouse with Game Chips & Bread Sauce

Tom Kitchin

COMPLEXITY: MODERATE | PREP TIME: 30 MINUTES | COOK TIME: 25 MINUTES | SERVES: 4

INGREDIENTS

GAME CHIPS

4 floury potatoes, such as Maris Piper, very thinly sliced, ideally using a mandoline

vegetable oil, for deep-frying

GROUSE

4 oven-ready young grouse (or partridge as a substitute)

4 large slices/rashers pancetta

olive oil

sea salt and freshly cracked black pepper

watercress sprigs, to garnish

1 recipe bread sauce (p. 465), to serve

JOSH'S NOTES

Preparation: Make the game chips and bread sauce in advance.

Key element: Wrap the pancetta neatly around the breast, and truss it to hold it in place so it cooks evenly.

Tip: Caramelize the pancetta well so that it holds its shape and doesn't tear.

Complements: Red wine sauce goes well with this, p. 468.

METHOD

The game chips can be made a day in advance and stored in an airtight container until required. After slicing the potatoes, use kitchen paper to pat them dry. Heat enough oil for deep-frying in a deep-fat fryer or a heavy-based saucepan until a potato slice sizzles instantly. Add as many potato slices as will fit without over-crowding and fry, stirring constantly, until they are golden brown. Drain well on kitchen paper and sprinkle with salt while they are still hot. Continue until all the slices are fried.

When you're ready to roast the birds, pre-heat the oven to 325°F (170°C) fan or 375°F (190°C) regular bake.

Using a small, sharp knife, remove the wishbone from each grouse. Season the cavities with salt and pepper, then cover the breasts of each with 1 folded pancetta rasher. Tie the bacon securely to the birds with kitchen string, then truss the legs for even cooking.

Heat a large, well-seasoned, ovenproof frying pan over a medium-high heat, then add a splash of oil. When it is hot, add the birds and fry until they and the pancetta are nicely coloured all over.

Turn the grouse onto one breast, place the pan in the oven and roast for 3 minutes. Turn the birds over onto the other breast and roast for a further 3 minutes. Depending on the size and age of the birds, they may need another minute or two. If you feel the breasts at the bottom, they should have a little spring in them.

Leave the birds to rest for 5 minutes, covered with tinfoil.

Meanwhile, heat the bread sauce, which might require a little extra milk. Untie the grouse, then serve garnished with watercress and with the game chips and bread sauce alongside.

"Every year at The Kitchin we put the grouse on the menu from the twelfth of August, the Glorious Twelfth, which is the first day of the shooting season. In my opinion, roasting it whole like this and serving it with bread sauce and game chips is, quite simply, the best way to eat grouse."

– TOM KITCHIN

Rosemary Roast Chicken with Baked Fennel & Potatoes

Marcus Wareing

COMPLEXITY: EASY | PREP TIME: 15 MINUTES, PLUS UP TO 24 HOURS BRINING
COOK TIME: ABOUT 1 HOUR 15 MINUTES | SERVES: 4 TO 6

INGREDIENTS

3½ tbsp (50 g) butter, softened, plus extra for greasing

2 cloves garlic, finely grated

sea salt and freshly ground black pepper

1 bunch of rosemary, half the needles finely chopped

3 to 4 lb (1.4 to 1.8 kg) chicken, giblets removed, brined (p. 479)

4 large King Edward or Chippies Choice or other floury potatoes, scrubbed and cut into large wedges

½ tsp fennel seeds, crushed

1 bulb fennel, cut into slices ½ in (1 cm) thick

1¼ cups (300 ml) chicken stock (p. 482)

2 tbsp (30 ml) heavy/double cream

JOSH'S NOTES

Key element: Get a good dark golden colour on the skin; if needed, increase the temperature at the end to achieve this.

METHOD

Pre-heat the oven to 400°F (200°C) fan or 425°F (220°C) regular bake, and lightly grease a large roasting tray with a little butter.

Mix the softened butter in a bowl with the garlic, a generous pinch each of salt and pepper, and the chopped rosemary, until well combined. Rinse the chicken under cold running water and pat it dry with kitchen paper. Use your hands to smear two-thirds of the flavoured butter under the skin of the chicken and all over the flesh of the breasts and legs. Smear the remaining third over the top of the chicken.

Season the cavity and the outside of the bird with a little more salt and pepper. Sit the chicken in the greased roasting tray and roast in the oven for 20 minutes, until it starts to take on a golden colour. Remove from the oven and reduce the oven temperature to 350°F (180°C) fan or 400°F (200°C) regular bake. Add the potatoes, fennel seeds, and rosemary sprigs to the roasting tray, season well and place back in the oven.

Continue to roast for a further 30 minutes. Turn the potatoes, then add the sliced fennel to the roasting tray and place back in the oven for a further 15 minutes, turning the fennel halfway through. To check that the chicken is cooked, insert a skewer into the thickest part of the thigh – if the juices run clear, it is ready. If not, continue to cook for a further 15 to 20 minutes and test again. Remove the chicken, fennel, and potatoes from the tray to a large dish. Loosely cover with foil and leave to rest for 5 minutes.

Put the roasting tray directly on the stovetop over a medium heat and stir in the stock. Bring to the boil and simmer for 5 minutes. Pass the gravy through a sieve to remove the rosemary, then whisk in the double cream and season to taste.

Carve the chicken and serve it with the fennel, potatoes, and gravy.

Perfect Roast Turkey

Martha Stewart

COMPLEXITY: MODERATE | PREP TIME: 20 MINUTES, PLUS STANDING TIME
COOK TIME: 5 HOURS | SERVES: 12 TO 14

INGREDIENTS

1 x 20 to 21 lb (9 to 9½ kg) fresh whole turkey, giblets and neck removed from cavity and reserved

12 oz (3 sticks/340 g) unsalted butter, melted, plus 4 tbsp (60 g) unsalted butter at room temperature

1 bottle dry white wine

2 tsp salt

2 tsp freshly ground black pepper

classic turkey stuffing (p. 445)

1 cup (240 ml) dry red or white wine for gravy (optional)

giblet stock (see overleaf)

Ingredients continued overleaf

METHOD

Rinse the turkey with cool water and dry with paper towels. Let stand for 2 hours at room temperature.

Place a rack on the lowest level in the oven and pre-heat the oven to 450°F (230°C). Combine the melted butter and white wine in a bowl. Fold a large piece of cheesecloth into quarters and cut it into a four-layer square measuring 17 in (43 cm) on each side. Immerse the cheesecloth in the butter and wine, and let it soak.

Place the turkey, breast side up, on a roasting rack in a heavy metal roasting pan. If the turkey comes with a pop-up timer, remove it; an instant-read thermometer is a much more accurate indication of doneness. Fold the wing tips under the turkey. Sprinkle ½ teaspoon each of salt and pepper inside the turkey. Fill the large cavity and neck cavity loosely with as much stuffing as they hold comfortably; do not pack tightly. (Cook the remaining stuffing in a buttered baking dish for 45 minutes at 375°F/190°C.) Tie the legs together loosely with kitchen string (a bow will be easy to untie later). Fold the neck flap under and secure with toothpicks. Rub the turkey with the softened butter and sprinkle with the remaining 1½ teaspoons salt and pepper.

Lift the cheesecloth out of the liquid and squeeze it slightly, leaving it very damp. Spread it evenly over the breast and about halfway down the sides of the turkey; it can cover some of the leg area. Place the turkey, legs first, in the oven and cook for 30 minutes. Using a pastry brush, baste the cheesecloth and exposed parts of the turkey with butter and wine. Reduce the oven temperature to 350°F (180°C) and continue to cook for a further 2 hours 30 minutes, basting every 30 minutes and watching the pan juices; if the pan gets too full, spoon out the juices, reserving them for the gravy.

After the third hour of cooking, carefully remove and discard the cheesecloth. Turn the roasting pan so that the breast is facing the back of the oven. Baste the turkey with pan juices. If there are not enough juices, continue to use the butter and wine. The skin gets fragile as it browns, so baste carefully. Cook for 1 more hour, basting after 30 minutes.

After this fourth hour of cooking, insert an instant-read thermometer into the thickest part of the thigh. Do not poke into a bone. The temperature should reach at least 180°F (82°C) (stuffing should be between 140 and 160°F/60 to 70°C) and the turkey should be golden brown. The breast does not need to be checked for temperature. If the legs are not yet fully cooked, baste the turkey, return it to the oven, and cook for another 20 to 30 minutes.

When fully cooked, transfer the turkey to a serving platter and let rest for about 30 minutes. Meanwhile, make the gravy. Pour all the pan juices into a glass measuring cup. Let stand until grease rises to the surface, about 10 minutes, then skim it off. Meanwhile, place the roasting pan over a medium-high heat. Add the dry red or white wine, or water, to the pan. Using a wooden spoon, scrape the pan until the liquid boils and all the crispy bits are unstuck from the pan. Add the giblet stock, stir well and bring back to the boil. Cook until the liquid has reduced by half, about 10 minutes. Add the defatted pan juices and cook over a medium-high heat for 10 minutes more. You will have about 2½ cups (600 ml) of gravy. Season to taste, strain into a warm gravy boat, and serve with the turkey.

––––––––––

"If your roasting pan only fits sideways in the oven, turn the pan every hour so that the turkey cooks and browns evenly."
– MARTHA STEWART

Continued overleaf

Perfect Roast Turkey cont.

....

Giblet Stock

MAKES: ABOUT 2 CUPS (480 ML)

giblets (heart, gizzard, and liver) and neck reserved from turkey

4 tbsp (60 g) unsalted butter

1 onion, peeled and cut into ¼-in (5-mm) dice

1 stalk celery with leaves, stalk cut into ¼-in (5-mm) dice, leaves roughly chopped

1 small leek, trimmed, washed, and cut into ¼-in (5-mm) dice

salt and freshly ground black pepper

1 bay leaf

Trim any fat or membrane from the giblets. The liver should not have the gallbladder, a small green sac, attached. If it is, trim it off carefully, removing part of the liver if necessary. Do not pierce the sac; the liquid it contains is very bitter. Rinse the giblets and neck and pat dry with paper towel.

In a medium-sized saucepan, melt 3 tablespoons (45 g) butter over a medium heat. Add the onion, celery and leaves, and leeks. Cook, stirring occasionally, until the onions are translucent, about 10 minutes. Add ½ teaspoon salt and ¼ teaspoon pepper and cook for another 5 minutes. Add 4 cups (960 ml) water, the bay leaf, and the gizzard, heart, and neck (do not add the liver; it needs to be cooked separately or it makes the stock bitter). Bring to the boil, then reduce to a high simmer. Cook for 45 minutes, or until the gizzard is tender when pierced with the tip of a knife.

Meanwhile, chop the liver finely. Melt the remaining tablespoon (15 g) of butter in a small frying pan over a medium-low heat. Add the liver and cook, stirring constantly, for 4 to 6 minutes, until the liver no longer releases any blood and is fully cooked. Set aside.

After the 45 minutes of simmering, the liquid should have reduced to about 2½ cups (600 ml). If it has not, increase the heat and cook for another 10 to 15 minutes. Strain the broth. Chop the gizzard and heart very fine and add to the strained broth along with the chopped liver. Pick the meat off the neck and add to the broth. Set aside until needed for gravy.

_____

"The giblets are edible when properly prepared and are the secret to a fine broth and gravy. Make this while the turkey roasts."

– MARTHA STEWART

INGREDIENTS

DUCK CONFIT

18 oz (500 g) coarse
sea salt

1 sprig of thyme

1 sprig of rosemary

4 cloves garlic

1 tsp black peppercorns,
crushed

6 duck legs (about
5⅔ oz/160 g each)

4½ lb (2 kg) duck fat

DUCK LEG

7 oz (200 g) string/
French beans, trimmed
and cut into 1½-in
(4-cm) lengths

1 Morteau sausage
(about 10½ oz/300 g)

7 oz (200 g) garlic
sausage

7 oz (200 g) unsmoked
bacon lardons

¾ tbsp (10 g) unsalted
butter

2 French black
puddings, 5 oz/150 g
each

6 tbsp (90 ml) classic
vinaigrette (p. 476)

2 heads curly frisée
(white part only), leaves
separated

2 tbsp chopped parsley

sea salt and freshly
ground white pepper

6¾ tbsp (100 ml) red
wine jus

3 tbsp (45 ml) extra
virgin olive oil

Crisp Confit Duck Leg, Black Pudding & Salad Lyonnaise

Chris & Jeff Galvin

COMPLEXITY: MODERATE | PREP TIME: 45 MINUTES, PLUS REFRIGERATION TIME
COOK TIME: 3 HOURS 30 MINUTES | SERVES: 6

METHOD

First, prepare the duck confit – this needs to be started 2 days in advance. In a blender or food processor, blend the salt, thyme, rosemary, garlic, and peppercorns together until the herbs and garlic have completely broken down. Pour half of this mixture onto a tray large enough to hold all the duck legs side by side, then place the duck legs on top. Cover with the remaining salt mixture. Cover with plastic wrap, then leave in the fridge for 24 hours. Remove the legs from the salt, brushing off any excess, and discard the salt mixture. Rinse the legs thoroughly under cold running water.

Pre-heat the oven to 265°F (130°C). Melt the duck fat in a large casserole, add the duck legs and return the fat to a slow simmer. Cover with a lid and cook in the oven for 3 hours, or until the meat is tender (you should be able to remove the thigh bone easily with your fingers).

Carefully remove the casserole from the oven and leave to cool to room temperature. Line a tray with plastic wrap. Using a slotted spoon, remove the duck legs to the tray, placing them skin side down, then cover and refrigerate for 24 hours or until completely chilled.

On the day of serving, pre-heat the oven to 400°F (200°C).

Blanch the string/French beans in a large pan of salted boiling water for 5 minutes, then refresh in iced water, drain and set aside.

Put the Morteau sausage in a pan, cover with cold water and bring to the boil, then immediately refresh under cold water for 5 minutes. Drain. Cut both the cooked Morteau sausage and the garlic sausage into quarters lengthwise, then into slices ⅛ in (3 mm) thick.

Continued overleaf

Crisp Confit Duck Leg, Black Pudding & Salad Lyonnaise cont.

Place a frying pan over a high heat until very hot. Add the bacon lardons along with the butter and cook for a few minutes until golden, then drain and set aside.

Place an ovenproof frying pan over a high heat until very hot. Add the duck legs skin side down (you don't need any fat in the pan) and cook for 2 minutes, then transfer to the oven for 12 minutes to heat through. Remove from the oven and use a fish slice to ease the skin from the bottom of the frying pan. If the skin isn't golden enough, cook over a medium heat on the stovetop until golden and crisp. Remove from the pan and keep warm.

Turn the oven to the grill setting on a medium heat. Lightly oil a baking tray. Cut the black pudding into slices ½ in (1 cm) thick. Lay these on the baking tray and grill for 4 minutes, or until heated through.

To serve, heat the string/French beans, sausages, and bacon lardons together in a saucepan over a medium heat until warmed through. Transfer to a mixing bowl, add the vinaigrette, frisée, parsley, and some seasoning, and gently toss together. Divide the salad between 6 serving plates, place the duck legs on top and the black pudding around. Spoon the red wine jus around the outside of the plates and finish with a drizzle of extra virgin olive oil.

JOSH'S NOTES

Preparation: The duck legs need to be prepared up to two days in advance.

Key element: Source good-quality Morteau, garlic sausage, and black pudding.

Tip: Keep the skin of the duck intact for best results.

INGREDIENTS

DRY-AGED DUCKS

2 Normandy ducks, heads and feet on, about 5¾ lb (2.6 kg) each

DUCK SPICE

1½ oz (40 g) Szechuan peppercorns

2¼ oz (65 g) coriander seeds

1½ oz (40 g) cumin seeds

1 oz (30 g) dried lavender

CHICKEN JUS

6¾ tbsp (100 ml) rapeseed/canola oil

1¼ lb (560 g) onion, diced ¾ in (2 cm)

9¼ oz (260 g) carrot, peeled and diced ¾ in (2 cm)

9¼ oz (260 g) celery diced ¾ in (2 cm)

6¾ tbsp tomato purée/paste

3⅛ cups (750 ml) red wine

10 lb (4½ kg) chicken wings

5½ lb (2½ kg) chicken feet

3½ gallons (13½ litres) water

2 bay leaves

10 sprigs of thyme

25 black peppercorns

Ingredients continued overleaf

Duck Honey-glazed with Cherries & Onions

Daniel Humm

COMPLEXITY: DIFFICULT | PREP TIME: 2 HOURS, PLUS HANGING TIME
COOK TIME: 6 HOURS | SERVES: 8

Using meat hooks, hang the ducks by their necks in the refrigerator with good air circulation until the skin of the ducks is thoroughly dried, 10 to 14 days. Cut the heads and necks from the ducks, discarding the heads and reserving the necks for the cherry duck jus. Cut the mid-wing section, wing tips, and feet from the ducks, reserving the wing pieces for the jus. Remove and discard the wishbones. Truss the ducks with butcher's twine.

For the duck spice, separately coarsely grind the Szechuan peppercorns, coriander seeds, and cumin seeds, just enough to crack each of the spices. Sift the ground spices through a coarse-meshed tamis and discard the dust. Mix the ground spices with the lavender and set aside.

For the chicken jus, pre-heat a convection oven to 400°F (200°F), high fan. Heat the oil in a large roasting pan over a high heat. Add the onion, carrots, and celery, and sauté until they caramelize, about 12 minutes. Add the tomato purée/paste and sauté until caramelized, 3 minutes. Add the red wine and bring to a simmer. Reduce by half, about 10 minutes. Set the wine and vegetable mixture aside.

Spread the chicken wings in a single layer on 2 large, rimmed, unlined baking trays and roast in the oven until caramelized, about 50 minutes, turning the tray once. Drain, and discard any rendered fat. Scrape the roasted wings into a large stockpot and combine with the chicken feet and water. Bring to a simmer over a medium heat and skim the stock of all impurities and fats that rise to the top. Add the wine and vegetable mixture to the stock, along with the bay leaves, thyme, and peppercorns. Simmer the stock over low heat, uncovered, for 6 hours, skimming every 30 minutes.

Strain the stock through a chinois, return to the heat in a large, clean saucepan, and reduce over low heat to 1 quart (1 litre). Prepare an ice bath. Strain the reduced jus through a chinois again and chill over the ice bath. Reserve in an airtight container, refrigerated, for up to 3 days or freeze for up to 30 days.

Continued overleaf

INGREDIENTS CONT.

WHITE BALSAMIC PICKLING LIQUID

1 cup plus 2 tsp (250 ml) white balsamic vinegar

½ cup (100 g) sugar

6¾ tbsp (100 ml) water

4¼ tsp salt

ONION PETALS

1 onion

kosher/flaky salt, to taste

1¾ oz (50 g) smoked duck fat

2 tsp white soy sauce

¾ cup plus 1¼ tbsp (200 ml) water

¾ cup plus 1¼ tbsp (200 ml) white balsamic pickling liquid

DAIKON RIBBONS

1 daikon radish

6¾ tbsp (100 ml) white balsamic pickling liquid

6¾ tbsp (100 ml) water

kosher/flaky salt, to taste

CHERRY RELISH

18 oz (500 g) pitted sour cherries

kosher/flaky salt, to taste

6¾ tbsp (100 ml) white balsamic vinegar

Duck Honey-glazed with Cherries & Onions cont.

For the white balsamic pickling liquid, combine all the ingredients in a mixing bowl and whisk to fully dissolve the sugar and salt. Reserve, refrigerated, for up to 2 weeks.

For the onion petals, pre-heat a combi oven to 198°F (92°C), full steam, and prepare an ice bath. Cut the onion into quarters, through the root. Pull the onion layers apart and cut into petals or strips about ¾ in (2 cm) thick. Season the petals with salt, combine with the duck fat and soy sauce in a sous vide bag, and seal airtight. Cook in the steam oven until tender, about 20 minutes. Shock the onion petals in the bag in the ice bath. When cool, but before the fat has solidified, remove the onion petals from the bag and drain. Combine the onion petals with the water and pickling liquid in a sous vide bag and compress. Drain.

For the daikon ribbons, use a deli slicer or a mandolin to cut the radish into thin strips. Trim the strips so that they measure ⅝ x 2¼ in (1½ x 6 cm). Combine the daikon ribbons with the water and pickling liquid in a sous vide bag and compress. Drain.

For the cherry relish, pre-heat a combi oven to 198°F (92°C), full steam. Season the cherries with salt, combine with the vinegar in a sous vide bag and seal airtight. Cook the cherries in the steam oven for 25 minutes. Strain the cherries, and reserve the liquid for the sauce. Squeeze any excess moisture from the cherries and roughly chop. Season the cherries with some of the reserved liquid and additional salt as necessary. Keep warm.

For the cherry duck jus, heat the oil in a large saucepan over a medium heat. Sear the duck necks and wings in the oil, turning occasionally, until thoroughly caramelized, about 20 minutes. Drain off any rendered fat from the pan, reduce the heat to low, and add the shallots to the pan. Cook, stirring frequently, until the shallots have softened, about 2 minutes. Add the black garlic and cherries and roast until fragrant. Add the chicken jus, bring to a simmer, and cook until reduced to a sauce consistency, about 25 minutes. Season with the cherry vinegar and salt. Keep warm.

To finish, pre-heat a convection oven to 400°F (200°C), high fan. Thoroughly rub the honey into the skin of the ducks, making sure to make a complete, thin, and even layer. Coat the ducks evenly with the duck spice and season generously with salt. Space the ducks evenly on a wire rack set over a baking tray. Roast the ducks in the oven for 16 minutes, turning the tray once. A cake tester inserted against the breastbone should feel warm to the touch once removed. Remove the ducks from the oven and let rest at room temperature for 20 minutes before serving.

Pre-heat a conventional oven to 325°F (170°C). Line a baking sheet with parchment paper and lay out the onion petals and daikon ribbons on the paper in a single layer. Brush generously with the melted duck fat. Place in the oven until heated through, about 5 minutes.

Carve the breasts from the duck and trim away any connective tissue. Slice each breast in half lengthwise. Brush each portion with the brown butter and season with the *fleur de sel*. Spoon about 1 heaped tablespoon cherry relish towards the top left of each plate. Weave the onion petals and daikon ribbons over the cherry relish to cover. Garnish the arrangement with onion flowers. Place 1 duck breast portion to the right of the garnish. Sauce with the cherry duck jus.

INGREDIENTS CONT.

CHERRY DUCK JUS

3 tbsp plus 1 tsp (50 ml) rapeseed/canola oil

10½ oz (300 g) duck necks and wings reserved from the dry-aged ducks

1¾ oz (50 g) sliced shallots

1 qt (1 litre) chicken jus

3 cloves black garlic

1¾ oz (50 g) pitted cherries

3 tbsp plus 1 tsp (50 ml) cherry vinegar, reserved from the cherry relish

kosher/flaky salt, to taste

TO FINSIH

3 tbsp honey

kosher/flaky salt, for seasoning the ducks

48 onion petals

32 daikon ribbons

smoked duck fat, melted

TO SERVE

brown butter, melted

fleur de sel

onion flowers

JOSH'S NOTES

Key element: Remove the duck carefully from the bone.

Tip: Take your time carving, and follow the bone structure with a smaller knife.

Duck with Orange Sauce
Canard à l'Orange

Josh Emett

COMPLEXITY: MODERATE | PREP TIME: 20 MINUTES | COOK TIME: 1 HOUR 15 MINUTES
SERVES: 2

INGREDIENTS

1 whole fresh duck, about 4½ lb (2 kg)

rapeseed/canola oil as needed

sea salt as needed

4 tsp red wine vinegar

4 tsp Cointreau or Grand Marnier liqueur

½ cup (120 ml) fresh orange juice

⅓ cup (80 ml) beef stock (p. 484)

1 orange, skin julienned and flesh cut into segments

¾ tbsp (10 g) unsalted butter, softened

JOSH'S NOTES

Preparation: Prepare the duck first; make the sauce once it's finished roasting.

Key element: Take your time over crisping the skin, and control the heat carefully.

Tip: Let the duck cool before carving; it will hold together better and won't dry out as much.

METHOD

Pre-heat the oven to 400°F (200°C).

Remove the wing tips from the duck, and discard. Place the duck on a rack over a roasting pan, rub with a generous amount of rapeseed/canola oil and season to taste with sea salt. Roast for 20 minutes, then reduce the temperature to 350°F (180°C) for another 40 minutes. Remove from the oven and leave to cool to room temperature.

While the duck is cooling, make the sauce. Heat a small pot over a medium heat until hot, add the vinegar and simmer rapidly until reduced by half, about 30 seconds. Add the liqueur and orange juice, bring back to the boil and simmer rapidly until reduced by half, about 1 minute.

Add the beef stock and bring back to the boil, then simmer rapidly until reduced by one-third, to a nice sauce consistency, about 1 minute. Finish the sauce by adding the julienned orange, orange segments, butter, and a touch of seasoning, stirring gently to incorporate the butter into the sauce. Set aside.

Divide the duck into portions by removing the breasts with wings attached, then removing the legs. Remove the thigh bone from the leg and trim the drumsticks, cleaning the meat off the knuckle bone on the end.

Heat a lightly oiled frying pan over a medium heat until fairly hot. Place the duck portions in the pan to crisp up the skin of the legs and breasts, about 5 to 6 minutes.

Carve the breasts and arrange on a serving plate with the leg portions. Pour the sauce over the top.

"The sweetness of the orange sauce is a perfect complement to the crispy skin and richness of the duck, and should be complemented with anything green and refreshing that is in season."
– JOSH EMETT

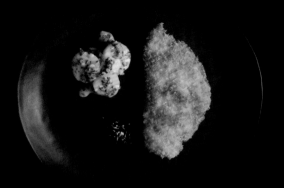

Chicken Schnitzel, p. 200

Spicy Chicken, p. 210

Veal with Tuna Sauce, p. 246

Slow-roasted Lamb Shoulder, p. 269

Pork & Cabbage Dumplings, p. 242

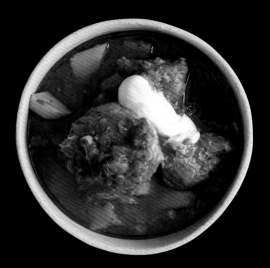

Veal Shoulder Goulash, p. 265

Tasha's Livers on Toast, p. 295

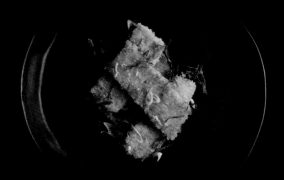

Crumbed Tripe, p. 297

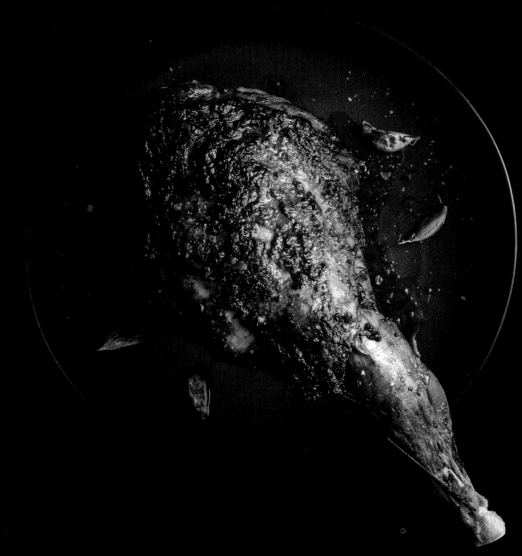

Leg of Lamb, p. 273

Meat & Offal

Meat has overtaken staples as the principal component in
virtually every meal we eat today, but these recipes are the
ones you simply must cook at least once in your life. From true
classics such as moussaka, osso buco, porcetta, rogan josh,
and shepherd's pie, to modern interpretations of beef tartare,
barbecue ribs, and even offal – which deserves a chance if you're
brave enough to give it a try. As with any ingredient, quality
and provenance are vital to creating a memorable dish, but
learning how to handle meat with respect and listen to what it's
telling you, will result in dishes truly worthy of the animals who
sacrificed their lives to produce them.

INGREDIENTS

4 tbsp (60 ml) extra virgin olive oil

½ small leek, diced as small as possible – ⅛-in (3-mm) pieces

2½ oz (70 g) Ibérico or other air-dried ham, diced very small

½ cup (60 g) all-purpose/plain flour

⅓ cup (75 ml) ham or vegetable stock

1⅓ cups (325 ml) whole milk

freshly grated nutmeg

sea salt and freshly ground black pepper

TO COAT & FRY

⅔ cup (75 g) all-purpose/plain flour

2 large eggs, beaten

2⅔ oz (75 g) breadcrumbs

oil, for frying

JOSH'S NOTES

Preparation: Make ahead of time, to allow to chill.

Key elements: Good quality jamón. Take time to cook the roux to achieve the right flavour.

Tip: Don't fry too many at once, and let them rest for a minute to cool before eating.

Ham Croquettes
Jamón Croquetas

José Pizarro

COMPLEXITY: EASY | PREP TIME: 30 MINUTES, PLUS CHILL TIME
COOK TIME: 20 MINUTES | SERVES: 4

METHOD

Heat the olive oil in a pan until it starts to shimmer, then add the leek and sauté until soft but not coloured. Stir in the ham, fry for another minute, then stir in the flour and fry over a medium heat until the mixture is golden but not burnt. This will take about 5 minutes. It is important that the flour in the roux is cooked properly, otherwise the croquetas will taste of flour.

Combine the stock and milk in a small pan and heat until hot but not boiling. Season the liquid with a few scrapes of nutmeg. Gradually add the liquid to the roux, a few tablespoons at a time, stirring the mixture all the time. Once you have incorporated all the liquid, continue to cook the sauce for about 5 minutes until it thickens and leaves the sides of the pan when you stir it. At this stage, add a couple of turns of the pepper mill, taste the sauce and adjust the salt if necessary – the ham can be very salty to start with. The sauce is now done. It should be really thick because you don't want the croquetas to turn into pancakes!

Smooth the sauce onto a baking tray (12 x 8 in/30 x 20 cm is fine), then cover with plastic wrap to stop the mixture drying out. Leave it to cool before putting it in the fridge for 1 hour.

When you are ready for the next stage, line up three bowls: one with the flour, the other with the beaten egg, and the third with the breadcrumbs. Dust your hands with flour, take a scoop of chilled sauce and roll it between your palms. The size of the croquetas is up to you, but the easiest is a walnut-sized ball. Next, dunk the croqueta into the flour – you want more of a dusting than a coating – followed by the egg and then the breadcrumbs. Put the croquetas on a tray and when you've used up all the mixture, put them all back in the fridge for 30 minutes.

If you have a deep-fat fryer, heat the oil to 325°C (170°C) and fry the croquetas for a couple of minutes. If not, heat the oil in a frying pan until it starts to shimmer, then add 3 or 4 croquetas at a time and fry until they are golden all over. You don't want them to cook too quickly, otherwise the centres won't be hot enough.

INGREDIENTS

18 oz (500 g) pork belly, skinned and chopped

2 lb (850 g) game mix – ask your butcher for boneless, skinless mixed venison, pheasant, hare and so on

9 oz (250 g) pork liver

3½ tbsp (50 g) butter

2 onions, finely chopped

3 cloves garlic, finely chopped

6 juniper berries

2 dried bay leaves

2 cloves

1½ tsp thyme leaves

1 tsp cracked black pepper

2 tbsp (30 ml) brandy

2 tbsp (30 ml) red wine

2 tsp salt

¹⁄₁₆ oz (2 g) saltpetre (optional)

CRANBERRY COMPOTE

¾ cup (200 g) light-brown cane sugar/Demerara sugar

6¾ tbsp (100 ml) freshly squeezed orange juice

¾-in (2-cm) piece of fresh ginger, peeled and finely chopped

14 oz (400 g) cranberries, defrosted if frozen

½ nutmeg

1 orange

Ingredients continued overleaf

Game Terrine Glazed in Port Jelly with Cranberry Compote

Tom Kerridge

COMPLEXITY: DIFFICULT | PREP TIME: 45 MINUTES
COOK TIME: 2 HOURS, PLUS REFRIGERATION TIME | SERVES: 12

METHOD

Pre-heat the oven to 265°F (130°C) and bring a kettle of water to the boil. Line a 10 x 4 in (25 x 10 cm) terrine or a 1¼ quart (1.2 litres) ovenproof dish with plastic wrap, then leave to one side.

Mince the pork belly, game mix, and pork liver together and put in a large bowl, then leave to one side.

Melt the butter in a frying pan over a low heat. Add the onion and garlic and fry, stirring, for at least 5 minutes, until softened but not coloured. Remove the pan from the heat and leave the onion and butter mix to cool, then add to the bowl with the ground/minced meats.

Grind the juniper berries, bay leaves, cloves, thyme, and black pepper together in a spice grinder. Add this spice and herb mix to the ground/minced meats. Add the brandy, red wine, salt, and saltpetre, if using. Get your hands in and combine thoroughly. The salt will begin to break down the meat and you will find that the mixture becomes a little tighter in your hands.

Push the meat mix into the lined terrine, trying not to have any air bubbles. Bring the plastic wrap over the top to seal, then place the terrine's lid on top (if it has one). Place the terrine in a roasting tray and pour in enough boiling water to come halfway up the sides. Place the tray in the oven and cook the terrine for 1 hour 30 minutes to 2 hours, until the centre of the terrine has reached 158°F (70°C) on an instant-read thermometer. Remove the terrine from the tray, take the lid off and put a heavy weight on the top to press the meat down. Leave to cool completely, then place in the fridge for 12 hours, still with the weight on top.

Meanwhile, make the cranberry compote. Place the sugar, orange juice, and ginger in a saucepan over a high heat and bring to the boil, stirring to dissolve the sugar. Stir in the cranberries and grate in the nutmeg.

Continued overleaf

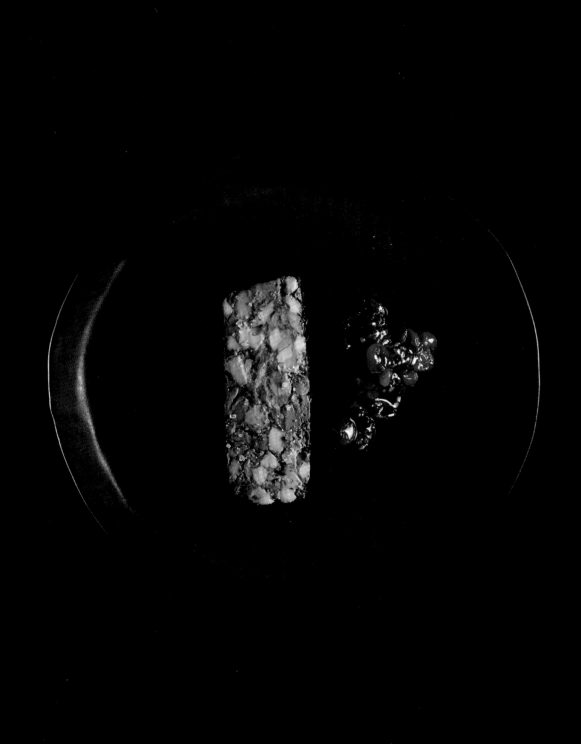

INGREDIENTS CONT.

PORT JELLY

1⅓ cups plus 2 tbsp
(350 ml) port

¼ cup (50 g) superfine/
caster sugar

3 gelatine leaves

TO SERVE

hot toast

Game Terrine Glazed in Port Jelly with Cranberry Compote cont.

Simmer, uncovered and stirring frequently, for about 15 minutes until the cranberries soften and form a chutney-like appearance. Grate in the zest of the orange, then transfer the compote to a bowl and leave to cool.

To make the port jelly, place the port and sugar in a saucepan over a high heat and bring to the boil, stirring to dissolve the sugar. When the sugar has dissolved, remove the pan from the heat and leave to one side.

Soak the gelatine leaves in cold water for about 5 minutes, until softened. Squeeze out the water, then add the gelatine to the warm port mix and stir until it has dissolved. Pass through a fine sieve into a bowl.

Remove the terrine from its mould and scrape off any excess fat or jelly. Use a ladle to pour the port jelly over the top of the terrine. Place the terrine back in the fridge for about 10 minutes, until the jelly sets. You will need to do this three or four times to get a good layer of jelly.

After the jelly has set, use a long, thin knife to trim the sides of the terrine so that it looks smart, then slice and serve with cranberry compote and toast.

TIP

If you want to get ahead over the holiday period, the cranberry compote will keep in a covered container in the fridge for up to a week.

JOSH'S NOTES

Preparation: Chop all the meat evenly. Set the terrine overnight.

Key elements: Cook time to reach the correct internal temperature; Press the terrine flat and evenly with an appropriate weight.

Tip: Cool the jelly over ice until it begins to thicken and almost set, before pouring over the terrine.

Pork Rillettes
Rillettes de Cochon

Stéphane Reynaud

COMPLEXITY: MODERATE | PREP TIME: 25 MINUTES | COOK TIME: 6 HOURS, PLUS CHILL TIME
SERVES: 8

INGREDIENTS

1⅛ lb (510 g) pork loin

1 pork hock or shank (about 1⅓ lb/600 g)

3½ oz (100 g) slab bacon

3½ oz (100 g) pork belly

2⅓ cups (480 g) lard

2 onions, chopped

3 sprigs of thyme, picked

4 cups (960 ml) white wine

salt and freshly ground black pepper

METHOD

Chop all of the meat into 1-in (2½-cm) cubes.

Melt 2 cups of the lard in a pot set over a low heat. Add the onion, all the meat, and the thyme leaves. Cook, covered, very gently for 5 to 6 hours, adding the wine at regular intervals and stirring frequently; the longer and more gently the mixture is cooked, the better the pork rillettes will be. Season with salt and pepper once the meat has cooked down and the mixture has a uniform texture.

Drain the meat from the fat, and cool down. Once cool enough to handle, break up slightly and remove any skin. Season and add a small amount of fat back into the meat.

Spoon into six small pots, pressing down well. Melt the remaining lard and pour over to cover and seal each pot. Chill for 48 hours before serving.

JOSH'S NOTES

Preparation: Allow plenty of time to cook the pork.

Key element: Low and slow cooking will ensure the meat is falling apart and tender.

Tip: Press the meat down to be as flat as possible, and use a hot palette knife to smooth it over.

INGREDIENTS

BEEF

distilled white vinegar

4 marrow bones

7 oz (200 g) blade steak

7 oz (200 g) chuck steak

3½ oz (100 g) boneless rib of beef

2 qt (2 litres) vegetable stock

2 onions, trimmed, peeled, and halved

2 carrots, trimmed, peeled, and quartered

1 bouquet garni (thyme, rosemary, bay leaf, etc.)

3 cloves garlic, crushed

3 cloves

3 peppercorns

1½ tsp coarse salt

VEGETABLES

4 baby carrots

4 baby leeks

4 baby turnips

2 stalks celery

4 potatoes

HORSERADISH CREAM

5 oz (150 g) fromage blanc (quark)

½ tsp grated horseradish

1 tbsp chives, finely chopped

1 tbsp parsley, finely chopped

fine salt and freshly ground black pepper

TO SERVE

fleur de sel

roughly crushed black pepper

Pot-au-feu with Sharp Horseradish Cream

Anne-Sophie Pic

COMPLEXITY: EASY | PREP TIME: 40 MINUTES, PLUS OVERNIGHT SOAKING
COOK TIME: 50 MINUTES, OR 3 HOURS IF USING CASSEROLE DISH | SERVES: 4 OR MORE

METHOD

Fill a large bowl with cold water, add a little white vinegar, then immerse the marrow bones in it and leave them to soak overnight in the fridge. The next day, cut all the meat into pieces, put it in a pressure cooker and cover with vegetable stock. Bring to a simmer over a medium heat, then skim off any foam from the surface. Add onions, carrots, bouquet garni, garlic, cloves, peppercorns, and salt. Follow the manufacturer's instructions for bringing the cooker up to pressure, then cook for 45 minutes on the 'vegetables' setting. Leave the pressure cooker to rest for 10 minutes, off the heat, before carefully opening. If not using a pressure cooker, simmer the pot, covered, for at least 3 hours, stirring occasionally and topping up the liquid with a little boiling water if necessary.

Drain the soaked marrow bones and remove the marrow from the bones. Poach the marrow for 3 minutes in some of the beef cooking liquid from the pressure cooker, then set aside.

Peel and trim the vegetables as required, leaving a little of the leaves on the carrots and turnips. Cook the vegetables in boiling salted water until tender, about 10 minutes, then refresh in cold water and drain.

Meanwhile, mix the fromage blanc with the grated horseradish, chives, and parsley. Season with salt and pepper.

To finish, skim the fat from the beef cooking liquid, then strain through a fine sieve. Divide the meats and vegetables between 4 bowls, plates, or dishes, and add a little marrow and broth to each one. Season with fleur de sel and roughly crushed black pepper. Serve hot with the horseradish cream.

"Traditionally, pot-au-feu is cooked for a long time to soften and tenderize the cheaper cuts of meat. But if you make it in a pressure cooker, the tenderizing process is accelerated. I like to cook the meat and vegetables separately, adding marrow bones for flavour."

– ANNE-SOPHIE PIC

Pork & Cabbage (Beijing) Dumplings
Guotie & Jiaozi

Ken Hom

COMPLEXITY: MODERATE | PREP TIME: 1 HOUR | COOK TIME: 15 MINUTES
MAKES: 30 TO 32 DUMPLINGS

INGREDIENTS

DOUGH

2¼ cups (275 g) all-purpose/plain flour, plus extra for dusting

1 cup plus 2 tsp (250 ml) very hot water

STUFFING

8 oz (225 g) ground/minced fatty pork

6 oz (175 g) Chinese cabbage (Chinese leaves), finely chopped

2 tsp fresh ginger, finely chopped

1 tbsp (15 ml) Shaoxing rice wine or dry sherry

1 tbsp (15 ml) dark soy sauce

1 tsp light soy sauce

1 tsp salt

½ tsp freshly ground black pepper

3 tbsp green onion/spring onion, finely chopped

2 tsp sesame oil

1 tsp sugar

2 tbsp (30 ml) cold chicken stock (p. 482)

METHOD

First make the dough. Put the flour in a large bowl and stir the hot water gradually into it, mixing all the while with a fork or chopsticks until most of the water is incorporated. Add more water if the mixture seems dry. Remove the mixture from the bowl and knead it with your hands until smooth, dusting with a little flour if it is sticky. This should take about 8 minutes. Put the dough back in the bowl, cover with a clean, damp kitchen towel and let it rest for about 20 minutes.

While the dough is resting, combine the stuffing ingredients in a large bowl, mixing them together thoroughly.

After the resting period, remove the dough from the bowl and knead again for about 5 minutes, until smooth, dusting with a little flour if it is sticky. Form the dough into a log about 9 in (23 cm) long and about 1 in (2½ cm) in diameter. Cut the log into equal segments; there should be about 30 to 32.

Roll each of the dough segments into a small ball with your hands, then roll each ball out into a small, round, flat 'pancake' about 2½ in (6 cm) in diameter. Arrange these, nicely spaced apart, on a large, lightly floured tray and cover with a damp kitchen towel to keep them from drying out until you are ready to use them.

Put about 2 teaspoons of filling in the centre of each 'pancake' and then fold in half. Moisten the edges with water and pinch together with your fingers. Pleat around the edge, pinching to seal well. The dumpling should look like a small Cornish turnover/pasty with a flat base and a rounded top. Replace the finished dumpling on the floured tray and keep it covered until you have stuffed all the dumplings.

Image on p. 231

Heat a large frying pan (with a lid, and preferably non-stick) over a high heat until hot. Add about 1 tablespoon (15 ml) of oil and place half the dumplings flat-side down into the pan. Turn down the heat to medium and cook for about 2 minutes, until they are lightly browned on the bottom. Add half of the water, cover the pan tightly and cook for about 12 minutes or until most of the liquid has been absorbed. Uncover the pan and continue to cook for a further 2 minutes. Remove the dumplings to a warmed plate, wipe the pan with kitchen paper and repeat for the second batch.

Serve straight away. Provide each person with three small bowls containing some Chinese white rice vinegar, chilli oil, and light soy sauce. The idea is to concoct your own dipping sauce by mixing these three ingredients exactly to your taste.

INGREDIENTS CONT.

TO COOK

1 to 2 tbsp (15 to 30 ml) groundnut/peanut oil

⅔ cup (150 ml) water

TO SERVE

Chinese rice wine vinegar

chilli oil

light soy sauce

JOSH'S NOTES

Preparation: Make the dough slightly in advance to allow plenty of time to form the dumplings.

Key element: Foaming the dumplings; try watching an online demonstration to perfect the technique.

Tip: Try and get plenty of colour on the dumplings when they're first in the pan – the colour will dilute when the water is added.

Beef Carpaccio with Caponata

Rodney Dunn

COMPLEXITY: EASY | PREP TIME: 10 MINUTES | SERVES: 6

INGREDIENTS

6 × 3½-oz (100-g) pieces beef sirloin, sliced ½ in (1 cm) thick

sea salt and freshly ground black pepper

extra virgin olive oil, for drizzling

finely grated Parmesan, to serve

caponata (p. 131), to serve

METHOD

Place the sirloin slices, one at a time, in a clean plastic bag and use a meat mallet or rolling pin to flatten until they are about ¹⁄₁₆ in (1 to 2 mm) thick.

Arrange the sirloin slices on plates, season with salt and pepper, scatter with caponata, and drizzle with extra virgin olive oil. Finely grate a little Parmesan over the top, then serve immediately.

———————

"I have used sirloin for this carpaccio as it holds together when pounded flat, but there are many other cuts you could use, such as topside. The caponata is more like a relish, with the vegetables cut small, providing sweet and sour highlights."

– RODNEY DUNN

JOSH'S NOTES

Key element: Beat the meat thinly enough so it will almost melt in your mouth.

Tip: Beat the meat gently in the direction you want it to go, and depending on the cut.

Complements: Serve with toasted crusty bread.

INGREDIENTS

BROTH

1 medium-sized carrot, chopped small

2 stalks celery, chopped small

1 medium-sized onion, chopped small

½ leek, chopped

1 bay leaf

6 cups (1½ litres) water

VEAL

2⅔ lb (1.2 kg) *magatello* (cut of veal, usually from the thigh. It is one large piece that you will tie up.)

salt and freshly ground black pepper

oil, for cooking

5 whole cloves garlic

18 oz (500 g) canned tuna fillets (in olive oil)

6 Cantábrico anchovies (large Spanish anchovies in olive oil)

2 oz (60 g) capers

3 gherkins

2 bay leaves

10 sprigs of Italian parsley

zest of 2 lemons (not grated but strips)

1 cup plus 2 tsp (250 ml) dry white wine

MAYONNAISE

2 egg yolks, at room temperature

1 tsp lemon juice

1 cup plus 2 tsp (250 ml) sunflower oil

2 tsp white wine vinegar

1 tsp fine salt

pinch of freshly ground black pepper

Veal with Tuna Sauce
Vitello Tonnato

Stefano Baiocco

COMPLEXITY: DIFFICULT | PREP TIME: 1 HOUR | COOK TIME: 4 HOURS | SERVES: 10 OR MORE

METHOD

To prepare the broth, put all the ingredients in a pot, bring to a gentle boil over a medium heat, and cook, uncovered, for about an hour – don't add salt. Strain out all the vegetables and put the broth aside. Pre-heat the oven to 140°F (60°C).

To prepare the veal, tie it up with string to help it hold its shape, and season with salt and pepper. Using a pan that can also be used inside the oven, heat 1½ tablespoons (22½ ml) of oil over a medium-high heat. Put the veal and garlic into the pan, and brown the veal on all sides for 2 to 3 minutes. Add the drained tuna, anchovies, capers, gherkins, the remaining herbs, and the strips of lemon zest. Gently break up the tuna fillets, and when it is all browned add the white wine. Bring to a gentle boil and reduce by about half, then slowly add the broth.

Now put into the oven and cook with 50 per cent humidity (if you don't have a combination oven, add a tray of water on the bottom shelf) until the temperature in the heart of the veal reaches 130°F (54°C) – this takes about 3 hours. Remove from the oven, remove veal from the pot and cool in the refrigerator to 37°F (3°C). Remove parsley, bay leaves, lemon zest, and garlic from the bottom of the pan. Pour what remains into a blender and blend until it becomes a smooth creamy consistency. Refrigerate until needed.

Now to prepare the mayonnaise – put the egg yolks (make sure they are at room temperature) in a high-rimmed bowl, add the lemon juice and mix with an electric beater. Keep the beater going while you start adding the sunflower oil to the egg mixture, slowly, in a fine drizzle and in small quantities at a time so that the mixture doesn't separate/curdle/go crazy. When you have mixed 40 to 50 per cent of the sunflower oil in, the mixture should be quite dense. Add the vinegar a little at a time in order to dilute it, then continue adding the sunflower oil in the same way as before – a slow, fine drizzle – until finished. Lastly, add the salt and pepper. To complete the salsa tonnata, take the tuna mixture you previously blended from the fridge and add it to the mayonnaise. The quantity to mix is 2 parts of tuna mixture to 1 part of mayonnaise.

To serve, slice the veal thinly. Present it on a serving platter, covering the bottom of the platter rather than piling the meat slices on top of each other, and spoon the salsa tonnata on top.

Image on p. 230

INGREDIENTS

GROUND SPICE MIX

1 tbsp fennel seeds

2 tbsp coriander seeds

1 tsp cumin seeds

1 tsp black peppercorns

SPICE PASTE

10 dried chillies, soaked in boiling water for 10 minutes

3 stalks lemongrass

2 in (5 cm) fresh ginger

2 in (5 cm) fresh galangal (or extra ginger)

2 in (5 cm) fresh turmeric (or 2 tsp ground turmeric)

3 cloves garlic

1 tsp shrimp paste, dry-toasted (or 2 tsp fish sauce)

½ medium-sized onion, roughly chopped

BEEF

6 tbsp (90 ml) vegetable oil

1 stalk lemongrass, bruised

4 green cardamom pods

28½ oz (800 g) beef (rump is best), diced

6¾ tbsp (100 ml) coconut milk

1 tbsp dark coconut sugar or molasses sugar

1 tsp fine sea salt

6¾ tbsp (100 ml) water

TO FINISH

4 tablespoons *kerisik* (roasted coconut)

4 kaffir lime leaves, bruised (or strips of rind from 2 limes)

Perak Beef Rendang

Norman Musa

COMPLEXITY: MODERATE | PREP TIME: 30 MINUTES | COOK TIME: 1 HOUR
SERVES: 4 TO 6

METHOD

Dry-toast the spice mix ingredients in a small pan until fragrant, then grind the seeds using a spice grinder until they have turned to a fine powder.

Blitz the spice paste ingredients in a food processor until smooth. Mix the ground spice mix and the spice paste in a bowl to form a curry paste.

Heat the oil in a large saucepan over a medium heat, add the lemongrass and cardamom pods and sauté for 30 seconds to infuse the oil. Add the curry paste and sauté for about 5 minutes, until the oil separates.

Add the beef, coconut milk, sugar, and salt along with 6¾ tablespoons (100 ml) of water, giving it all a good stir. Simmer, uncovered, on a low heat for 45 minutes, or until the beef is tender.

Finally add the *kerisik* and lime leaves, and simmer for 2 minutes over a low heat. Serve with steamed jasmine rice.

INGREDIENTS

1¾ lb (800 g) whole piece of beef fillet

2 mild onions

1 tbsp Dijon mustard

2 tbsp tomato ketchup

½ cup plus 1 tsp (125 ml) olive oil

3 egg yolks

1 tbsp capers

1 tbsp chopped chives

Tabasco sauce

salt and pepper

JOSH'S NOTES

Complements: Serve with toasted or grilled crusty bread, with a touch of olive oil.

Beef Tartare Bistro-style
Tartare de Bœuf Bistrot

Stéphane Reynaud

COMPLEXITY: EASY | PREP TIME: 15 MINUTES | SERVES: 6

Chop the beef into small, evenly sized cubes. Dice the onions finely.

Combine the mustard with tomato ketchup, olive oil, and egg yolks. Add the capers, chives, and onions.

Combine the dressing and meat gently, and season with salt, pepper, and Tabasco. Shape into a mound and serve with a salad of fresh herbs.

INGREDIENTS

3 qt (3 litres) water or beef stock
2¼ lb (1 kg) beef short ribs
3 tbsp plus 1 tsp (50 ml) vegetable oil
4½ oz (120 g) Green Curry Paste (p. 461)
2½ cups (600 ml) coconut milk
2 to 3 tsp Thai fish sauce
½ tsp palm sugar
¾ oz (20 g) pea eggplants or berry eggplants
2 to 3 kaffir lime leaves, veins removed and torn into halves
10 Thai basil leaves
1 red finger chilli pepper, de-seeded and julienned
steamed jasmine rice, to serve

Beef Green Curry
Kaeng Kheaw Wan Nua

Ian Kittichai

COMPLEXITY: EASY | PREP TIME: 30 MINUTES | COOK TIME: 2 TO 3 HOURS | SERVES: 4

In a large saucepan, bring the water or stock to the boil over a high heat. Add the ribs, reduce the heat to medium-low and simmer gently for 2 to 3 hours or until tender. Set aside.

Heat a frying pan over a medium heat, and add the vegetable oil and curry paste. Cook, stirring, for 5 to 10 minutes. Add the coconut milk, stir in and bring to the boil.

Add the Thai fish sauce to taste, palm sugar, cooked ribs, eggplants, kaffir lime leaves, and Thai basil leaves, and bring back to the boil. Ladle into bowls and garnish with chilli pepper. Serve with steamed jasmine rice on the side.

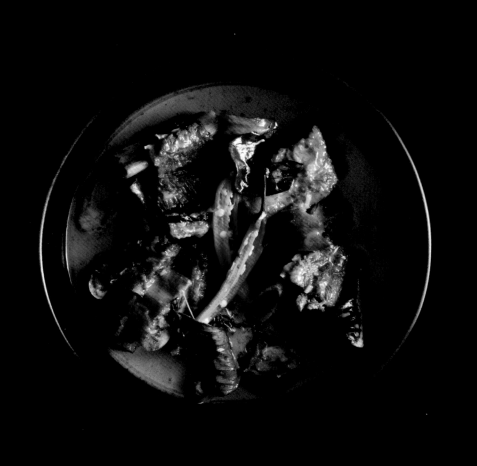

INGREDIENTS

4 lamb shanks, fat removed

9 oz (250 g) lamb shoulder meat, cut into 1½-in (3½-cm) cubes

4 tbsp (60 ml) vegetable oil

1 tsp fennel seeds

1 tsp cumin seeds

1 blade of mace

2 cloves

4 green cardamom pods

2 black cardamom pods

1 in (2½ cm) stick cinnamon

1 bay leaf

3 onions, sliced

1 tbsp ginger paste

1 tbsp garlic paste

1 tsp turmeric powder

1 tsp red chilli powder

1 tsp cumin powder

1 tsp cilantro/coriander powder

salt

2 tbsp tomato purée/paste

1 tbsp (15 ml) lemon juice

½ tsp garam masala

1 tsp granulated sugar

TO SERVE

chopped fresh cilantro/coriander

thin strips of fresh ginger

JOSH'S NOTES

Preparation: Make in advance to allow the flavours to develop.

Tip: Add more chilli if you love spice.

Lamb Shank Rogan Josh

Vineet Bhatia

COMPLEXITY: EASY | PREP TIME: 30 MINUTES | COOK TIME: 1 HOUR 30 MINUTES
SERVES: 4

METHOD

Wash and drain the lamb shanks and diced meat. Heat the oil in a large pan, add the whole spices and bay leaf, and cook briefly until they start to crackle. Add the sliced onions and cook, stirring occasionally, until they turn pale yellow. Add the meat to the pan and cook, stirring occasionally, until browned.

Add the ginger and garlic pastes, and cook for a minute longer. Stir in the ground spices and some salt, and cook, stirring, for 2 minutes. Add enough water to cover the meat, bring to a simmer and cook gently for about 40 minutes, until the meat is three-quarters done.

Stir in the tomato purée/paste and simmer until the meat is fully cooked and the liquid has thickened, about another 40 minutes. Add the lemon juice, garam masala, and sugar. Check the seasoning and serve, garnished with the cilantro/coriander and ginger.

"Rogan josh (or rogan gosht) is classically a lamb stew of Persian origin brought in by the Mughals, making its way to northern India and Kashmir (as the Mughals frequently retreated to Kashmir during the unrelenting summer heat) and beyond. 'Roughan' means 'clarified butter' or 'oil' in Persian, while 'jus' (romanized to josh) means to 'stew' or 'braise'."

– VINEET BHATIA

INGREDIENTS

1⅓ lb (600 g) dried
Tarbais beans or lingot
beans, soaked overnight
in cold water

7 oz (200 g) pork fat or
unsmoked fatty bacon,
chopped

7 oz (200 g) air-dried
ham like Bayonne,
chopped

2 onions, chopped

2 carrots, chopped

1 ham bone, about
1⅓ lb (600 g)

2 cups plus 1¼ tbsp
(500 ml) duck or chicken
(p. 482) stock, or water

1 whole head garlic,
cloves separated and
crushed

sea salt and freshly
ground black pepper

4 ripe tomatoes,
crushed in a Mouli

5 Toulouse sausages,
halved

5 confit duck legs,
bones removed,
halved (p. 221)

1¾ oz (50 g) duck fat,
to serve

JOSH'S NOTES

Tip: Cook in two
separate casseroles
if you don't have one
large enough.

Family Cassoulet

Pascal Aussignac

COMPLEXITY: MODERATE I PREP TIME: 25 MINUTES, PLUS OVERNIGHT SOAKING
COOK TIME: 4 HOURS I SERVES: 10 TO 12

METHOD

Pre-heat the oven to 300°F (150°C).

Drain the soaked beans and place in a large saucepan. Add water
to cover, bring to the boil over a medium heat, then simmer,
uncovered, for about 5 minutes. Drain and set aside.

In a large, stovetop-safe casserole over a medium-low heat,
sauté the pork fat, ham, and chopped vegetables until softened.
Add the drained beans, ham bone, stock, and garlic. Season
lightly with salt and pepper and bring to a light boil. Tip the
crushed tomatoes on top, cover, and place in the oven for 1 hour.
(Alternatively, turn the oven down to 200°F (90°C) and cook for
3 hours – it is better this way.)

When beans have softened a little, add the sausages and duck
pieces, cover again, and cook for 50 minutes until beans are totally
'fondant' – soft but still holding their shape. The dish should be still
juicy; if not, crush some more tomatoes, strain out the seeds and
add the juice. Remove the bone and season again.

Ideally, cool the cassoulet and store in the fridge for at least 1 day,
so that the flavours mature. Then reheat gently until hot and
bubbling, and mix in some duck fat to enrich. If you really do like
a crusty top, heat the cassoulet under a hot grill for a few minutes
(add some breadcrumbs if you wish). If you need anything else ...
a green salad with French dressing would be good.

"There is not one ultimate cassoulet recipe but dozens, and each
town in the south-west will claim that theirs is the original.
As I don't want to stir up this hornet's nest, I give you my
mother's own personal favourite, which does not have a crust
or breadcrumbs (my family likes the cassoulet moist and saucy)."

– PASCAL AUSSIGNAC

Steak & Kidney Pudding

Nathan Outlaw

COMPLEXITY: MODERATE | PREP TIME: 10 MINUTES
COOK TIME: 3 HOURS 30 MINUTES | SERVES: 4

INGREDIENTS

FILLING

oil for cooking, plus extra to oil the basin

2 red onions, peeled and chopped

2 carrots, peeled and diced

2 tbsp all-purpose/plain flour

sea salt and freshly ground black pepper

18 oz (500 g) chuck steak, cut into chunks

7 oz (200 g) ox kidney, cut into chunks

2 cups plus 1¼ tbsp (500 ml) beer (I use Sharp's Doom Bar)

2 bay leaves

PASTRY

2¼ cups (275 g) all-purpose/plain flour

3 tsp baking powder

1 tsp English mustard powder

½ tsp fine sea salt

3½ oz (100 g) suet, chopped

about ¾ cup plus 1¼ tbsp (200 ml) cold water

JOSH'S NOTES

Key elements: Roll the pastry out to the exact thickness; and line the basin.

Tip: Gently crimp the pastry top by brushing with water and folding on itself, making sure there aren't any gaps. Tie the string lengths into a handle before cooling, as they will expand.

METHOD

For the filling, heat a large flameproof casserole or pan over a medium heat and add a good drizzle of oil. When the oil is hot, add the onion and carrot and cook, stirring occasionally, until softened and caramelized. Remove and set aside.

Season the flour with salt and pepper. Toss the steak and kidney in the flour to coat, shaking off any excess. Heat up the casserole again, add a little more oil and brown the meat in small batches on all sides, then remove and set aside.

Deglaze the casserole with the beer, scraping up any meaty bits from the bottom of the pan. Return the meat and vegetables to the pan and add the bay leaves. Simmer gently over a low heat for 2 hours until the meat is tender. Check the seasoning and leave to cool completely.

Meanwhile, make the suet pastry (it is best made a few hours before assembling). Put the flour, baking powder, mustard powder, and salt in a large bowl and rub in the suet using your fingertips. Using a table knife, mix in enough cold water to bring the mix together to make a firm dough.

Take a quarter of the dough, wrap it in plastic wrap and set aside. Lightly oil a 1-quart (1-litre) pudding basin and line with 2 layers of plastic wrap. Roll out the rest of the dough to about ⅛ in (3 mm) thick and use to line the basin, without stretching it. Spoon in the filling up to ¾ in (2 cm) from the rim. Roll out the other piece of dough and position over the filling, dampening the edges with cold water and pressing them together to seal.

Cover with a round of baking parchment, pleated in the centre, and then a pleated round of foil. Secure under the rim of the basin with kitchen string, leaving a length of string to use as a handle. Pour enough water into a saucepan (large enough to take the pudding basin) to one-quarter fill it and bring to a simmer. Lower the basin into the pan, cover with a tight-fitting lid and simmer gently for 1 hour 30 minutes, checking the water level every so often and topping up as necessary.

When the pudding is ready, remove the foil and paper, then turn out onto a warmed plate and bring to the table. I like to serve it with mash, peas, and horseradish sauce.

INGREDIENTS

18 oz (500 g) braising beef, cut into 1-in (2½-cm) cubes

1 onion, chopped into brunoise

4 carrots, chopped into ½-in (1-cm) dice

18 oz (500 g) button onions, left whole

2 stalks celery, chopped into ½-in (1-cm) dice

2 cloves garlic, finely chopped

1 bottle (16 fl oz/450 ml) Guinness

salt and freshly ground black pepper

2 tbsp (30 ml) vegetable oil, for frying

2 qt (2 litres) beef stock (p. 484)

8 rock oysters

12 x 20 in (30 x 50 cm) sheet puff pastry

JOSH'S NOTES

Preparation: Marinate the beef overnight for maximum flavour.

Tip: Don't boil the meat mixture too vigorously, and skim the surface during the cooking process.

Complements: Serve with a wintery mashed potato or similar vegetable side.

Guinness & Oyster Pie

Richard Corrigan

COMPLEXITY: MODERATE | PREP TIME: 25 MINUTES, PLUS MARINATING OVERNIGHT
COOK TIME: 20 MINUTES | SERVES: 3 TO 4

METHOD

The day before, place the beef, vegetables, and Guinness in a large, non-reactive bowl. Stir to mix, cover and place in the fridge to marinate for 12 hours or overnight.

Drain off the marinade and set aside. Remove the beef to a separate bowl and season it with salt and pepper. Heat a good splash of oil in a large stovetop-safe casserole dish over a medium to high heat. When hot, add the beef, in batches, and fry until browned on all sides, using a slotted spoon to transfer each batch to a clean bowl when done.

Add a splash more oil if necessary, then add the vegetables and fry until nicely caramelized, about 15 minutes. Add the reserved Guinness marinade and stir to deglaze the bottom of the dish. Add the browned beef and beef stock. Bring just to the boil, and simmer, covered, for 1 hour 30 minutes, until tender.

Using a slotted spoon, transfer the beef and vegetables to a large bowl. Turn up the heat and gently boil the remaining stock until reduced by three-quarters. Shuck the oysters, reserving the juice. Add the beef back to the reduced sauce, then add the shucked oysters and juice. Allow the mixture to cool and set, 2 to 3 hours.

When the mixture has set, pre-heat the oven to 350°F (180°C). Cut out a round of puff pastry 6 in (15 cm) in diameter and place on a baking tray. Place the meat mixture on the pastry and mould into a slightly flattened ball, leaving ½ in (1 cm) of pastry clear around the edge. Cut the remaining pastry to a round large enough to cover the ball easily. Carefully place over the meat ball and press the pastry edges tightly together. Decorate with leftover pastry if desired, moistening with a little water to help it stick. Bake the pie for 15 minutes, until the pastry is nicely browned and the meat is heated through.

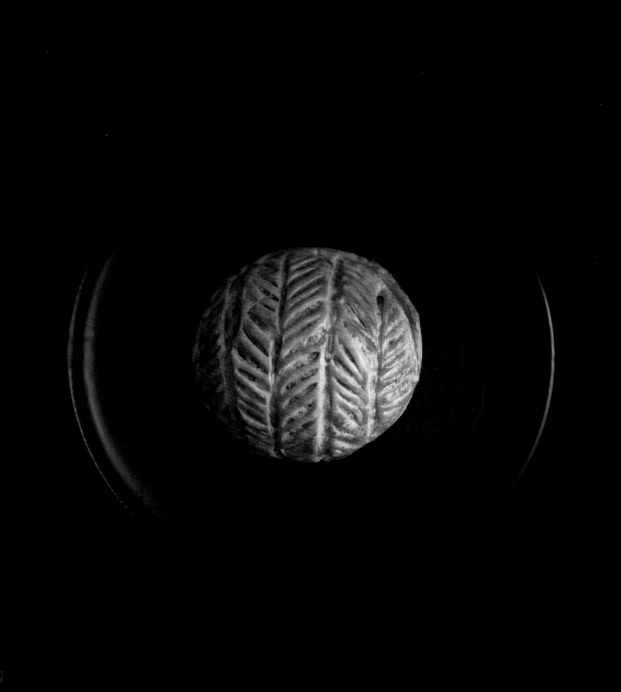

INGREDIENTS

olive oil as needed

1 onion, finely diced

2 cloves garlic,
finely diced

1 tbsp lemon thyme,
chopped

1 tbsp rosemary,
chopped

10½ oz (300 g) lamb
mince

3½ oz (100 g) pork
mince

3½ oz (100 g) veal
mince

2 tbsp tomato purée/
paste

2 sticks cinnamon

9 oz (250 g) crushed
tomatoes

salt, to taste

2 eggplants/aubergines,
sliced ½ in (1 cm) thick

3 medium-sized Desiree
potatoes, sliced ½ in
(1 cm) thick

BÉCHAMEL SAUCE

3½ oz/7 tbsp (100 g)
butter

¾ cup plus 2½ tsp (100 g)
all-purpose/plain flour

2½ cups (600 ml) milk,
warmed

3 eggs, beaten

3½ cups (100 g) grated
kefalograviera cheese

JOSH'S NOTES

Key element: Cook the
aubergine/eggplant and
potatoes until tender.

Tip: Bake until very
golden brown; take a
little longer if needed.

Moussaka

George Calombaris

COMPLEXITY: MODERATE I PREP TIME: 1 HOUR I COOK TIME: 1 HOUR 30 MINUTES
SERVES: 4

METHOD

In a large frying pan, heat 1 tablespoon (15 ml) oil over a medium heat and sauté the onion, garlic, lemon thyme, and rosemary until soft, about 5 minutes. Proceed to add all the ground/minced meat and brown it for 15 minutes. Add the tomato purée/paste, cinnamon, and crushed tomatoes. Reduce the heat to low and allow to simmer, uncovered, for 1 hour. Remove the cinnamon and season to taste with salt.

Melt the butter for the béchamel in a heavy-based saucepan over a low heat. Add the flour and stir over the low heat for 2 minutes. Slowly add the warm milk, stirring constantly, and continue stirring and cooking until thick, about 5 minutes. Cover with a lid and allow to cool for 10 minutes. Whisk in the beaten egg and kefalograviera cheese, and season to taste with salt.

Pre-heat the oven to 400°F (200°C).

Brush the aubergine/eggplant and potatoes with olive oil. Lay the slices in separate ovenproof trays and bake until tender. Oil a casserole dish and lay the half of the baked aubergine/eggplant over the bottom. Add a layer of half the prepared meat sauce. Add a layer of half the sliced potato over the meat sauce. Repeat the layers, then top with béchamel sauce and bake for 45 minutes, until golden brown.

Shepherd's Pie

Adam Byatt

COMPLEXITY: MEDIUM | PREP TIME: 45 MINUTES | COOK TIME: 3 HOURS | SERVES: 8

INGREDIENTS

MASH

3⅓ lb (1½ kg) large King Edward potatoes

1 cup plus 1¼ tbsp (250 ml) milk

4 tbsp (60 g) butter

sea salt and freshly ground black pepper

LAMB

2 large carrots

1⅓ lb (600 g) turnips

7 oz (200 g) celery root/celeriac

2 onions

olive oil

1 x 5½ lb (2½ kg) lamb shoulder on the bone (without the shank end)

sea salt and freshly ground black pepper

18 oz (500 g) ground/minced breast of lamb (ask your butcher to prepare this for you)

¾ cup plus 1¼ tbsp (200 ml) balsamic vinegar

2 heads garlic

5 cups (1.2 litres) brown chicken stock (p. 482)

a few sprigs of thyme

2 sprigs of rosemary

1 bay leaf

METHOD

Make the mash: Cut the potatoes into approximately ¾-in (2-cm) dice, place in a saucepan and cover with cold water. Bring to the boil over a medium heat and boil gently for about 20 minutes, or until tender when pierced with a fork. Drain and leave for a few minutes to steam dry. Put the potatoes through a ricer, then add the milk and butter and beat with a wooden spoon just until combined and the mash is smooth. Check and adjust the seasoning, and set aside at room temperature until ready to use.

Pre-heat the oven to 300°F (150°C) fan or 325°F (170°C) regular bake.

Peel the carrots, turnips, and celery root/celeriac, and dice roughly into ¾-in (2-cm) cubes. Peel and thinly slice the onions.

Heat a splash of olive oil in a large flameproof casserole, season the shoulder of lamb with salt and pepper, and brown slowly over a medium heat in the hot oil. Lift the shoulder out of the casserole, then add the ground/minced lamb and season with salt and pepper. Cook over a high heat until well coloured, then remove and set aside to drain in a colander placed over a bowl.

Put the carrots, turnips, and celery root/celeriac in the casserole and brown them over a high heat, then remove and set aside to drain.

Add the onions to the casserole (you may need to add a touch more olive oil at this point) and brown them lightly, then add the balsamic vinegar and simmer to reduce in volume by one-third.

Put the ground/minced lamb back in the casserole and mix with the onions, then place the lamb shoulder on top, together with the whole heads of garlic. Pour in the stock, add the thyme, rosemary, and bay leaf, and cover with a 'lid' of parchment paper.

Place the casserole in the oven and cook for 2 hours, then spoon the juices over the shoulder and check that the meat is coming away from the bone with ease – it should then need a further 30 minutes to cook through completely. Remove from the oven and leave until the meat is cool enough to handle.

Increase the oven temperature to 400°F (200°C) or 425°F (220°C) regular bake.

Take the shoulder out of the casserole and scrape all of the meat into a large bowl, fat and all. Discard any sinew and bones. Lift the garlic out and squeeze the flesh into the meat in the bowl. Discard the garlic skins together with the thyme, rosemary, and bay leaf. Now add the ground/minced lamb, cooking juices, and onions to the bowl and stir well to mix.

Place the meat mixture in a clean casserole or baking dish to finish the pie. Place the vegetables on top and cover with the mash. Use a palette knife to smooth the mash down, then make light indents in the top with the side of the knife.

Place the pie in the oven and cook for 15 minutes, or until the mash is golden brown.

JOSH'S NOTES

Preparation: You can prepare the lamb shoulder the day before.

Key element: If the lamb is extra fatty, remove some of the excess fat.

Tip: Leave the pie in the oven until the top is lovely and golden.

Lancashire Hotpot

Marco Pierre White

COMPLEXITY: MODERATE | PREP TIME: 1 HOUR
COOK TIME: 2 HOURS 30 MINUTES | SERVES: 6

INGREDIENTS

6 neck fillets of lamb, trimmed of all sinews

salt and freshly ground black pepper

3 tbsp (45 ml) olive oil, not extra virgin

1 carrot, peeled and chopped

1 onion, peeled and chopped

1 stalk celery, chopped

2 cloves garlic, crushed

1 sprig of thyme

1 sprig of rosemary

1 bay leaf

6 black peppercorns

1 tbsp tomato purée/paste

6 cups (1½ litres) lamb stock

POTATO TOPPING

3½ tbsp (50 g) unsalted butter

1 large onion, peeled and thinly sliced

4 large Maris Piper potatoes

½ cup plus 2 tbsp (150 ml) chicken stock (p. 482)

METHOD

Pre-heat the oven to 350°F (180°C).

Season the lamb neck fillets with salt and pepper. Heat half the olive oil in a hot pan and seal the lamb on all sides until golden brown in colour. Drain off any excess fat and place the neck fillets in a casserole dish.

In the same pan that you used to seal the lamb, heat the remaining olive oil and fry off the carrot, onion, and celery until they are golden brown, about 10 minutes. Transfer these to the casserole dish with the lamb and add the garlic, herbs, peppercorns, and tomato purée/paste. Pour the lamb stock over. Cover with a tight-fitting lid and cook in the oven for 1 hour 30 minutes to 2 hours, until the meat becomes very soft and tender.

Remove the neck fillets and keep to one side. Pass the cooking liquor through a fine sieve into a clean pan. Over a medium heat, bubble to reduce by two-thirds, until the liquor becomes thick enough to coat the back of a spoon. Keep to one side.

In the meantime, make the potato topping in either one large tray or six small blini pans, 4 in (10 cm) in diameter. If using a large tray, cut out the discs once cooked. Line the pans or tray with silicone paper and smear a little of the butter onto each one. Melt the remaining butter in a frying pan over a medium heat, add the thinly sliced onions and slowly caramelize, stirring occasionally. Gently warm the reduced chicken stock.

Peel and slice the potatoes paper-thin using a mandoline. Arrange the potatoes into the tray or pans, adding some of the caramelized onion at every other layer. When they reach a thickness of about ⅔ in (1½ cm), stop. Poke two or three holes in the top of each dish (or the equivalent for a large tray), and pour just enough chicken stock over the top to moisten the potatoes. Cover individually with a sheet of greased silicone paper.

Cook the potatoes on the stovetop until they begin to bubble, then continue cooking them in the oven (at 350°F/180°C) for 25 to 35 minutes, until the potatoes are soft when tested with the point of a knife. The natural starches of the potatoes should stick the slices together to form a solid 'cake'. Leave them to one side to cool.

Reheat the neck fillets in the reduced cooking liquor, taking care not to reduce the sauce too far as it will become sticky and difficult to eat. Gently warm the potatoes back up in the oven, then turn them out so the bottom becomes the top and divide into six portions if they have been cooked in one tray. They should be golden brown in colour – if need be, they can be coloured gently with a little olive oil in a non-stick pan over a medium heat.

Slice each fillet into four pieces and arrange them in the centre of each plate. Pour the cooking liquor over the meat and around the plate, and place one serving of potato on top with the golden surface up. I like to serve this with braised red cabbage on the side.

————————

"Hotpot originated in the Lancashire cotton industry in the 1800s when female mill-workers would prepare the dinner in the morning, put it in the oven and eat many hours later. I guess it was a fore-runner of the slow cooker. Others suggest that it was a dish prepared for pit workers to take to the mines wrapped in a blanket to keep the 'pot hot', which they would then have for lunch. The aristocracy claimed that it was the perfect dish to take to the races, in tall pots and also wrapped in a blanket. Farmers maintain that it was a family dish eaten by shepherds on the moors using the same 'blanket' principle. Whatever its origins, it's one of those dishes that started out as food for the poor and is in fact fit for a king."

– MARCO PIERRE WHITE

INGREDIENTS

2 oz (60 g) margarine
(substitute with butter
or 1 tbsp/15 ml oil if
preferred; the margarine
is used because it has a
high burning point but
absorbs like butter)

3⅓ lb (1½ kg) gravy beef
or oyster blade, cut into
large cubes

1 onion, chopped

1 heaped tbsp all-
purpose/plain flour

1⅔ cups (400 ml) red wine

1¼ cups (300 ml) beef
stock (p. 484)

bouquet garni (thyme,
rosemary, bay leaf, etc.)

1 beef bouillon/stock
cube

1 heaped tsp tomato
purée/paste

3 shallots, finely chopped

1 large clove garlic, finely
chopped

salt and freshly milled
black pepper

12 to 15 pickling onions
(or whole shallots)

2 oz (60 g) bacon or speck
(sometimes known as
continental bacon) cut
into bite-size pieces

a little butter

5 oz (150 g) champignons

1 tsp sugar

2 tbsp chopped parsley,
to serve

Beef Burgundy
Bœuf Bourguignon

Diane Holuigue

COMPLEXITY: MODERATE | PREP TIME: 30 MINUTES | COOK TIME: 2 HOURS | SERVES: 6

METHOD

In a large casserole or deep frying pan with a lid, heat the margarine over a medium-high heat and fry the beef until well-browned. Add the onion and brown well also. Sprinkle the flour over all, and stir to the bottom of the pan to form a roux. Add the liquids, the bouquet garni, bouillon/stock cube, tomato purée/paste, shallots, and garlic, and season lightly with salt and pepper. Place the lid on the casserole and simmer gently for about 2 hours, turning the pieces once.

During the cooking, boil the pickling onions in salted water until softened; drain and set aside. When the beef is cooked, use a small frying pan to fry the bacon until crispy and rendered. Add to the beef. In the rendered bacon fat, plus more butter if necessary, fry the champignons – whole if tiny, or cut into chunky pieces. When fried, add to the casserole. Fry the boiled onions, adding a tiny bit of sugar to caramelize them a little, then add to the casserole.

To serve, transfer the beef and garnish pieces to a serving platter. Boil down the cooking liquid in the casserole to a sauce consistency. Taste and adjust the seasoning, then coat the beef with the sauce and garnish. Sprinkle with chopped parsley.

"The most famous dish from the beautiful wine-producing area of Burgundy, bœuf bourguignon, along with its chicken counterpart coq au vin teaches the epitome of the world's great dishes."

– DIANE HOLUIGUE

JOSH'S NOTES

Preparation: If time
allows, try marinating
the beef overnight
in the wine for extra
flavour.

INGREDIENTS

3½ lb (1.6 kg) piece of chuck beef, trimmed of excess fat and sinew

marinade (see below)

salt and freshly ground black pepper

6¾ tbsp (100 ml) olive oil

1 onion, cut into large dice

4 cloves garlic, finely chopped

2 carrots, peeled and cut into large dice

2 stalks celery, cut into large dice

5 oz (150 g) smoked bacon, diced

1 tsp picked thyme leaves

3 tbsp plus 1 tsp (50 ml) red wine vinegar

1 cup plus 2 tsp (250 ml) red wine

2 tbsp tomato purée/paste

2 cups plus 1¼ tbsp (500 ml) chicken stock (p. 482)

14 oz (400 g) ripe truss tomatoes, skins removed, chopped

2⅔ oz (75 g) pitted Niçoise or Kalamata olives

2 tbsp picked rosemary leaves

MARINADE

2½ cups (600 ml) red wine

2 sprigs of thyme

4 strips of orange zest (cut using a peeler)

6 whole cloves

½ stick cinnamon

1 bay leaf

Beef Stew Provençale-style
Bœuf en Daube Provençale

Simon Wright

COMPLEXITY: MODERATE | PREP TIME: 35 MINUTES, PLUS MARINATING OVERNIGHT
COOK TIME: 4 HOURS | SERVES: 6

METHOD

Cut the beef into large pieces, about 2 in (5 cm) square, place in a large bowl with the marinade ingredients and mix together, pressing the meat down so that it is covered with the marinade. Cover and refrigerate overnight.

Pre-heat the oven to 125°F (60°C).

Remove the beef from the marinade, keeping the marinade to one side. Dry the beef with a clean cloth and season well with salt and pepper. Heat a little olive oil in a frying pan over a high heat and sear the beef, in batches, until nicely caramelized. Transfer each batch to a bowl and keep to one side.

Heat the remaining oil in a large ovenproof casserole dish over a medium heat. Add the onion, garlic, carrot, and celery, and cook until the vegetables are soft and slightly caramelized, about 10 minutes. Add the bacon and thyme and cook for a few minutes until the bacon has browned slightly.

Add the vinegar and allow to reduce until completely evaporated, then add the red wine and reserved marinade. Bring to a light boil and reduce the liquid by about two-thirds, or until it becomes slightly thick and syrupy. Add the tomato purée/paste, stir to combine, then add the beef, chicken stock, and chopped tomatoes. Bring the mixture to a simmer, check the seasoning and adjust as necessary.

Cover the meat mixture with a piece of baking paper the same size as the dish, place the lid on and cook in the oven for 3 to 3 hours 30 minutes, until the beef is tender. Remove from the oven and allow to cool for about 15 minutes. This will allow excess fat to rise to the surface of the daube so that it can easily be removed. Use a spoon to remove the fat from the surface, then strain the liquid of the daube into a clean saucepan, bring it to a light boil and reduce until it has thickened slightly and is rich in flavour. Pour the reduced liquid back onto the meat, stir in olives and rosemary and gently warm together over a low heat.

Serve with buttered egg pasta, fresh herbs, baby onions, and roasted carrots.

INGREDIENTS

1 boneless veal shoulder (weight 2½ lb/1 kg)

coarse sea salt or kosher/flaky salt

2 tbsp (30 g) unsalted butter

½ tsp freshly ground black pepper

5¼ oz (150 g) slab bacon, roughly chopped

2¼ oz (62½ g) paprika

1 onion, peeled and chopped

4 cloves garlic, peeled and chopped

1 tsp caraway seeds

1 tsp dried marjoram

5 plum tomatoes, chopped

1 green bell pepper/ capsicum, cored, seeded and roughly chopped

1 red bell pepper/ capsicum, cored, seeded and roughly chopped

1 yellow bell pepper/ capsicum, cored, seeded and roughly chopped

2 cups (480 ml) water

1 lb (450 g) Yukon Gold potatoes (about 2), roughly chopped

2 bay leaves

2 sprigs of fresh thyme

sour cream, for serving

Veal Shoulder Goulash

Daniel Boulud

COMPLEXITY: MODERATE | PREP TIME: 35 MINUTES | COOK TIME: 3 HOURS
SERVES: 4 TO 6

METHOD

Centre a rack in the oven and pre-heat the oven to 300°F (150°C).

Season the veal with salt. In a small cast-iron pot or Dutch oven set over a high heat, melt the butter. When the butter begins to foam, stir in the black pepper. Add the veal shoulder and sear on all sides. After about 7 minutes, sprinkle the bacon around the veal shoulder. Continue cooking until the veal is golden brown, about 15 minutes total cooking time. Transfer the veal shoulder to a platter.

Lower the heat to medium-high. Add the paprika, onion, garlic, caraway seeds, and marjoram and cook, stirring, until the onion is translucent, 6 to 7 minutes. Add the tomatoes and bell peppers/capsicum and cook, stirring, for 4 minutes. Pour in the water and stir to incorporate the brown bits from the bottom of the pot. Add the potatoes, bay leaves, and thyme and stir to combine. Return the veal to the pot and bring to a simmer. Cover the pot and transfer it to the oven.

Braise until the veal is tender, about 2 hours 30 minutes. Serve with the sour cream on the side.

———————

"Goulash is part of the French *repertoire de cuisine*, so I learned how to make it when I was a 15-year-old apprentice. Later, I sampled a version that was slightly different from the classic. The paprika-flavoured sauce was thickened with vegetables and simmered until it became almost like a savoury jam or compote clinging to the meat. It was just wonderful."

– DANIEL BOULUD

JOSH'S NOTES

Tip: You can cook this well in advance; it lasts extremely well.

Image on p. 231

all-purpose/plain flour,
for dusting
salt and freshly ground
black pepper
4 x 12½ oz (350 g)
centre-cut pieces
venison shanks
vegetable oil

SAUCE

1 onion, peeled and cut
into ½-in (1-cm) cubes
1 clove garlic, peeled
and crushed
1 medium-sized carrot,
peeled and cut into
½-in (1-cm) cubes
3½ oz (100 g) celery,
peeled and sliced
½ in (1 cm) thick
2 tbsp (30 g) butter
pinch of saffron
2 tbsp picked thyme
leaves
1½ oz (40 g) tomato
purée/paste
6¾ tbsp (100 ml) white
wine
2 qt (2 litres) strong
brown chicken stock
(p. 482)

POLENTA

1 qt (1 litre) milk
1 qt (1 litre) chicken
stock (p. 482)
2 cloves garlic, crushed
sprig of thyme
pinch of salt
18 oz (500 g) fine
polenta
4 tbsp mascarpone
6¾ tbsp (100 ml) olive
oil
3 tbsp plus 1 tsp (50 ml)
cream
9 oz (250 g) Parmesan
4 egg yolks
truffle oil to taste

GREMOLATA

½ bunch flat-leaf parsley
1 lemon
4 cloves garlic
salt and freshly ground
black pepper

Veal Osso Bucco with Truffled Polenta & Gremolata

Mark Sargeant

COMPLEXITY: MODERATE | PREP TIME: 1 HOUR | COOK TIME: 3 HOURS | SERVES: 4

METHOD

Pre-heat the oven to 320°F (160°C).

Lightly flour and season the pieces of venison. In a heavy-based casserole, fry them in the vegetable oil over a high heat for about 8 minutes, until nicely coloured on both sides. Set aside.

In the casserole, gently cook the onion, garlic, carrot, and celery in the butter over a medium-low heat until soft, about 10 minutes. Add the saffron, thyme, and tomato purée/paste and cook for a minute or so. Add the white wine and bubble to reduce completely, then add the brown chicken stock and the pieces of venison.

Cook slowly in the oven for 2 to 2 hours 30 minutes, until tender. Remove from the oven and cool slightly, then take the shanks out. Over a medium heat, reduce the cooking liquor for about 15 minutes until it thickens, 15 minutes, then pour back over the shanks to heat.

For the polenta, place the milk, stock, garlic, thyme, and salt in a saucepan over a medium heat. Bring just to the boil, then turn the heat off and leave to infuse for 15 minutes. Strain into a bowl, add the polenta and stir in for 8 minutes, then add the remaining polenta ingredients and stir in.

To make the gremolata, pick the parsley leaves from stalks, finely chop and place in a mixing bowl. Using a microplane or fine grater, grate in the zest of the lemon and the garlic. Season with a little salt and pepper.

GARNISHING VEGETABLES

12 small waxy potatoes, such as Kipfler

1½ tbsp (20 g) butter

12 small carrots, peeled

3 to 6 small turnips, halved or quartered, according to size

½ cup (80 g) shelled peas

2 tbsp freshly chopped flat-leaf parsley

Navarin of Lamb with Spring Vegetables cont.

Scoop the lamb into a large bowl and strain the sauce over. The navarin can be refrigerated overnight or for several hours. (The shank has added important gelatinous juices to the sauce.

You can decide to remove it and eat it separately as a small salad the next day, or alternatively cut the meat from the shank and add it to the navarin.) Reheat the navarin in the oven at 320°F (160°C) for 45 minutes.

Meanwhile, prepare the garnishing vegetables. Parboil the potatoes in a saucepan of simmering water for 10 to 15 minutes, or until three-quarters cooked. Drain. Heat the butter in a heavy-based saucepan over a medium heat, then cook the carrots and turnips, covered, for 5 minutes, shaking or stirring every so often to prevent them burning.

Add the potatoes, carrots, and turnips to the casserole of navarin and cook for a further 20 minutes. During the final 5 minutes, pour boiling water over the peas, then drain and add to the navarin. Taste the sauce for salt and pepper and season if necessary.

Serve in some pre-warmed bowls, and scatter each portion with chopped parsley. It would be a good idea to set each place at the table with a spoon as well as a knife and fork.

JOSH'S NOTES

Preparation: Prepare the meat and vegetables well in advance.

Key element: Submerge the garnishing vegetables in the navarin cooking liquor to ensure even cooking.

Tip: Ensure you get a good colour on the lamb and vegetables in the first few steps of cooking.

Complements: I love serving this with Dijon mustard on the side.

Leg of Lamb Rubbed with Rosemary & Anchovies

Jean-André Charial

COMPLEXITY: EASY | PREP TIME: 10 MINUTES, PLUS REFRIGERATION TIME
COOK TIME: 3 TO 4 HOURS | SERVES: 6 TO 8

INGREDIENTS

PASTE RUB

1 sprig of fresh rosemary leaves (or 1 tbsp dried rosemary)

10 anchovy fillets in olive oil, drained

3 cloves garlic, peeled

freshly ground black pepper to taste

2 tsp balsamic vinegar

2 tsp olive oil

1 tbsp Dijon mustard

MEAT

2⅔ lb (1.2 kg) leg of lamb

4 cloves garlic, unpeeled

JOSH'S NOTES

Key element: Monitor during cooking to make sure the lamb doesn't darken too early.

Comment: Lamb and anchovies is a classic combination, and this dish improves with charring.

Complements: Great with a salsa verde, p. 440, and potatoes.

METHOD

In a blender (in short bursts, scraping down the sides of the bowl when necessary), mix the rosemary, anchovies, garlic, pepper, vinegar, olive oil, and mustard until the mixture forms a paste that is not too smooth.

Place the meat in an ovenproof dish and rub the paste into it, making sure to cover all the sides. Cover with plastic wrap and refrigerate for at least 1 hour, preferably 3 to 4 hours.

About 30 minutes before cooking, take the meat from the refrigerator and rest it at room temperature. Pre-heat the oven to 425°F (220°C).

Remove the plastic wrap and place the unpeeled garlic under and around the meat. Bake for 20 minutes, then lower the temperature to 265°F (130°C) and cook for a further 2 hours 30 minutes, basting the meat every 30 minutes. If the meat is browning too quickly, cover it with tinfoil.

Take the dish from the oven, and if you have not already done so, cover it lightly in tinfoil and leave it to rest for at least 5 minutes.

To serve, cut the meat at the table, serving it with the pan juices and a potato gratin, p. 133.

Image on p. 232

Honey Glazed Ham

Gordon Ramsay

COMPLEXITY: EASY | PREP TIME: 20 MINUTES | COOK TIME: 4 HOURS | SERVES: 8 TO 10

INGREDIENTS

6⅔ lb (3 kg) unsmoked, boneless gammon joint, tied with string to hold its shape

4 medium-sized carrots, peeled and roughly chopped

1 leek, cleaned and roughly chopped

1 onion, peeled and roughly chopped

1 tsp black peppercorns, lightly crushed

1 tsp coriander seeds, lightly crushed

1 stick cinnamon, broken in half

3 bay leaves

handful of cloves

HONEY GLAZE

½ cup (100 g) light-brown cane sugar/ Demerara sugar

3 tbsp plus 1 tsp (50 ml) Madeira wine

5 tsp sherry vinegar

½ cup (125 g) honey

METHOD

Put the gammon in a large saucepan and pour on enough cold water to cover it. Add the carrots, leek, onion, peppercorns, coriander seeds, cinnamon, and bay leaves. Bring to the boil, turn down to a simmer and cook, uncovered, for 3 hours, topping up with more boiling water if necessary. From time to time, skim off the froth and any impurities that rise to the surface. If cooking in advance, leave the ham to cool in the stock overnight. Otherwise, allow it to cool a little, then remove from the pan. Strain the stock (and save for soups, sauces, etc.).

To make the glaze, put the sugar, Madeira, sherry vinegar, and honey in a pan and stir over a low heat to combine. Bring to the boil, lower the heat and simmer for 3 to 4 minutes, until you have a glossy dark syrup. Do not leave unattended, as it can easily boil over.

Pre-heat the oven to 375°F (190°C). Lift the ham onto a board. Snip and remove the string, then cut away the skin from the ham, leaving behind an even layer of fat. Lightly score the fat all over in a criss-cross, diamond pattern, taking care not to cut into the meat. Stud the centre of each diamond with a clove.

Put the ham in a roasting tray and pour half of the glaze over the surface. Roast for 15 minutes. Pour on the rest of the glaze and return to the oven for another 25 to 35 minutes until the ham is golden brown, basting with the pan juices frequently. It also helps to turn the pan as you baste, to ensure that the joint colours evenly.

Remove from the oven and leave to rest for 15 minutes before carving and serving with your preferred accompaniments.

———

"A lovely glazed ham is a great staple over Christmas, not least because it's also delicious cold with a good chutney. Roast on the day if serving hot, or up to 2 days ahead if serving cold."

– GORDON RAMSAY

Roasted Pork Belly with Homemade Apple Sauce

Curtis Stone

COMPLEXITY: EASY | PREP TIME: 15 MINUTES | COOK TIME: 2 HOURS 30 MINUTES
SERVES: 8

INGREDIENTS

3-lb (1.4-kg) piece
of pork belly (skin
removed)

1 tbsp kosher/flaky salt

1 tsp garlic powder

1 tsp freshly ground
black pepper

homemade apple sauce
(p. 466)

METHOD

Pre-heat the oven to 350°F (180°C).

Using a small, sharp knife, score the fat that covers the pork belly in a crosshatch pattern. In a small bowl, mix the salt, garlic powder, and pepper to blend. Rub the spice mixture all over the pork belly, working it into the scored surface.

Place a wire rack on a rimmed baking tray, set the pork belly on the rack, fat side up, and cover it with tinfoil. Roast for about 2 hours, or until the pork is tender.

Increase the heat to 400°F (200°C), remove the foil from the pork, and continue roasting for about 30 minutes, or until the pork belly is browned all over and pull-apart tender. Remove from the oven and let rest for about 15 minutes.

Carve the pork and serve with the apple sauce.

GET CREATIVE

I've purposely kept my roasted pork belly simple so that you can take it in any direction you'd like. For example, for the rich intoxicating flavours of Mexican cuisine, mix 2 teaspoons each of ancho chilli powder and kosher/flaky salt, 1½ teaspoons ground cumin, and ½ teaspoon each of freshly ground black pepper and garlic powder, and rub this spice mixture over the pork belly. You'll want to dice the pork, or pull it apart, and tuck it into tacos, burritos, quesadillas, or enchiladas.

Or, for five-spice pork belly, simply coat the pork belly with 1 tablespoon five-spice powder and 2 teaspoons kosher/flaky salt. This is especially delicious in banh mi sandwiches.

MAKE AHEAD

The pork belly can be roasted up to 2 days ahead, cooled, covered, and refrigerated. To re-warm, cut the pork into portions and sear them in a non-stick frying pan over a medium heat until golden brown on all sides and heated through, or roast them in a 350°F (180°C) oven, or grill them.

Porchetta

Guy Grossi

COMPLEXITY: EASY | PREP TIME: 30 MINUTES, PLUS REFRIGERATION TIME
COOK TIME: 3 HOURS | SERVES: 12

INGREDIENTS

1 loaf sourdough
(p. 498) broken into
pieces

2 cloves garlic

1 tsp ground cloves

1 tsp ground nutmeg

1 tsp ground star anise

3½ oz (100 g) sage
leaves

14 oz (400 g) flat-leaf
parsley

6¾ tbsp (100 ml)
olive oil, plus extra for
drizzling

3½ oz (100 g) grated
Parmigiano Reggiano

salt and cracked black
pepper

6⅔ lb (3 kg) pork belly

JOSH'S NOTES

Preparation: The pork
needs to be seasoned,
and dried in the fridge
overnight.

Key element: Blend the
bread mixture in two or
more batches so it forms
a good consistency.

Tip: Ask for a wide,
flat piece of pork belly
if possible, which will
make it easier to roll.

Complements: Simple
potatoes and greens.

METHOD

Place the sourdough, garlic, spices, herbs, olive oil, and Parmigiano
Reggiano in a food processor and pulse until well combined and
mixture clings together when pinched. Season with salt and pepper,
and keep in the fridge until needed.

Lay the pork belly out skin side down. Starting at one end, separate
the skin from the meat to about half way, leaving the meat attached
to the rest of the belly. Season the meat with salt and pepper and
spread the bread paste evenly over it. Leaving the separated skin
behind, roll the pork meat over itself into a log, then fold the skin
over to cover – this is done so that the skin is not rolled into the
centre of the porchetta.

Cut 4 pieces of butcher's twine, each long enough to tie around the
pork roll. Lay the twine on a work surface at even intervals and place
the rolled pork on top. Bring up each piece of twine and tie a knot
to secure the pork firmly, so that it will hold its shape during cooking.
Season the pork skin with salt and leave uncovered in the fridge for
24 hours to dry out the skin.

Pre-heat a fan-forced oven to 325°F (170°C). Place a wire rack inside
a roasting tray, place the pork roll on the rack, seam side down,
drizzle with olive oil and cook for 2 hours 30 minutes until the skin
is crackling and the meat is soft and tender.

Remove from the oven and allow to rest for 15 minutes
before carving.

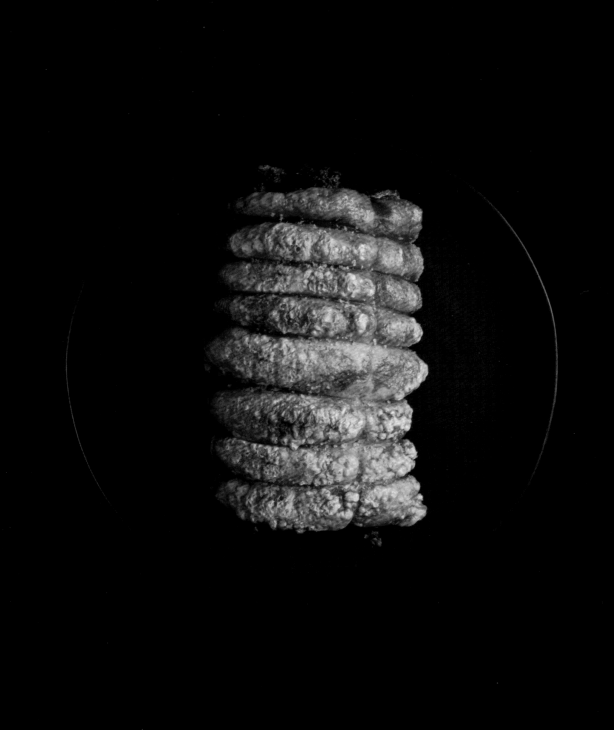

INGREDIENTS

PIG CHEEKS & MUSHROOMS

8 x 7 oz (200 g) pig cheeks

1¼ cups (300 ml) chicken stock (p. 482)

2 cups plus 1¼ tbsp (500 ml) reduced veal stock (glaze) (see overleaf)

9 oz (250 g) shiitake mushrooms

9 oz (250 g) enoki mushrooms

9 oz (250 g) nameko mushrooms

¾ cup plus 1¼ tbsp (200 ml) dry vermouth (Noilly Prat)

6¾ tbsp (100 ml) grapeseed oil

fine sea salt

CELERIAC CREAM

4 French shallots, finely diced

2 white celery stalks (inner stalks), finely chopped

1 garlic clove, finely chopped

7 oz/1¾ sticks (200 g) unsalted butter

1 celery root/celeriac head

2 cups plus 1¼ tbsp (500 ml) chicken stock (p. 482)

10 tbsp (150 ml) cream

sea salt, to taste

Ingredients continued overleaf

Slow-braised Pig Cheek with Celeriac Cream & Mushrooms

Peter Gilmore

COMPLEXITY: DIFFICULT | PREP TIME: 1 HOUR | COOK TIME: 10 HOURS | SERVES: 8

METHOD

Prepare the veal stock (see overleaf).

Prepare the pig cheeks by trimming around the meaty part, leaving a 1¼ in (3 cm) circumference of fat and skin around the meat. Set up a bowl of iced water. Bring a saucepan of water to the boil and blanch the pig cheeks in the boiling water for just 1 minute. Refresh in the iced water and dry well.

Place the pig cheeks in two vacuum bags, with 10 tablespoons (150 ml) chicken stock and 3 tablespoons plus 1 teaspoon (50 ml) of veal glaze (see overleaf) in each bag. Seal in a vacuum sealer and steam in a temperature-controlled combi oven at 185°F (85°C) for 10 hours. Alternatively, if cooking conventionally, you could use more chicken stock and veal glaze and braise the pig cheeks in a casserole dish with a lid in a 200°F (100°C) oven for 6 hours. Once the pig cheeks have cooked, allow to cool completely, then place them in the refrigerator until required.

Remove all the stalks from the shiitake, enoki, and nameko mushrooms, and set aside. Put the vermouth in a small saucepan and bubble to reduce it down to 2 tablespoons (30 ml), then add the remaining 1⅔ cups (400 ml) veal glaze and set aside.

Sweat the shallots, celery, and garlic in a frying pan with 3½ oz/⅞ stick (100 g) butter over a medium-low heat, stirring occasionally, being careful not to add any colour. Peel and dice the celery root/celeriac into ¾-in (2-cm) cubes and add to the pan. Add the chicken stock, and simmer gently until almost all the stock has evaporated. Place the contents of the pan into a blender and blend on high for 1 minute. Add the remaining 3½ oz/⅞ stick (100 g) butter and blend for a further minute. Pass the purée through a drum sieve. Taste and season with sea salt, then set aside.

Pre-heat the oven to 350°F (180°C). Remove the pig cheeks from the bags and remove any jellied stock.

Continued overleaf

REDUCED VEAL STOCK

1 brown onion, chopped

1 carrot, chopped

3 tbsp plus 1 tsp (50 ml) grapeseed oil

1 lb 2 oz (500 g) veal or beef trimmings

4 cloves garlic, bruised with the back of a knife

2 cups plus 1¼ tbsp (500 ml) good-quality red wine

8 qt (8 litres) veal stock (p. 485)

6 ripe tomatoes, cut in half

2 sprigs of thyme

Slow-braised Pig Cheek with Celeriac Cream & Mushrooms cont.

Trim the cheeks, removing the skin and cutting around the fat so that there is only ½ in (1 cm) fat surrounding and covering the top of the meat. Season the cheeks with sea salt.

Heat 3 tablespoons plus 1 teaspoon (50 ml) of grapeseed oil in an ovenproof saucepan and sauté the cheeks, fat side down, until golden brown. Remove the cheeks and the oil from the pan. Return the cheeks to the pan with 1¼ cups (300 ml) of the vermouth-enriched veal glaze. Place the saucepan and cheeks in the oven and allow the cheeks to warm through for about 10 minutes.

To finish the celeriac cream, whip the cream until soft peaks form. Re-heat the celeriac purée, then fold through the whipped cream.

Sauté all the mushrooms in the remaining 1¾ fl oz (50 ml) grapeseed oil. When the mushrooms are light brown, add the remaining vermouth-enriched glaze and reduce until the mushrooms are well glazed. Season with sea salt. Remove the cheeks from the oven and finish reducing the glaze on the stovetop. Spoon the glaze over the cheeks as you go, until the cheeks are well glazed.

Place a spoonful of celeriac cream in the centre of each serving plate and top with a glazed cheek. Place a couple of spoonfuls of mushrooms next to the cheek and serve immediately.

....

Reduced Veal Stock (Demi-glace and Glaze)

In a large stockpot set over a medium heat, sauté the onion and carrot in the grapeseed oil until lightly browned. Add the veal or beef trimmings and continue to sauté until the meat is well browned. Add the garlic and red wine. Bubble to reduce the wine until there is only 6¾ tablespoons (100 ml) of liquid left, then add the stock, tomatoes, and thyme. Continue to reduce the stock on a medium simmer until the stock has halved in quantity. Strain through a fine conical strainer lined with muslin cloth. You should now have a demi-glace (half-reduced stock).

To make a glaze, place the demi-glace in a clean pot and reduce over a high heat until you have the required viscosity for glazing and saucing meats. Generally from 4 quarts (4 litres) of demi-glace you will need to reduce it to somewhere between 3⅓ cups (800 ml) and 2 cups plus 1¼ tablespoons (500 ml) to achieve a glaze. The further you reduce, the heavier the glaze.

"This is a relatively simple recipe for autumn. The earthy flavours of celeriac and mushrooms really complement the texture and flavour of the slow-braised pig cheeks."

– PETER GILMORE

Roasted Rib of Beef with Yorkshire Puddings & Horseradish Cream

Tom Kitchin

COMPLEXITY: MODERATE | PREP TIME: 30 MINUTES | COOK TIME: 1 HOUR | SERVES: 6

INGREDIENTS

6⅔ lb (3 kg) rib of beef on the bone

sea salt

2 tbsp freshly cracked pepper

vegetable oil for cooking

4 large potatoes, peeled and halved

⅔ cup (150 ml) chicken stock (p. 482)

TO SERVE

Yorkshire puddings (see overleaf)

horseradish cream (see overleaf)

Ingredients continued overleaf

METHOD

Heat the oven to its highest setting (probably 465°F/240°C).

Put a large roasting tray into the oven to heat up. Meanwhile, season the rib of beef well with salt and cracked pepper, rubbing the seasoning into the meat.

Using oven gloves, transfer the roasting tray to the stovetop over a medium-high heat and add a drizzle of oil. Place the rib of beef in the roasting tray and colour all over, turning as necessary. This may take 8 to 10 minutes, but it's very important not to skimp on this stage.

Now add the potatoes to the tray and turn to colour on all sides. Transfer the roasting tray to the very hot oven and roast for 15 minutes. This allows the beef to take on colour quickly and will create a lovely crust.

Reduce the oven setting to 350°F (180°C) and roast for a further 30 minutes or until the beef is cooked to your liking. To check, insert a metal needle into the thickest part for 30 seconds, then remove and place it against your lip. If the needle is slightly warm, the meat is ready to come out if you want it pink. If it's hot or very hot, it will be medium to well done. If it is cold, it needs longer in the oven.

When the beef is ready, transfer it and the potatoes to a warm platter and set aside to rest in a warm place for about 20 minutes. Pour off any fat from the roasting tray into a bowl (save to use to roast potatoes or make Yorkshire puddings another day). Place the tray over a medium heat and add the chicken stock, stirring to deglaze and scrape up the tasty sediment from the bottom of the pan to make a light gravy.

Carve the beef and serve with the roast potatoes, a seasonal green vegetable or two, Yorkshire puddings, and horseradish cream.

JOSH'S NOTES

Comment: Who doesn't love a Sunday roast? This one is superb.

Continued overleaf

YORKSHIRE PUDDINGS

1 cup (115 g) all
purpose/plain flour

2 large free-range eggs

½ cup plus 1 tsp
(125 ml) milk

⅔ tsp salt

freshly ground black
pepper

4 tbsp beef dripping
or vegetable oil

HORSERADISH CREAM

1 cup plus 2 tsp (250 ml)
whipping cream

1 tsp red wine vinegar

1 tbsp freshly grated
horseradish

1 tsp crème fraîche

sea salt

Roasted Rib of Beef with Yorkshire Puddings
& Horseradish Cream cont.

Yorkshire Puddings

COMPLEXITY: EASY | PREP TIME: 10 MINUTES, PLUS REFRIGERATION TIME
COOK TIME: 25 MINUTES | MAKES: 6

Pre-heat the oven to 430°F (220°C) and put a baking tray inside to
heat up.

Put the flour into a mixing bowl and make a well in the middle.
Add the eggs with half of the milk, and beat until smooth. Now add
the rest of the milk and season with the salt and a grind of pepper,
mixing well. Place the batter in a refrigerator and leave to stand for
3 to 4 hours.

Spoon about 1 tablespoon of beef fat or vegetable oil into each
compartment of a non-stick 6-hole Yorkshire pudding tray. Slide the
tray onto the hot baking tray in the oven and heat for 5 minutes or
until smoking hot.

Now, quickly ladle the batter into the tray to three-quarters fill each
compartment. Immediately return the tray to the oven and bake for
20 minutes or until well puffed and golden brown. Serve at once.

Horseradish Cream

COMPLEXITY: EASY | PREP TIME: 5 MINUTES | SERVES: 6

Whip the cream in a bowl until it holds firm peaks, then add
the vinegar and whisk briefly to incorporate. Fold in the grated
horseradish and crème fraîche, and season with salt to taste.

"This traditional roast beef accompaniment tastes so much better
if it is made with fresh horseradish. You can buy this from farmers'
markets and some supermarkets – or better still, grow your own."
– TOM KITCHIN

INGREDIENTS

RIB MARINADE

1¾ oz (800 g) baby back
   pork ribs
4 tsp Chinese five spice
3 tbsp plus 1 tsp (50 ml)
   light soy sauce
3 tbsp plus 1 tsp (50 ml)
   kecap manis (sweet
   soy)
4 cloves garlic, minced
2 tsp minced fresh
   ginger
2 tsp salt
2 tsp ground black
   pepper

RIB COOKING LIQUOR

1 qt (1 litre)
   chicken stock (p. 482)
cilantro/coriander stalks
   from the garnish
1¾ oz (50 g) ginger,
   peeled and roughly
   chopped
1 stalk lemongrass
3 lime leaves
1 fresh red chilli,
   deseeded
3 tbsp plus 1 tsp (50 ml)
   light soy sauce

RIB GLAZE

4½ oz (125 g) miso
   paste
⅓ cup (75 ml) vegetable
   stock
6¾ oz (190 g) honey
   (I use Chinese honey)
1¾ oz (50 g) maltose
1 tbsp *kecap manis*

FOR SMOKING

wood chips

TO SERVE

handful of fresh cilantro/
   coriander leaves
1 red chilli, thinly sliced
4 green onions/spring
   onions, thinly sliced
¾ oz (20 g) toasted
   sesame seeds

The Ivy's
Sticky Smoked
BBQ Short Ribs

Gary Lee

COMPLEXITY: MODERATE | PREP TIME: 30 MINUTES, PLUS MARINATION TIME
COOK TIME: 2 HOURS | SERVES: 4

METHOD

Using a sharp knife, make incisions between the rib bones on both
sides, being careful not to cut all the way through. Mix together the
rib marinade ingredients and rub all over the ribs, including into the
incisions. Cover and marinade in the fridge for 24 hours.

Remove the ribs from the fridge and wipe off all excess marinade.
Place the rib cooking liquor ingredients in a pan large enough to
hold the ribs, and bring the liquor to the boil. Add the ribs and
reduce the heat to a gentle simmer. Cook the ribs for 1 hour, or until
the meat is tender, then remove from the liquid and allow to cool.

Meanwhile, make the glaze by heating the miso with the vegetable
stock in a pan over a medium heat, whisking well to combine. Gently
simmer to reduce the liquid until most has evaporated, then remove
from the heat and stir in the remaining ingredients.

Rub some of the glaze onto the cooked ribs. If you have a smoker
then follow the manufacturer's instructions; alternatively, a simple
stove-top smoker can be made out of normal kitchen utensils. Place
2 handfuls of wood chips in the centre of a roasting tray, place a
wire rack over the top and put the ribs on the rack. Place this on the
stovetop and turn on to a moderate to low heat. Once the chips start
smoking, cover the tray with foil and leave to gently smoke for about
1 hour, making sure to brush more of the glaze onto the ribs every
10 minutes. The ribs should be nice and sticky once finished.

Serve the ribs with the garnish ingredients scattered over the top.

INGREDIENTS

all-purpose/plain flour,
for dusting

18 oz (500 g) puff pastry

3½ oz (100 g) baby
spinach

3 tbsp plus 1 tsp (50 ml)
vegetable oil

9 oz (250 g) mixed
wild mushrooms, finely
chopped

1⅔ lb (750 g) chestnut
mushrooms, finely
chopped

sea salt and freshly
ground black pepper

6¾ tbsp (100 ml)
Madeira wine

2 shallots, finely diced

1 clove garlic, finely
chopped

½ bunch thyme

3⅓ lb (1½ kg) thick
centre-cut beef fillet,
trimmed of any sinew

2 tbsp prepared English
mustard

3 egg yolks beaten with
1 tbsp (15 ml) water
(egg wash)

SAVOURY CRÊPES

1¼ cups (150 g) all-
purpose/plain flour

1⅓ cups (325 g) semi-
skimmed milk

1 egg

salt and freshly ground
black pepper

2 tbsp (30 g) unsalted
butter, melted

Classic Beef Wellington

Calum Franklin

COMPLEXITY: MODERATE | PREP TIME: 45 MINUTES, PLUS REFRIGERATION TIME
COOK TIME: 1 HOUR | SERVES: 6 TO 8

METHOD

With a light dusting of flour, roll out the puff pastry to a rectangle measuring 16 x 12 in (40 x 30 cm) and place in the fridge to rest.

Make the savoury crêpes. Whisk the flour, milk, and whole egg together till smooth, season with salt and pepper, then whisk in 1½ tablespoons (20 g) of the melted butter. Rub a little of the remaining butter around a large, non-stick frying pan, place over a low-medium heat and carefully pour in just enough batter to make a thin 8-in (20-cm) diameter crêpe. Colour lightly, about 45 seconds, then flip over and cook for another minute until done. Remove from the pan. Repeat until you have 4.

On a clean, flat work surface, lay out the crêpes into a rectangular shape measuring 14 x 10 in (35 x 25 cm), overlapping the bottom two crêpes onto the top two. Evenly cover the crêpes with the uncooked baby spinach.

In the large frying pan, heat 2 tablespoons (30 ml) vegetable oil over a high heat, add the mushrooms and season with salt and pepper. Cook until there is no moisture left at all in the mushrooms, then add the Madeira and reduce to a gentle simmer.

In a small pot, heat 1 tablespoon (15 ml) vegetable oil and sweat down the shallots, garlic, and thyme till soft, about 5 minutes, then add this to the mushroom mix. When the Madeira has completely reduced and the mixture is almost dry again, remove the pan from the heat and quickly scatter the mushroom mix evenly over the baby spinach. The heat from the mushrooms will gently wilt the spinach. When the mushrooms have cooled, gently pat down to compact.

Wipe out the frying pan and return it to a high heat. Season beef fillet well and then rub all over with vegetable oil. When the pan is smoking hot, carefully put the beef fillet in it and sear all over for 20 to 30 seconds, just to get a little colour all over. Remove the beef fillet and lay horizontally across your mushroom mix. When cooled, rub the beef all over with the English mustard.

Continued overleaf

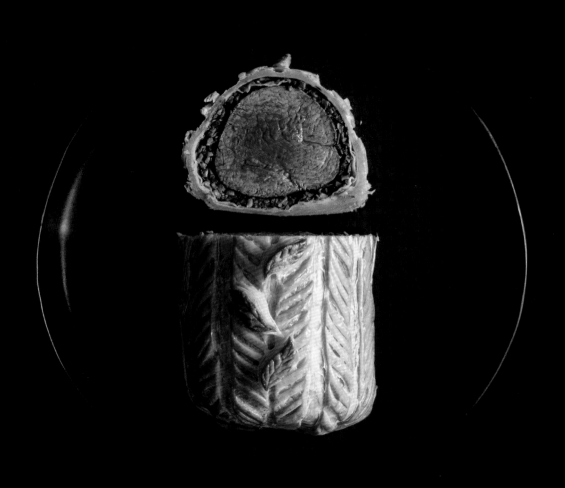

Classic Beef Wellington cont.

Remove the pastry from the fridge and place on a baking tray lined with parchment paper. Gently dust off any excess flour and brush liberally with the egg wash. Roll the beef/spinach/mushroom crêpes into a tight cigar shape and quickly lift and transfer to lie horizontally across the bottom of the pastry. Roll the pastry upwards, keeping it tight to the cigar until the seam is across the bottom with about 1¼ in (3 cm) of overlapped pastry. Trim off any excess.

Carefully crimp down each end of the Wellington and trim so that there is just enough to tuck back under itself, and brush all over with egg wash. Any of the remaining trimmed pastry can be used for decoration across the top. Put the Wellington in the fridge for 2 hours to rest and chill in the centre, then remove and give a final brush with egg wash and sea salt.

Pre-heat the oven to 365°F (185°C) fan and bake the Wellington for 40 minutes, or until the centre reads 95°F (35°C) with a temperature probe. Slide the Wellington, still on its parchment paper, onto a cooling rack and leave to rest for at least 25 minutes before slicing with a sharp serrated knife and serving with gravy and roast potatoes.

JOSH'S NOTES

Key element: Make the crêpes as thin as you can, and try not to overlap them too much.

Tip: Lay baking paper underneath the crêpes so you can roll the cigar really tightly.

Complements: Serve with beef jus and any potato side dish.

Corned Beef & Pickled Tongue

Hugh Fearnley-Whittingstall

COMPLEXITY: EASY | PREP TIME: 20 MINUTES
COOK TIME: 3 HOURS, PLUS BRINING AND SOAKING TIME | SERVES: 10 OR MORE

INGREDIENTS

4 to 6 lb (1.8 to 2.7 kg) piece of beef (brisket, flank, or a whole beef tongue)

1 bouquet garni (thyme, rosemary, bay leaf, etc.)

1 carrot, chopped

1 onion, chopped

1 stalk celery, chopped

1 leek, chopped

½ head garlic

BRINE

5 qt (5 litres) water

16 oz (450 g) Demerara or light brown sugar

3 lb (1.4 kg) coarse sea salt

1 tsp black peppercorns

1 tsp juniper berries

5 cloves

4 bay leaves

sprig of thyme

3 tbsp saltpetre (optional)

JOSH'S NOTES

Preparation: 5 to 10 days to brine, and 24 hours to soak.

Comment: The brine imparts a great flavour, so don't rush it or shorten the timeframe.

METHOD

Put all the ingredients for the brine in a large saucepan and stir well over a low heat until the sugar and salt have dissolved. Bring to the boil, allow to bubble for 1 to 2 minutes, then remove from the heat and leave to cool completely.

Place your chosen piece of meat in a non-metallic container, such as a large Tupperware or a clay crock. Cover the meat completely with the cold brine, weighting it down if necessary with a piece of wood. Leave in a cool place for 5 to 10 days (joints of less than 6 lb/2.7 kg should not be left for more than a week, or they will become too pickled).

Before cooking, remove the meat from the brine and soak it in fresh cold water for 24 hours, changing the water at least once (you could make that 48 hours if it had the full 10-day immersion). Then put it in a pan together with the bouquet garni, vegetables, and garlic, cover with fresh water, and bring to a gentle simmer.

Poach very gently on top of the stove – or in a very low oven (275°F/140°C) if you prefer. A 6 lb (2.7 kg) piece of beef will take 2 hours 30 minutes to 3 hours. A salted tongue may take even longer. In either case, cook until the meat is completely tender and yielding when pierced with a skewer. The coarse skin of a boiled tongue must be peeled off and discarded before it is served.

Serve hot, carved into fairly thick slices, with lentils, beans, horseradish mash, or boiled potatoes, and either creamed fresh horseradish or good English mustard. Also excellent cold.

Bone Marrow with Sea Urchin & Purslane

Lennox Hastie

COMPLEXITY: DIFFICULT | PREP TIME: 45 MINUTES, PLUS BRINING TIME
COOK TIME: 30 MINUTES | SERVES: 4

INGREDIENTS

SALT BRINE

1 cup (250 g) non-iodized table sea salt

5 qt (5 litres) filtered water

SHINBONES & SEA URCHIN

4 grass-fed shinbones, split lengthways (see tips)

1 qt (1 litre) salt brine (see below), chilled

3 live sea urchins

FERMENTED CHILLI CAPER DRESSING

⅓ oz (10 g) finely chopped shallot

3 tbsp plus 1 tsp (50 ml) Chardonnay vinegar

zest of ½ lemon

¾ oz (20 g) capers, finely chopped

¾ oz (20 g) caperberries, finely chopped

½ tsp fermented chilli paste (p. 460)

¼ bunch flat-leaf parsley, finely chopped

6¾ tbsp (100 ml) fruity, mild extra virgin olive oil, such as Arbequina or Koroneiki

TO SERVE

3½ oz (100 g) purslane, washed and picked

METHOD

First make the salt brine. In a large, deep saucepan, combine the salt with 2 quarts (2 litres) water. Bring to the boil, stirring to dissolve the salt. Remove the pan from the heat and pour in the remaining water. Allow to cool and refrigerate to chill completely before using for brining.

Place the shinbones in the chilled salt brine for 6 hours or overnight. Remove and pat dry with paper towels.

Ignite a fire in your wood-fired oven. Leave it to burn until medium embers are produced – you are aiming to bring the oven to a temperature of 570°F (300°C).

Prepare the sea urchins. Locate the surface with the central mouth and cut a large circular opening around it with a pair of sharp, pointed scissors. Carefully remove the orange roe, which you will find hidden within. Rinse the roe in chilled filtered water and reserve. Discard the shell.

Prepare the dressing. Rinse the shallot in water and leave to soak in a bowl with the vinegar for 20 minutes. Drain the shallot well, add the lemon zest, capers, caperberries, fermented chilli paste, parsley, and olive oil, and mix to combine.

Place the bone marrow in a cast-iron pan and roast in the wood-fired oven until the fat begins to render. The marrow is done when it turns a sienna-brown colour and starts to bubble around the edges. Remove from the oven and brush the marrow with a spoonful of the fermented chilli and caper dressing. Top with the sea urchin and purslane. Serve immediately.

TIPS

Ask your butcher to split your shinbones lengthways. The shinbones need time to chill in the brine solution, so begin this recipe at least 6 hours ahead of time.

"Bone marrow indicates the quality of the animal, so it is important to select bones from high-quality grass-fed cows."

– LENNOX HASTIE

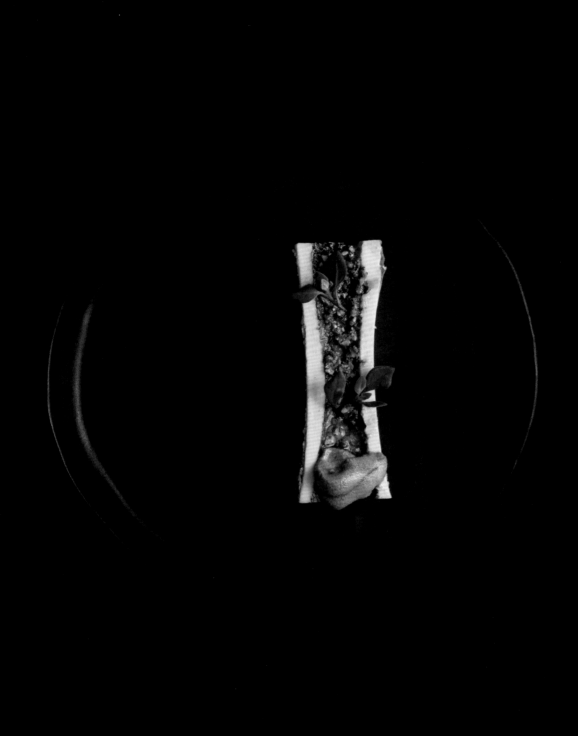

Chicken Livers with Capers, Parsley & Guanciale

Nancy Silverton

COMPLEXITY: EASY | PREP TIME: 30 MINUTES | COOK TIME: 10 MINUTES
MAKES: ENOUGH FOR 24 CROSTINI

INGREDIENTS

16 oz (450 g) chicken livers

kosher/flaky salt and freshly ground black pepper

1 cup (240 ml) extra virgin olive oil

2 oz (60 g) pancetta, chopped

2 cloves garlic, finely chopped

2 tbsp (30 ml) brandy or Cognac

2 tbsp fresh flat-leaf parsley, finely chopped

2 tbsp shallots, finely chopped

2 tbsp capers (preferably salt-packed), soaked for 15 minutes if salt-packed, rinsed, and drained

grated zest of 1 lemon

1 tbsp (15 ml) fresh lemon juice

12 thin slices guanciale or pancetta (about 6 to 8 oz/175 to 225 g)

24 crostini bagnati (see overleaf)

Ingredients continued overleaf

METHOD

Use a small knife to remove the connective veins from the chicken livers, discard the veins, and place the chicken livers on a plate lined with paper towels. Pat them with the paper towels to get out the excess moisture, and discard the towels. Season the livers very generously with salt and pepper and toss to coat them all over with the seasoning.

Heat ¼ cup (60 ml) of the olive oil in a large sauté pan over a medium-high heat until the oil is almost smoking and slides easily in the pan, 2 to 3 minutes. One by one, carefully add the chicken livers to the pan. (By adding them one at a time the pan doesn't cool down too much, and it also ensures you will have room for all of the livers, as they shrink immediately when they hit the pan. You should be able to fit them all in the pan at the same time.)

Cook the livers for about 3 minutes per side, until they're deep brown. Add the pancetta, reduce the heat to low, and cook for 1 to 2 minutes, until the fat is rendered from the pancetta. Add the garlic and cook for about 1 minute, stirring constantly to prevent it from browning. Add the brandy, shake the pan or stir the livers to deglaze the pan, and cook for about 30 seconds to burn off the alcohol. Turn off the heat and turn the contents of the pan out onto a large cutting board, making sure to get all the bits out of the bottom of the pan.

Pile the parsley, shallots, capers, and lemon zest on top of the mound of chicken livers and pancetta and drizzle with the lemon juice and ¼ cup (60 ml) of olive oil. Run a large knife through the mound five or ten times to roughly chop the livers and all the other ingredients. Drizzle another ¼ cup (60 ml) of olive oil over the mound and continue to chop, gathering the ingredients into a mound from time to time. Add the remaining ¼ cup (60 ml) of olive oil and chop until the livers are the consistency of a coarse paste, almost puréed. Serve the chicken liver spread now, or transfer to an airtight container and refrigerate for up to 3 days; bring to room temperature before assembling the crostini.

Continued overleaf

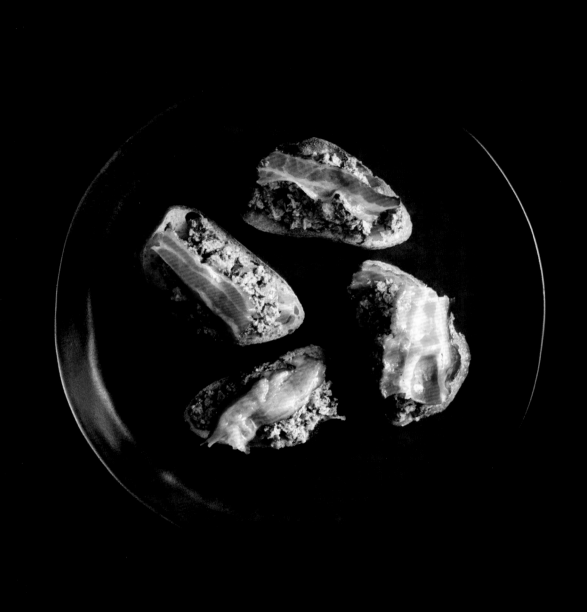

CROSTINI BAGNATI

24 x ½-in (1-cm) slices
from a loaf of rustic
white bread such as
ciabatta, cut on the bias

extra virgin olive oil,
for bread

1 clove garlic, halved

4 tbsp (60 ml) finishing-
quality extra virgin
olive oil

Maldon sea salt or
another flaky sea salt
such as fleur de sel

Chicken Livers, Capers, Parsley & Guanciale cont.

Adjust the oven rack to the middle position and pre-heat the oven to 350°F (180°C), or pre-heat a sandwich press. (You will need the oven to finish the dish.)

Place the bread slices on a baking tray, brush the tops with olive oil, and bake for 15 to 20 minutes, until golden brown and crisp. Remove from the oven and rub the oiled side with garlic. Alternatively, brush both sides of the bread with olive oil, toast in the sandwich press, and rub one oiled side with garlic. Drizzle with 1 tablespoon (15 ml) finishing-quality olive oil, and sprinkle liberally with sea salt.

Place the guanciale slices on a baking tray and put in the oven until they are cooked through but not crisp, 3 to 5 minutes. Remove from the oven and transfer to paper towels to drain.

To assemble, lay the crostini oiled side up on a work surface and spoon a heaped tablespoon of the chicken liver spread in an uneven layer on the toast, leaving the edges exposed. Tear 1 piece of guanciale in half and lay both halves at an angle on top of the chicken liver, slightly overlapping in a natural-looking way. Repeat with the remaining crostini, chicken liver, and guanciale, and serve.

"I was totally happy with our crostini until I went to the Spotted Pig in New York City and had theirs. April Bloomfield, the chef, served her chicken livers on bread that was doused with – not drizzled and not brushed, but drowned in – olive oil, which made the chicken liver taste that much better. When I came back from that trip, we started doing the same thing, drowning the toast for our chicken liver pâté in the best finishing-quality olive oil we have."
– NANCY SILVERTON

JOSH'S NOTES

Key elements: Clean the livers well, and have all the the elements to hand before you start.

Tip: A high heat for the pan will give good colour without over-cooking the livers.

Tasha's
Livers on Toast

Natasha Sideris

COMPLEXITY: EASY | PREP TIME: 30 MINUTES | COOK TIME: 5 MINUTES | SERVES: 4

INGREDIENTS

olive oil

knob of butter

1 small white onion, finely chopped

2 cloves garlic, crushed

18 oz (500 g) chicken livers

1 tsp beef stock powder

1 tsp dried thyme

salt and freshly ground pepper

1 tsp all-purpose/plain flour

lemon juice

½ cup plus 2 tbsp (150 ml) water

2 tbsp (30 g) butter

4 tbsp flat-leaf parsley, chopped

4 fried eggs (optional)

4 slices ciabatta toast, buttered

METHOD

Heat a little olive oil in a pan set over a medium heat and add the knob of butter. Add the onion and fry gently; when it begins to soften, add the garlic, chicken livers, beef stock powder, and thyme. Season with salt and pepper to taste.

Sprinkle the flour over the livers in the pan, add a squeeze of lemon juice and the water. Cook over a medium heat until the sauce has thickened, about 1 minute. Stir in the extra butter to glaze the sauce. When it has melted, add the parsley and stir in.

Fry the eggs to your liking (if including), and toast the ciabatta.

Top the ciabatta toast with the livers and cover with the sauce. The egg can be served either on top or on the side.

_____

"This is an old family favourite that reminds me of happy mornings. Oven-roasted tomatoes and a fried egg are great additions to the iron-rich livers. It's a hearty breakfast that easily doubles up as a quick but filling brunch."

– NATASHA SIDERIS

JOSH'S NOTES

Key element: A runny egg is desirable, as it enriches the sauce.

Tip: Don't overcook the livers, and make sure they're evenly sized.

Image on p. 231

Devilled Kidneys

Gary Rhodes

COMPLEXITY: EASY | PREP TIME: 20 MINUTES | COOK TIME: 10 MINUTES | SERVES: 4

INGREDIENTS

8 lambs' kidneys

1 oz/1¾ tbsp (25 g) butter, melted

salt and cayenne pepper

1 tbsp English mustard

2 tsp white wine vinegar

1 tsp Worcestershire sauce

drop of groundnut/ peanut oil, if pan-frying

4 thick slices hot buttered toast, to serve

"Devilled kidneys is one of the best-known Victorian and Edwardian breakfast dishes, often to be found sizzling gently in a silver chafing dish on a country-house breakfast sideboard. The kidneys can be cooked in a number of ways, some shallow-fried, some grilled or even baked."

– GARY RHODES

METHOD

The outer skin of the kidneys should first be removed, cutting away any gristle.

For grilling, simply split the kidneys open, cutting three-quarters of the way through. The open shape can now be held by threading it with a cocktail stick. Soak the sticks in water before using, to prevent them from catching alight. For sautéing, cut the kidneys in two, giving you four halves per portion.

To grill, pre-heat an oven grill to hot. Brush the 8 pieces with the melted butter and season with a pinch of salt and cayenne pepper. Sit under the grill to cook for 3 minutes on each side.

While the kidneys cook, mix together the mustard, vinegar, and Worcestershire sauce. Half of this mixture can now be brushed on the kidneys and they can be cooked for a further 1 to 2 minutes. Turn the kidneys and brush with the remaining mustard mix. Replace under the grill and cook for 1 minute. The devilled kidneys can be presented on the toasts, removing the cocktail sticks before serving.

To pan-fry, season the kidneys with the salt and cayenne pepper. Heat a frying pan to a medium heat with the groundnut/peanut oil. Once the oil is close to smoking, place the kidneys in the pan. These will seal very quickly in the hot oil. Turn after 2 minutes and continue to fry. After 3 to 4 minutes of cooking, add the butter. Continue to pan-fry, turning the kidneys. Mix the mustard, vinegar, and Worcestershire sauce together. After 5 to 6 minutes, this dressing can be added to the pan. Roll the kidneys so that they are totally covered. Cook for a further minute and present them on the warm buttered toasts.

TIP

If you are a kidney fan but prefer them just grilled or pan-fried, then simply omit the mustard, Worcestershire sauce, vinegar, and cayenne pepper. Season just with salt and pepper and then follow the cooking methods and times as for devilled kidneys.

Crumbed Tripe
Tablier de Sapeur

Stéphane Reynaud

COMPLEXITY: EASY | PREP TIME: 25 MINUTES | COOK TIME: 3 HOURS | SERVES: 6

INGREDIENTS

2¼ lb (1 kg) rumen tripe, bleached by the butcher

4 carrots, peeled and cut into 1-in (2½-cm) pieces

3 brown onions, thickly sliced

1 leek, thickly sliced

1 stalk celery

bouquet garni (thyme, rosemary, bay leaf, etc.)

2 eggs

1 tbsp (15 ml) sunflower oil

6 medium-sized French toast crackers

5¼ oz/1⅓ sticks (150 g) butter, chopped

3 green onions/spring onions, thinly sliced

fine sea salt

METHOD

Put the tripe in a large saucepan with the carrots, onion, leek, celery, and bouquet garni. Cover with water, cover, and cook for 3 to 4 hours, topping up the pan with a little boiling water from time to time if necessary. When ready, the tripe should be soft. Drain. Discard the cooking liquid and vegetables, and slice the tripe into 3 long, thin strips. Pat dry with paper towels and cut into 6 evenly sized rectangular pieces.

Whisk the eggs with the sunflower oil in a shallow bowl. Finely chop the crackers in a food processor to a fine crumb. Transfer to a shallow bowl. Dip the tripe in the eggs, then in the crumbs. Place these crumbed 'aprons' on a tray lined with baking paper.

Heat the butter in a large frying pan over a medium heat until melted. Add the green onions/spring onions and crumbed tripe. Cook the 'aprons' for 3 minutes on each side, or until browned. Sprinkle with sea salt and serve.

Serve with steamed potatoes and a good Béarnaise sauce, p. 472.

JOSH'S NOTES

Key element: Cooking the tripe until tender.

Tip: Cool the tripe before you crumb, and double-crumb if you want more texture; I prefer to let it cool in the liquid to retain moisture.

Image on p. 231

INGREDIENTS

BROTH

1 whole chicken, about 2⅔ lb (1.2 kg)

3 cloves garlic, crushed

5 parsley stalks

2 onions, coarsely chopped

1 carrot, coarsely chopped

2 stalks celery, coarsely chopped

1 leek, coarsely chopped

3 bay leaves

2 sprigs of thyme

5 black peppercorns

SWEETBREADS

14 oz (400 g) veal sweetbreads

1 tbsp (15 g) butter

salt and freshly ground white pepper

MUSHROOMS

2 tbsp (30 g) butter

salt and freshly ground black pepper

10½ oz (300 g) Parisian mushrooms, cut into segments

7 oz (200 g) shiitake mushrooms, cut into strips

2 tsp lemon juice

JOSH'S NOTES

Key element: Take care when layering up the vol au vent cases so that the pastry rises evenly.

Tip: Be flexible with the oven time for the pastry, season well and don't be shy with the herbs.

Fried Veal Sweetbreads with Vol au Vents

Peter Goossens

COMPLEXITY: DIFFICULT | PREP TIME: 1 HOUR 30 MINUTES
COOK TIME: 2 HOURS 30 MINUTES | SERVES: 4

METHOD

1 day in advance, wash the chicken and pat dry with paper towel. Put the chicken with the garlic and parsley stalks in a large pan and cover with water. Add the remaining broth ingredients and bring to the boil, skimming the foam off regularly. Turn down the heat as soon as the broth stars to boil, and let it simmer, uncovered, for about 90 minutes. Allow to cool and put in the refrigerator overnight.

Place the sweetbreads in salted water for 12 hours, changing the water after 6 hours. Bring a pan of salted water to the boil, add the sweetbreads and poach gently for 10 minutes, then drain and cool under cold running water. Clean the sweetbreads by cutting all the membrane and pieces of fat from them. Place the sweetbreads between kitchen paper, cover with a weight and put them in the fridge for one night. If making your own puff pastry, do that now and rest it overnight.

Cut the sweetbreads into large pieces, fry in the butter for 5 to 6 minutes, and season with salt and pepper. Set aside.

Put a knob of butter in another pan and fry the mushrooms until a nice light brown, adding the shiitake after 2 minutes. Season with salt and pepper and add the lemon juice, then remove from the heat.

Pre-heat the oven to 375°F (190°C). Roll out the puff pastry to ⅛ in (2 to 3 mm) thick. Using a 2¾ in (7 cm) cutter, cut 4 rounds for the base of the vol au vents. Then make 12 rings by cutting 12 rounds with the 2¾ in (7 cm) cutter and then removing the centres with a 2 in (5 cm) cutter. Prick holes in the large rounds with a fork and coat them with beaten egg. Place a ring on each base and coat with egg. Repeat until every round has 3 rings on top. Bake the puff pastries for 25 minutes, until golden brown.

Remove the broth from the refrigerator and scoop the fat from the surface. Warm until the broth is liquid, then remove the chicken and sieve the broth. Set 2 cups plus 1¼ tablespoons (500 ml) of broth aside and boil the rest to reduce it to one-third. Remove the skin from the chicken and remove the meat.

To make the balls, season the ground/minced veal with salt and pepper. Knead in the egg and breadcrumbs and form into small balls. Place the reserved chicken broth in a small saucepan, heat to boiling point and poach the balls for about 2 minutes.

For the roux, melt the butter, beat the flour through it and let it dry for a few minutes over a medium heat. While stirring continuously, pour the reduced broth (18 to 20 fl oz/500 to 600 ml) in slowly and combine with the flour-butter mixture. Let the sauce boil briefly, then season with salt, pepper, and lemon juice. Add the cream and cook briefly again.

To make the Dutch sauce, place the egg yolks and water in a saucepan over a low heat and beat to form a nicely bound sauce. Remove from the heat and stir in the lumps of cold butter. Season with salt, pepper, and lemon juice.

To serve, put the chicken pieces, mushrooms, balls and sweetbreads in the cream sauce. Fill each puff pastry with the mixture. Finish with Dutch sauce, shrimps, and chopped parsley.

INGREDIENTS CONT.

PUFF PASTRIES

1⅓ lb (600 g) puff pastry (ready-made or see p. 513)

1 egg, beaten

BALLS

14 oz (400 g) ground/minced veal

salt and freshly ground black pepper

1 egg

3 tbsp breadcrumbs

ROUX

3½ tbsp (45 g) butter

½ cup (70 g) all-purpose/plain flour

salt and freshly ground black pepper

2 tsp lemon juice

2 tsp cream

DUTCH SAUCE

3 egg yolks

2 tbsp (30 ml) water

3½ tbsp (45 g) cold butter, cubed

salt and freshly ground black pepper

2 tbsp lemon juice

TO SERVE

10½ oz (300 g) cooked, unpeeled grey shrimp

4 tbsp chopped parsley

INGREDIENTS

4 pigs' back trotters (feet), deboned (ask your butcher to do this)

3½ oz (100 g) carrots, diced

3½ oz (100 g) onions, diced

½ cup plus 2 tbsp (150 ml) dry white wine

1 tbsp (15 ml) port

½ cup plus 2 tbsp (150 ml) veal stock (p. 485)

knob of unsalted butter

STUFFING

5¼ tbsp (75 g) unsalted butter, plus extra for the sauce

8 oz (225 g) veal sweetbreads, blanched and chopped

20 dried morels, soaked in cold water until soft, then drained

1 small onion, finely chopped

1 skinless chicken breast, about 7 oz (200 g) diced

1 egg white

¾ cup plus 1¼ tbsp (200 ml) heavy/double cream

salt and freshly ground black pepper

TO SERVE

mashed potato (p. 258)

JOSH'S NOTES

Key element: Braise the trotters until you can just press your fingers through the fat.

Tip: Once the trotters are cooked, scrape away any excess fat from the inside.

Tante Claire
Stuffed Pig's Trotter
Pied de Cochon Tante Claire

Pierre Koffmann

COMPLEXITY: DIFFICULT | PREP TIME: 45 MINUTES, PLUS REFRIGERATION TIME
COOK TIME: 3 HOURS 30 MINUTES | SERVES: 4

METHOD

Heat the oven to 325°F (160°C).

Place the trotters in a casserole or Dutch oven together with the carrot, onion, wine, port, and stock. Cover and transfer to the oven to braise for 3 hours.

Meanwhile, make the stuffing. Heat the butter in a large frying pan, add the sweetbreads and fry for 5 minutes. Add the morels and onions and cook for another 5 minutes. Remove from the pan and set aside to cool.

Place the chicken breast in a food processor together with the egg white and cream. Season with salt and pepper and blitz until smooth, then mix with the sweetbread mixture to make the stuffing.

Lift the trotters out of the casserole and pass the cooking liquid through a sieve into a saucepan. Set aside. Open the trotters out flat and lay each on a piece of tinfoil. Leave to cool, then fill each trotter with the stuffing. Wrap tightly in the foil. Chill in the refrigerator for at least 2 hours.

To reheat the trotters, you can either steam them by sitting the parcels in a steamer basket until heated through, or put them in an oven pre-heated to 425°F (220°C) . If using the oven, place the foil parcels in a large casserole or Dutch oven, cover and place in the oven for 15 minutes.

Meanwhile, prepare the mashed potato following the recipe, and make the sauce. For the sauce, place the reserved trotter cooking liquid over a high heat and bubble to reduce it by half, then whisk in a knob of butter.

To serve, unwrap the trotters and serve on warm plates with the hot sauce poured over and a scoop of mashed potato alongside.

"When you buy your trotters, ask your butcher for hind trotters and for him to debone them for you. The hind trotters are longer than the front ones, which are too small."

– PIERRE KOFFMANN

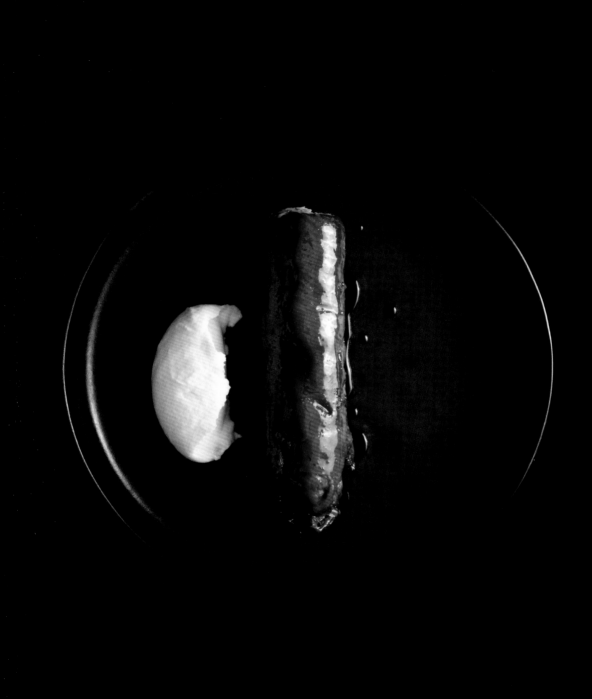

Mogador Macaron, p. 320

Baking

There is a technical aspect to baking that demands attention
and precision – neglecting to include exactly the right amount
of baking powder, added at precisely the right moment, can be
the difference between a light, fluffy, melt-in-the-mouth gateau,
and a flat, dense one that is more cookie than cake. Take heed
of the weights, measures, temperatures, tips, and tricks the chefs
have provided here. They will help you master these classic
tarts, pies, biscuits, cookies, and cakes, from the perfect pizza,
to mouthwatering macaron and scrumptious sticky buns. Put the
kettle on, and enjoy the fruits of your labours.

Cheese Beignets

Tom Aikens

COMPLEXITY: EASY | PREP TIME: 15 MINUTES | COOK TIME: 25 MINUTES | MAKES: 25

INGREDIENTS

1 cup plus 2 tsp
(250 ml) water

3½ tbsp (50 g)
unsalted butter

½ cup plus 1 tbsp (70 g)
all-purpose/plain flour

3½ oz (100 g)
Parmesan, grated

1 whole egg

3 egg yolks

½ tsp English mustard

salt and pepper

fine polenta, for dusting

vegetable oil, for frying

METHOD

In a medium-sized saucepan, bring the water to a simmer along with the butter, then remove from the heat and add the flour. Cook slowly, stirring, for about 8 minutes until the mixture leaves the sides of the pan.

Remove from the heat and stir in the grated Parmesan. Add the whole egg, egg yolks, mustard, salt, and a generous amount of pepper, and beat to combine.

Spread a generous amount of polenta over a tray. Pipe balls of the mixture onto the polenta and coat the beignets with polenta.

Using a deep-fat fryer or large, deep pan, heat the deep-frying oil to 350°F (180°C). Add the beignets, in batches so as not to overcrowd the pan, and fry for 2 minutes, or until crisp. Drain well on paper towel before serving.

JOSH'S NOTES

Preparation: Technically these are fried, not baked, but they're so light and fluffy we've included them here. The frying may take longer than expected depending on size and the temperature of the oil.

Key element: Use a strong, good-quality cheese for optimum flavour.

Tip: Place the mixture in the fridge to set, before you try to mould it.

INGREDIENTS

GOUGÈRES

1 cup plus 3 tbsp
(285 ml) water

½ cup/1 stick (125 g)
butter

½ tsp salt

1⅓ cups plus 1¾ tbsp
(180 g) flour

10½ oz (300 g) eggs

4½ oz (125 g) Gouda,
grated

CHLOROPHYLL

4 bunches spinach

GREEN TOMATO MARMALADE

3½ lb (1.6 kg) green
tomato chutney (p. 454)

1 bunch chervil,
finely chopped

1 bunch chives,
finely chopped

1 bunch tarragon,
finely chopped

all the chlorophyll from
the 4 bunches of spinach

TO SERVE

clarified butter

nice hard cheese
(Gouda or pecorino)
to shave on top

JOSH'S NOTES

Preparation: Make the
chutney ahead of time.

Key element: Cook the
gougères until they
are hollow-sounding
inside. Turn the oven off
and leave them a little
longer to dry out.

Tip: Use a knife to
pierce the bottom of
each gougère before
piping in the chutney.

Gouda & Sweet Chutney Gougères

Daniel Puskas

COMPLEXITY: MODERATE | PREP TIME: 45 MINUTES | COOK TIME: 30 MINUTES
MAKES: 10 OR MORE

METHOD

Pre-heat the oven to 325°F (170°C), low fan if you have a combi oven.

In a medium-sized pot, bring the water and butter to the boil over a medium heat, then add the flour. Cook, stirring, until it pulls away from the sides of the pot. Remove from the heat and allow to cool. Add egg a little at a time, beating to combine before adding more. Add the grated cheese and stir in well.

Transfer to a piping bag fitted with a small nozzle. Pipe small rounds (like half a golf ball) onto baking sheets and bake for 20 minutes at 325°F (170°C) fan 2, then for a further 4 minutes at full fan (if you have this available). Remove from the oven and set to one side to cool.

To make the chlorophyll, blend the spinach with a tiny amount of water until smooth. Strain the liquid into a pot and gently boil until the chlorophyll separates out. Pass this through a fine sieve and filter bag to collect the chlorophyll.

Mix the marmalade ingredients together in a bowl, making sure to whisk vigorously to break up all the chlorophyll and mix the herbs through evenly. Transfer to a piping bag fitted with a medium-sized nozzle and place in the fridge.

To serve, we flash the gougères in a hot oven, then fill them with green tomato marmalade from the piping bag. Heat the clarified butter until nicely hot, then brush it on the top of the gougères and use a microplane to shave a lot of cheese on top.

Tomato Tart
with Goat's Cheese

Tarte Fine à la Tomate,
Fromage de Chèvre

Pierre Koffmann

COMPLEXITY: EASY | PREP TIME: 20 MINUTES | COOK TIME: 12 TO 25 MINUTES
MAKES: FOUR 5 IN (12 CM) TARTS

INGREDIENTS

All-purpose/plain flour,
for dusting

1⅓ lb (600 g) puff pastry
(ready-made or see
p. 513)

4 large tomatoes, finely
sliced

2 tbsp (30 ml) olive oil

pinch of Espelette
pepper

1 egg yolk, beaten, to
glaze

7 oz (200 g) goat cheese
log, sliced

handful of wild arugula/
rocket leaves, to garnish

salt

METHOD

Pre-heat the oven to 325°F (170°C). Line a baking sheet with
baking parchment.

Lightly dust a work surface with flour and roll out the pastry until
it is ¹⁄₁₆ to ⅛ in (2 to 3 mm) thick (or use ready-rolled). Using a 5-in
(12-cm) cutter, cut out 4 pastry discs. Cover each disc with tomato
slices, overlapping them slightly and leaving a ¼-in (5-mm) border
free around the edge of the pastry. Drizzle with the oil, then season
with salt and the Espelette pepper.

Brush the exposed pastry with the beaten egg, then transfer the
discs to the prepared baking sheet and bake for 12 minutes, until
the pastry is risen and golden and the tomatoes are very soft.

Remove the tray from the oven and scatter over the slices of goat
cheese while the tarts are hot so that the cheese melts slightly.
Garnish with a few arugula/rocket leaves and serve immediately.

"In September there is always a surplus of tomatoes in Gascony,
and this simple tart makes a nice change from salad. It's a very,
very easy dish to prepare but one that for me recalls warm days
and the joy of simple flavours."

– PIERRE KOFFMANN

JOSH'S NOTES

Key element: As always
with pastry, get a nice
golden colour for the
best flavour.

Tip: The cook time
depends on the pastry
you use, the ripeness of
the tomatoes and how
thickly they are cut.

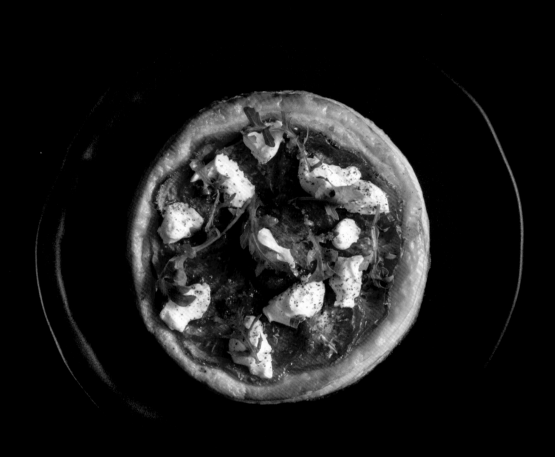

Pizza Pomodoro

Travis Lett

COMPLEXITY: EASY | PREP TIME: 10 MINUTES | COOK TIME: 5 MINUTES
MAKES: ONE 10 TO 12 IN (25 TO 30 CM) PIZZA

INGREDIENTS

semolina flour for
dusting

one 6½ oz (185 g) ball
Gjelina pizza dough
(p. 502), proofed and
stretched to 10 to
12 in (25 to 30 cm) in
diameter

⅓ cup (75 ml)
pomodoro sauce
(p. 464)

½ cup (80 g) confit
tomatoes (p. 455)

2 tbsp (30 ml) best-
quality olive oil

¼ tsp dried oregano,
preferably Sicilian

¼ tsp flaky sea salt

¼ cup (7 g) fresh basil
leaves

crushed red pepper
flakes for serving

METHOD

Place a pizza stone on the middle rack of your oven and pre-heat
the oven to the highest possible setting, at least 500°F (260°C)
for 1 hour. Lightly dust a pizza peel or a rimless baking sheet with
semolina flour. Using your forearms or the backs of your hands,
transfer the stretched round of dough to the prepared peel.

With a large spoon, gently spread the pomodoro sauce evenly across
the dough, leaving a 1-in (2½-cm) border without any sauce. Sprinkle
the tomato confit in areas where there is less sauce. Drizzle with half
of the olive oil and sprinkle with half the oregano and all the sea salt.

Slide the dough onto the pizza stone in the oven and bake, allowing
it to bubble up and rise. Once the rim starts to look pillowy and airy,
use the pizza peel or baking sheet to turn the pizza 180 degrees to
ensure that it browns evenly all over. It's ready when the rim is a deep
golden brown and beginning to char and the bottom of the pizza is
crisp, 4 to 5 minutes in total.

Using the peel or baking sheet, transfer the pizza to a cutting board.
Sprinkle with the remaining oregano and the basil and drizzle the rest
of the olive oil over the top. Slice and serve hot, with crushed red
pepper flakes on the side.

JOSH'S NOTES

Preparation: Make the
pizza dough, pomodoro,
and confit tomatoes in
advance.

Key element: A very,
very hot pre-heated
oven.

Tip: Adjust the cooking
time according to how
hot you can get your
oven.

Pissaladière

Josh Emett

COMPLEXITY: EASY | PREP TIME: 35 MINUTES | COOK TIME: 1 HOUR | SERVES: 8

INGREDIENTS

1 sheet puff pastry cut to 12 x 8 in (30 x 20 cm), defrosted if frozen

2 tbsp plus 2 tsp (40 ml) olive oil

3 onions, finely sliced

2 tbsp (30 ml) sherry vinegar

3½ tbsp (30 g) granulated brown sugar

pinch of sea salt

cracked pepper to taste

⅓ cup (60 g) pitted Kalamata olives, halved lengthwise

few sprigs of thyme, leaves picked

2 white anchovies, cut into ½-in (1-cm) pieces

1 egg yolk

METHOD

Crimp the edges of the puff pastry sheet to raise them slightly to hold in the filling. Place in the fridge until needed.

In a frying pan, heat the olive oil until hot, then add the onion. Cook, stirring often, until caramelized and golden brown, then add the vinegar and brown sugar, sea salt, and cracked pepper. Cook, stirring, until moisture has evaporated and the mix is golden, shiny, and completely caramelized, about 35 minutes. Remove from the heat and allow to cool.

Pre-heat the oven to 400°F (200°C).

Bring out the puff pastry and prick the base gently with a fork. Spread the cooled onion mix evenly across the pastry, leaving a crimped edge of about 1 cm (½ in). Place the olives, thyme leaves, and anchovy randomly around the tart. Glaze the crimped edges with egg yolk. Bake for 20 to 25 minutes until golden brown all over. Rest for 15 minutes and serve at room temperature.

JOSH'S NOTES

Key elements: Make sure the onion has a beautiful dark caramel colour, which will impart the best flavour. Season well – taste as you cook to get it just right.

Tip: The tart should be caramelized and golden brown all over – leave it in the oven for as long as it takes, as oven temperatures often vary.

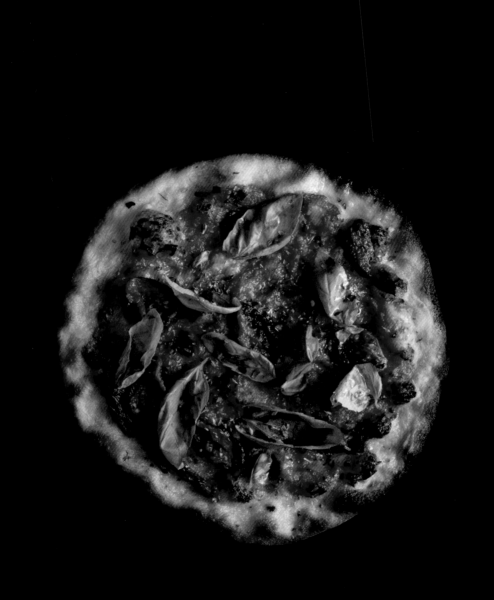

Twice-baked Goat Cheese Soufflé

Carl Koppenhagen

COMPLEXITY: MODERATE | PREP TIME: 35 MINUTES | COOK TIME: 1 HOUR | MAKES: 8

INGREDIENTS

3½ oz/7 tbsp (100 g) unsalted butter, plus extra, softened, to butter ramekins

½ cup (70 g) all-purpose/plain flour

2⅓ cups (560 ml) milk, heated to just simmering

¼ cup (15 g) mixed chopped chervil, chives, and parsley

¼ cup (25 g) grated Grana Padano

9 oz (250 g) soft goat cheese, whipped until smooth

8 eggs, separated

sea salt and freshly ground black pepper

TO SERVE

2 cups plus 1¼ tbsp (500 ml) cream

1 cup (90 g) grated Grana Padano

2 handfuls frisée (curly endive)

½ cup (10 g) flat-leaf parsley leaves

3 tbsp caramelized red onion

¼ cup (60 ml) Dijon vinaigrette

sea salt and freshly ground black pepper

JOSH'S NOTES

Preparation: Add a little flour when buttering the moulds, to prevent sticking.

Key element: Having a strong-flavoured goat cheese will ensure a rich taste.

METHOD

Pre-heat the oven to 330°F (165°C). Thickly butter 8 aluminium ramekins (or teacups) of 1 cup plus 1¼ tablespoon (250 ml) capacity and refrigerate for at least 30 minutes.

In a medium-sized heavy-based saucepan over a medium heat, melt the butter, then add the flour and stir for 2 minutes, until foaming but not coloured. Gradually whisk in the heated milk, then reduce the heat and simmer for 5 to 10 minutes, stirring occasionally, until the sauce has thickened. Remove from the heat, add the herbs, Grana Padano, and goat cheese, and whisk until smooth. Allow to cool for 5 minutes, then beat in the egg yolks and season the mixture well.

Whisk the egg whites to soft peaks. Add one-third of the egg white to the goat cheese mixture and mix thoroughly. Gently fold in the remaining egg white until completely incorporated.

Ladle the soufflé mix into the prepared ramekins and smooth off the tops with a palette knife. Run your thumb around the rim of the moulds to create a clean edge for even rising. Place the ramekins in a baking dish lined with a clean tea towel, then fill the dish with hot, not boiling, water to come two-thirds of the way up the sides of the ramekins. Bake in the oven for 15 to 20 minutes, until puffed and golden. Cool the soufflés until deflated, then run a knife around the inside edge of the ramekins and tip each soufflé into a gratin dish or ovenproof bowl.

When ready to serve, pre-heat the oven to 425°F (220°C). Pour ¼ cup (60 ml) cream and sprinkle about 2 tablespoons Grana Padano over each soufflé, then bake for 10 to 12 minutes until puffed, golden, and bubbling. Serve immediately with a salad of frisée, parsley, and caramelised onion, dressed with Dijon vinaigrette and seasoned well.

"It is imperative that the mixture is seasoned well – it should be bordering on over-seasoned. Once the egg whites are added, they tend to dilute the seasoning. The quantity of this mixture may vary due to egg quality and size, how much the milk reduces while heating or how much your roux is cooked."

– CARL KOPPENHAGEN

Quiche Lorraine

Annie Smithers

COMPLEXITY: MODERATE | PREP TIME: 35 MINUTES, PLUS REFRIGERATION TIME
COOK TIME: 1 HOUR 15 MINUTES | MAKES: ONE 9½ IN (24 CM) QUICHE

INGREDIENTS

PÂTE BRISÉE (PIE PASTRY)

2 cups (240 g) all-purpose/plain flour

pinch of salt

¾ cup plus 1½ sticks (180 g) unsalted butter, cubed

¼ cup (60 ml) cold, sparkling mineral water

QUICHE FILLING

1 small onion, finely diced

oil, for cooking

6 thin slices/rashers of streaky bacon, cut into lardons

1¼ cups (300 ml) cream

3 egg yolks

1 whole egg

salt and freshly ground black pepper

JOSH'S NOTES

Key element: The dough needs to be very cold before you roll it.

Tip: Leave the dough overhanging the sides when blind-baking, then trim it with a bread knife before filling.

Complements: Serve with a crisp, green salad and tomato chutney.

METHOD

To make the pastry, sieve the flour and salt into a mixing bowl. Chop the unsalted butter through the flour. Make a well in the centre and add the sparkling mineral water. Carefully bring the flour mixture in from the outside until the dough comes roughly together. Push the dough outwards with the palm of your hand to roughly blend in the butter – you should be able to see large streaks of butter in the dough. Cut into two pieces, shape each into a disc and wrap in plastic wrap. Refrigerate for 1 hour.

Roll one disc of pastry out to about ⅛ in (2 to 3 mm) thick. Line a 9½ in (24 cm) flan tin with a removable base with the pastry, folding the top edge neatly. Refrigerate for 30 minutes.

Pre-heat the oven to 400°F (200°C). Line the pastry case with baking paper and fill with baking beans. Blind-bake the tart shell for about 18 minutes, then remove the baking beans and return to the oven for about 10 minutes to make sure that the pastry is an even golden colour. Remove from the oven and reduce the oven temperature to 325°F (160°C).

Sweat the onion in a frying pan in a little oil until soft. Add the bacon and cook for another couple of minutes. Drain off any excess oil. Arrange the onion and bacon over the pastry case. Mix the cream, egg yolks, and egg together, then season with salt and black pepper. Pour into the pastry case and put in the oven. Cook for 30 to 40 minutes. The filling will puff up and turn golden brown. Remove from the oven when there is the slightest wobble. Let rest for a minute or two when out of the oven before removing from the tin and serving.

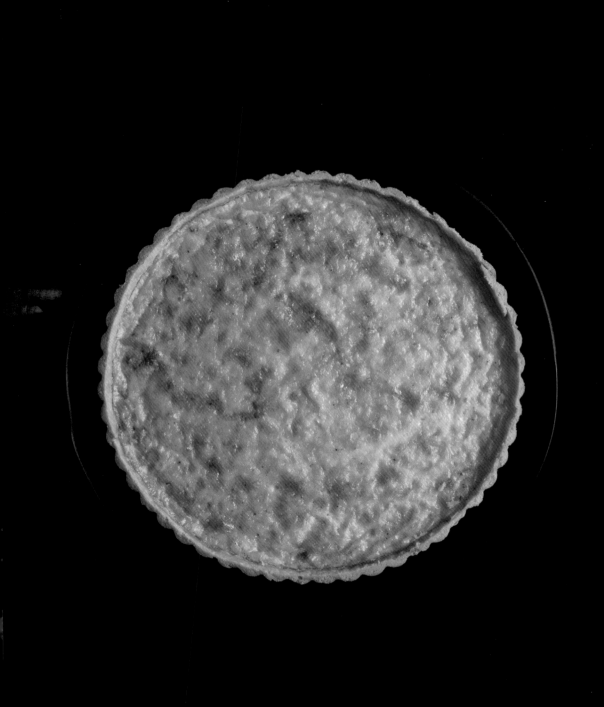

Madeleines

Shannon Bennett

COMPLEXITY: EASY | PREP TIME: 15 MINUTES, PLUS REFRIGERATION TIME
COOK TIME: 6 MINUTES | MAKES: 30

INGREDIENTS

3½ oz/7 tbsp (100 g) cultured butter

½ cup (125 g) superfine/caster sugar

3 eggs

2 cups (250 g) all-purpose/plain flour, plus extra for moulds

1 tsp baking powder

zest and juice of ½ lemon

seeds from 1 vanilla bean

pinch of salt

butter for moulds

METHOD

In a mixing bowl, cream the butter and sugar together until pale. Add the eggs and beat until combined. If the mixture curdles, don't be alarmed. Sift in the flour and baking powder and beat on low speed to combine. Mix in the lemon zest and juice, vanilla bean seeds, and salt. Cover and place in the refrigerator until cold.

Pre-heat the oven to 350°F (180°C).

Brush madeleine moulds with butter and dust with flour. Place a teaspoonful of mixture in each mould. Place in the oven and bake for 5 to 6 minutes, or until golden. Remove from the moulds by carefully tapping the underside.

Serve immediately with a cup of espresso.

———

"Legend has it that this recipe was developed by a peasant girl named Madeleine who lived outside the castle of Commercy in a small village in Lorraine, France. The ruler at the time, Stanislaw Leszcynski, was so taken by the cakes that he made them a part of the royal repertoire. Other flavours to consider are honey, hazelnut, maple syrup, orange, chocolate, or pistachio."

– SHANNON BENNETT

JOSH'S NOTES

Preparation: The dough can be stored in the fridge for up to 2 days prior to baking.

Key element: Butter and flour the tin meticulously so that the madeleines are crispy.

Tip: Use the top shelf of the oven; this ensures they will be a good colour.

Shortbread

Nick Nairn

COMPLEXITY: EASY | PREP TIME: 15 MINUTES | COOK TIME: 15 MINUTES
MAKES: 20 PIECES

INGREDIENTS

9 oz/2¼ sticks (250 g) unsalted butter, at room temperature

1 cup (125 g) powdered sugar/icing sugar

dash of vanilla essence

2 cups (250 g) all-purpose/plain flour, sifted, plus extra for dusting

1 cup (125 g) cornstarch/cornflour, sifted

pinch of salt

superfine/caster sugar to dust

METHOD

Pre-heat the oven to 320°F (160°C). In a stand mixer, mix the butter, powdered/icing sugar, vanilla, and salt on low speed until smooth. Increase the mixer speed to medium and cream the butter mix for 3 to 4 minutes, until it's soft and very pale. You can do this in a bowl with a hand-held mixer, too.

Take the mixer speed back to low and add the sifted flours, mixing only just enough to incorporate the flours. Don't overwork the dough. Finish by hand, bringing the dough together. Then roll out carefully on a floured surface, dusting the roller with a little flour as you go. The lighter your touch, the better the shortbread. Roll the dough to about ½ in (1 cm) thick and cut with a round cutter dipped in flour before each cut. Lightly press with the back of a fork if you want the prong-pattern.

Lay the cookies/biscuits on a very lightly greased baking sheet and bake until light golden brown around the edges, about 15 minutes. As the cookies/biscuits are removed from the oven, dust with superfine/caster sugar – use a palette knife to transfer to a cooling rack and allow to cool before storing.

———————

"Everyone loves these. Light, short, wonderful."

– NICK NAIRN

JOSH'S NOTES

Key element:
Don't over-mix the dough, and cut the shortbreads neatly.

Tip: Flour everything. I used a floured spatula to transfer the cut shortbreads to a tray.

Almond Biscotti

Dorie Greenspan

COMPLEXITY: EASY | PREP TIME: 25 MINUTES
COOK TIME: 30 MINUTES, PLUS COOLING TIME | MAKES: 30

INGREDIENTS

1¾ cups (210 g) all-purpose/plain flour

1½ tsp baking powder

¼ tsp salt

½ cup (75 g) yellow maize meal/cornmeal

1 stick (½ cup/115 g) unsalted butter, at room temperature

1 cup (200 g) sugar

2 large eggs

1½ tsp pure almond extract

¾ cup (85 g) sliced almonds, blanched or unblanched

JOSH'S NOTES

Key element: Even shaping of the logs for the first bake will result in a better shape for the final biscotti.

Tip: Turn the baking sheet 180° halfway through the first cook, to ensure a nice even colour.

METHOD

Centre a rack in the oven and pre-heat to 350°F (180°C). Line a baking sheet with baking parchment or a silicone mat.

Whisk the flour, baking powder, and salt together. Add the maize meal/cornmeal and whisk again. Working with a stand mixer fitted with a paddle attachment, or with a hand mixer in a large bowl, beat the butter and sugar together at medium speed for 3 minutes, until very smooth. Add the eggs and continue to beat, scraping down the bowl as needed, for another 2 minutes, or until the mixture is light, smooth, and creamy. Beat in the almond extract. Reduce the mixer speed to low and add the dry ingredients, mixing just until they are incorporated. You'll have a soft stick-to-your-fingers dough that will ball up around the paddle or beaters. Scrape down the paddle and bowl, toss in the almonds and mix just to blend.

Scrape half the dough onto one half of the baking sheet. Using your fingers and a rubber spatula, work the dough into a log about 12 in (30 cm) long and 1½ in (3½ cm) wide. The log will be more rectangular than domed, and bumpy, rough, and uneven. Form a second log with the remaining dough on the other half of the baking sheet.

Bake for 15 minutes, or until the logs are lightly golden but still soft and springy to the touch. Transfer the baking sheet to a rack and cool the logs on the baking sheet for 30 minutes.

If you turned off the oven, bring it back up to 350°F (180°C). Using a wide metal spatula, transfer the logs to a cutting board and, with a long, serrated knife, trim the ends and cut the logs into slices ¾ in (2 cm) thick. Return the slices to the baking sheet – this time standing them up like a marching band – and slide the sheet back into the oven.

Bake the biscotti for another 15 minutes, or until they are golden and firm. Transfer them to racks and cool to room temperature.

VARIATIONS

- Spiced biscotti: Whisk some spice into the flour mixture – ground cinnamon, ginger, cardamom, or even black pepper.

- Lemon or orange biscotti: Rub the grated zest of 2 lemons or 1 orange into the sugar before beating the butter and sugar together.

Mogador
Macaron

Pierre Hermé

COMPLEXITY: MODERATE | PREP TIME: 1 HOUR, PLUS REFRIGERATION TIME
COOK TIME: 25 MINUTES, PLUS STANDING TIME | MAKES: ABOUT 72 MACARON

INGREDIENTS

MACARON SHELLS

2⅓ cups plus 3½ tsp (300 g) powdered sugar/icing sugar

10½ oz (300 g) ground almonds

4 oz (110 g) liquefied egg whites

1 tsp lemon-yellow liquid food colouring

about ⅛ tsp red liquid food colouring (½ coffee spoon)

4 oz (110 g) 'liquefied' egg whites

¼ cup plus 1 tbsp (75 ml) still mineral water

1⅓ cups (300 g) superfine/caster sugar

MILK CHOCOLATE & PASSIONFRUIT GANACHE

3½ oz/7 tbsp (100 g) 'La Viette' butter (sweet butter from Charentes), at room temperature

1¼ lb (550 g) Valrhona Jivara chocolate, or milk chocolate with 40% cocoa solids

10 passionfruit (for 9 oz/250 g juice)

TO SERVE

cocoa powder

METHOD

Sift together the powdered/icing sugar and ground almonds.

Stir the food colouring into the first measure of liquefied egg whites. Pour them over the mixture of powdered/icing sugar and ground almonds but do not stir.

Place the second portion of liquefied egg whites in the bowl of a stand mixer. Bring the water and sugar up to boil at 244°F (118°C). When the syrup reaches 239°F (115°C), start whisking the second portion of liquefied egg whites to soft peaks.

When the sugar syrup reaches 244°F (118°C), keep the mixer going and pour the syrup over the egg whites. Continue whisking while allowing the meringue to cool down to 122°F (50°C), then fold it into the ground almond-icing sugar mixture. Spoon the batter into a piping bag fitted with a small plain nozzle.

Line several baking trays with baking parchment. Pipe rounds of batter about 1½ in (3½ cm) in diameter onto the trays, spacing them ¾ in (2 cm) apart. Rap the baking trays on a work surface covered with a tea towel. Using a sieve, sprinkle the shells with a light dusting of cocoa powder. Leave the shells to stand for at least 30 minutes until they form a skin.

Pre-heat the oven to 350°F (180°C) fan, then put the trays in the oven. Bake for 12 minutes, quickly opening and shutting the oven door twice during cooking time. Out of the oven, slide the shells on their parchment onto the work surface.

For the ganache, cut the butter into pieces. Chop up the chocolate with a serrated knife. Halve the passionfruit and scoop out the seeds with a teaspoon. Strain the fruit to obtain 9 oz (250 g) juice. Weigh the juice and bring it to the boil.

Partially melt the chopped chocolate in a bowl set over a pan of barely simmering water. One third at a time, pour the hot juice over the chocolate. When the temperature of the mixture reaches 140°F (60°C), add the pieces of butter, a few at a time. Stir to obtain a smooth ganache.

Pour the ganache into a gratin dish and press plastic wrap over the surface of the ganache. Place in the fridge for the ganache to thicken, about 2 hours. When thickened, spoon the ganache into a piping bag fitted with a small plain nozzle. Pipe a generous mound of ganache on to half the shells. Top with the remaining shells.

Store the macaron for 24 hours in the fridge and bring back out 2 hours before serving.

LIQUEFIED EGG WHITES

Separate the whites from the yolks. Weigh out the necessary quantity of egg whites into two bowls. Cover the bowls with plastic wrap. Using the point of a sharp knife, pierce the film with holes. Place the bowls in the fridge. It is best to prepare the egg whites several days in advance, preferably a week, so that they lose their elasticity.

TIPS

Make sure you weigh out 9 oz (250 g) of juice when you strain the fresh passionfruit. You can sometimes find frozen passionfruit juice in delicatessens. Check that it contains no more than 5 per cent sugar.

Milk chocolate brings out every aspect of passionfruit: Its fragrance and its subtle, tangy sweetness. The different flavours blend to create a vibrant harmony and complement one another.

JOSH'S NOTES

Preparation: Make the liquefied egg whites several days in advance; it's a perfect way to use up unused egg whites.

Tip: Rapping the sheets on the work surface will remove bubbles from the mixture and smoothe out any piping imperfections.

Image on p. 302

Millefeuille

à la Baumanière

Jean-André Charial

COMPLEXITY: MODERATE | PREP TIME: 1 HOUR | COOK TIME: 10 MINUTES | MAKES: 6

INGREDIENTS

CREAM FILLING

1 cup plus 2 tsp (250 ml) milk

1 tbsp (15 g) butter

1 vanilla bean

¼ cup (50 g) granulated sugar

2 or 3 egg yolks

¼ cup (25 g) all-purpose/plain flour

generous ¾ cup (200 ml) whipping cream

CARAMEL ICE CREAM

1¼ cups (250 g) granulated sugar

6¾ tbsp (100 ml) cream

8 egg yolks, medium-sized eggs, beaten

½ cup plus 1 tsp (125 ml) condensed milk

PUFF PASTRY RECTANGLES

1 recipe puff pastry (p. 513)

confectioners' sugar for dusting

METHOD

For the cream filling, place the milk, butter, and vanilla bean in a saucepan and bring to the boil over a medium heat. Meanwhile, in a bowl beat together the sugar, egg yolks, and flour. When the milk comes to the boil, add some to the egg mixture, mix well, and return to the saucepan. Bring back to the boil, then remove from the heat and let cool. Whip the cream, fold into the cooled mixture and refrigerate.

For the caramel ice cream, first caramelize the sugar. Place the sugar in a medium-sized pan and heat over a medium heat until the sugar starts to caramelize and turn golden – take care, as it burns easily. When caramelized, deglaze the pan with the cream. Add the beaten egg yolks, then cook as you would a custard. Add the condensed milk and process in an ice cream machine. Freeze until needed.

For the puff pastry rectangles, when the pastry is ready, roll it out again – it should be about ½ in (5 mm) thick. Transfer to baking sheets and bake at 350°F (180°C) for about 10 minutes. Remove from the oven, score into 18 rectangles measuring about 7 x 1¼ in (12 x 3 cm) with a knife, sprinkle with confectioners' sugar and return to the oven until the sugar caramelizes. Cut into the marked rectangles.

Assemble each millefeuille by layering 3 rectangles of puff pastry with 2 layers of cream filling. Serve with the caramel ice cream.

JOSH'S NOTES

Preparation: Make early to allow the filling to set.

Tip: Cook the custard until it's relatively thick, as it will soften it once the cream is added.

King Cake
Galette des Rois

Rachel Khoo

COMPLEXITY: DIFFICULT | PREP TIME: 30 MINUTES, PLUS REFRIGERATION TIME
COOK TIME: 50 MINUTES | MAKES: ONE 11 IN (28 CM) CAKE

INGREDIENTS

12½ oz (350 g) puff
pastry (p. 513)

5 oz (150 g) shelled and
blanched hazelnuts

⅓ cup plus 2 tsp (75 g)
sugar

pinch of salt

3½ oz/7 tbsp (100 g)
very soft butter, plus a
little extra for greasing

1 egg

1 apple, unpeeled,
cored and finely sliced

METHOD

Line the bottom of an 11 in (28 cm) cake tin with baking paper and
butter the sides. Cut the puff pastry in half and roll out one half to
fit the base of the cake tin, trimming away any excess. Roll out the
other half to a rectangle measuring 6 x 14 in (15 x 35 cm) and cut
it in half lengthways.

Line the sides of the cake tin with one of the pastry strips, allowing
a little overlap where the base meets the side. Use your fingertip
to press down the overlap to make sure the pastry seals. Push the
second strip around the bottom of the tin, where the sides and
base join, allowing a little overlap.

Using a sharp knife, cut out triangles from the side to create a crown
shape. Make sure to leave a band of pastry at least 1½ in (3½ cm)
high around the base, as otherwise the hazelnut cream will spill out.
Chill the lined tin in the fridge for 30 minutes.

Toast the hazelnuts in a dry pan until golden. Leave to cool slightly
before blending to a fine powder. Beat together the sugar, hazelnut
powder, salt, and butter until smooth, then incorporate the egg.
Spread the mixture evenly over the base of the pastry. Hide a small
ceramic figure or a clean penny in the pastry cream and cover with
the sliced apple.

Place a baking tray in the oven and pre-heat it to 400°F (200°C).
Put the cake in the oven on the hot tray and reduce the temperature
to 350°F (180°C). Bake for 45 minutes, or until golden brown.
If the pastry browns too quickly, cover it with some greased foil.

JOSH'S NOTES

Key element: Rest the
pastry properly, work
fast and be gentle when
lining the tin.

Tip: Roll out the pastry
to be long enough
to circle the inside of
your tin.

Baklava

Claudia Roden

COMPLEXITY: MODERATE I PREP TIME: 45 MINUTES
COOK TIME: 45 MINUTES, PLUS COOLING TIME I MAKES: ABOUT 50 PIECES

INGREDIENTS

SYRUP

2¼ cups (500 g) sugar

1¼ cups (300 ml) water

2 tbsp (30 ml) lemon juice

2 tbsp (30 ml) orange blossom or rose water

BAKLAVA

18 oz (500 g) phyllo/filo pastry, in large sheets

¾ cup/1½ sticks (180 g) unsalted butter, melted

13 oz (375 g) pistachio nuts, walnuts, or almonds, ground or finely chopped

JOSH'S NOTES

Preparation: It takes time to make the layers, but the effort is worth it.

Key element: Good-quality pistachios make all the difference.

Tip: Chop the nuts quite small – it will make it easier to portion the pastry afterwards.

METHOD

Pre-heat the oven to 350°F (180°C).

Prepare the syrup first. In a pan over a medium heat, dissolve the sugar in the water with the lemon juice, and simmer a few minutes until it thickens enough to coat a spoon. Add the orange blossom or rose water and simmer for half a minute. Allow to cool, then chill in the refrigerator.

One at a time, lay half the sheets of filo in a greased baking tray a little smaller than the sheets of filo, brushing each with melted butter and letting the edges come up the sides of the tray or overhang.

Spread the nuts of your choice evenly over the sheets. Cover with the remaining sheets, brushing each, including the top one, with melted butter. Using a sharp knife, cut parallel lines 1½ to 2 in (4 to 5 cm) apart diagonally into diamond shapes, right through to the bottom.

Bake the baklava for 30 to 45 minutes, or until it is puffed up and golden. Remove from the oven and pour the cold syrup over the hot baklava along the slashed lines. If you prefer to use less, pour on three-quarters or half the amount and let people help themselves to more if they wish to. Leave to cool.

When cold and ready to serve, cut the pieces of pastry out again and lift them out one by one onto a serving dish, or turn the whole pastry out (by turning it upside down onto a large sheet and then turning it over again on the serving dish) and cut out again along the original lines.

VARIATIONS

- In Iraq and Iran they flavour the almond with 1 tablespoon ground cardamom.

- In Greece they stir a spoonful or two of honey into the syrup.

- When using walnuts you can mix 2 teaspoons cinnamon into the filling.

Image on p. 364

Portuguese Custard Tarts
Pastéis de Nata
Nuno Mendes

COMPLEXITY: MODERATE | PREP TIME: 45 MINUTES | COOK TIME: 30 MINUTES | MAKES: 6

INGREDIENTS

melted butter, for greasing

1 x 11¼ oz (320 g) sheet all-butter puff pastry, about ⅛ in (2 to 3 mm) thick

CUSTARD

1 cup plus 2 tsp (250 ml) whole milk

1 stick cinnamon

a few strips of lemon zest

1½ tbsp (20 g) unsalted butter

2 tbsp all-purpose/ plain white flour

1 tsp cornstarch/ cornflour

2 egg yolks

SUGAR SYRUP

1 cup (225 g) superfine/ caster sugar

1 stick cinnamon

a few strips of lemon zest

TO SERVE

sugar and ground cinnamon, for dusting

JOSH'S NOTES

Tip: Keep the pastry thin, and avoid stretching it too much when placing in the tins, to avoid shrinkage during cooking.

METHOD

Brush 6 individual muffin tins generously with melted butter, then chill them in the fridge. (If you don't have individual tins, use half of a 12-hole muffin tin.)

Make sure the pastry is in a large rectangle about ⅛ (2 to 3 mm) thick, rolling it out a little if necessary, then roll it up lengthways into a tight sausage shape about 2 in (5 cm) in diameter. Slice this into 6 discs ½ to ¾ in (1 to 2 cm) thick (any leftover pastry can be frozen to use another day). Press the discs into the tins with your fingers, stretching or rolling them out to fit, making sure they come to just below the top of the tins. Chill them while you make the custard.

To make the custard, heat ½ cup plus 2 tablespoons (150 ml) of the milk in a pan over a medium heat together with the cinnamon, lemon zest, and half the butter, bringing it to just below boiling point. Remove from the heat and leave to infuse for 10 minutes. Remove the cinnamon and lemon zest.

In a bowl, mix the flour and cornstarch/cornflour to a thin paste with the remaining milk, adding the milk gradually to prevent lumps forming. Pour the warm infused milk over the paste, stirring well, then pour the mixture back into the pan. Cook, stirring gently, over a low heat for a few minutes, or until it thickens to a heavy/ double cream consistency. Whisk in the remaining butter and remove from the heat.

To make the sugar syrup, put the ingredients in a pan with 5 tablespoons (75 ml) water and cook over a medium heat for 5 minutes, until the sugar dissolves. Cook over a low heat until you have a light brown, fragrant caramel, swirling the pan occasionally.

Carefully add 5 tablespoons (75 ml) water and return the pan to a gentle heat to dissolve any solid caramel, then strain it into a heatproof bowl. Pour half the syrup into the custard and whisk well. (The leftover syrup will keep in the fridge in an airtight container for 4 weeks.)

Continued overleaf

Portuguese Custard Tarts cont.

Pre-heat the oven to its highest setting and put a baking sheet on the top shelf. Just before cooking the tarts, pour the custard into a measuring jug and stir in the egg yolks. Add a splash of milk to bring the quantity up to 1¼ cups (300 ml), if necessary. Pour the custard into the pastry-lined muffin tins and bake on the hot baking sheet for 9 to 13 minutes, or until the tops are quite dark, rotating them if necessary to make sure they colour evenly.

Brush the tarts with a little of the remaining sugar syrup, then leave to cool slightly in the tins before removing and cooling on a wire rack. The custard will continue to set as it cools, but should still be creamy and quite soft in the centre. Sprinkle with sugar and cinnamon just before serving, as we do in Portugal.

"When you mention Portuguese food, most people think of *pastéis de nata*, our glorious custard tarts. They became popular in the mid-nineteenth century when monks at the Mosteiro dos Jerónimos in Belém began selling them to help make a living. The filling here has a soft scent of citrus and should be really runny – just perfect for small boys with coffee spoons."

– NUNO MENDES

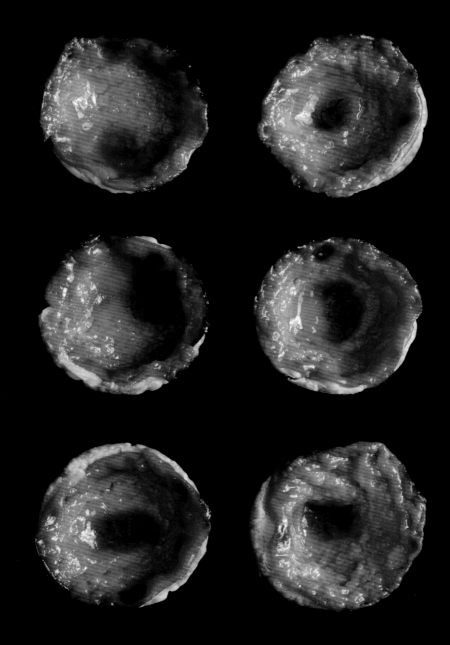

French Custard Mini Cakes
Canelés

Pascal Aussignac

COMPLEXITY: DIFFICULT | PREP TIME: 25 MINUTES, PLUS REFRIGERATION TIME
COOK TIME: 1 HOUR | MAKES: 12

INGREDIENTS

2 cups plus 1¼ tbsp
(500 ml) whole milk

seeds from 2 vanilla
beans

3½ tbsp (50 g) unsalted
butter, plus extra for
greasing

2 large free-range eggs

2 egg yolks

2 cups (250 g)
powdered sugar/icing
sugar

4 tbsp (60 ml) brown
rum (I use Negrita Dark)

1 cup (100 g) soft/pastry
flour (type 45)

JOSH'S NOTES

Preparation: Plan ahead
– the batter should be
made 2 days in advance
for best results.

Key element: Prepare
the moulds properly;
if you want to make
perfect canelés, use
beeswax.

Tip: Never wash copper
moulds – wipe them
with a tea towel or put
them back in the oven
for a few minutes. If you
treat them with care,
they will last a lifetime.

METHOD

Place the milk in a saucepan along with the seeds scraped from the
vanilla beans. Over a medium heat, bring just to boiling point then
mix in the butter, stirring until it has melted. Remove from the heat
and leave to cool.

In a bowl, beat together the eggs, egg yolks, powdered/icing
sugar, rum, and flour to a thick batter (this can be done in a food
processor). Strain the buttery milk into the bowl and beat together
until smooth. Cover and chill in the fridge for 2 days, to maximize
the flavour.

When ready to bake, pre-heat the oven to 410°F (210°C) or
convection oven to 356°F (180°C). Brush the inside of the moulds
with butter; you can also put a little unscented wax on the bottom to
help get the *canelés* crusty. Place the moulds on a baking sheet to
hold them steady, then pour in the chilled batter almost to the top.

For large moulds (2¼ in/5½ cm) bake for 10 minutes, then reduce the
temperature to 350°F (180°C) and bake for up to 40 to 50 minutes
more. For small moulds (1⅜ in/3½ cm) bake for 10 minutes then
reduce oven as above and bake for up to 30 minutes. Carefully, turn
them out onto a rack and leave to cool down.

They are eaten at room temperature – they should be crusty outside
and gooey inside.

"These famous light-as-a-feather cakes from Bordeaux are
traditionally baked in ridged copper moulds, which you buy from
specialist kitchenware suppliers. But shape apart, the mixture rises
nicely in dariole or brioche moulds or muffin tins; for the best results,
let the mixture mature for two days in your fridge before baking."

– PASCAL AUSSIGNAC

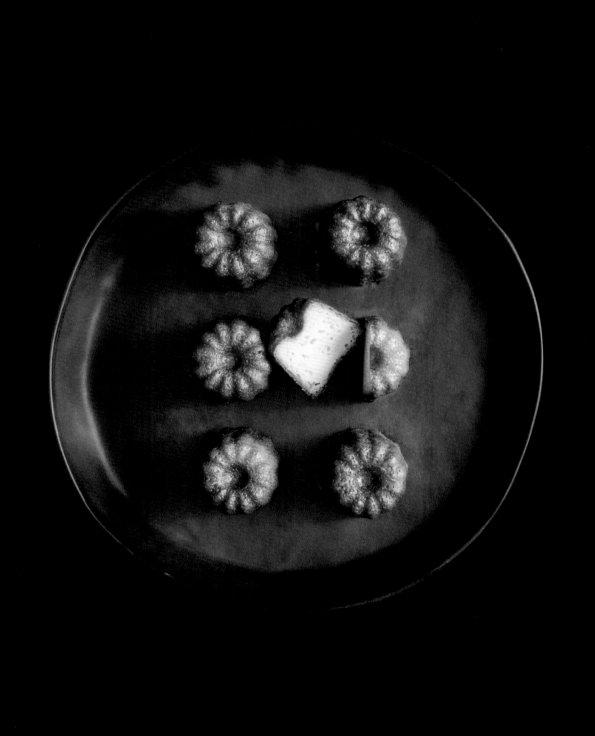

Sticky Sticky Buns

Joanne Chang

COMPLEXITY: MODERATE | PREP TIME: 1 HOUR, PLUS PROVING TIME
COOK TIME: 45 MINUTES | MAKES: 8

INGREDIENTS

GOO

¾ cup (1½ sticks/170 g) unsalted butter

1½ cups (350 g) light brown sugar

⅓ cup (110 g) honey

⅓ cup (80 ml) cream

⅓ cup (80 ml) water

¼ tsp salt

BUNS

1 recipe brioche dough (see opposite)

all-purpose/plain flour, for rolling out

¼ cup (60 g) light brown sugar

¼ cup (50 g) granulated sugar

⅛ tsp ground cinnamon

1 cup (100 g) pecan halves, toasted and chopped

JOSH'S NOTES

Preparation: Make the brioche dough in advance.

Key element: Allow enough time for the goo to cool.

Tips: If the goo has set when you come to turn the buns out, heat the tin slightly over a low heat to melt. The reserved dough will keep in the refrigerator for up to 1 week, or in the freezer for up to 2 months.

METHOD

To make the goo, melt the butter in a medium-sized saucepan over a medium heat, then whisk the brown sugar until dissolved. Remove the pan from the heat and whisk in the honey, cream, water, and salt. Let cool to room temperature before using, about 30 minutes. Goo can be made up to 2 weeks in advance and stored in an airtight container in the refrigerator.

Line a baking sheet with non-stick baking paper. Divide the brioche dough in half, reserving the other half for another use. On a floured work surface, roll the dough into a tall rectangle, about 12 x 16 in (30 x 40 cm) and ¼ in (5 mm) thick. It will have the consistency of cold, damp Play-Doh and should be fairly easy to roll out.

In a small bowl, mix together both sugars, the ground cinnamon, and half the chopped pecans. Sprinkle this mixture evenly over the entire surface of the brioche rectangle.

Starting from the top (short edge) of the rectangle and working your way down, roll dough over on itself, tightly, like a jelly/jam roll, until the entire sheet is rolled up. Trim both edges of the brioche roll slightly to even out the ends. Using a bench scraper or chef's knife, cut the roll into 8 equal pieces. (At this point, the unbaked buns can be tightly wrapped and frozen for up to 1 week. When ready to bake, remove the buns from freezer. Leaving them wrapped, let them defrost in the refrigerator overnight, or at room temperature for 2 to 3 hours; then proceed as below.)

Pour the prepared goo into a 9 x 13 in (23 x 33 cm) baking pan/tin and sprinkle the remaining pecans evenly over goo. Place the buns in the pan, evenly spaced and laying them on a cut side. Cover tin with plastic wrap and let the buns prove at warm room temperature for about 2 hours, until the dough is puffy, pillowy, and soft and the buns are touching each other.

Heat the oven to 350°F (180°C) and position a rack in the middle of the oven. Bake the buns for 35 to 45 minutes, until golden brown. Remove from the oven and let cool for 20 to 30 minutes in the tin. One at a time, invert the buns onto a serving platter and spoon any extra goo and pecans on top. Serve warm – best served right away, or within 4 hours of baking.

Brioche Dough

COMPLEXITY: EASY | PREP TIME: ABOUT 20 MINUTES, PLUS PROVING TIME
MAKES: ENOUGH FOR 16 STICKY STICKY BUNS

Combine the flour, bread flour, yeast, sugar, salt, water, and 5 eggs in the bowl of a stand mixer fitted with a dough hook attachment. Mix on low speed until all of the ingredients come together, about 3 to 4 minutes. Add up to an additional ½ cup (70 g) as needed. Scrape the bowl if necessary to ensure the flour is incorporated into the wet ingredients. Mix on low speed for another 3 to 4 minutes until the mixture is very stiff.

Add the butter to the flour mixture piece by piece, and continue mixing on low speed until the butter is completely blended into the dough, about 10 minutes. If necessary, stop the mixer occasionally, scrape the sides of the bowl and break the dough up with your hands.

Once the butter is completely incorporated into the dough, mix on medium speed for another 15 minutes, until the dough becomes sticky, soft, and somewhat shiny. Turn the mixer to medium-high speed for about 1 minute. You should hear the dough make a slap-slap-slap sound as it hits the sides of the bowl. Test the dough by pulling at it – it should stretch a bit and have a little give. If it seems wet and loose and more like a batter than a dough, add a few tablespoons of flour and mix until it comes together. If it breaks off into pieces when you pull at it, continue to mix it on medium speed for another 2 to 3 minutes, until it develops more strength and stretches when you grab it. You should be able to gather it all together and pick it up as one piece when it's ready.

Place the dough in a large bowl or plastic container and cover with plastic wrap – the plastic wrap should be directly on top of the dough, touching it. Let the dough prove (i.e., grow and develop flavour) in the refrigerator for at least 6 hours, or overnight.

INGREDIENTS CONT.

BRIOCHE DOUGH

2½ cups (300 g) all-purpose/plain flour, plus and additional ½ cup (70 g) as needed

2½ cups (325 g) high-gluten bread flour

3¼ tsp active dry yeast (or 28 g fresh cake yeast)

⅓ cup plus 1 tbsp (90 g) superfine/caster sugar

1 tbsp salt

⅔ cup (160 ml) cold water

5 large eggs, plus 1 egg for egg wash

2¾ sticks (310 g) unsalted butter at room temperature, cut into 10 to 12 pieces

Image on p. 365

INGREDIENTS

3 cups plus 2 tbsp (472 g) strong/bread flour

2 tbsp kosher/flaky salt

about 1⅓ cups (313 g/ml) water, very cold

26 tbsp/3¼ sticks (365 g) unsalted butter (84% butterfat), softened

1½ tsp instant dried yeast (preferably SAF Gold Label) [1]

non-stick cooking spray as needed

all-purpose/plain flour (for dusting) as needed

about 1¾ cups (360 g) granulated sugar

Dominique's

Kouign Amanns

DKAs

Dominique Ansel

COMPLEXITY: DIFFICULT | PREP TIME: 3 HOURS, PLUS PROOFING
COOK TIME: 30 MINUTES | MAKES: 10 TO 12

METHOD

MAKE DOUGH

Combine the strong/bread flour, salt, water, 1 tablespoon (15 g) butter, and the yeast in a stand mixer fitted with a dough hook. Mix on low speed for 2 minutes to combine. Increase the speed to medium-high and beat for 10 minutes. When finished, the dough will be smooth and slightly tacky and will have full gluten development. Test by stretching it – the dough will have some elasticity.

Lightly grease a medium-sized bowl with non-stick cooking spray and transfer the dough to the bowl. Cover loosely with plastic wrap and prove at room temperature until doubled in size, about 1 hour.

Punch down the dough by folding the edges into the centre, releasing as much of the gas as possible, and turn it out onto a large sheet of plastic wrap. Using your palms, press it to form a 10-in (25-cm) square. Wrap it tightly in the plastic wrap and place in the freezer for 15 minutes. Flip the dough and return it to the freezer for another 15 minutes so that it chills evenly.

MAKE BUTTER BLOCK

While the dough is chilling, draw a 7-in (18-cm) square on a piece of parchment paper with a pencil. Flip the parchment over so that the butter won't come in contact with the pencil marks. Place the remaining 25 tablespoons (350 g) butter in the centre of the square and spread it evenly with an offset spatula to fill the square. Refrigerate the butter until firm but still pliable, about 20 minutes.[2]

Remove the butter from the refrigerator. It should still be soft enough to bend slightly without cracking. If it is too firm, lightly beat it with a rolling pin on a lightly floured work surface until it becomes pliable. Make sure to press the butter back to its original 7-in (18-cm) square after working it.

[1] Instant yeast is often used for doughs with higher sugar content, because this yeast needs less water to react and sugar tends to pull water from the dough. You can substitute the same quantity of active dry yeast, but may get a denser final product.

[2] Whenever you are laminating dough, it is important that the consistency and temperature of the dough matches that of the butter.

Continued overleaf

Dominique's Kouign Amanns cont.

SPECIAL TOOLS

stand mixer with dough hook attachment

ruler

large offset spatula

silicone baking mat

10 to 12 round ring moulds, 2 in (7 cm) in diameter

stainless steel tongs

ROLL DOUGH

Remove the dough from the freezer; make sure it is very cold throughout. Place the dough on a lightly floured work surface. Arrange the butter block in the centre of the dough so it looks like a diamond in the centre of the square (rotated 45 degrees, with the corners of the butter facing the centre of the dough sides). Pull the corners of the dough up and over to the centre of the butter block. Pinch the seams of the dough together to seal the butter inside. You should have a square slightly larger than the butter block.

With a rolling pin, using steady, even pressure, roll the dough out from the centre so that it triples in length. This will take several passes. Use extra flour to dust the work surface to ensure that nothing sticks. When finished, you should have a rectangle about 24 x 10 in (60 x 25 cm) and ¼ in (5 mm) thick.[3]

MAKE FIRST THREE FOLDS

Place the dough so that the longer sides run left to right. From the right side fold one-third of the dough onto itself, keeping the edges lined up with each other. From the left side fold the remaining one-third of the dough on top of the side that has already been folded. Line up all the edges so that you are left with an even rectangle. The dough is being folded as if it were a piece of paper going into an envelope; this is called a 'letter fold'. Do not rest the dough and immediately move on to the next fold.[4]

Starting with the seam of the dough on the right, roll out the dough, vertically from top to bottom, to a rectangle about 24 x 10 in (60 x 25 cm) and ¼ in (5 mm) thick. Repeat the letter fold.

Immediately roll out the dough again to a rectangle about 24 x 10 in (60 x 25 cm) and ¼ in (5 mm) thick, exactly as in the previous step. Repeat the letter fold. Wrap the dough in plastic wrap and refrigerate for 30 to 40 minutes to rest.

MAKE FOURTH FOLD

Sprinkle sugar in a thin, even layer on the work surface (as if you were flouring the work surface, but using sugar instead). Lay out the dough on the sugar. Starting with the seam of the dough on the right, roll out the dough once more, vertically from top to bottom, to a rectangle about 24 by 10 in (60 x 25 cm) and ¼ in (5 mm) thick. Sprinkle a thin, even layer of sugar on the top. Repeat the letter fold.[5]

[3] Keeping the dough's rectangular shape is very important at this point to ensure even layers throughout the process. You will need a large area to roll out the dough.

[4] When making the DKA, speed is very important. Work the dough as quickly as possible, otherwise it will soften and the butter will push out of the seams. This results in a dense and doughy product.

[5] Work quickly when you add the sugar, as it will start to draw out moisture from the dough and make the surface wet.

Sprinkle another thin, even layer of sugar on the work surface. Place the dough on the sugar. Starting with the seam on the right, roll out the dough one final time to a rectangle about 24 x 10 in (60 x 25 cm) and ¼ in (5 mm) thick. Sprinkle another thin layer of sugar on top.

Using a chef's knife, cut the dough into 4-in (10-cm) squares. Each square should weigh about 3½ ounces (100 g). Sprinkle a little bit more sugar on the work surface. Fold in the corners of each square to meet at the centre, pushing the centre down firmly. Repeat with the new corners that were formed, again pushing down firmly in the centre.

Line a baking sheet with a silicone baking mat. Spray lightly with non-stick spray and sprinkle with enough granulated sugar to just lightly coat it. Place the ring moulds 4 in (10 cm) apart on the baking sheet.

Place a square of dough in the centre of each ring. The dough will hang over the edges of the mould. Fold the excess dough into the centre of the DKA and press down firmly. Proof at room temperature, 15 to 20 minutes.

While the DKAs are proofing, place a rack in the centre of the oven and pre-heat the oven to 365°F (185°C) for conventional or 340°F (170°C) for convection ovens.

Bake the DKAs on the centre rack for 15 minutes. Rotate the pan 180 degrees and bake for 15 minutes more. The DKAs are finished when they turn golden brown and have about doubled in size.

Remove from the oven. Using a pair of stainless-steel tongs, unmould the DKAs onto a baking tray while still hot: Grab the metal rings with the tongs and flip the DKAs over so that the flat side is up. Remove the rings. Let the DKAs cool completely, still inverted.

Enjoy at room temperature. If you are looking for more adventure, slice a DKA in half horizontally and add a scoop of ice cream to make an ice cream sandwich. DKAs should be consumed within 6 hours of baking.

"I love making this recipe . . . because it can only be eaten fresh and will change your life when you do."

– DOMINIQUE ANSEL

Ginger Loaf
Best Gingerbread in the World

Al Brown

COMPLEXITY: EASY | PREP TIME: 25 MINUTES | COOK TIME: 1 HOUR 10 MINUTES | MAKES: 1 LARGE LOAF OR 2 SMALL

INGREDIENTS

2½ cups (300 g) all-purpose/plain flour

1 cup (200 g) brown sugar

1 tsp baking soda

1 tsp baking powder

1½ tbsp ground ginger

½ tsp mixed spice

½ tsp grated nutmeg

1 tsp ground cinnamon

12 oz (335 g) cane sugar syrup/golden syrup

1 cup/2 sticks (225 g) butter, cut into rough dice, plus extra for greasing

2 eggs, lightly beaten

1 cup plus 2 tsp (250 ml) milk

METHOD

Pre-heat your oven to 300°F (150°C). Grease 2 standard loaf tins (or 1 large one) with butter and line with baking paper.

Into a large bowl, sift the flour, brown sugar, baking soda, baking powder, ginger, mixed spice, nutmeg, and cinnamon. Whisk to combine.

Place the cane sugar syrup/golden syrup and butter in a small saucepan and melt over a low heat.

Add the cane sugar syrup/golden syrup and butter mix, followed by the lightly beaten eggs and milk, to the spiced flour. Whisk to combine, then pour into your prepared loaf tin(s).

Bake for 1 hour 10 minutes, or until a skewer inserted into the centre comes out clean. If you're making 1 large loaf, your cooking time will definitely go up.

Remove from the oven and let cool in the tin for 30 minutes before turning out.

Serve warm or cold, slathered in butter!

———————

"This recipe is simply a knockout. It gets made in our family at least once a month. Super-easy to make, it's a recipe that falls into that 'fail-safe' category. The ginger loaf is incredibly moist, freezes well and is generally served with a lick of butter and a cuppa tea."

– AL BROWN

JOSH'S NOTES

Key element: Rest the loaf before demoulding.

Tip: Using a darker baking pan/tin gives you a darker, more even colour around the outside.

Complements: Definitely butter, and a little salt.

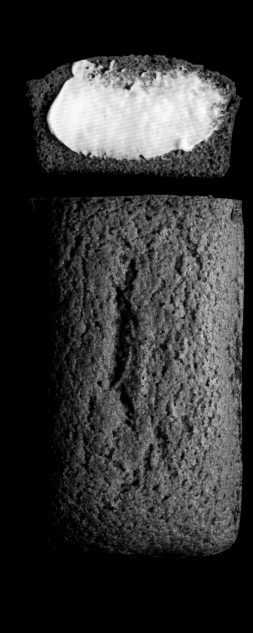

Carrot Cake

Ron Paprocki

COMPLEXITY: EASY | PREP TIME: 30 MINUTES
COOK TIME: 50 MINUTES, PLUS COOLING TIME | MAKES: ONE 12 X 8 IN (30 X 20 CM) CAKE

INGREDIENTS

CARROT CAKE

2½ cups (500 g) sugar

1⅓ cups plus 2¼ tsp (340 g) vegetable oil

9 oz (250 g) eggs

3 cups (375 g) strong/ bread flour (T55)

1 tbsp baking soda

1 tbsp baking powder

2 tsp ground cinnamon

¼ tbsp salt

18 oz (500 g) finely grated carrots

cooking spray

CREAM CHEESE FROSTING

1⅓ cups/2⅔ sticks (300 g) butter

8 oz (225 g) Philadelphia cream cheese

2 cups plus 1½ tbsp (300 g) powdered sugar/ icing sugar

seeds from 1 vanilla bean

METHOD

Pre-heat the oven to 350°C (180°C). In a large bowl, mix the sugar, oil, and eggs to a smooth paste. Sift the dry ingredients together and add to the paste, stirring to combine. Add the grated carrot and fold through until combined.

Line a 12 x 8 in (30 x 20 cm) square cake tin with baking paper, and spray the edges with cooking spray. Place on the middle shelf and bake for 50 minutes, or until a skewer inserted into the centre comes out clean. Leave for 10 to 15 minutes before removing from the tin. Leave to cool.

For the cream cheese frosting, beat the butter until soft and creamy, then add the cream cheese and vanilla bean seeds, and beat to combine. Add the powdered/icing sugar and continue to beat until smooth.

When the cake is cool, ice and cut.

JOSH'S NOTES

Key element: Make sure the butter for the frosting is soft, and all the ingredients are the same temperature.

Tip: Smooth the icing on the top of the cake with a hot palette knife.

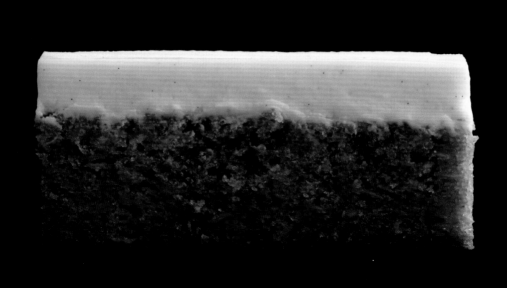

Traditional Christmas Cake

Charmaine Solomon

COMPLEXITY: DIFFICULT | PREP TIME: 3 HOURS
COOK TIME: 2 HOURS 30 MINUTES, PLUS COOLING TIME | MAKES: ONE 10 IN (25 CM) CAKE

INGREDIENTS

CAKE

9 oz (250 g) raisins, chopped

13½ oz (385 g) golden raisins/sultanas, chopped

9 oz (250 g) mixed glacé fruit such as pineapple, apricot, and quince (avoid using fig), chopped

9 oz (250 g) preserved ginger, chopped

18 oz (500 g) chow chow preserves (available at Asian grocery stores, or substitute with melon jelly/jam or ginger marmalade)

4½ oz (120 g) mixed peel, chopped

9 oz (250 g) glacé cherries, halved

9 oz (250 g) raw cashews or blanched almonds, finely chopped

½ cup plus 1 tsp (125 ml) brandy, plus 1 to 2 tbsp (15 to 30 ml) extra if desired

13 oz/3⅓ sticks (375 g) butter

2¼ cups (500 g) superfine/caster sugar

12 egg yolks (separately reserve 6 egg whites plus 1 egg white for almond paste)

2 tsp finely grated lemon zest

METHOD

Line a 10 in (25 cm) round or square cake tin with three layers of brown paper, then one layer of baking paper liberally brushed with melted butter. To insulate the tin even more, wrap the outside with a sheet of newspaper folded into three and secure it with kitchen string.

Combine the raisins, golden raisins/sultanas, mixed glacé fruit, preserved ginger, chow chow preserves, mixed peel, glacé cherries, and cashews in a large bowl. Pour the brandy over and set aside. (This step can be done the day before, allowing the fruit more time to soak in the brandy, if desired.)

Pre-heat the oven to 265°F (130°C). Cream together the butter and sugar until light and fluffy. Add the egg yolks, one at a time, beating well after each addition. Add the lemon zest, spices, vanilla and almond extracts, rose water, and honey, and mix well. Add the semolina and beat until well combined.

Transfer the mixture to a large bowl and use your hands to mix in the fruit until thoroughly combined — it's much easier than a spoon and professional pastry cooks do it this way.

In a separate bowl, beat the reserved egg whites until stiff peaks form, then fold through the fruit mixture until just combined. Pour into the prepared cake tin and bake for 2 hours 15 minutes to 2 hours 30 minutes, covering the cake with foil after the first hour to prevent over-browning. The cake will be very rich and moist when done. If you prefer a darker and drier result, bake for 4 hours 30 minutes to 5 hours — it will not be dry, but certainly firmer than if you cook for a shorter time.

Allow to cool completely, preferably overnight, then remove the paper and wrap the cake in foil. A tablespoon or two of brandy may be sprinkled over the cake just before wrapping. If desired, ice the cake with the almond paste. This cake can be stored in an airtight container for one year or longer.

To make the almond paste, mix together the almond meal and powdered/icing sugar in a large bowl. Add the egg, brandy, sherry, and almond extract, if using, then knead until the mixture holds together. Roll out half the almond paste on a work surface dusted with powdered/icing sugar and cut to fit the top of the cake. Brush the cake with egg white, then place the almond paste on top and press lightly with a rolling pin. Roll the remaining almond paste into a strip to fit around the side of the cake.

INGREDIENTS CONT.

CAKE CONT.

1½ tsp ground cardamom

1 tsp ground cinnamon

1 tsp freshly grated nutmeg

¾ tsp ground cloves

2 tbsp (30 ml) natural vanilla extract

1 tbsp (15 ml) natural almond extract

2 tbsp (30 ml) rose water, or to taste

1 tbsp honey

9 oz (250 g) fine semolina

6 egg whites (reserved previously)

ALMOND PASTE

2½ cups (250 g) almond meal

4 cups (500 g) powdered sugar/icing sugar, sifted, plus extra for dusting

1 small egg, beaten

1 tbsp (15 ml) brandy

1 tbsp (15 ml) sherry

½ tsp natural almond extract (optional)

1 egg white (reserved previously), beaten, for brushing

Black Forest Gateau

Harald Wohlfahrt

COMPLEXITY: MODERATE | PREP TIME: 1 HOUR 30 MINUTES | COOK TIME: 25 MINUTES
MAKES: ONE 10 IN (26 CM) CAKE

INGREDIENTS

SPONGE CAKE BASE

5 eggs

¾ cup plus 2 tbsp (175 g) sugar

1 cup (125 g) all-purpose/plain flour

2 tsp baking powder

1¾ oz (50 g) cornstarch/cornflour

2¾ tbsp unsweetened cocoa

2 tsp vanilla sugar

CHERRY FILLING

12½ oz (350 g) bottled sour cherries

1 oz (30 g) food starch

2 tbsp plus 1 tsp sugar

2 tbsp (30 ml) cherry brandy

CREAM FILLING

3⅓ cups (800 ml) cream

2 tbsp plus 1¼ tsp sugar

2 tsp vanilla sugar

7 oz (200 g) cream stiffener (available in specialist cookery shops)

DECORATION

1¾ oz (50 g) drained sour cherries

3½ oz (100 g) chocolate flakes

METHOD

SPONGE CAKE BASE

Separate the eggs. In a stand mixer fitted with a whisk attachment, beat the egg whites with half the sugar until stiff. In a separate bowl, beat the yolks with the remaining sugar until creamy. Add the yolk mix to the whites and mix to combine. Mix the flour with the baking powder, cornstarch/cornflour, and cocoa and sift on top of the egg mix. Add the vanilla sugar and mix carefully with a large spoon. Pre-heat the oven to 350°F (180°C). Line a springform tin approx. 10 in (26 cm) in diameter with baking paper. Pour the dough in and smooth the top. Bake for 25 minutes. Cover a flat work surface with baking paper. Remove the tin from the oven and flip it over onto the baking paper. Open and remove the tin, and let the cake cool. Don't remove the baking paper from the cake bottom.

CHERRY FILLING

Drain the liquid from the cherries into a bowl, and set 1 cup plus 2 teaspoons (250 ml) of the liquid aside. In a small bowl, mix the food starch with the sugar and 4 tablespoons (60 ml) of the reserved cherry liquid. Put the rest of the reserved cherry liquid into a pot and bring to the boil, then remove from the heat. Add the starch mixture, stir in and bring to the boil again. Remove from the heat, add the drained cherries and the brandy and let cool.

CREAM FILLING

Mix the cream with the sugar, vanilla sugar, and cream stiffener. Because it's a lot of cream, split into two parts and beat each until very stiff.

ASSEMBLY

Carefully remove the baking paper from the cake bottom. With a large, sharp knife, cut the cake horizontally into three pieces. Place the bottom piece of cake on a platter. (You can use the springform ring to help stack the cake.) Spread half the cherry filling on the bottom piece of cake. Top with one-quarter of the cream filling and smooth out until level. Add the middle piece of cake and press lightly. Add the remaining cherry filling and another quarter of cream filling, and smooth out until level. Add the top piece of cake and press lightly. Put 3 tablespoons of the cream filling into a piping bag and set aside. Cover the entire cake with the remaining cream filling. Decorate with the cream from the piping bag, cherries, and chocolate flakes.

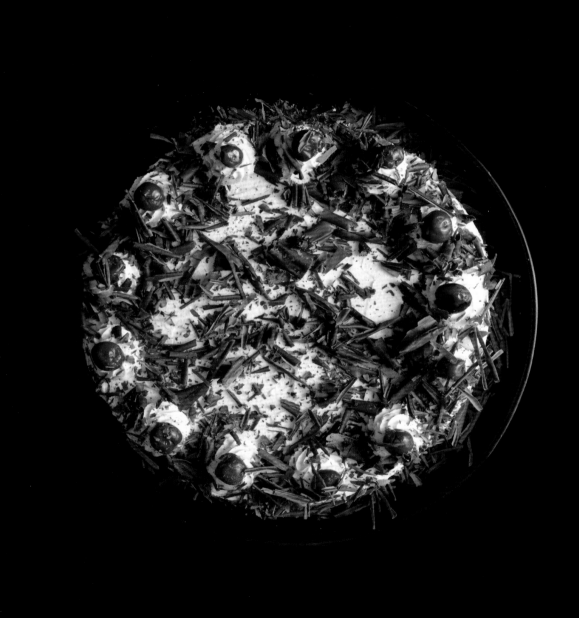

Easy Vanilla Cake

Ruth Reichl

COMPLEXITY: EASY | PREP TIME: 15 MINUTES | COOK TIME: 45 MINUTES
MAKES: ONE 9 IN (23 CM) CAKE

INGREDIENTS

1 cup/ 2 sticks (225 g) unsalted butter, at room temperature, plus extra for the tin

1 cup (200 g) sugar

3 eggs

2¼ cups (280 g) all-purpose/plain flour, plus extra for the tin

1 tsp baking soda

2 tsp baking powder

1 tsp salt

8½ oz (242 g) sour cream

5 tsp vanilla extract

METHOD

Pre-heat the oven to 350°F (180°C). Liberally grease a bundt cake tin and lightly dust with flour.

Cream the butter with the sugar until light and fluffy. Add the eggs, one at a time, blending well after each addition. Don't worry if the batter looks curdled.

Mix the dry ingredients together and add to the butter mixture. Gradually add the sour cream, stirring just until mixed in, and then the vanilla.

Spoon the very thick batter into the prepared bundt tin and bake for 35 to 45 minutes, or until golden and the cake, when touched, just springs back. Allow to cool on a wire rack for 5 minutes and then turn out of the tin onto a rack to cool thoroughly.

"This is the easiest, sturdiest, most versatile cake I know – and a perfect cake for a beginning baker. You can serve it plain for breakfast or dress it up at night for dessert by serving it with whipped cream and berries, or chocolate or caramel sauce."

– RUTH REICHL

JOSH'S NOTES

Key elements: Use a good-quality, natural vanilla essence; be gentle with the batter but ensure it is evenly mixed.

Tip: To reduce the cooking time, this recipe makes excellent cupcakes.

Image on p. 364

Baked Chocolate Tart

Simon Wright

COMPLEXITY: MODERATE | PREP TIME: 40 MINUTES
COOK TIME: 1 HOUR 15 MINUTES, PLUS COOLING TIME | MAKES: ONE 9 IN (23 CM) TART

INGREDIENTS

SWEET PASTRY

¾ cup plus 1½ sticks (180 g) cold butter, cut into small cubes, plus extra for tin

pinch of salt

⅓ cup (70 g) superfine/caster sugar

2 eggs

5 tsp cold water

2 cups plus 1 tbsp (300 g) all-purpose/plain flour, plus extra for tin

4 Graham crackers/digestive biscuits, finely crushed

Ingredients continued overleaf

METHOD

To make the pastry, place the butter, salt, and sugar in a food processor and process till smooth. Add 1 egg and the cold water, and mix until fully incorporated. Add the flour and pulse the machine until the mixture just comes together.

Tip the pastry out onto a clean work surface and gently knead into a ball. Try to not overwork the pastry, as the gluten in the flour will strengthen and make the pastry less crumbly. Flatten the pastry ball slightly with the palm of your hand, wrap in plastic wrap and refrigerate for 1 hour.

Remove the pastry from the fridge and allow it to come to a workable temperature, about 15 minutes. Preheat the oven to 350°F (180°C). Grease a 9-in (23-cm) diameter tart tin with a removable base with butter and lightly coat with flour, tipping out any excess flour.

Place half the crushed crackers/biscuits on a clean work surface, place the pastry on top and roll the pastry to a thickness of about ⅛ in (3 mm). Sprinkle the remaining biscuit crumbs over pastry and use your rolling pin to gently press crumbs into the pastry.

Roll the pastry over the rolling pin and drape over the tart tin. Using a small ball of excess pastry, gently ease the rolled pastry into the tin. This allows you to press the pastry into the tin without tearing it; the heat from your hands can make the pastry delicate. Trim some of the excess pastry from the edges but leave a good 2 in (5 cm) overlap to allow for shrinkage when baking. In a small bowl, beat the remaining egg and set aside.

Continued overleaf

INGREDIENTS CONT.

CHOCOLATE FILLING

1⅓ lb (600 g) good-quality dark chocolate (70% cocoa solids)

2¾ cups plus 1 tbsp (675 ml) cream

¾ cup plus 3 tbsp (225 ml) milk

½ cup (100 g) sugar

2 eggs

TO SERVE

vanilla ice cream

chocolate shavings

Baked Chocolate Tart cont.

Place the prepared tart case on a baking tray, line it with baking paper and fill with baking beans. Bake for about 10 minutes, or until the edges have started to colour. Remove from the oven, trim excess pastry from around the edges, lift out the baking paper and beans, brush the inside with the beaten egg and return the tart case to the oven for a further 10 to 15 minutes, until the pastry is golden brown. Remove from the oven and allow to cool. Turn the oven down to 225°F (110°C).

To make the filling, coarsely grate the chocolate into a large heatproof bowl. In a heavy-based saucepan bring the cream, milk, and sugar to the boil, pour onto the grated chocolate and stir until the mixture becomes dark and glossy, about 5 minutes. In a separate bowl, whisk the eggs together, then stir into the chocolate mixture and pass it through a fine sieve into your prepared tart case.

Bake for about 40 minutes, or until the tart has set around the outside but still has a slight wobble in the centre. Remove from the oven and allow to cool for about 2 hours before serving.

Serve with vanilla ice cream and garnish with chocolate shavings.

JOSH'S NOTES

Key elements: Line the tart tin carefully; monitor cooking time closely to ensure the tart is just right.

Tip: Place the tart tin on the oven rack before pouring in the filling.

Lemon Tart

Chris & Jeff Galvin

COMPLEXITY: MODERATE | PREP TIME: 25 MINUTES, PLUS REFRIGERATION TIME
COOK TIME: 1 HOUR 15 MINUTES | MAKES: ONE 10 IN (26 CM) TART

INGREDIENTS

1 recipe sweet pastry
(p. 510)

2 free-range egg yolks,
beaten

icing sugar, to dust

LEMON FILLING

finely grated zest and
juice of 10 unwaxed
lemons (you need
1¾ cups plus 2 tbsp/
450 ml juice)

2¼ cups (500 g)
superfine/caster sugar

1 qt (1 litre) heavy/
double cream

6 free-range eggs

6 free-range egg yolks

JOSH'S NOTES

Preparation: Make the
tart shell in advance, to
allow time for it to rest
and settle.

Tips: Skim the top of the
filling thoroughly to get
a perfect finish. If you
don't have a blowtorch,
dust the tart with
powdered/icing sugar.

METHOD

Roll the pastry out on a lightly floured work surface, then use to line a
10-in (26-cm) loose-bottomed flan tin about 2 in (4½ cm) deep (or a
cake ring placed on a baking tray lined with non-stick baking paper).
Leave excess pastry overhanging the edge of the tin – you will trim
this off after cooking the pastry. Refrigerate for 25 minutes.

Pre-heat the oven to 350°F (180°C). Line the pastry case with
greaseproof paper, then fill to the top with baking beans (or
uncooked dried beans or rice). Bake for 18 to 20 minutes, until pale
golden. Remove from the oven and lift out the paper and beans, then
return to the oven and bake for a further 5 minutes. Remove from the
oven again, brush the beaten egg yolk over the hot pastry and return
to the oven for 5 minutes. Remove once more and transfer to a rack
to cool. Reduce the oven temperature to 225°F (110°C).

To make the filling, put the lemon juice and superfine/caster sugar
in a saucepan and bring to the boil over a medium heat, stirring
occasionally. Remove from the heat, stir the lemon zest in and leave to
infuse for 3 to 4 minutes, then pass the mixture through a fine sieve.

Put the cream in a separate saucepan and bring to the boil over a
medium heat, then remove from the heat and allow to cool slightly.
Put the eggs and egg yolks in a large mixing bowl and whisk together.
While still whisking, pour the lemon juice/sugar mixture onto the
eggs. When fully incorporated, whisk in the cream and then pass the
mixture through a fine sieve. Skim off any bubbles from the top.

Place the cooled pastry case, in its tin, on a baking sheet and place this
on a shelf in the oven. Gently pour in the lemon filling, taking it to the
very top and being very careful to avoid any spillage. Bake for about
40 minutes, until only just set. The middle should wobble like a jelly
when the tart is cooked. Remove from the oven and leave to cool on
the baking sheet for at least 3 hours at room temperature – do not put it
in the fridge, or the pastry will go soggy. When cool, neatly trim off the
excess pastry from around the edge of the tart using a small paring knife.

Carefully remove the tart from the tin or ring, then cut it into wedges.
Dust with powdered/icing sugar and caramelize the top with a chef's
blowtorch just before serving.

Bakewell Tart

Jason Atherton

COMPLEXITY: EASY | PREP TIME: 25 MINUTES, PLUS REFRIGERATION TIME
COOK TIME: 1 HOUR 10 MINUTES | MAKES: ONE 9½ IN (23 CM) TART

INGREDIENTS

a little all-purpose/plain flour, for rolling

9 oz (250 g) sweet pastry (p. 510)

½ cup (160 g) warm apricot jam, for glazing

sifted powdered/icing sugar, for dusting (optional)

FILLING

½ cup/1 stick (125 g) unsalted butter, softened

½ cup (125 g) superfine/caster sugar

2 large eggs

4½ oz (125 g) ground almonds

3 tbsp all-purpose/plain flour

3 tbsp raspberry jam

½ cup (50 g) slivered/flaked almonds

JOSH'S NOTES

Preparation: Make the pastry in advance; the filling can also be made in advance.

Key elements: Take your time lining the tart shell, and don't be too shy with the jam.

Tip: Keep any excess pastry aside to patch up holes or cracks.

METHOD

On a lightly floured work surface, roll the pastry out to ¹⁄₁₆ in (2 mm) thick. Gently roll the pastry over the rolling pin, then lay it over a 9 to 9½ in (23 to 24 cm) round tart tin with a removable base. Gently press the pastry smoothly over the base and up the sides of the tin, leaving about ½ in (1 cm) hanging over the rim. Cover with plastic wrap and chill in the freezer for at least 1 hour, to let the pastry firm up.

Pre-heat the oven to 350°F (180°C) fan or 400°F (200°C) regular bake.

Take the pastry case out of the freezer and remove the plastic wrap. Line with baking parchment, then fill with baking beans. Bake for about 15 minutes, until the sides are lightly golden brown. Remove the baking beans and parchment, then return to the oven for a further 5 to 10 minutes, until the pastry is lightly golden with no grey patches of uncooked pastry. Remove from the oven, trim off the excess pastry round the rim with a sharp knife, and set aside. Reduce the oven temperature to 320°F (160°C) fan or 350°F (180°C) regular bake.

For the filling, lightly beat the butter and sugar together until light and fluffy, then beat in the eggs. Add the ground almonds and flour and fold through until evenly combined.

Spread a thin layer of raspberry jelly/jam over the base of the tart case, then fill with the almond mixture. Sprinkle the slivered/flaked almonds evenly over the top. Bake for 25 to 35 minutes, until the top is golden brown. Leave to cool slightly before brushing the top with warm apricot jam, then leave to cool completely. Dust with powdered/icing sugar before serving, if wished.

"I spent my early years in Sheffield, not far from the town of Bakewell, so I naturally have a soft spot for a good Bakewell tart. Here I'm using traditional raspberry jam in the filling, but I have also made some pretty good Bakewell tarts using gooseberry or damson jam."

– JASON ATHERTON

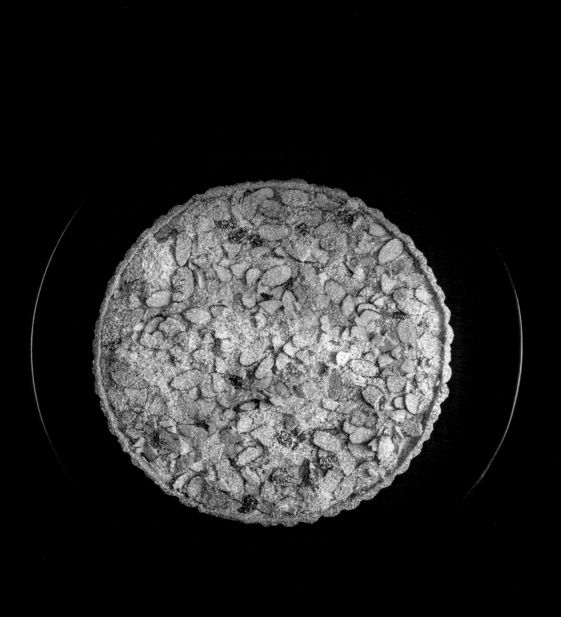

Dark Chocolate Brownie

Josh Emett

COMPLEXITY: EASY | PREP TIME: 20 MINUTES | COOK TIME: 20 MINUTES
MAKES: 10 OR MORE

INGREDIENTS

2¼ cups/4½ sticks (500 g) butter

14 oz (400 g) 70% dark chocolate

8 eggs

1⅔ cups (375 g) superfine/caster sugar

1¾ cups (150 g) cocoa powder

1¼ cups (150 g) soft all-purpose/plain flour

2 tsp baking powder

2 tsp vanilla essence

150 dark chocolate buttons or squares

METHOD

Pre-heat the oven to 350°F (180°).

Heat the chocolate and butter over a bain-marie over medium heat until melted and combined. Whisk the eggs and sugar together until creamy. Sieve the remaining dry ingredients together.

Fold the chocolate and butter through the eggs, followed by the dry ingredients. Fold through the vanilla and the chocolate buttons/squares.

Beat thoroughly so the mixture is well-combined and does not split.

Place in a lined baking tray and bake for about 15 minutes, or until a skewer comes out just clean. Cool on a rack, cut into even pieces, and serve warm or cold.

_____

"I use dark chocolate for my brownie as I prefer the flavour, but you can substitute with other chocolates depending on your preference."

– JOSH EMETT

JOSH'S NOTES

Key element: I prefer this brownie when it is slightly undercooked, so experiment and cook it to the degree that you prefer.

Tall & Creamy Cheesecake

Dorie Greenspan

COMPLEXITY: MODERATE | PREP TIME: 30 MINUTES | COOK TIME: 2 HOURS 45 MINUTES, PLUS REFRIGERATION TIME | MAKES: ONE 9 IN (23 CM) CHEESECAKE

INGREDIENTS

CRUST

6 oz (175 g) Graham cracker/digestive biscuit crumbs

3 tbsp sugar

pinch of salt

½ stick/4 tbsp (55 g) unsalted butter, melted

CHEESECAKE

2 lb (900 g) cream cheese, at room temperature

1⅓ cups (265 g) superfine/caster sugar

½ tsp salt

2 tsp pure vanilla extract

4 large eggs, at room temperature

1⅔ cups (325 g) sour cream or heavy/double cream, or a combination of the two

JOSH'S NOTES

Preparation: Make a day ahead as it is best to set it overnight.

Key element: Spread the biscuit layer thinly and gently up the sides, and ensure there are no lumps.

Tip: Use large tinfoil to ensure that no water can get in during baking.

METHOD

To make the crust, butter a 9 in (23 cm) springform tin – choose one that has sides that are 2¾ in (7 cm) high (if the sides are lower you will have cheesecake batter left over). Wrap the bottom of the tin (on the outside) in a double layer of tinfoil.

Stir the crumbs, sugar, and salt together in a medium-sized bowl. Pour over the melted butter and stir until all of the dry ingredients are uniformly moist. Turn the ingredients into the tin and use your fingers to pat an even layer of crumbs over the bottom of the tin and about halfway up the sides. Don't worry if the sides are not perfectly even or if the crumbs reach slightly above or below the midway point on the sides. Put the tin in the freezer while you preheat the oven. (The crust can be covered and frozen for up to 2 months.)

Centre a rack in the oven, pre-heat the oven to 350°F (180°C). Place the tin on a baking sheet and bake for 10 minutes. Set the crust aside to cool on a rack while you make the cheesecake. Reduce the oven temperature to 325°F (170°C).

To make the cheesecake, put a kettle of water on to boil. Working with a stand mixer fitted with a paddle attachment, or with a hand mixer in a large bowl, beat the cream cheese at medium speed until soft and creamy, about 4 minutes.

With the mixer running, add the superfine/caster sugar and salt and continue to beat for another 4 minutes or so, until the cream cheese is light. Beat in the vanilla. Add the eggs one by one, beating for a full minute after each addition – you want a well-aerated batter. Reduce the mixer speed to low and mix in the sour cream and/or heavy/double cream.

Continued overleaf

Tall & Creamy Cheesecake cont.

Put the foil-wrapped tin in a roasting pan that is large enough to hold the tin with some space around it. Give the batter a few stirs with a rubber spatula, just to make sure that there is nothing left unmixed at the bottom of the bowl, and scrape the batter into the tin. It will reach the rim of the tin. Put the roasting pan in the oven and pour enough boiling water into it to come halfway up the sides of the tin.

Bake the cheesecake for 1 hour 30 minutes, at which point the top should be browned (and perhaps cracked), and may have risen just a little above the rim of the tin. Turn off the oven and prop the oven door open with a wooden spoon. Allow the cheesecake to luxuriate in its water bath for another hour.

After 1 hour, carefully pull the setup out of the oven, lift the tin out of the roaster – be careful, there may be some hot water in the foil – and remove the foil. Let the cheesecake come to room temperature on a cooling rack.

When the cheesecake is cool, cover the top lightly and refrigerate for at least 4 hours; overnight is better. At serving time, remove the sides of the springform tin – I use a hair dryer to do this – and set the cake on a serving platter.

VARIATIONS

- Chocolate crust: Replace the crumbs with chocolate wafer crumbs. You may want to add a pinch of cinnamon, nutmeg, or ginger to the mix as well.

- Lemon cheesecake: Add the grated zest of 2 lemons, the juice of 1 lemon, and ½ teaspoon pure lemon extract to the batter.

- Berry cheesecake: Pour half of the batter into the tin, drop in about 1 cup (190 g) of fresh raspberries, blueberries, or a combination of berries, and top with the remaining batter. Alternatively, you can very gently fold small berries into the batter, taking care not to crush the berries and colour the batter.

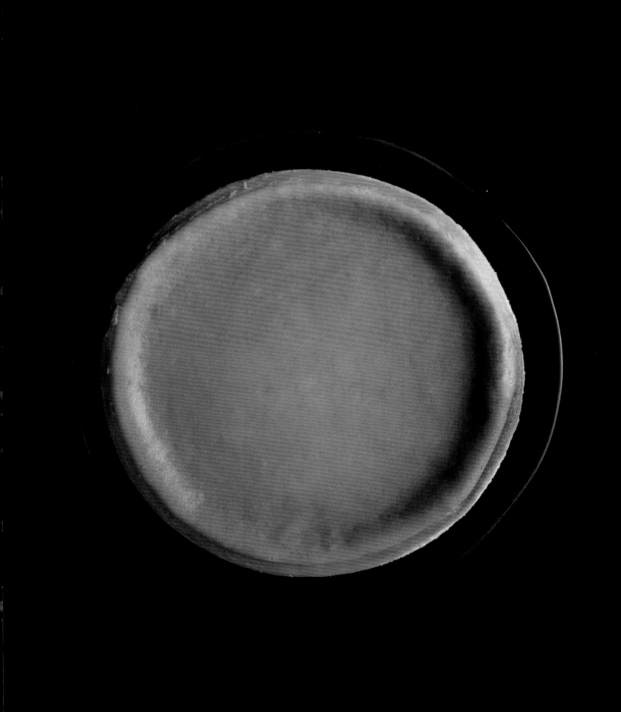

Pecan Pie

Josh Emett

COMPLEXITY: EASY | PREP TIME: 30 MINUTES, PLUS RESTING TIME
COOK TIME: 1 HOUR | MAKES: FOUR 4 TO 5 IN (10 TO 12 CM) PIES

INGREDIENTS

PASTRY SHELLS

1 recipe sweet pastry
(p. 510)

1 egg yolk, lightly
beaten with 1 tbsp
cream or milk
(egg wash)

FILLING & DECORATION

5 tsp dark rum

½ tsp salt

¾ cup (165 g) light-
brown cane sugar/
Demerara sugar

4½ tbsp (60 g)
unsalted butter

7 oz (200 g) glucose

5 oz (150 g) whole eggs
(about 3 medium-sized)

4½ oz (125 g) pecans,
roughly chopped

½ cup (60 g) whole
pecans, for decoration

JOSH'S NOTES

Key element: Use fresh
pecans – if they've been
sitting in the pantry for a
while they may be stale.

Tip: Pick out the whole
pecans to decorate the
top; any that are broken
can be used in the
filling.

Complements: Serve
with Chantilly cream or
plain whipped cream.

METHOD

Line four small tart tins 4 to 5 in (10 to 12 cm) in diameter with sweet pastry, leaving a little extending over the edges. Rest in the fridge for 1 hour.

Place the rum and salt in a heatproof bowl, stir and set aside. Melt the sugar, butter, and glucose together in a pot over a low to medium heat, stirring until the sugar is completely dissolved. Pour onto the rum and salt mix, and stir until combined. Set aside to cool to room temperature.

Meanwhile, pre-heat the oven to 350°F (180°C). Line the pastry cases with greaseproof paper and fill with baking beans. Bake for 30 to 35 minutes, then remove the beans and paper, brush the pastry with egg wash and return to the oven for 2 minutes to seal. Transfer the tins to a rack to cool. Turn the oven down to 330°F (165°C).

Beat the eggs together lightly until just combined. When the rum mix is cool, add the egg and chopped pecans and fold in. Place the tart shells, in their tins, on a baking sheet and fill with the pecan mix, stirring well before filling each one to make sure the mix is evenly spread. Decorate the top with whole pecans, then bake for 25 minutes, until set. Once set, cleanly slice off the rough pastry edges with a sharp serrated knife, and then demould and serve.

Banoffee Pie

Curtis Stone

COMPLEXITY: EASY | PREP TIME: 30 MINUTES, PLUS REFRIGERATION TIME
COOK TIME: 15 MINUTES | MAKES: ONE 8½ TO 9 IN (22 TO 23 CM) PIE

INGREDIENTS

CRUST

10 oz (280 g) Marie biscuits or Graham crackers/digestive biscuits

2⅓ cups/1⅓ sticks (150 g) butter, melted

TOFFEE SAUCE

½ cup (100 g) packed dark brown sugar

14 oz (395 g) can sweetened condensed milk

½ cup/1 stick plus 1 tbsp (125 g) butter

FILLING

1¼ cups (300 ml) cream

5 small ripe bananas (about 1⅔ lb/750 g total)

JOSH'S NOTES

Preparation: Prepare the crust an hour beforehand to allow time to grill.

Key element: Line the base correctly so that the rim of the pie will hold everything tightly.

METHOD

Line the bottom of an 8½ to 9 in (22 to 23 cm) springform tin with baking paper. Chop the cookies/biscuits in a food processor until they are finely ground. Pour the melted butter over the crumbs and process to blend well. The crumbs should stick together when pressed. Press the crumb mixture over the bottom and 1½ in (3½ cm) up the side of the tin. Refrigerate.

Combine the brown sugar and 2 tablespoons (30 ml) water in a medium-sized heavy-based saucepan. Stir over medium heat until the sugar dissolves. Raise the heat and boil without stirring, occasionally swirling the pan and brushing down the sides with a pastry brush dipped into water, until the syrup is a deep amber colour, about 5 minutes. Stir in the condensed milk and butter. Continue stirring for 5 minutes or until the sauce thickens slightly.

Remove the toffee sauce from the heat and spread 1 cup of sauce over the prepared crust. Refrigerate for about 1 hour, or until the toffee is semi-firm. Keep the remaining toffee sauce at room temperature.

Using an electric mixer, beat the cream in a large bowl until thick and very soft, billowy peaks form. Slice 3 of the bananas into very thin rounds. Fold the sliced bananas into the softly whipped cream, and spoon the filling into the prepared pie crust.

Slice the remaining 2 bananas, and arrange the slices decoratively over the pie. Re-warm the remaining toffee sauce gently over low heat. Drizzle some of the sauce decoratively over the pie. (If the sauce has thickened too much to drizzle, stir a few tablespoons of milk into it.) Cut the pie into wedges, and transfer them to plates. Drizzle each pie wedge with more sauce, and serve.

"This is the ultimate hybrid: a combination of banana and toffee in one incredible pie."

– CURTIS STONE

INGREDIENTS

about 10 cups quartered and cored skin-on heritage apples, to mound up high in the pie pan (2½ to 3 lb/1.2 to 1.4 kg)

½ cup (100 g) sugar, plus 1 to 2 tsp for sprinkling on top of the pie

½ tsp salt

1 tsp ground cinnamon

2 gratings of nutmeg

½ tsp ground allspice

1 tbsp (15 ml) artisanal apple cider vinegar (or 1 to 2 tsp fresh lemon juice)

1 to 2 tbsp (15 to 30 ml) Calvados or other apple liqueur (optional but really good)

½ cup (70 g) all-purpose/plain flour, plus extra for rolling out

1 recipe traditional pie dough (p. 507)

1 knob butter, the size of a small walnut, cut into small pieces

EGG WASH

1 egg white

2 tbsp (30 ml) water

JOSH'S NOTES

Key element: Roll the pastry to the correct thickness, and no thinner than ⅛ in (3 mm).

Tip: Use a good mix of apples, some sweet, some tart, some that hold their shape, and some that don't.

Quintessential Apple Pie

Kate McDermott

COMPLEXITY: EASY | PREP TIME: 35 MINUTES
COOK TIME: 1 HOUR, PLUS COOLING TIME | MAKES: ONE 9 IN (23 CM) PIE

METHOD

Cut the quartered apples into slices ½ in (1 cm) thick, or chunk them into pieces you can comfortably get into your mouth.

Put the apples, ½ cup (100 g) sugar, salt, cinnamon, nutmeg, allspice, vinegar, Calvados (if using), and flour in a large bowl and mix lightly until most of the surfaces are covered with what looks like wet sand.

On a lightly floured work surface, roll out 1 disc (half) of the pastry dough and place it in a deep, 9 in (23 cm) round pie dish. Pour the apple mixture into the unbaked pie crust, mounding it high, and dot with the small pieces of butter.

Roll out the remaining dough so that it will be large enough to cover the pie, lay it over the fruit, and cut 5 to 6 vents on top. Trim the excess dough from the edges and crimp them together. Cover the pie with plastic wrap and chill in the refrigerator while you pre-heat the oven to 425°F (220°C).

Using a fork, beat the egg white and water together to create an egg wash. Lightly brush some egg wash over the entire pie, including the edges, and bake for 20 minutes. Reduce the heat to 375°F (190°C) and bake for 30 minutes longer.

Open the oven and carefully sprinkle the remaining 1 to 2 teaspoons sugar evenly on top of the pie, then continue baking for 10 minutes more. Look for steam and a slight bit of juice coming out of the vents before removing the pie from the oven. Get your ear right down almost to the top of the pie and listen for the sizzle-whump, which some call the pie's heartbeat.

Cool the pie for at least 1 hour before serving.

Baklava, p. 326

French Meringues, p. 386

Chocolate & Banana Bombolini, p. 414

Easy Vanilla Cake, p. 346

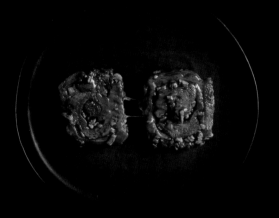

Sticky Sticky Buns, p. 332

Caramelized Pineapple Crêpes, p. 415

Chocolate Profiteroles, p. 412

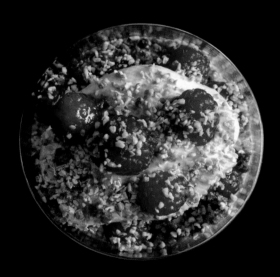

Cranachan, p. 379

Baked Alaska Bombe, p. 389

Desserts & Sweets

Whether you're a serious sugar fiend or not, everyone miraculously seems to be able to find room for dessert. Tiramisu, trifle, crème brûlée, bombolini, rum baba, chocolate molten cakes, crumble, clafoutis, crêpes Suzette, sticky toffee pudding, they're all here – and more. And oh, the possibilities for accompaniments; what dessert doesn't taste better with a dash of chocolate sauce, a scoop of homemade ice cream, or a quenelle of freshly whipped cream? And if your sweet tooth still isn't sated, try your hand at the chocolate truffles. Decadence at its darkest.

Crème Brûlée

Josh Emett

COMPLEXITY: EASY | PREP TIME: 20 MINUTES
COOK TIME: 45 MINUTES, PLUS REFRIGERATION TIME | MAKES: 5 TO 6

INGREDIENTS

2 cups plus 1¼ tbsp (500 ml) heavy/double cream

2 vanilla beans

10 egg yolks

⅔ cup (150 g) superfine/caster sugar

TO SERVE

⅓ cup plus 1¾ tbsp (100 g) superfine/caster sugar

METHOD

Pre-heat the oven to 210°F (100°C), half-fan if you have a combi oven.

Pour the cream into a pot, add the vanilla beans and heat until just below boiling point. In a heatproof bowl, whisk the egg yolks and sugar together, then pour the hot cream over the egg mix, stirring together well. Strain into a jug.

Pour the strained mix into flat brûlée dishes, using about 7 oz (200 g) per dish. Place the dishes in a deep roasting tray and pour hot water into the tray to come about halfway up the dishes. Cook for 35 minutes, until the custards are just set. Remove from the oven, allow to cool, then place in the fridge for at least 3 to 4 hours.

When ready to serve, remove from the fridge. Sprinkle sugar over the top of each dish and shake off the excess. Using a blowtorch, gently caramelize the sugar all the way around until golden and crispy. Serve straight away.

JOSH'S NOTES

Preparation: Make sure you have suitable dishes, shallow and with a wide base.

Key element: You will need a chefs' blowtorch – the brûlée on the top is essential.

Tip: Watch the oven carefully – when you think the custard is just set, tap the side of the tray gently until there isn't any movement in the centre of the brûlée.

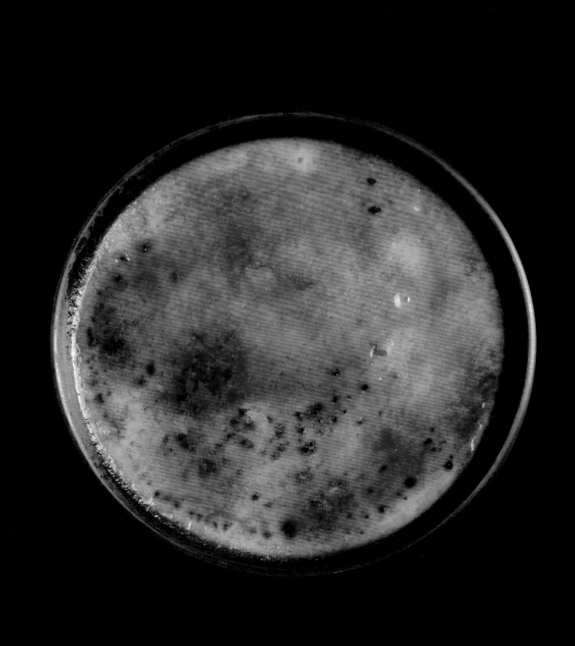

Calvados Crème Caramel

Shannon Bennett

COMPLEXITY: MODERATE | PREP TIME: 15 MINUTES, PLUS REFRIGERATION TIME
COOK TIME: 1 HOUR, PLUS REFRIGERATION TIME | MAKES: 6

INGREDIENTS

1 oz (30 g) currants

¾ cup plus 1¼ tbsp
(200 ml) Calvados

4 eggs

2 egg yolks

⅓ cup (80 g) superfine/
caster sugar

1 cup plus 2 tsp
(250 ml) milk

CARAMEL

1⅓ cups (300 g) sugar

6¾ tbsp (100 ml) water

METHOD

Macerate the currants in the Calvados for 24 hours.

Combine the eggs, egg yolks, and superfine/caster sugar in
a heatproof mixing bowl. Do not overbeat, as it will create air
bubbles in the caramel.

Warm the milk in a saucepan until just about to boil, then pour it
over the egg mixture, whisking constantly until combined. Strain
the Calvados from the currants and incorporate into the custard.
Pass the custard through a fine sieve and set aside.

To make the caramel, combine the sugar and half of the water
in a heavy-based saucepan and cook over a medium heat for
3 to 4 minutes, or until a light golden colour. Test with a sugar
thermometer – the temperature should be between 262 and 270°F
(128 and 132°C). Very carefully stir in the remaining water and boil
for 2 minutes.

Start the oven pre-heating to 210°F (100°C).

Place a teaspoonful of the caramel in the bottom of six dariole
moulds and set aside for 20 minutes to set.

Pour the custard over the caramel until the dariole moulds are
three-quarters full. Place a teaspoon of the currants in each
mould. Place the moulds in a baking tray. Pour boiling water into
the tray to come halfway up the sides of each dariole mould.
Bake for 45 minutes. Allow to cool, then place in the refrigerator
for 30 minutes or until ready to serve.

To unmould, place each dariole mould in warm water, then gently
invert onto a small serving plate. The crème caramels are best
served within 24 hours.

JOSH'S NOTES

Preparation: Macerate
the currants overnight.

Key element: Follow the
recipe steps precisely to
ensure you achieve the
correct consistency for
the caramel.

Tip: Bake until just
set, and allow time
to refrigerate before
serving.

"I cannot go past including a crème caramel in my dessert repertoire.
With this particular dessert, apple purée or poached apples make
the perfect accompaniment."

– SHANNON BENNETT

Crème Catalan

Dave Verheul

COMPLEXITY: MODERATE | PREP TIME: 30 MINUTES, PLUS REFRIGERATION TIME
COOK TIME: 1 HOUR, PLUS CHILLING TIME | MAKES: 8

INGREDIENTS

CUSTARD

2⅔ cups plus 1½ tbsp (625 g) heavy/double cream

¾ cup plus 2 tbsp (210 ml) milk

zest of 1 orange

zest of 1 lemon

1 tbsp toasted fennel seeds

½ cup plus 2 tsp (110 g) sugar

seeds from ½ vanilla bean

¼ cup (70 g) egg yolks

CARAMEL

1½ cups (300 g) sugar

6¾ oz (100 ml) water

METHOD

In a small pot, bring the cream, milk, zests, fennel seeds, sugar, and vanilla bean seeds up to just below the boil, then take off the heat and leave to infuse for 15 minutes. Strain the slightly cooled mix, then use a stick blender to blend in the yolks. Strain the mix again and chill overnight.

The following day, pre-heat the oven to 300°F (150°C).

For the caramel, place the sugar and 1 cup plus ¾ tablespoon (70 ml) water in a small pot and cook over a medium heat to a light golden caramel. Remove from the heat and let it cook through to a deep, dark colour. At this point carefully add in the remaining 2 tablespoons (30 ml) water and mix until combined. Pour a small amount of this caramel into the bottom of 8 dariole moulds and chill slightly, until set.

Gently pour the cream mix into each mould. Place the moulds in a high-sided oven dish, and fill this dish with hot water up to the level of the custard mix. Cover with foil and cook for 45 minutes; check at this point and cook longer as required – the custard should be lightly set. When done, remove from the bath and chill.

To turn out, gently heat the outside and top of the mould, then flip over above a serving plate, and pull one side of the crème Catalan away from the edge, which will allow air into the base and release the custard, which should fall out.

JOSH'S NOTES

Preparation: Prepare the custard the day before and chill overnight.

Key element: Make sure the caramel is dark enough, and the correct consistency.

Tip: Let the caramel set and cool sufficiently before adding the custard.

Chocolate Mousse

Anne-Sophie Pic

COMPLEXITY: MODERATE | PREP TIME: 20 MINUTES | COOK TIME: 2 HOURS
MAKES: 4 TO 6

INGREDIENTS

7 oz (200 g) dark
(bittersweet) chocolate

¼ cup plus 2 tbsp
(90 ml) heavy/double
cream

2 egg yolks

4¼ oz (120 g) egg white
(4 to 5 eggs)

3 tbsp superfine/
caster sugar

JOSH'S NOTES

Preparation: Bring
the eggs out of the
fridge beforehand to
bring them to room
temperature.

Key element: Focus on
achieving the correct
temperatures.

Tip: Chop the chocolate
very finely to ensure
it melts quickly and
evenly.

METHOD

Break the chocolate into pieces, then chop it finely with a knife and
put into a heatproof bowl. Pour the cream into a saucepan and bring
to the boil over a medium heat, then immediately pour it over the
chocolate. Mix well with a spatula until smooth and glossy, then
add the egg yolks, mix again and put to one side.

Put the egg white into a large bowl or an electric mixer (the bowl
used should be very clean, since any trace of fat will make it harder
to whisk the egg white), then whisk. As soon as peaks begin to form,
start to add the sugar, little by little. Don't over-whisk the egg white,
or it will be difficult to fold in the chocolate ganache.

Gently fold the whisked egg white into the chocolate ganache,
keeping as much air in the egg white as possible. Don't over-mix:
You need to just incorporate the two mixtures, no more. Leave the
mousse in the mixing bowl, or decant into ramekins or smaller bowls,
then chill in the fridge for 2 hours. Serve as it is – set, yet meltingly soft.

TIP

For the mousse to be properly light and airy, the chocolate ganache
and the egg white mixtures need to have the same consistency.
If you have a cooking thermometer, check the temperature of
the chocolate ganache before you add the whisked egg white:
It should be around 95 to 104°F (35 to 40°C).

VARIATION

Try adding mint or cinnamon to the mixture, or infuse the cream
with orange zest.

"There is no secret to this mousse: You just need really fresh eggs
and very good dark chocolate, preferably with 52 to 70 per cent
cocoa solids to give it real depth. Serve this with shortbread,
a banana smoothie, almond biscuits."

– ANNE-SOPHIE PIC

Chocolate & Orange Soufflé

Bruno Loubet

COMPLEXITY: MODERATE | PREP TIME: 20 MINUTES | COOK TIME: 12 MINUTES | MAKES: 4

INGREDIENTS

butter, to grease

⅓ cup plus 1 tbsp (90 g) superfine/caster sugar, plus extra to coat the ramekins

8 egg yolks

½ cup plus 1¼ tbsp (50 g) unsweetened cocoa powder, plus extra to dust

2 tbsp (30 ml) whisky

½ tsp finely grated orange zest

10 egg whites

pinch of salt

JOSH'S NOTES

Preparation: Butter and sugar the moulds in advance, and prepare them as directed.

Tip: Make sure you're ready to eat the soufflés, hot and straight from the oven.

METHOD

Pre-heat the oven to 350°F (180°C) fan or 400°F (200°C). With your finger, evenly butter the inside of four individual soufflé dishes, each 4 in (10 cm) in diameter and 2 in (5 cm) high. Put some sugar in one of the dishes and move it around to coat the whole surface. Tip all the excess sugar into another dish and coat it in the same way, then repeat with the other dishes. Set aside.

In a bowl, whisk together the egg yolks and ¼ cup (50 g) of the sugar until very smooth and pale. Add the cocoa, whisky, and orange zest, and mix well. In a large, clean bowl, whisk the egg whites with a tiny pinch of salt to soft peaks. Add the remaining sugar and continue whisking until the mixture becomes firm but not too stiff. Add a quarter of the egg whites to the egg yolk mixture. Mix with a whisk, then fold in the remaining egg whites (the best way is to use a pastry scraper).

Fill the prepared soufflé dishes with the mixture, right to the top, then above the rim by about ½ in (1 cm). Be careful not to get any of the mixture on the edges of the dishes, or the soufflés will stick to the dishes and will not rise evenly.

Place the dishes in a roasting tin and pour in about ½ in (1 cm) of hot water. Place the tin on top of the stove and bring the water to the boil, then transfer to the oven. Bake for about 12 minutes, reducing the oven setting to 325°F (170°C) fan or 375°F (190°C) as soon as the soufflés start to rise.

When the soufflés are puffed up, remove them from their bain-marie of hot water, quickly dry the dishes and place on serving plates. Dust some cocoa powder over the soufflés and serve immediately.

_____

"Soufflé is one of those legendary posh French dishes that seem incredibly difficult to achieve. This recipe is one of the simplest I know and gives a brilliant result. If your ingredients are at room temperature when you start, and the moulds are buttered properly, then there is not much space for mistakes."

– BRUNO LOUBET

Coconut Panna Cotta

Michael Meredith

COMPLEXITY: EASY | PREP TIME: 10 MINUTES
COOK TIME: 25 MINUTES, PLUS REFRIGERATION TIME | MAKES: 6

INGREDIENTS

3 leaves of gelatine 'titanium-strength'

1⅔ cups (400 ml) coconut cream

1¼ cups (300 ml) soy milk

1 kaffir lime leaf

seeds from ½ vanilla bean

7 oz (200 g) coconut sugar

JOSH'S NOTES

Key element: Don't whisk too much; this creates air bubbles.

Tip: Cool the mixture well before placing in the moulds, to prevent the fats splitting.

Soak the gelatine in cold water to soften; squeeze out excess water before using. In a pot bring the coconut cream, soy milk, kaffir lime leaf, and vanilla bean seeds to a light boil. Off the heat add the coconut sugar and gelatine and whisk in, then put back over a medium heat for 3 minutes, stirring gently. Remove from the heat, cover and leave to infuse for 20 minutes.

Set a bowl over another bowl containing ice. Strain the mixture into the top bowl and stir until the panna cotta is thickened in consistency, 8 to 10 minutes. Pour into dariole moulds and place in the fridge until fully set, 3 to 4 hours. Turn out onto serving plates and serve with a tropical fruit salad and some toasted shaved coconut.

Lemon Semifreddo

Ray McVinnie

COMPLEXITY: EASY | PREP TIME: 10 MINUTES | SERVES: 6 TO 8

INGREDIENTS

3 eggs, separated

½ cup (110 g) superfine/caster sugar

zest of 1 lemon

¼ cup plus 1 tsp (65 ml) limoncello

1½ cups plus 2 tsp (370 ml) cream, whipped

JOSH'S NOTES

Complements: Serve with fresh citrus fruits.

Beat the egg yolks, sugar, and zest together until thick, pale, and creamy. Stir in the limoncello.

In a clean bowl, beat the egg whites until they hold soft peaks. Fold the yolk mixture, whipped cream, and egg whites together, then pour into a shallow pan, cover and freeze until firm (5 hours). Serve in scoops.

"This is a great way to make 'ice cream' without using an ice cream machine. This simplified semifreddo is made with raw ingredients so doesn't keep weeks in the freezer like commercial ice cream, but it will keep for a few days so can be made in advance."
– RAY MCVINNIE

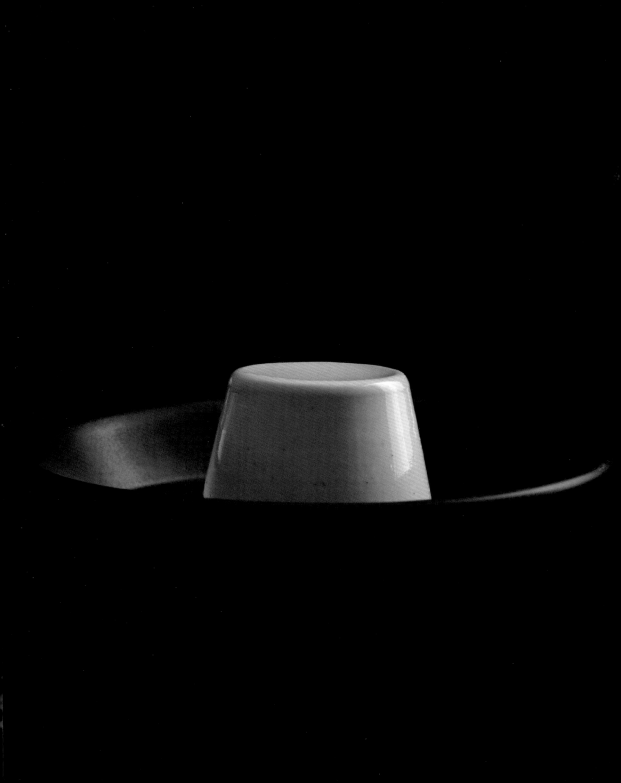

Pistachio Ice Cream

Ron Paprocki

COMPLEXITY: EASY | PREP TIME: 15 MINUTES | COOK TIME: 15 MINUTES
MAKES: 6 CUPS (1½ LITRES)

INGREDIENTS

3 cups plus 2 tbsp (750 ml) milk

2 cups plus 1¼ tbsp (500 ml) heavy/double cream

10½ oz (300 g) egg yolks

1¼ cups (250 g) sugar

2 oz (60 g) pistachio paste

1 tsp (5 g) *fleur de sel*

This recipe accompanies Ron Paprocki's Baked Alaska Bombe recipe, p. 389.

In a medium-sized pot, bring the milk and cream to the boil.

Meanwhile, beat the sugar and egg yolks in a bowl until combined. When the milk mixture starts to come to the boil, add a little to the egg mixture and stir in to temper the yolks, then add the contents of the bowl to the milk mixture and continue to heat, stirring constantly, until it reaches 183°F (84°C). Remove from the heat, add the pistachio paste and *fleur de sel*, and emulsify using a hand held blender.

Allow to cool, then refrigerate overnight. Spin in an ice cream machine according to the manufacturer's instructions. Freeze until required.

Classic Rice Pudding

Josh Emett

COMPLEXITY: MODERATE | PREP TIME: 20 MINUTES | COOK TIME: 25 MINUTES
SERVES: 4 TO 6

INGREDIENTS

6⅓ oz (180 g) short-grain rice

⅔ cup (150 g) superfine/caster sugar

2 cups plus 1¼ tbsp (500 ml) milk

2 cups plus 1¼ tbsp (500 ml) cream

2 vanilla pods, split open

150 g egg yolks (4 to 5 medium-sized eggs)

JOSH'S NOTES

Key elements: Once you add the egg yolks, don't let the mixture get too hot or boil; the final steps are key to perfecting the dish.

Place the rice, ⅓ cup (70 g) sugar, milk, cream, and vanilla in a pot. Place over a medium heat and bring to the boil, then simmer gently, uncovered, for 20 to 25 minutes until the rice is almost cooked with a small bite to it.

In a heatproof bowl, whisk the egg yolk and remaining sugar together until combined.

Remove the rice from the heat and stir in the egg yolk mix. Return to the heat and cook gently for a few more minutes, without letting it boil.

Once the rice is completely cooked, remove from the heat and serve straight away if possible.

Cranachan

Nick Nairn

COMPLEXITY: EASY | PREP TIME: 20 MINUTES | COOK TIME: 3 TO 4 MINUTES | MAKES: 4

INGREDIENTS

4½ oz (125 g) pinhead oatmeal

¼ cup plus 2 tsp (55 g) soft brown sugar

1¼ cup (300 ml) heavy/ double cream (or crème fraîche)

8 oz (225 g) fresh raspberries (or frozen raspberries, thawed)

2 tbsp (30 ml) Drambuie or Scotch whisky

extra raspberries, to decorate

METHOD

Pre-heat an oven grill to medium. Line a grill pan with foil. Spread the oatmeal in an even layer over the foil and sprinkle evenly with the soft brown sugar. Place under the grill for 3 to 4 minutes until the sugar begins to caramelize. Stir well and grill again until golden brown. Do not allow to burn! Cool completely then peel off the foil and break into chunks.

Softly whip the cream. Toss the raspberries with the liquor. Starting with the oatmeal, layer these three ingredients in tall glasses, ending with a layer of cream. Top with extra raspberries and serve immediately before the oatmeal goes soggy. Serve drizzled with extra Drambuie mixed with warm honey for true Scottish indulgence!

"This is simply the best way to make this classic Scottish dessert. I have tasted many dreadful cranachans over the years – soggy or gritty oatmeal, overwhipped cream, not enough booze – and have decided that there's nothing for it but to toast the oatmeal. Grilling the oatmeal gives it a nutty flavour and caramelizes the sugar onto it, giving a crunchy texture to the finished dish."

– NICK NAIRN

JOSH'S NOTES

Preparation: Make sure to use the pinhead oatmeal.

Key element: Toast the oatmeal as directed until golden brown.

Image on p. 365

Peach Melba

Maggie Beer

COMPLEXITY: EASY | PREP TIME: 25 MINUTES | COOK TIME: 15 MINUTES | SERVES: 4

INGREDIENTS

4 ripe yellow peaches

3 tbsp (40 g) unsalted butter

finely grated zest of 1 orange

3½ oz (100 g) mascarpone

3½ oz (100 g) natural probiotic yoghurt

½ tsp cinnamon powder

2 tbsp powdered sugar/icing sugar, sifted

3 tbsp slivered/flaked almonds

7 oz (200 g) fresh raspberries

METHOD

Pre-heat the oven to 400°F (200°C) fan-forced.

Cut the peaches in half and remove the stones. Place the peach halves, cut side up, on a baking tray. Place a small piece of butter in each peach half, and bake for 12 to 15 minutes or until golden and just soft. While still warm, slip the skins off the peaches. Slice the peaches and set aside.

In a bowl, mix the orange zest, mascarpone, yoghurt, cinnamon, and powdered/icing sugar until smooth and combined. Place the slivered/flaked almonds in a small, dry frying pan and toast lightly over a medium heat, shaking the pan to prevent them burning.

Divide the peaches and berries between serving plates together with a generous dollop of mascarpone cream and a scattering of slivered/flaked almonds.

"I've written this recipe for baked peaches largely to compensate for the often-disappointing flavour of fresh peaches. Unless you buy them from a farmers' market, peaches are usually offered for sale before they are ripe – simply, but sadly, because of the logistics of getting fruit to market. Baking will bring out their flavour and perfume, but if you have perfectly ripe fresh peaches you can eliminate that step entirely."

– MAGGIE BEER

JOSH'S NOTES

Key element: Good-quality peaches and raspberries elevate this dish.

Tip: Check the peaches aren't bruised when you buy them, and handle them very gently.

INGREDIENTS

JELLY, FRUIT & SPONGE

5 sheets bronze-grade
leaf gelatine

10½ oz (300 g)
raspberries

14 oz (400 g)
strawberries, hulled and
halved if large

10½ oz (300 g)
blackberries

6¾ tbsp (100 ml)
medium sherry

1⅓ cups plus 2 tbsp
(350 ml) water

¾ cup plus 2¼ tbsp
(200 g) superfine/caster
sugar

seeds from 1 vanilla bean

7 oz (200 g) Madeira
cake (store-bought,
or cream cake recipe,
p. 389)

CUSTARD

1⅔ cups (400 ml) whole
milk

¾ cup plus 1¾ tbsp
(200 ml) heavy/double
cream

8 large free-range egg
yolks

⅓ cup (80 g) superfine/
caster sugar

1 heaped tbsp
cornstarch/cornflour

CREAM

1⅔ cups (400 ml) heavy/
double cream

seeds from 1 vanilla bean

⅓ cup (80 g) superfine/
caster sugar

½ cup (60 g) powdered
sugar/icing sugar, sifted

TO SERVE

½ cup (50 g) slivered/
flaked almonds, toasted

Sherry Trifle

Nathan Outlaw

COMPLEXITY: EASY | PREP TIME: 35 MINUTES | COOK TIME: 15 MINUTES | SERVES: 8

METHOD

To make the jelly, soak the gelatine leaves in cold water to soften. Meanwhile, put half of each fruit into a blender (set the rest aside for later). Add the sherry, water, sugar, and vanilla bean seeds to the blender and blitz to a purée, then pass through a sieve into a pan to remove the pips. Bring to the boil, then measure out 2 cups plus 1¼ tablespoons (500 ml). Squeeze the gelatine leaves to remove excess liquid, add to the measured liquid while it is still hot and whisk until dissolved.

Cut the Madeira cake into slices and lay in the bottom of a glass serving bowl, then pour the fruit jelly over the sponge. Leave the jelly to cool and partially soak into the sponge, then refrigerate to set.

To make the custard, pour the milk and cream into a heavy-based pan and slowly bring to the boil over a medium-low heat. In the meantime, whisk the egg yolks and sugar together in a large bowl, then whisk in the cornstarch/cornflour. As the creamy milk comes to the boil, pour it into the egg mixture, whisking as you do so. Pour the custard back into the cleaned pan and cook, stirring, over a medium heat until it thickens; do not boil. Pass through a sieve into a bowl, cover the surface with plastic wrap or baking paper to prevent a skin forming and leave to cool.

Once the custard is cold, take the trifle bowl from the fridge and arrange two-thirds of the remaining fruit on top of the jelly. Pour or spoon on the custard and return to the fridge to set.

When the custard is set, put the cream, vanilla bean seeds, superfine/caster sugar, and powdered/icing sugar into a medium-large bowl and whisk until soft peaks form. Spoon the cream on top of the trifle and top with the rest of the berries and the toasted slivered/flaked almonds.

Traditional Tiramisu

Marc Vetri

COMPLEXITY: EASY | PREP TIME: 30 MINUTES, PLUS STANDING TIME | SERVES: 12

INGREDIENTS

8 eggs, separated

1½ cups (300 g) sugar

2 lb (900 g) mascarpone, at room temperature

24 store-bought ladyfingers, plus a few for garnish

1 qt (1 litre) brewed espresso or strong brewed coffee, cooled

¼ cup (25 g) unsweetened cocoa powder, plus more for garnish

JOSH'S NOTES

Preparation: Make the coffee ahead of time so it has time to cool.

Key element: Soaking the ladyfingers – if they are wet it makes the dish lighter, but balance this against having too much liquid.

Tip: Pour the coffee into a shallow tray to make it easier to soak the ladyfingers.

METHOD

Put the egg yolks in the bowl of a stand mixer along with 1 cup (200 g) sugar. Beat with the paddle attachment on medium-high speed until nice and thick, 1 to 2 minutes. Transfer to another bowl.

Put the mascarpone in the mixer bowl and beat with the paddle attachment briefly to soften it. Beat in the yolk mixture on medium speed until smooth, about 1 minute.

In a clean mixer bowl, beat the egg whites and remaining ½ cup (100 g) sugar with the whisk attachment until glossy and thick, about 5 minutes. Using a rubber spatula, fold the whites into the mascarpone mixture in 3 batches.

Soak the ladyfingers in the espresso just until softened and saturated, about 1 minute. Make a layer of soaked ladyfingers in a 3-quart (3-litre) serving dish or bowl, or in 12 individual serving dishes or bowls. Top with half the mascarpone mixture, another layer of ladyfingers, and a final layer of mascarpone. Let stand at room temperature for 30 minutes before serving.

Sprinkle the top with the cocoa. Garnish each portion with another ladyfinger, dusted on one side with a little cocoa.

PREP AHEAD

I use Forno Bonomi ladyfingers, which you can pick up at Italian grocery stores or at Amazon and other online retailers. The tiramisu keeps for about 3 days in the refrigerator. Let the tiramisu stand at room temperature for at least 10 minutes before serving to take the chill off.

BEVERAGE

Miscela d'Oro Espresso/Caffe Corretto: The espresso in a classic tiramisu calls for not much more than espresso to drink. However, if you're like me and enjoy the digestive powers of grappa, pour 1 oz (30 ml) in your coffee and make a caffe corretto.

"If there's one thing I learned in Italy, it's that store-bought ladyfingers work best for tiramisu."

– MARC VETRI

French Meringues

Josh Emett

COMPLEXITY: EASY | PREP TIME: 20 MINUTES
COOK TIME: 30 MINUTES, PLUS COOLING TIME | MAKES: 24

INGREDIENTS

4 egg whites, at room temperature

½ cup (110 g) superfine/caster sugar

1 cup (110 g) powdered sugar/icing sugar

1 tsp vanilla extract

METHOD

Pre-heat the oven to 300°F (150°C).

Place the egg whites in a very clean bowl and whisk to stiff peaks. Add both types of sugar, spoon by spoon, whisking each spoonful in before adding the next. When all the sugar is in, continue whisking for a further 4 to 5 minutes, until the meringue is smooth and glossy.

Line 2 or more baking sheets with non-stick baking paper. Transfer the meringue to a piping bag fitted with a small nozzle, and pipe 24 rounds onto the baking paper.

Turn the oven down to 265°F (130°C) and bake the meringues for 30 minutes. Switch the oven off, leaving the meringues inside and the door closed. Leave until cool, or ideally overnight.

Store the crispy meringues in an airtight container until needed. They will keep for about a week.

JOSH'S NOTES

Preparation: Use a little drop of meringue to hold the baking paper to the trays.

Key element: Ensure the eggs are at room temperature.

Tip: I like to do these overnight, and come back to them in the morning for the best results.

Image on p. 364

Italian Meringue

Michael Caines

COMPLEXITY: EASY | PREP TIME: 20 MINUTES | COOK TIME: 5 MINUTES
MAKES: 4 TO 5 CUPS

INGREDIENTS

1¾ cups (400 g)
superfine/caster sugar

½ cup plus 2 tbsp
(150 ml) water

8 egg whites

METHOD

Put the water and sugar in a small saucepan and heat to 250°F (120°C), until the sugar has melted but has not taken on any colour.

Start to whip the egg whites to light peaks, then gradually pour the cooked sugar liquid onto the egg whites while still whisking. Continue to whisk until the meringue is cold, and then it's ready to use.

———————

"Unlike most meringues, Italian meringue uses cooked sugar to cook the egg white, which stabilizes the eggs and creates a firm marshmallow-like texture. This gives you a key advantage when using it in a fruit mousse: it makes the mousse stable, reducing the amount of gelatine and cream needed, leaving you with a fuller fruit-flavoured mousse, improving its texture. It's also a favoured meringue for baked Alaska and lemon meringue tart, as the meringue is served soft."

– MICHAEL CAINES

Eton Mess

Josh Emett

COMPLEXITY: EASY | PREP TIME: 45 MINUTES | SERVES: 6

INGREDIENTS

18 oz (500 g)
strawberries

1 tsp superfine/caster
sugar

1¼ cups (300 ml) cream

1 tbsp powdered sugar/
icing sugar

½ vanilla bean

6 French meringues
(p. 386), gently crushed

METHOD

Separate out 5 oz (150 g) of the most ripe or over-ripe strawberries – there are usually some in every basket/punnet. Finely slice these into a bowl and sprinkle with the superfine/caster sugar. Leave for 30 minutes, then blend to a smooth purée consistency.

Cut the remaining strawberries into halves or quarters, depending on size.

Put the cream and powdered/icing sugar in a bowl and scrape the seeds from the vanilla bean into the bowl. Whisk to soft peaks.

Put the sliced strawberries, whipped cream, and crushed meringues in a large bowl and fold gently together, then pour in the strawberry purée and swirl through. Pour into a clean bowl, and serve.

JOSH'S NOTES

Preparation: Make the meringues a day in advance to allow them to become nice and crisp overnight.

Key element: Over-ripe strawberries for the purée.

Tip: Mix gently, to maintain swirls of colour through the cream.

Baked Alaska Bombe

Ron Paprocki

COMPLEXITY: DIFFICULT | PREP TIME: 1 HOUR 30 MINUTES, PLUS FREEZING TIME
COOK TIME: 35 MINUTES | SERVES: 10

INGREDIENTS

CREAM CAKE

1 cup (200 g) sugar

7 oz (200 g) eggs

9 oz (250 g) whipped
cream

2 cups (250 g) all-
purpose/plain flour (T55)

¼ oz (8 g) baking
powder

RASPBERRY SORBET

1¾ cups plus 2 tbsp
(450 ml) water

9 oz (250 g) powdered
glucose

⅓ oz (10 g) sorbet
stabilizer (available
in specialist cookery
stores)

6¾ tbsp (100 ml) lemon
juice

2¼ lb (1 kg) sieved
raspberry purée

6¾ tbsp (100 ml)
glucose syrup

ITALIAN MERINGUE

2½ cups (500 g) sugar

6¾ tbsp (100 ml) water

9 oz (250 g) egg whites

TO ASSEMBLE

pistachio ice cream
(p. 378)

Image on p. 366

METHOD

Pre-heat the oven to 350°F (180°C). Line a baking pan/tin measuring 9 x 13 in (23 x 33 cm) with parchment paper.

For the cream cake, whisk the eggs and sugar together until light and fluffy and have achieved full volume. Fold half of the whipped cream into the egg mixture.

Sift the flour and baking powder into the mixture and fold in gently. Fold in the remaining whipped cream, then spread evenly over the lined baking pan. Bake for approximately 25 minutes, until lightly golden, then remove from the oven and allow to cool completely.

For the sorbet, place the water in a medium-sized pot and bring up to just below boiling. Combine the glucose and sorbet stabilizer and whisk into the water; heat to 183°F (84°C), then remove from the heat and add the lemon juice, purée, and glucose mixture, stirring to combine. Allow to cool, then refrigerate overnight. Spin in an ice cream machine according to manufacturer's instructions.

For the meringue, place the sugar and water in a small pot and heat to soft-ball stage, about 244°F (118°C).

Place the egg whites in a stand mixer fitted with a whisk attachment. When the sugar reaches temperature, have the mixer running on medium speed and the egg white at soft peak stage, then pour the sugar syrup in a thin stream into the egg white. Continue to mix on high speed until the bowl is cool.

To assemble, use a 2¼ in (6 cm) ring cutter to cut 12 rings of cream cake from the pan. Trim and discard the browned top and bottom layers so that only approximately ½ in (1 cm) of the centre remains. Set aside.

Pipe the pistachio ice cream directly onto the cream cake, followed by the raspberry sorbet. Place in the freezer and allow to freeze thoroughly, 3 to 4 hours.

One by one, remove from the freezer and use a small offset spatula to completely cover with the Italian meringue. Brown the meringue with a kitchen blowtorch and place in the freezer until ready to serve.

Pavlova with Strawberries & Rhubarb

Curtis Stone

COMPLEXITY: EASY | PREP TIME: 35 MINUTES | COOK TIME: 1 HOUR 30 MINUTES
SERVES: 6 TO 8

INGREDIENTS

MERINGUE

6 large egg whites

1¾ cups (395 g) superfine/caster sugar

1 tsp distilled white vinegar

½ tsp pure vanilla extract

½ tsp kosher/flaky salt

2 tbsp plus 2 tsp cornstarch/cornflour

TOPPING

3 tbsp (45 ml) amaretto or other almond-flavoured liqueur

3 tbsp honey (preferably lavender honey)

6 oz (175 g) fresh rhubarb, thinly sliced diagonally

8 oz (225 g) small fresh strawberries, hulled and halved

1½ cups (360 ml) heavy/double cream

1 tsp pure almond extract

2 tbsp toasted pistachios, finely chopped

powdered sugar/icing sugar, for sifting

METHOD

To make the meringue, position a rack in the lower third of the oven and pre-heat the oven to 300°F (150°C). Line a large baking sheet with baking paper and draw an 8 in (20 cm) circle on the paper. Place it face down on the baking sheet.

In the bowl of a stand mixer fitted with the whisk attachment, beat the egg whites until foamy. Gradually add the sugar, beating on medium-high speed for about 10 minutes, or until firm glossy peaks form. Beat in the vinegar, vanilla, and salt. Sift the cornstarch/cornflour over the meringue and gently fold it in.

Using a large spoon, dollop the meringue into the centre of the circle on the prepared baking sheet. Spread the meringue decoratively, keeping it within the circle (the meringue will expand slightly as it bakes).

Place the meringue in the oven, immediately reduce the oven temperature to 225°F (110°C), and bake for about 1 hour, or until the meringue is crisp on the outside but still has a marshmallow-like centre and puffs ever so slightly. Turn off the oven, prop the oven door open with a wooden spoon, and leave the meringue in the oven for 30 minutes, then remove from the oven and cool completely.

To prepare the fruit, whisk the amaretto and honey in a medium-sized heavy-based saucepan over a medium-high heat until the mixture simmers. Add the rhubarb and return the mixture to a simmer, then immediately remove the pan from the heat. Set aside for about 5 minutes, or until the rhubarb softens slightly but does not become mushy.

Transfer the rhubarb mixture to a medium-sized bowl. Add the strawberries and toss to coat with the honey mixture. Set aside, tossing occasionally, for at least 30 minutes, or until the strawberries have softened slightly.

To assemble the pavlova, place the cream and almond extract in a large bowl and use a handheld mixer to beat just thick enough to form loose dollops. Set the meringue on a platter and spoon the cream over it. Using a slotted spoon, arrange the strawberry-rhubarb mixture on the cream; reserve the juices in the bowl. Sprinkle the pavlova with the pistachios and sift powdered/icing sugar over it.

Cut the pavlova into wedges and transfer to plates. Drizzle some of the reserved strawberry-rhubarb juices around each wedge and serve immediately.

PAVLOVA PERFECTION

So here's a thing or two about pavlova: If the meringue is overbaked, it puffs too much and creates a big gaping air pocket inside, robbing you of that desirable marshmallowy centre that contrasts beautifully with the crisp exterior. To get it just right, I suggest using an oven thermometer to make sure that your oven is at the correct temperature. Oven thermometers can be found in the baking aisle in many supermarkets or at housewares stores for only a few dollars – a good investment for the perfect pav and one that will come in handy every time you bake.

"Good ol' Aussie pav . . . or is it good ol' New Zealand pav?! This dessert was created to honour Anna Pavlova, the amazing Russian ballerina, who first toured Australia and New Zealand in 1926. There is debate to this day over which country invented it. Whatever the case, this billowy meringue with its marshmallowy centre and crisp, delicate crust is a must-make."

– CURTIS STONE

JOSH'S NOTES

Preparation: The meringue can be made up to 8 hours ahead, and then cooled, covered, and stored at room temperature.

Complements: You can also serve with passionfruit curd, or your choice of seasonal fruits.

Crumble with Poached Rhubarb

Colin Fassnidge

COMPLEXITY: EASY I PREP TIME: 30 MINUTES I COOK TIME: 25 MINUTES I SERVES: 6

INGREDIENTS

CRUMBLE

4 cups (500 g) all-purpose/plain flour

8¾ oz/2¼ sticks (250 g) cold unsalted butter, chopped

1¼ cups (250 g) light-brown cane sugar/Demerara sugar

3½ oz (100 g) hazelnuts, crushed

3½ oz (100 g) rolled oats

pinch of ground cinnamon

pinch of ground ginger

POACHED RHUBARB

2 bunches rhubarb, stalks trimmed and diced

2½ cups (600 ml) ginger beer

¾ oz (20 g) fresh ginger, peeled and chopped

4 star anise

1 stick cinnamon

1 vanilla bean, split and seeds scraped

1 cup (200 g) superfine/caster sugar

TO SERVE

6 tbsp crème fraîche

METHOD

To make the crumble, pre-heat the oven to 350°F (180°C), and grease a 1¼-in (3-cm) deep baking tray. Use your fingertips to mix the flour and butter to a sandy texture. Mix in the sugar, then the remaining ingredients.

Spread the crumble over the prepared tray and cook for 10 minutes, or until golden. If not using immediately, cool completely and store in an airtight container.

For the poached rhubarb, place all ingredients in a saucepan (including the vanilla bean). Bring to a simmer over a medium heat and cook for 4 minutes, or until the rhubarb is just tender. Transfer to an ovenproof dish and remove the star anise, cinnamon, and vanilla bean.

Sprinkle the crumble mixture over the rhubarb and return to the oven for about 5 minutes, to reheat. Remove from the oven and serve with crème fraîche.

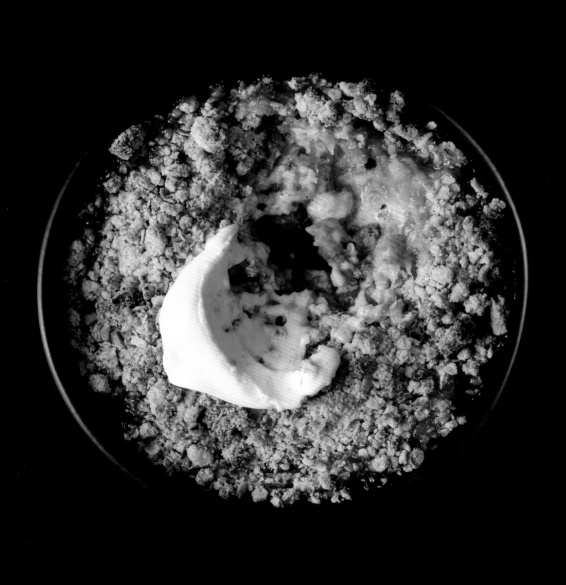

Apple Tarte Tatin with Crème Normande

Chris & Jeff Galvin

COMPLEXITY: MODERATE | PREP TIME: 20 MINUTES
COOK TIME: 1 HOUR 30 MINUTES, PLUS COOLING TIME | MAKES: ONE 8 IN (20 CM) TART

INGREDIENTS

a little plain (all-purpose) flour, for rolling

4¼ oz (120 g) puff pastry

7¾ tbsp (110 g) salted butter, softened

½ cup plus 1¼ tbsp (130 g) superfine/ caster sugar

7 Braeburn apples, peeled, halved, and cored

crème Normande (p. 490)

METHOD

On a lightly floured surface, roll the puff pastry out to a round 8½ in (21 cm) in diameter. Transfer the pastry to a flat tray lined with non-stick baking paper, prick all over with a fork, and place in the fridge to rest for 40 minutes.

Pre-heat the oven to 320°F (160°C).

Spread the butter over the bottom of an 8 in (20 cm) tarte tatin mould or non-stick ovenproof frying pan. Sprinkle superfine/caster sugar over in an even layer, then arrange the apple halves over the sugar, cut side up, with two halves in the middle.

Lay the pastry round over the apples, tucking the edges down the side. Place the mould or pan over a medium heat for about 10 minutes, until the sugar starts to caramelize. Transfer to the oven and bake for 1 hour 30 minutes.

Remove the tart from the oven and leave to cool for at least 30 minutes.

Invert the tarte tatin onto a chopping board and cut it into four portions. Serve warm with a generous spoonful of crème Normande.

JOSH'S NOTES

Key elements: If you can't source Braeburns, use apples that aren't too acidic, and good-quality puff pastry. Line the pan neatly with the apples – they lose a third of their volume when cooked.

Tip: Cook the caramel until it's a toffee colour on the stovetop, which will ensure it is beautifully caramelized at the end.

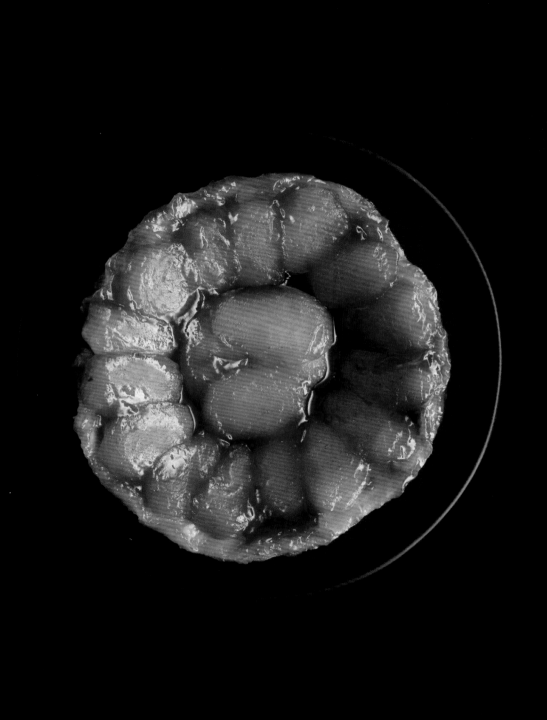

Plum Clafoutis

Marcus Wareing

COMPLEXITY: EASY | PREP TIME: 15 MINUTES | COOK TIME: 20 MINUTES | MAKES: 4

INGREDIENTS

3½ tbsp (50 g) butter, plus extra for greasing

4 tbsp light-brown cane sugar/Demerara sugar

6 ripe plums, halved and stones removed

½ cup plus 2 tbsp (150 ml) heavy/double cream

½ cup plus 2 tbsp (150 ml) milk

seeds from 1 vanilla bean

grated zest of 1 lemon

2 eggs

3¼ tbsp superfine/caster sugar

⅓ cup (45 g) all-purpose/plain flour

1 tbsp powdered sugar/icing sugar, for dusting

ice cream, to serve

METHOD

Lightly grease four 5-in (12- to 13-cm) ovenproof blini pans or ramekins with butter. Pre-heat the oven to 320°F (160°C) fan or 350°F (180°C) regular bake.

Put the light-brown cane sugar/Demerara sugar in a small, heavy-based saucepan or frying pan. Place over a medium heat and leave to melt and caramelize to a deep golden colour, swirling the pan occasionally (do not stir) to get even caramelization – this will take 5 to 8 minutes. Add the butter, whisk well and simmer for 1 to 2 minutes until well combined.

Pour a quarter of the caramel into each blini pan or ramekin, then quickly – while the caramel is still hot – place 3 plum halves, cut side down, into the caramel.

Put the cream, milk, vanilla bean seeds, and lemon zest in a small saucepan and gently bring to the boil. Remove from the heat.

In a deep bowl, whisk together the eggs and superfine/caster sugar. Whisk in the flour, then gradually add the hot milk and cream, whisking continuously.

Pour the batter over the plums in each pan or ramekin, then place in the oven for around 15 minutes, until golden and cooked through. Remove from the oven, dust with powdered/icing sugar and serve immediately with your favourite ice cream.

JOSH'S NOTES

Key element: If you don't have quite the right sized dishes, adjust the amount of plums and batter.

Tip: If fresh plums are out of season, this dish works just as well with preserved plums.

INGREDIENTS

CAKES

5½ tsp fresh yeast, or 2¾ tsp dried yeast

1 tbsp (15 ml) warm water

2 cups (250 g) T45 flour (soft/cake flour)

½ tsp salt

¼ cup (45 g) light-brown cane sugar/Demerara sugar

5 medium-sized eggs, whisked

6 tbsp (85 g) unsalted butter, melted, plus extra for greasing

SYRUP

1⅓ cups plus 2 tbsp (350 ml) water

¾ cup plus 2 tsp (170 g) sugar

¼ cup plus 2 tsp (70 ml) dark rum

1 vanilla bean

zest of 1 orange

1 stick cinnamon

VANILLA CREAM

1 cup plus 2 tsp (250 ml) cream

1 tsp powdered/icing sugar

seeds from ½ vanilla bean

Rum Baba

Josh Emett

COMPLEXITY: MODERATE | PREP TIME: 45 MINUTES, PLUS PROVING TIME
COOK TIME: 2 HOURS 30 MINUTES | MAKES: 8 TO 10

METHOD

To make the cakes, dissolve the yeast in warm water and set aside for a few minutes until frothy on top.

Place the flour, salt, sugar, and eggs in the bowl of an electric mixer and use the paddle to mix for 1 minute, until combined. Add the yeast mix and mix until combined. Add the melted butter and continue mixing until the dough comes together loosely. Cover the bowl and leave in a warm place for about 1 hour 30 minutes, or until doubled in size.

When the dough is nearly doubled, grease muffin moulds with a little butter. Knock the dough down, then pour into the muffin moulds, filling them no more than two-thirds full. Cover and leave in a warm place to proof, about 45 minutes.

When the cakes are nearly ready, pre-heat the oven to 400°F (200°C) and bake for 12 minutes, until golden all over. Remove from the oven and take the cakes out of the moulds. Allow to cool.

To make the syrup, place all the ingredients in a pot and bring to the boil over a medium heat, stirring to dissolve the sugar. Cool to room temperature.

To make the vanilla cream, place the cream, powdered/icing sugar, and vanilla bean seeds in a bowl and whisk to soft peaks.

Soak cakes in the cooled syrup for 5 minutes, then place on a plate with a drizzle of syrup and serve with a quenelle of vanilla cream.

JOSH'S NOTES

Preparation: Find a warm spot to allow the dough to prove properly and in enough time.

Chocolate Molten Cakes

Jean-Georges Vongerichten

COMPLEXITY: EASY | PREP TIME: 15 MINUTES | COOK TIME: 15 MINUTES | MAKES: 4

INGREDIENTS

½ cup/1 stick (115 g) butter, plus some for buttering the moulds

4 oz (115 g) bittersweet chocolate, preferably Valrhona

2 eggs

2 egg yolks

¼ cup (50 g) sugar

2 tsp all-purpose/plain flour, plus more for dusting

METHOD

In the top of a double boiler set over simmering water, heat the butter and chocolate together until the chocolate is almost completely melted. While that's heating, beat together the eggs, egg yolks, and sugar with a whisk or electric beater until light and thick.

Beat together the melted chocolate and butter; it should be quite warm. Pour in the egg mixture then quickly beat in the flour, just until combined.

Butter and lightly flour four 4-oz (½-cup) moulds, custard cups, or ramekins. Tap out the excess flour, then butter and flour them again. Divide the batter among the moulds. (At this point you can refrigerate the desserts until you are ready to serve, for up to several hours; bring them back to room temperature before baking.)

Pre-heat the oven to 450°F (230°C). Place the moulds on a tray and bake for 6 to 7 minutes; the centre will still be quite soft but the sides will set. Invert each mould onto a plate and let sit for about 10 seconds. Unmould by lifting up one corner of the mould; the cake will fall out onto the plate. Serve immediately.

JOSH'S NOTES

Preparation: These are great to make ahead of time, but allow enough time to bring them back to room temperature.

Key element: Prepare the moulds well, to prevent sticking.

Tip: The more you make these, the better you will get at achieving a perfect liquid centre.

SAUCE

8 tbsp/1 stick (115 g) unsalted butter

⅓ cup plus 1 tsp (75 g) golden superfine/caster sugar

1½ oz (40 g) dark muscovado sugar

½ cup plus 1¼ tbsp (140 ml) heavy/double cream

pinch of salt

PUDDING

6 oz (175 g) Medjool dates, stoned and roughly chopped

1 tsp bicarbonate of soda

1¼ cups (300 ml) boiling water

3½ tbsp (50 g) unsalted butter, softened, plus extra for greasing

3 oz (80 g) dark muscovado sugar

2 large free-range eggs, beaten

1½ cups (175 g) all-purpose/plain flour

1 tsp baking powder

pinch of ground cloves

pinch of salt

2⅔ oz (75 g) walnut halves, roughly chopped

JOSH'S NOTES

Key element: Grilling at the end will get the best flavour, but watch it carefully, as it colours quickly.

Tip: If you don't have dates, you can substitute with other ingredients such as raisins or nuts.

Sticky Toffee Pudding

Felicity Cloake

COMPLEXITY: EASY | PREP TIME: 35 MINUTES | COOK TIME: 35 MINUTES | SERVES: 6

METHOD

Pre-heat the oven to 350°F (180°). Butter a deep baking dish approximately 9½ in (24 cm) square.

Make the sauce by putting all the ingredients in a pan and heating slowly until the butter has melted, then turning up the heat and bringing to the boil. Boil for about 4 minutes, until the sauce has thickened enough to coat the back of a spoon. Pour half the sauce into the base of the dish and put it into the freezer.

Put the dates and bicarbonate of soda in a heatproof dish and cover with the boiling water. Leave to soften while you prepare the rest of the pudding.

Beat together the butter and sugar until fluffy, then beat in the egg, a little at a time. Sift in the flour, baking powder, cloves, and salt and mix until well combined, then add the dates and their soaking water, and the walnuts, and mix well.

Take the baking dish out of the freezer and pour the batter on top of the toffee sauce. Put in the oven for 30 minutes, until firm to the touch, then take out of the oven and heat the grill to medium.

Poke a few small holes evenly over the surface of the pudding with a skewer or fork, and pour over the rest of the sauce. Put briefly under the grill, keeping an eye on it as it burns easily. Serve with vanilla ice cream.

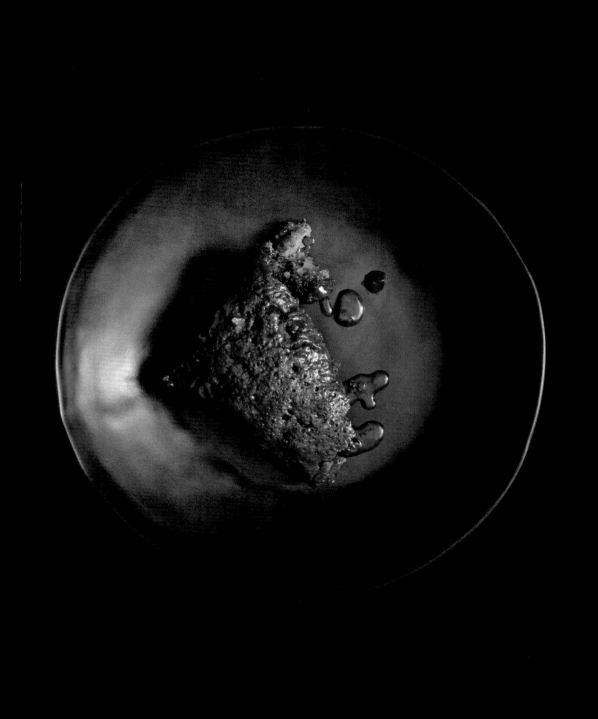

INGREDIENTS

6 tbsp/¾ stick (85 g) butter, melted, plus extra for greasing

1 cup plus 2 tbsp (140 g) self-raising flour

⅓ cup plus 1¾ tbsp (100 g) superfine/caster sugar

1 tsp baking powder

¾ cup plus 1¼ tbsp (200 ml) milk

1 egg, beaten

3 Granny Smith apples

3 sticks cinnamon

½ cup plus 2 tbsp (90 g) golden raisins/sultanas (steeped in Calvados overnight, if wished)

½ cup plus ¾ tbsp (120 g) dark brown sugar

6¾ tbsp (100 ml) boiling water

CUSTARD

2 cups plus 1¼ tbsp (500 ml) milk

¾ cup plus 1¼ tbsp (200 ml) cream

1 vanilla bean, split and seeds scraped

8 egg yolks

⅔ cup (150 g) superfine/caster sugar

1 tsp cornstarch/cornflour

JOSH'S NOTES

Preparation: If you wish to soak the golden raisins/sultanas in Calvados, do this the night before.

Apple Sponge Pudding

Reuben Riffel

COMPLEXITY: EASY | PREP TIME: 30 MINUTES | COOK TIME: 45 MINUTES | SERVES: 8 TO 10

METHOD

Pre-heat the oven to 350°F (180°C). Grease a large (2-quart/2-litre) baking dish with a little melted butter.

Place the flour, superfine/caster sugar, and baking powder in a large bowl and mix to combine.

In a separate bowl, mix the milk, beaten egg, and melted butter. Pour this into the dry ingredients and stir to form a batter.

Peel and core the apples, then slice into ½-in (1-cm) segments. Place the apple in the base of the baking dish together with cinnamon and golden raisins/sultanas. Pour the batter over the apples.

Stir the dark brown sugar into the boiling water until dissolved. Pour over the top of the batter. Bake for 45 minutes, until the sponge springs back when lightly pressed with a finger. Remove from the oven and allow to cool slightly.

For the custard, put the milk, cream, and vanilla bean in a saucepan and bring to simmering point over low heat. Meanwhile, whisk the egg yolks, sugar, and cornstarch/cornflour in a heatproof bowl until pale and creamy.

When the milk mixture is at simmering point, whisk it into the egg mixture to incorporate. Stand the bowl over a pan of simmering water set over a gentle heat, and continue to whisk until the custard thickens. Pour through a sieve and serve with warm apple sponge pudding, removing the cinnamon sticks as you serve.

_____

"This dessert was served during the cold winter months. My Aunt Bekka used to make this, and it was always a hit. Sweet, but also with a slight tartness to it. I often asked her to make this for me. I actually never got her recipe, but this one is close."

– REUBEN RIFFEL

Summer Pudding with Clotted Cream

Mark Sargeant

COMPLEXITY: MODERATE | PREP TIME: 45 MINUTES | COOK TIME: 5 MINUTES | MAKES: 4

INGREDIENTS

3½ oz (100 g) blackcurrants

3½ oz (100 g) blueberries

3½ oz (100 g) raspberries

3½ oz (100 g) blackberries

3½ oz (100 g) strawberries

1 stick cinnamon

⅓ cup (80 g) superfine/caster sugar

1 piece of lemon peel

1 piece of orange peel

1 vanilla bean

3 tbsp cornstarch/cornflour, mixed with a little water to form a paste

1 brioche loaf, crusts removed, cut into thin slices

some berries to garnish

clotted cream to serve

JOSH'S NOTES

Preparation: Make this a day ahead, so the brioche has time to absorb all the juices.

Tip: Line the dish with plastic wrap for easy removal of the puddings from the moulds.

METHOD

Place the berries in a pan with the cinnamon, superfine/caster sugar, citrus peel, vanilla bean, and a splash of water. Cover with a lid and cook over a low heat for 2 to 3 minutes, until the berries are becoming slightly soft and the juices are coming out.

Remove and discard the pieces of citrus peel and the vanilla bean. Add the cornstarch/cornflour, cook out, stirring, until thickened, then remove from the heat and allow to cool.

To prepare the brioche, remove the crusts from the loaf and cut into 2, vaguely square-shaped, halves. Cut each square into slices ¼ in (5 mm) thick. Out of the biggest slices, use 2-in (5-cm) cutters to stamp out 8 circles – these will be used for the tops and the bottoms of the puddings. Cut the rest of the slices in half to create rectangular strips, roughly ¾ x 3¼ in (2 x 8 cm).

Press a circle of bread firmly into the base of each of four moulds, then use the rectangular strips to line the edges. If there are any gaps, use smaller pieces of brioche to fill them (make sure the bread is firmly pressed against the moulds for this whole process).

Spoon berry juice over the brioche in the moulds to make it moist, saving some for the final step, then spoon in the berries. Finally place the last circles of brioche on top. Apply small weights to the top of the puddings, ensuring that the edges of the brioche are sealed, and place in the fridge to set overnight.

When ready to serve, remove the puddings from their moulds, place on plates and drizzle the reserved berry juice over the tops so that they are nicely covered. Arrange the berries around the puddings and finish with a scoop of clotted cream.

Bread & Butter Pudding

Gordon Ramsay

COMPLEXITY: EASY | PREP TIME: 25 MINUTES | COOK TIME: 40 MINUTES | SERVES: 6 TO 8

INGREDIENTS

2 to 3 tbsp apricot jam

3½ tbsp (50 g) softened butter, plus extra to grease

6 *pains au chocolat*, cut into slices ½ in (1 cm) thick

1 to 2 tbsp ground cinnamon

4 tbsp light-brown cane sugar/Demerara sugar

¼ cup (35 g) golden raisins/sultanas

2 cups plus 1¼ tbsp (500 ml) whole milk

½ cup (120 ml) heavy/double cream

6 eggs

seeds from 2 vanilla beans

METHOD

Pre-heat the oven to 350°F (180°C). Lightly butter a 7 x 9 in (18 x 23 cm) baking dish.

Heat the jelly/jam in a pan over a low heat for a couple of minutes until melted. Set aside.

Butter the slices of *pain au chocolat* on one side, place them in a large bowl and set aside. Now sprinkle about 2 teaspoons of the cinnamon into the buttered serving dish along with 2 tablespoons of the sugar and all the golden raisins/sultanas. Pour over most of the melted jam, reserving a small amount for glazing at the end.

Whisk together the milk, cream, eggs, vanilla bean seeds, and 1 teaspoon of the cinnamon and pour half of this mixture all over the bread. When it has soaked in slightly, arrange the bread in the serving dish so that the pieces are overlapping. Continue layering the bread until all the pieces have been used, then pour over the rest of the egg mixture and scatter the surface with the remaining sugar and a light dusting of cinnamon.

Place in the preheated oven and bake for 35 to 40 minutes until golden.

To serve, brush the pudding with the reserved melted jelly/jam and serve immediately.

"Bread and butter pudding was absolutely my favourite when I was growing up. My mother always made it with cheap sliced white bread, but I've experimented with all sorts since: baguette, panettone, brioche, croissants. *Pain au chocolat* is my current favourite."

– GORDON RAMSAY

INGREDIENTS

CUSTARD CREAM

1 cup plus 2 tsp
(250 ml) milk

3 tbsp cornstarch/
cornflour

2 tbsp plus 2½ tsp sugar

¼ cup (60 g) egg yolk

1¾ tbsp (25 g) butter,
cut into small cubes

ALMOND CREAM

½ cup/1 stick plus
1 tbsp (125 g) butter

1 egg

1 egg yolk

5 oz (150 g) custard
cream (see above)

1⅓ oz (125 g) almond
flour

2 tsp rum

1 vanilla bean

Ingredients continued
overleaf

JOSH'S NOTES

Preparation: Buy good-
quality brioche, or make
your own, p. 508, ahead
of time.

Key element: Soaking
for the brioche.

Tip: Monitor the
temperature of the pan
and cook 1 or 2 *torrijas*
at a time until you
get used to the heat
and how quickly they
caramelize.

Caramelized
French Toast Spanish-style
Torrijas Caramelizadas

Andoni Luis Aduriz

COMPLEXITY: MODERATE | PREP TIME: 1 HOUR, PLUS SOAKING TIME
COOK TIME: 35 MINUTES | SERVES: 10

METHOD

For the custard cream, bring about ⅔ cup (150 ml) milk to the boil in
a pot. In a bowl, mix the cornstarch/cornflour, sugar, and the rest of
the milk together. Once the milk comes to the boil, add the contents
of the bowl, while stirring, and cook for 15 minutes.

In a clean bowl, beat the egg yolks until combined, then add a
little of the cooked mixture. Mix in quickly and pour back into the
pot. Combine everything well, then remove from the heat. Allow
the mixture to cool to 140°F (60°C) then add the butter and stir to
combine. Spread over a tray and cover with plastic wrap, touching
the surface of the custard cream.

For the almond cream, warm the butter by leaving it at room
temperature or working it with a spatula until it acquires the
consistency of whipped cream. Mix together with the remaining
ingredients. Cover and chill until needed.

To soak the brioche, mix the milk, cream, egg, and sugar until well
combined and the sugar has dissolved. Place in a large dish, put the
brioche slices in the bath and soak for 4 to 6 hours.

For the goat milk ice cream, bring the milk to the boil, then remove
from the heat and allow to cool. Warm it again to 104°F (40°C) and
add the sugar, glucose, and milk powder. Stir to combine, then heat
to 185°F (85°C) and allow to cool again. Freeze overnight and whip
in a Paco jet, or follow the instructions for your ice cream machine.

Continued overleaf

INGREDIENTS CONT.

FOR SOAKING THE *TORRIJAS*

1 loaf brioche, sliced
1¼ to 1½ in (3 to 4 cm),
wrapped in plastic wrap
and refrigerated for
4 days

2 qt (2 litres) milk

2 qt (2 litres) cream

1½ lb (720 g) egg

2 cups (440 g) sugar

goat milk ice cream

5¼ cups plus 2¼ tbsp
(1.3 litres) goat milk

¾ cup plus 2¼ tbsp
(200 g) sugar

2 oz (60 g) glucose

1¼ oz (35 g) milk
powder

salt

CANDIED LEMON PEEL

peel of ½ lemon

6¾ tbsp (100 ml) water

⅓ cup plus 1¾ tbsp
(100 g) sugar

2 tsp salt

TO FINISH

⅓ cup plus 1¾ tbsp
(100 g) sugar

3½ tbsp (50 g) butter

Caramelized French Toast Spanish-style cont.

For the candied lemon peel, cut the peel into thin strips (juliennes). Place in a pot, cover with cold water and bring to the boil. Strain off the water, replace with more cold water and bring back to the boil. Repeat this once more, then strain and set aside. Place the water, sugar, and salt in the pot, and bring to the boil and simmer to make a light syrup. Add the peel to the hot syrup for 1 minute, then remove with a slotted spoon and allow to cool.

To finish, remove the *torrijas* from the custard cream, heat a frying pan over a medium heat and sprinkle a little sugar on each side of the *torrijas*. Place a little butter in the pan and seal the *torrijas* on all sides until golden coloured and warmed through. Plate by putting some almond cream on each plate and the *torrijas* on top. Place ice cream to one side with the candied lemon peel.

"In this recipe you can avoid making the brioche at home. It can be purchased from a good bakery, always keeping in mind that it has to be made with butter."

– ANDONI LUIS ADURIZ

Chocolate Profiteroles

Diane Holuigue

COMPLEXITY: MODERATE | PREP TIME: 20 MINUTES | COOK TIME: 35 MINUTES
MAKES: ABOUT 35

INGREDIENTS

1 recipe chou pastry
(p. 512), still warm

melted butter, for
greasing

1 egg

1 tbsp (15 ml) milk

CRÈME PÂTISSIÈRE

1¾ cups plus 2 tbsp
(450 ml) milk

4 egg yolks

3 tbsp sugar

2 tbsp all-purpose/
plain flour

TO SERVE

chocolate sauce (p. 490)

METHOD

Pre-heat the oven to 400°F (200°C). Lightly grease a baking tray
(or two) with butter.

Transfer the warm chou pastry to a piping bag with a ½ in (1 cm)
nozzle and pipe onto the tray in dollops measuring ⅝ to 1¼ in
(1½ to 2 cm) across. The dough may also be formed by dropping
from a teaspoon. You should get about 35 puffs.

Beat the egg and milk together in a cup, and glaze the puffs with a
pastry brush. Bake for 20 minutes, then turn the tray and leave in the
oven for a further 15 minutes to dry out. If the puffs are already well
browned, the drying out can be done at 350°F (180°C).

When cooked, tap the tray to release the puffs, then quickly pierce
each one immediately in one side, towards the base, with the handle
of a teaspoon to allow the steam to escape; otherwise the puffs may
collapse. Cool on a cake rack while making the crème pâtissière.
The puffs may be made in advance and stored in an airtight tin for
1 or 2 days, or frozen.

CRÈME PÂTISSIÈRE

Scald the milk. Break the 4 yolks into a bowl and blend first with
the sugar, then with the flour. Delay (blend) with a little of the milk,
stirring well, then return all to the saucepan and stir to the boil,
using a whisk to blend well. The mixture thickens when it comes to
the boil; remove from heat and add the vanilla. Cool slightly and
transfer to the icing bag with the 7 mm nozzle.

JOSH'S NOTES

Preparation: The puffs
can be made one or two
days in advance; they
freeze very well.

Key element: Make sure
the crème patissière
boils, otherwise it may
not be thick enough.

TO ASSEMBLE

Pipe the cream into the puffs through the hole made with the teaspoon handle. Never cut small puffs open, as they don't ice neatly. The only exception is when filling them with ice cream.

Dip each puff into the sauce while it is still hot. You may serve 3 small puffs per person, or build puffs into a loose pyramid on a serving platter. Start with a base of about nine puffs, then seven, then five, etc. They don't stick in the way they would if dipped in a caramel instead of a chocolate sauce, but stacking them makes a spectacular presentation.

Finish by dribbling some sauce over the pyramid and thin the rest with a further 2 or 3 tablespoons (30 to 45 ml) of water, stirred in the sauce over heat. Serve this thinner sauce in a sauceboat.

"This is the full recipe with crème pâtissière at the centre of each puff. Some people choose a simpler dessert by simply baking the puffs, cutting them in half and filling at the last minute with vanilla ice cream, serving three per guest and then pouring the hot chocolate sauce over them at table."

– DIANE HOLUIGUE

Image on p. 365

Chocolate & Banana Bombolini

Massimo Mele

COMPLEXITY: EASY | PREP TIME: 15 MINUTES, PLUS FREEZING TIME
COOK TIME: 10 MINUTES | MAKES: 20

INGREDIENTS

3 oz (90 g) peeled banana

⅓ oz (10 g) superfine/caster sugar

6¾ tbsp (100 ml) milk

3½ oz/7 tbsp (100 g) unsalted butter

¾ cup plus 2½ tsp (100 g) all-purpose/plain flour

3 eggs

40 small plain chocolate buttons, 55% cocoa solids

2 cups plus 1¼ tbsp (500 ml) neutral-flavoured oil, for deep-frying

JOSH'S NOTES

Preparation: Start a day in advance, so they can freeze overnight.

Key element: Good ice trays that have a good 'doughnut' shape.

Tip: Rest the fried bombolini on a paper towel for a minute, which allows them to cool slightly on the outside.

METHOD

In a blender, purée the banana with the sugar until smooth. Put the milk and butter in a small saucepan on medium heat and heat until melted. Add the banana mixture and bring to the boil, then add the sifted flour and fold in slowly, making sure all of the flour is combined. The mixture will come together like choux pastry. Cook for 2 to 3 minutes, until you can no longer taste the flour, then transfer the mixture to a stand mixer. Using the paddle attachment, start mixing. Gradually add the eggs one at a time until they are all incorporated.

Once cooled, place the mixture in a piping bag and pipe into soft, flexible mini muffin trays, filling each hole three-quarters full. Place two chocolate buttons in each cube, making sure that the chocolate is completely covered by the mixture. Cover with plastic wrap and freeze overnight.

Heat the oil in a deep-fryer to 320°F (160°C). Check that the temperature is okay by putting in one frozen doughnut. After 5 minutes, take it out and cut it in half. The chocolate should be oozing out of the middle. If not cooked, adjust the cooking time slightly.

Fry the cubes in small batches and place on a plate covered with paper towels to drain. Dust with cinnamon sugar or serve with custard.

Image on p. 364

Caramelized Pineapple Crêpes with Crème Fraîche

Eric Ripert

COMPLEXITY: EASY | PREP TIME: 30 MINUTES
COOK TIME: 35 MINUTES, PLUS 1 HOUR TO REST | MAKES: 12 CRÊPES

INGREDIENTS

CRÊPES

6 tbsp/¾ stick (80 g) unsalted butter, plus extra for cooking

¾ cup (90 g) all-purpose/plain flour

2 tbsp sugar

½ tsp fine sea salt

3 large eggs

1½ cups (360 ml) milk

2 tbsp (30 ml) dark rum

SAUCE

1 cup (230 g) crème fraîche

1 tbsp sugar

1 vanilla bean, halved lengthwise

about 2 tbsp/¼ stick (30 g) unsalted butter

FILLING

½ cup (100 g) sugar

4 tbsp/½ stick (60 g) unsalted butter

2 tbsp (30 ml) dark rum

1 pineapple, peeled, cored, and cut into juliennes

METHOD

For the crêpes, melt the butter in a small pot over a medium heat. Simmer the butter until the milk solids turn brown. Set aside.

Sift the flour, sugar, and salt together in a bowl. Make a well in the dry ingredients, add the eggs, and whisk until incorporated. Whisk in the milk. Whisk in the browned butter and rum. Cover the batter and let rest in the refrigerator for at least an hour.

Meanwhile, for the sauce, whisk the crème fraîche lightly with the sugar until it becomes liquid. Scrape the seeds from the vanilla bean and stir them gently into the crème fraîche. Cover and refrigerate until ready to serve.

To cook the crêpes, melt ½ teaspoon butter in an 8-in (20-cm) non-stick frying pan over a medium-high heat. Ladle in ¼ cup of the crêpe batter and swirl to distribute evenly. Cook for 1 minute, or until it is golden on the bottom. Flip the crêpe and cook for another minute, or until golden on the second side. Transfer to a plate and repeat with the remaining batter, adding more butter to the pan as necessary and stacking the cooked crêpes. You will need a total of 12 crêpes. Cover the crêpes with plastic wrap until ready to serve.

For the filling, melt the sugar without stirring in a medium-sized pot over a medium-high heat, then simmer gently until the sugar has caramelized and is deep brown. Add the butter and rum and whisk to incorporate. Add the pineapple and cook until it is well coated and tender. Remove from the heat.

To assemble the dessert, place a crêpe on a work surface and spread ¼ cup of the pineapple down the centre. Roll up the crêpe and place on a plate with the seam down. Continue with the remaining crêpes, placing 2 crêpes on each plate. Drizzle the crème fraîche over the crêpes and serve immediately.

Image on p. 365

Crêpes Suzette

Jacques Pépin

COMPLEXITY: EASY | PREP TIME: 20 MINUTES | COOK TIME: 20 MINUTES
MAKES: 12 TO 15 CRÊPES

INGREDIENTS

CRÊPES

¾ cup (90 g) all-purpose/plain flour

2 large eggs

½ cup (120 ml) milk

1 tbsp (15 g) butter, melted

⅛ tsp salt

½ tsp sugar

⅓ cup (80 ml) cold water

2 tbsp (30 ml) rapeseed/canola oil

about 1 tbsp (15 g) butter, for the pan

ORANGE BUTTER

6 tbsp/¾ stick (80 g) unsalted butter, softened

¼ cup (25 g) sugar

1 tbsp grated orange rind

juice of 1 orange (about ⅓ cup/80 ml)

METHOD

To make the crêpes, combine the flour, eggs, ¼ cup (60 ml) milk, melted butter, salt, and sugar in a bowl and mix well with a whisk. (The mixture will be thick and smooth.) Add the remaining milk, the cold water and oil. Stir well.

Heat a 6-in (15-cm) crêpe pan or shallow frying pan, preferably non-stick, and butter it lightly (butter it only for the first crêpe.) Pour about 3 tablespoons of batter into one side of the pan and immediately tilt the pan, shaking it at the same time, to make the batter run all over the bottom. (The speed at which the batter spreads determines the thickness of the crêpe; if you do not move the pan fast enough, the batter will set before it has a chance to spread and the crêpe will be thicker than desired.)

Cook over a medium-high heat for about 1 minute, until browned. To flip, bang the pan on a pot holder set on the corner of the stove to loosen the crêpe, then flip it over. Or, lift up an edge of the crêpe with your fingers or a fork, grab the crêpe between your thumb and forefinger, and turn it over. Cook for about 30 seconds on the other side and transfer it to a plate. Notice that the side of the crêpe that browned first has the nicer colour; be sure to serve the crêpes so that this is the side that is visible. Repeat with the remaining batter, stacking the crêpes.

To make the orange butter, put the butter, sugar, and grated orange rind in a food processor and process until the mixture is a uniform orange colour. With the machine running, add the juice slowly, so that the butter absorbs it. Spread approximately 1 tablespoon of the orange butter on each crêpe. Fold the crêpes into quarters.

To finish, pre-heat the oven grill to hot. Butter a large ovenproof platter about 17 x 10 in (43 x 25 cm) with the softened butter and sprinkle it with 1½ tablespoons of the sugar. Arrange the filled crêpes on it, overlapping them slightly and leaving a space at the end of the platter where the sauce can accumulate. Sprinkle the crêpes with the remaining sugar and place them under the grill (approximately in the middle of the oven, so they won't burn) for 2 to 3 minutes, until the surface of the crêpes caramelizes.

Pour the liqueur on the very hot crêpes and carefully ignite with a long match. Bring the platter to the table and incline slightly so that the flaming juices gather in the space you left. Spoon up the liquid and pour it back, still flaming, onto the crêpes. When the flame subsides, serve the crêpes, 2 to 3 per person, with some of the sauce.

INGREDIENTS CONT.

TO SERVE

1 tbsp (15 g) unsalted butter, softened

3½ tbsp sugar

¼ cup (60 ml) Grand Marnier, Cointreau, or homemade orange liqueur

Ruth's
Very Rich Pancakes

Ruth Reichl

COMPLEXITY: EASY | PREP TIME: 5 MINUTES | COOK TIME: 5 MINUTES
MAKES: 10 TO 12 PANCAKES

INGREDIENTS

4 oz/1 stick (115 g) unsalted butter, plus extra for cooking

1 cup (240 ml) milk

3 tbsp (45 ml) neutral vegetable oil

2 eggs

1 cup (125 g) all-purpose/plain flour

4 tsp baking powder

4 tsp sugar

1 tsp salt

maple syrup, to serve

METHOD

Melt the butter in the milk and allow to cool. Whisk in the vegetable oil and eggs.

In a medium-sized bowl, whisk the dry ingredients together. Lightly whisk the milk mixture into the dry ingredients, just until combined. Do not overmix.

Melt ½ teaspoon of butter in a non-stick frying pan set over a moderate heat, until hot but not smoking. Pour the batter in – to whatever size you like – and cook until bubbles form on the top and then break. Flip over and cook for about another minute, until the bottom is golden.

Serve hot with real maple syrup.

"I like these best hot from the pan – but in a pinch you can keep them warm in a 200°F (100°C) degree oven."

– RUTH REICHL

JOSH'S NOTES

Preparation: Use the batter straight away – there is no need to rest it.

Key element: The temperature of the pan is key; you need to maintain a medium-high heat.

Tip: Don't make the pancakes too large, otherwise they will be difficult to cook evenly.

Carrot Halwa
Gajar Halwa

Sid Sahrawat

COMPLEXITY: MODERATE | PREP TIME: 30 MINUTES | COOK TIME: 2 HOURS 30 MINUTES
SERVES: 8 TO 10

INGREDIENTS

3⅓ lb (1½ kg) carrots, peeled and coarsely grated

2⅓ cups (560 ml) evaporated milk

½ cup (75 g) raisins

1½ cups (300 g) granulated sugar

3½ oz (100 g) *khoa* (also known as *mawa*: milk solids, from the frozen section of Indian grocers), grated

2 tbsp ghee (clarified butter)

1 tsp ground cardamom

pinch of saffron (optional)

¼ cup (30 g) slivered almonds

¼ cup (40 g) cashews

edible flowers (optional), for garnish

vanilla ice cream (optional), for serving

JOSH'S NOTES

Tip: Ensure that the heat is very low, otherwise the liquid will evaporate too quickly.

METHOD

Stir the carrot and evaporated milk together in a large, heavy-based saucepan. Bring to the boil, then reduce the heat to low and simmer for around 40 minutes until the carrot is soft, stirring occasionally. Meanwhile, cover the raisins in hot water and leave to soak for at least 15 minutes.

Stir the sugar into the carrot mix and simmer for a further 10 minutes, stirring often. Drain the raisins, and reserve a few tablespoons of raisins and *khoa* for garnish. Stir the remaining raisins and *khoa*, plus the ghee, cardamom, and saffron, into the carrot mix. Reduce the heat to very low and cook for about 1 hour 30 minutes until all of the milk is absorbed, stirring occasionally.

Meanwhile, set a medium-sized frying pan over a medium-low heat and toast the nuts, separately, until golden brown, stirring frequently. Remove from the pan and set aside to cool.

To serve, spoon the carrot halwa into a mound in one large or multiple individual serving bowls. Garnish with the reserved raisins and *khoa*, toasted nuts, and edible flowers. Enjoy warm with vanilla ice cream, or cold.

Leftover halwa will keep in an airtight container in the fridge for 3 days. Garnish with nuts only when serving, to keep the nuts crunchy.

TIP

Halwa can be prepared 1 to 2 days in advance and stored in the refrigerator, which will further develop the flavour. Reheat gently to serve warm (my preference), or eat cold.

Brandy Snaps

Josh Emett

COMPLEXITY: MODERATE | PREP TIME: 25 MINUTES, PLUS RESTING TIME
COOK TIME: 7 MINUTES | MAKES: 10 OR MORE

INGREDIENTS

¾ cup/1½ sticks
(175 g) unsalted butter,
softened

1⅓ cups (300 g)
superfine/caster sugar

½ cup (150 g) liquid
honey

1¼ cups (150 g) all-
purpose/plain flour

TO SERVE

¾ cup plus 1¼ tbsp
(200 ml) heavy/double
cream

2 tbsp powdered sugar/
icing sugar

few drops of vanilla
essence

METHOD

Using an electric mixer, beat the soft butter and sugar together until mixed but not pale. Add the honey and beat in, then add the flour and fold in, making sure that there are no lumps at all. Leave to rest for 1 hour.

Pre-heat the oven to 350°F (180°C). Line a couple of baking trays with non-stick baking mats. Using a thin, circular flat mould (you can cut one out of an old lid), about 6 in (15 cm) in diameter, spread the mix into about 8 thin rounds on the mats using a palette knife.

Bake one tray at a time for 6 to 7 minutes. Carefully lift each round from the tray with a fish slice, then roll while still hot around a brandy snap roller or clean broom handle. Carefully slide off onto a rack, and allow to set and become crispy. Repeat until all the brandy snaps are rolled.

Whip the cream with the powdered/icing sugar and vanilla to soft peaks, and transfer to a piping bag. When ready to serve, pipe the vanilla cream inside each brandy snap and serve immediately.

JOSH'S NOTES

Preparation: You can make the brandy snaps in advance and keep them in an airtight container until required.

Tips: Start with 4 or so brandy snaps on each tray so you have time to roll them while still hot. If they firm up before you can roll them, warm them slightly in the oven.

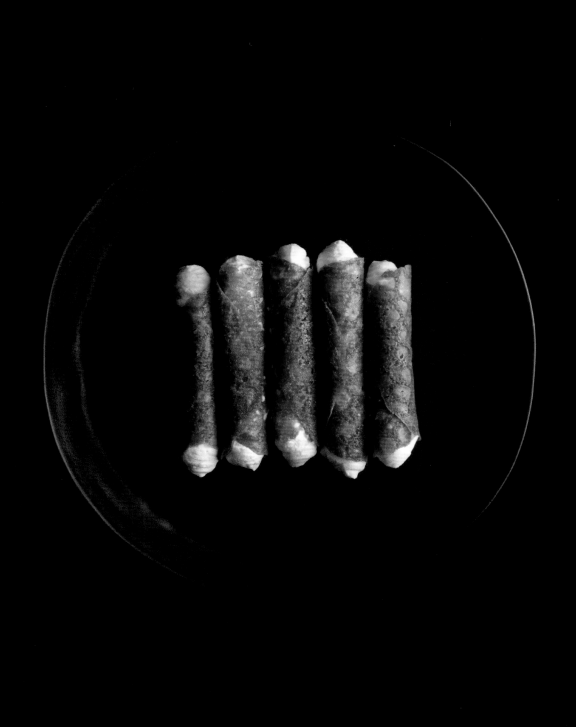

Chocolate Truffles

Natalia Schamroth

COMPLEXITY: EASY | PREP TIME: 30 MINUTES, PLUS 3 DAYS REFRIGERATION AND FREEZING TIME
COOK TIME: 10 MINUTES | SERVES: 25 TO 30

INGREDIENTS

DAY ONE

10½ oz (300 g) 55% chocolate, coarsely chopped

3½ oz (100 g) 64% chocolate, coarsely chopped

1 cup plus 2 tsp (250 ml) heavy/double cream

1 double shot (4 tbsp/60 ml) espresso, freshly made

DAY THREE

10½ oz (300 g) 64% chocolate, coarsely chopped

9¾ oz (275 g) best-quality cocoa

JOSH'S NOTES

Key element: Imperfect shapes are great; they don't have to be perfectly round and show the truffles have been handmade.

Tip: Once dipped, allow the shell to set in the chocolate before coating in the cocoa.

METHOD

On day one, place the chocolate in a heatproof bowl. Heat the cream until almost boiling, then pour the cream and espresso over the chocolate. Leave to sit for 5 minutes, then whisk until smooth.

Pour the chocolate mix through a fine sieve into a shallow glass or ceramic container. Allow to cool completely, then refrigerate until set (preferably overnight).

On day two, line a flat tray with non-stick baking paper. Heat a teaspoon in a bowl of very hot water, dry the spoon and use it to roll the mixture into truffle shapes (or use a melon-baller for perfect rounds). Place the truffles on the prepared tray and freeze overnight.

On day three, place the chocolate in a heatproof bowl set over a saucepan of simmering water, without letting the bowl touch the water. Once the chocolate has melted, stir it briefly until smooth, then remove from the heat. Place the cocoa in a separate bowl, preferably a wide one. Line a suitable storage container with baking paper.

Remove the truffles from the freezer. Working quickly, drop truffles into the melted chocolate one by one. Remove with a fork, shaking off any excess chocolate, and drop into the cocoa. Leave in the cocoa until the chocolate has set (around 5 minutes), then transfer to the storage container. Cover and refrigerate until ready to serve.

The cocoa can be sieved and reused, and any leftover melted chocolate can be eaten or kept for another use.

TIP

The number of truffles you make depends on the size and how much melted chocolate gets eaten along the way!

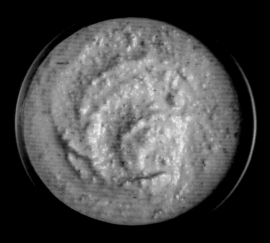

Salsa Romesco, p. 462

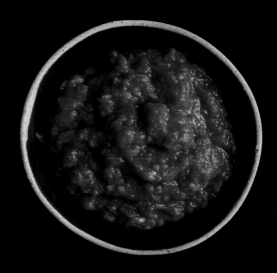

Napolitana Sauce, p. 463

Taramosalata, p. 435

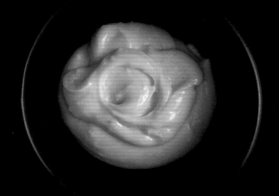

Aïoli, p. 475

Basics

Basics are the foundation for all other types of cooking, and mastering them will unlock the door to the cooking kingdom. Learning how to make your own condiments, curd, brines, bread, stocks, sauces, pastries, and even how to pickle your own vegetables, not only broadens your skills; it gives you an understanding of the various components that go into a recipe, and an appreciation for the ingredients that create classic underlying flavour profiles. Taking the time to create your own go-to fridge, freezer, and pantry basics will provide that elusive *je ne sais quoi* element that store-bought substitutes just can't beat.

Hummus

Claudia Roden

COMPLEXITY: EASY | PREP TIME: 10 MINUTES | COOK TIME: 20 MINUTES
SERVES: 8 OR MORE

INGREDIENTS

9 oz (250 g) dried garbanzo beans/chickpeas, rinsed and soaked in plenty of water overnight

½ tsp baking soda/bicarbonate of soda

10½ oz (300 g) light tahini

juice of 2 lemons

4 cloves garlic, crushed

salt

METHOD

Drain the soaked garbanzo beans/chickpeas and put them in a pan with plenty of fresh water and the baking soda/bicarbonate of soda. Bring to the boil, remove the scum, and simmer for 20 minutes or until they are very soft. Drain, reserving the cooking water.

Put the tahini, lemon juice, and garlic in a food processor and blend – the tahini will stiffen into lumps. Set aside a few whole garbanzo beans/chickpeas for a garnish, and add the rest to the blender. Blend, adding some salt and enough of the cooking water – about ¾ to 1 cup (200 to 250 ml) – to get a soft creamy paste.

Pour the hummus into a shallow dish and garnish with the whole garbanzo beans/chickpeas.

GARNISH VARIATIONS

- Dribble on 4 tablespoons (60 ml) of extra virgin olive oil.

- Sprinkle with ground cumin and paprika, or a sprinkling of sumac and a little chopped flat-leaf parsley.

JOSH'S NOTES

Preparation: Make this ahead of time – it will last in the fridge for 5 days.

Key elements: Good-quality garbanzo beans/chickpeas.

Tip: Add the water a little at a time to avoid the hummus becoming too runny.

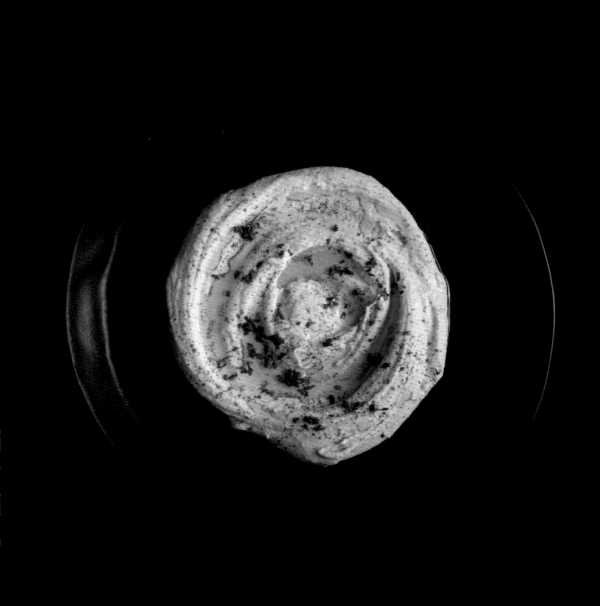

Guacamole

Grace Ramirez

COMPLEXITY: EASY | PREP TIME: 10 MINUTES | SERVES: 4

INGREDIENTS

2 ripe avocados

1 tbsp (15 ml) fresh lime or lemon juice

salt and freshly ground black pepper

½ red onion, peeled and diced (about ¼ cup/40 g)

1 jalapeño, serrano or other chilli, minced (optional)

2 tbsp cilantro/coriander leaves, finely chopped, plus extra for garnish

GARNISH

1 tbsp pomegranate seeds

1 tsp black sesame or toasted sesame seeds

flaky sea salt, to taste

JOSH'S NOTES

Key elements: Use fresh ingredients and perfectly ripe avocados.

Tip: Add the lemon or lime juice to the avocado right away, to keep it super-green.

METHOD

Halve the avocados, remove the stones and scoop the flesh out, putting it in a mixing bowl. Using a fork, mash the avocado, adding some lemon or lime juice, and season with salt and pepper to taste. Add the red onion, chilli, and cilantro/coriander. Just before serving, finish by garnishing with the pomegranate and sesame seeds, some extra cilantro/coriander, and flaky sea salt.

To prevent oxidation (browning), put the avocado stone in the middle of the guacamole. Acid also prevents oxidation, so feel free to add a thin layer of lemon or lime juice on top, folding this through just before serving.

If you need to refrigerate your guac (up to 2 days), put it in a bowl that has a tight-fitting lid. Pack the guacamole tightly in the bowl, pressing out any air bubbles. Dribble in some lukewarm water, making sure that the water covers the surface of the guacamole to about ½ in (1 cm) deep. Put some plastic wrap directly over the guac, then put the lid on and refrigerate. When ready to eat, take the lid off and gently pour out the water. Stir the guacamole to incorporate any extra moisture.

TIPS

- Do not over-mash your guacamole; leave it a bit chunky. It will have more texture and better taste.

- Chillies vary individually in their hotness. Start with half of one, and taste. Be careful when handling chillies – wash your hands, and do not rub your eyes!

- If pomegranates are not in season, simply leave them out. Another great flavour combo is *pepitas* with blue cheese on top.

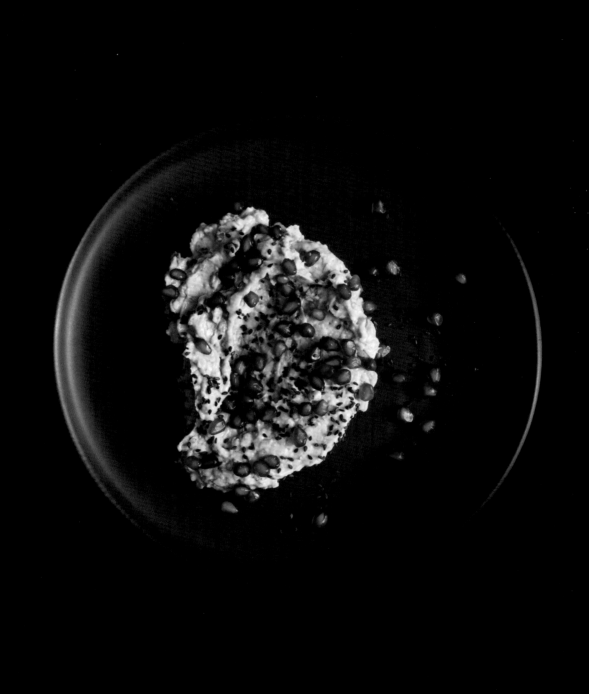

Baba Ghanoush

Greg Malouf

COMPLEXITY: EASY | PREP TIME: 20 MINUTES | COOK TIME: 20 MINUTES
MAKES: 2 CUPS (480 G)

INGREDIENTS

4 medium eggplants/
aubergines (about
2¼ lb/1 kg)

1 large clove garlic
crushed with ½ tsp
sea salt

7 oz (200 g) plain
unsweetened yoghurt

juice of 1 to 1½ lemons

3 tbsp tahini

sea salt and freshly
ground black pepper

extra virgin olive oil

JOSH'S NOTES

Key elements: Take
your time roasting the
eggplants/aubergines
over the open flame
and cook the eggplants/
aubergines until very
soft all the way through.

Tip: You can roughly
chop the aubergine/
eggplant pulp before
mixing.

Comment: I prefer it
chunky, so it's more of
an accompaniment,
than a dip.

METHOD

Prick the eggplants all over with a fork and then sit them directly on the naked flame of your stove burners. Set the flame to low-medium heat, and cook for at least 10 minutes, constantly turning until each whole aubergine/eggplant is blackened and blistered and has collapsed in on itself. Remove them from the flame and place them on a small cake rack in a sealed container or plastic bag (so the juices can drain off). Allow the eggplants/aubergines to cool for about 10 minutes.

If you prefer a milder smoky flavour, then you can char the eggplants/ aubergines on the flame for 5 minutes and finish off the roasting in an oven preheated to 350°F (180°C) for about 10 minutes.

When the eggplants/aubergines are cool, gently peel away the skin from the flesh with a small, sharp knife. Allow the skin to peel away naturally, and do not scrape the flesh directly off the skin, as it will have a burnt flavour. For this reason, too, be careful not to allow any pieces of the skin itself into the mix. Dip the peeled aubergine/ eggplant into acidulated water (4 cups/1 litre cold water plus ½ squeezed lemon), gently washing to remove any black pieces as it also helps keep the aubergine/eggplant white. Transfer the pulp to a colander and allow to sit for 20 to 30 minutes to drain further.

When you are ready to assemble the dish, mix the garlic paste with the yoghurt, then mix this into the aubergine/eggplant pulp together with the lemon juice and tahini. Season with salt and pepper and mix to combine – the dip should be coarse, not smooth and creamy. Don't be afraid to taste and adjust the seasoning, as it should taste sharp.

Tip into a bowl and with the back of a soup spoon make a large well. Tip in a big splash of extra virgin olive oil and serve as a dip with plenty of fresh Arabic bread or as a deliciously different accompaniment to grilled or roast lamb.

"Also called *moutabal*, versions of this superb dip are found throughout the Middle East, Eastern Mediterranean, and Iran. Local variations abound – with the addition of yoghurt, mint, and cumin on top of the basic oil, lemon, garlic, and tahini."
– GREG MALOUF

INGREDIENTS

1 cup (180 g) pitted
Moroccan oil-cured
olives

1 oil-cured white
anchovy fillet

juice of ½ lemon

1 tsp chopped garlic

½ cup plus 1 tsp
(125 ml) extra virgin
olive oil

───────────

This recipe accompanies
Marc Forgione's Niçoise
Salad recipe, p. 112.

Olive Tapenade

Marc Forgione

COMPLEXITY: EASY | PREP TIME: 10 MINUTES | MAKES: 1½ CUPS (370 ML)

In a food processor fitted with a metal blade, pulse the olives,
anchovy, lemon juice, and garlic until finely chopped.

With the motor running, slowly drizzle in the olive oil
until incorporated.

INGREDIENTS

¼ cup plus 1 tsp
(65 ml) good extra
virgin olive oil

5 cloves garlic, sliced

3 shallots, sliced

6¾ tbsp (100 ml)
white wine

2½ oz (70 g) canned
anchovy fillets

6¾ tbsp (100 ml) cream

JOSH'S NOTES

Tip: Slice the garlic and
shallots to the same size
so they cook evenly.

Complements: Serve
with fresh radishes,
crudités, endive. Also a
delicious accompaniment
to roast lamb.

Anchoiade

Josh Emett

COMPLEXITY: EASY | PREP TIME: 15 MINUTES | COOK TIME: 10 MINUTES
MAKES: 1 CUP (240 G)

Place the olive oil in a small pot and warm over a medium-low
heat, then add the garlic and shallots, and sweat down gently until
softened. Add the wine and simmer to reduce by half. Add the
anchovies and the cream, bring back up to the boil, then transfer
to a blender and blend until smooth, but still with a little texture.

Tzatziki

Ray McVinnie

COMPLEXITY: EASY | PREP TIME: 15 MINUTES | MAKES: 4 CUPS (980 G)

INGREDIENTS

1 medium-sized cucumber

2 cups (500 g) plain unsweetened additive-free yoghurt

1 tbsp (15 ml) extra virgin olive oil

1 tbsp (15 ml) white wine vinegar

sea salt

3 tbsp thinly sliced mint leaves, sliced just before needed, plus extra for serving

Peel the cucumber, split in half lengthways and scoop out the seeds with a teaspoon. Coarsely grate the cucumber and squeeze dry in handfuls.

Put all the ingredients into a bowl, mix well, taste and season with salt.

Serve sprinkled with a few extra mint leaves.

———————

"This is the classic Greek dip found on most Greek meze tables. It is also good as a sauce for grilled chicken, fish, lamb chops, or steamed vegetables."

– RAY MCVINNIE

Taramosalata

George Calombaris

COMPLEXITY: EASY | PREP TIME: 1 HOUR 5 MINUTES | MAKES: 3⅓ LB (1½ KG)

INGREDIENTS

5 oz (150 g) 2-day-old bread

⅓ cup (80 ml) cold water

⅓ cup plus 2 tbsp (110 ml) strained lemon juice

¼ brown onion, roughly chopped

6⅓ oz (180 g) taramosalata paste (use white cod roe only)

5 cups (1.2 litres) neutral oil

To begin, soak the bread in the water and lemon juice for about 1 hour, until well soaked. Transfer to a blender, add the onion and taramosalata paste, and blitz until very smooth.

While still blending, slowly add the oil to emulsify until a thick and whipped consistency is achieved.

Serve with pita. Do not use this in a vacuum siphon.

JOSH'S NOTES

Tip: Use a strong white bread such as ciabatta to achieve the right consistency.

Image on p. 426

Café de Paris Butter

Josh Emett

COMPLEXITY: EASY | PREP TIME: 25 MINUTES | COOK TIME: 3 MINUTES
MAKES: 2⅓ CUPS (550 G)

INGREDIENTS

1 tbsp (15 ml) olive oil

3½ oz (100 g) shallots, cut into brunoise

2 cloves garlic, cut into brunoise or microplaned

1 tsp chopped thyme leaves

1 tsp chopped rosemary leaves

17⅔ oz/4 sticks plus 3¼ tbsp (500 g) salted butter, at room temperature

1 oz (30 g) capers, rinsed and chopped

4 anchovy fillets, chopped

1 tbsp chopped parsley

1 tbsp chopped chives

1 tbsp chopped tarragon

1 tsp Dijon mustard

1 tbsp ketchup

1 tsp Worcestershire sauce

1 tsp port

1 tsp brandy

pinch of paprika

pinch of cayenne pepper

zest of 1 lemon

sea salt to taste

METHOD

Place the olive oil in a small pan and heat over a medium-low heat. Add the shallots, garlic, thyme, and rosemary and sweat down for 2 to 3 minutes, until soft. Remove from the pan and set aside to cool.

Place the butter in the bowl of a stand mixer fitted with the paddle attachment, and beat until softened.

Add the shallot mix then add all the other ingredients, and beat again on medium speed until it has come together. Season with sea salt.

Roll some plastic wrap out on a work surface, nice and flat with no creases.

Lay the butter along the plastic wrap in a neat line close to one edge. Starting from the point closest to you and rolling away, use the wrap to roll the butter into a tube about the diameter of a golf ball. Tie the ends neatly, squeezing out any air in the process.

Refrigerate for a few hours until firm and ready to use.

Herbed Garlic Butter

Josh Emett

COMPLEXITY: EASY | PREP TIME: 5 MINUTES | COOK TIME: 15 MINUTES
MAKES: ABOUT 9 OZ (250 G)

INGREDIENTS

1 tbsp (15 ml) olive oil

4 cloves garlic

8¾ oz/2¼ sticks (250 g) butter

1 tsp parsley, finely chopped

1 tsp chives, finely chopped

1 tsp thyme, finely chopped

1 tsp rosemary, finely chopped

Place a small pot over a medium heat and add the olive oil, then the garlic cloves. Cook gently, stirring occasionally, for about 15 minutes until the garlic cloves are a light golden colour and soft. Remove from the heat and mash the cloves finely with a fork or spoon. Allow to cool.

Place all the ingredients in a blender and blend until smooth and combined. Refrigerate in a sealed container until needed.

Basil Pesto

Josh Emett

COMPLEXITY: EASY | PREP TIME: 15 MINUTES | MAKES: 1 CUP (ABOUT 250 G)

INGREDIENTS

1 bunch (1½ oz/40 g) basil leaves

½ bunch (¾ oz/20 g) parsley leaves

⅛ cup (20 g) pine nuts, toasted

⅓ cup (30 g) grated Parmesan

½ cup plus 1 tsp (125 ml) extra virgin olive oil

1 clove garlic, finely grated

pinch of sea salt

JOSH'S NOTES

Tip: Make a double batch if you're able. It will keep for up to a week in the fridge.

Blanch the basil and parsley leaves in boiling water for 1 minute, refresh in iced water, then drain and squeeze out excess water.

Place the basil, parsley, and all the other ingredients in a high-speed blender and blitz until a smooth texture is achieved.

Chimichurri

Ben O'Donoghue

COMPLEXITY: EASY | PREP TIME: 20 MINUTES | MAKES: 1 CUP (ABOUT 250 G)

INGREDIENTS

1 tbsp dried wild oregano flowers or dried oregano

2 tbsp oregano or sweet marjoram, finely chopped

3 cloves garlic, finely chopped

3 shallots, finely chopped

½ tsp chilli flakes

½ tsp coarsely ground black pepper

¼ cup (60 ml) white wine vinegar

½ cup (120 ml) extra virgin olive oil

salt

METHOD

Rub the oregano flowers (if using) between your fingers to break them up. Combine with the chopped fresh herbs in a non-metallic bowl.

Add the garlic, shallots, chilli flakes, and pepper. Pour in the vinegar, stir gently to combine and let stand for 10 minutes.

Stir in the olive oil and season with salt to taste.

This sauce is best used straight away, as the acidity of the vinegar overpowers the freshness of the herb flavours if kept for too long.

———————

"This South American barbecue sauce is used right across the continent, from the southern Pampas region to as far north as Honduras. It has as many variations as, say, the Italian salsa verde, but in its purest form it is just dried oregano, vinegar, chilli flakes, black pepper, and olive oil."

– BEN O'DONOGHUE

JOSH'S NOTES

Key element: When chopping, keep everything small and equally sized.

Complements: Ideal for red meats.

Tip: Substitute the oregano with different herbs, depending on what's in season.

Salsa Verde

Sylvia Casares

COMPLEXITY: EASY | PREP TIME: 15 MINUTES | COOK TIME: 30 MINUTES
MAKES: ABOUT 4 CUPS (1 KG)

INGREDIENTS

1½ lb (675 g) tomatillos

½ large white onion, chopped

½ jalapeño, cut into 4 pieces (do not remove the seeds)

1 large tomato, cut into 4 pieces

3⅛ cups (750 ml) water

3 cloves garlic, minced

leaves from ½ bunch fresh coriander/cilantro

1¼ tsp sea salt

METHOD

Remove the papery outer skin from the tomatillos, rinse the fruit and cut it in half. Place the tomatillos, onion, jalapeño, tomato, and the water in a large saucepan over a medium heat. Bring to the boil, then lower the heat and simmer for 20 minutes or until all the ingredients are very soft. Set aside, off the heat, to cool for about 10 minutes.

Using a blender or good food processor, blend the garlic, coriander/cilantro, and salt until smooth. Add the tomatillo mixture. Blend on high speed until very smooth, about 1 minute.

Set aside for at least 10 minutes to let the flavours mellow before serving. Reheat gently, if needed, on the stovetop or in a microwave on low power until heated through.

The sauce may be refrigerated for up to 1 week or frozen for up to 3 months.

JOSH'S NOTES

Preparation: You may not be able to source tomatillo if they're not in season.

Tip: Remove the jalapeño seeds if you prefer this less hot.

Complements: Everything! I have this on my eggs in the morning.

Classic Skordalia with Bread

Diane Kochilas

COMPLEXITY: EASY | PREP TIME: 15 MINUTES | SERVES: 6

4 thick (2-in/5-cm) slices stale country bread, preferably sourdough

5 to 6 cloves garlic (to taste)

sea salt

¼ to 1 cup (65 to 250 ml) Greek extra virgin olive oil (as needed to taste)

4 to 6 tbsp (60 to 90 ml) red wine vinegar (to taste)

Run the bread under flowing tap water to dampen it, then squeeze dry and crumble. (You can remove the crusts, if desired, before dampening.)

Place the garlic in a large mortar and, using the pestle, pound with 2 pinches of salt to form a paste. Slowly add the bread, olive oil, and vinegar, alternating between each and seasoning to taste with salt as you continue to pound. The end result should take about 10 minutes and should be dense and spreadable.

Sambal

Josh Emett

COMPLEXITY: MODERATE | PREP TIME: 20 MINUTES | COOK TIME: 2 HOURS
MAKES: 36 OZ (1 KG)

INGREDIENTS

10½ oz (300 g) brown onion, peeled

10½ oz (300 g) red onion, peeled

2 oz (60 g) garlic, peeled

10½ oz (300 g) fresh red chilli, green stalk removed

1½ oz (40 g) candlenuts (optional)

1⅓ cups plus 2 tbsp (350 ml) rapeseed/canola oil

¼ cup (50 g) sugar

2 tsp salt

JOSH'S NOTES

Tip: Once cooked, blend it again for an extra-smooth paste.

In a bar blender, blend the onions, garlic, chilli, and candlenuts (if using) to a smooth paste. You may need to add a touch of the oil to get it moving in the blender.

Heat the oil in a large wok or pan over a medium heat, then add the paste and cook, stirring constantly, for about 45 minutes to 1 hour.

Add the sugar and salt, and keep cooking, still stirring, for about another hour, until the oil is staring to separate and you have a smooth, dark sambal.

Leave to cool before storing in an airtight container. It will keep for approximately 1 month in the fridge.

Thai Chilli Jam
Nam Prik Pao

Teage Ezard

COMPLEXITY: EASY | PREP TIME: 20 MINUTES | COOK TIME: 3 HOURS
MAKES: 1 CUP (320 G)

INGREDIENTS

18 oz (500 g) Roma tomatoes, roughly chopped

10 cloves garlic, peeled

2½ oz (70 g) fresh ginger, peeled and roughly chopped

4 large red chillies, roughly chopped

1 red bird's-eye chilli, roughly chopped

4 red bell peppers/capsicums, de-seeded and roughly chopped

12½ oz (350 g) red shallots, roughly chopped

10½ oz (300 g) pale palm sugar, grated

½ cup plus 2 tbsp (150 ml) fish sauce

½ cup plus 2 tbsp (150 ml) lime juice

METHOD

Place tomatoes, garlic, ginger, chillies, bell peppers/capsicums and shallots in a large saucepan set over a low heat and cook, stirring frequently. Cover the pan with a lid and cook until tender, about 1 hour.

Remove the lid and continue to cook, stirring occasionally so that it doesn't stick, for about 3 hours, until it has reduced and is starting to look like a jam.

Add the palm sugar and cook for a further 35 minutes. Allow to cool, then transfer to a food processor and blend until smooth. Stir in the fish sauce and lime juice.

Place the jelly/jam in an airtight container until needed. Pour some vegetable oil over the top to keep out the air, allowing it to keep for several weeks.

JOSH'S NOTES

Tip: The consistency of the jelly/jam should be smooth to ensure the flavour and texture are just right.

XO Sauce

Andrew McConnell

COMPLEXITY: MODERATE | PREP TIME: 30 MINUTES, PLUS SOAKING TIME
COOK TIME: 35 MINUTES | MAKES: ABOUT 1½ CUPS, PLUS 1 TBSP (375 ML)

INGREDIENTS

1 oz (25 g) dried scallops

3 oz (75 g) dried shrimp/prawns

½ cup plus 1 tsp (125 ml) vegetable oil

15 cloves garlic, sliced

5 red shallots, finely sliced

1¾ oz (50 g) *jamón* or prosciutto scraps, finely chopped

6 fresh long red chillies, de-seeded and finely chopped

6 dried long red chillies, soaked, de-seeded and finely chopped

10 dried bird's eye chillies, finely chopped

1 tsp roasted shrimp paste

3 tsp sugar, or to taste

JOSH'S NOTES

Preparation: Soak the dried seafood overnight to save on time.

Tip: Take the time to cut everything finely to achieve the right texture.

Comment: Love the very deep, smoky taste of this sauce.

Complements: Most things, but especially, Andrew McConnell's Fried Rice with Crab recipe, p. 76.

METHOD

Soak the dried scallops and dried shrimp/prawns separately, each in ½ cup plus 1 teaspoon (125 ml) of hot water, until they are plump (about 1 hour).

Drain the scallops and reserve the soaking water. Tear the drained scallops into fine shreds, pat dry on absorbent paper and set aside.

Drain the shrimp/prawns and reserve the soaking water. Finely chop the shrimp/prawns and set aside.

Heat the oil in a wok or large saucepan over a medium-high heat. Add the garlic and shallots, and cook, stirring, until pale gold in colour. Add the scallops and shrimp/prawns, and cook, stirring continuously, until golden brown (4 to 5 minutes).

Stir through the *jamón* and fresh and dried chillies, frying for 1 minute before adding the shrimp paste, sugar, and reserved scallop and shrimp/prawn water.

Lower the heat and cook, stirring occasionally, until the sauce is fragrant and the water has completely evaporated (10 to 20 minutes).

Remove from the heat and strain, reserving the oil. Transfer the solids to a sterile jar, then pour in enough of the reserved oil to cover.

The XO sauce will keep refrigerated in a sealed container for 1 month.

———————

"This version of XO sauce is very spicy, so if you would like to temper this somewhat, simply reduce the number of bird's-eye chillies."

– ANDREW MCCONNELL

Caramelized Onions

Marc Forgione

Marc Forgione

COMPLEXITY: EASY | PREP TIME: 15 MINUTES | COOK TIME: 40 MINUTES
MAKES: ABOUT 1 CUP (150 G)

INGREDIENTS

1 sprig fresh thyme

1 fresh or ½ dried bay leaf

rapeseed/canola oil

1 large onion, halved and julienned as thinly as possible

2 tbsp (30 ml) sherry vinegar

kosher/flaky salt and freshly ground black pepper

pinch of sugar

Using kitchen twine, tie together the thyme and bay leaf. Add enough oil to a 2-quart (2-litre) pot to cover the bottom of the pot, and set it over a high heat. Just before the oil starts to smoke, add the onion to the pot and give everything one good stir. Reduce the heat to medium-low, add the herb bundle and cook, stirring from time to time, for about 40 minutes or until the onion is golden, wilted, and caramelized. Be sure to stir the onion every 5 minutes.

Add the vinegar and 2 tablespoons (30 ml) of water, and stir to incorporate. Season to taste with salt and pepper, and add the sugar. Taste for seasoning and adjust if necessary. Remove from the heat and set aside until needed. Use immediately, or transfer to an airtight container and store in the refrigerator for up to 1 week.

Horseradish Gremolata

Travis Lett

Travis Lett

COMPLEXITY: EASY | PREP TIME: 10 MINUTES | COOK TIME: 20 MINUTES
MAKES: 2¼ OZ (65 G)

INGREDIENTS

CROUTONS

2 slices bread, stale is acceptable, cut into ½-in (1-cm) dice

2 tbsp (30 ml) olive oil

sea salt

GREMOLATA

½ oz (15 g) chopped fresh flat-leaf parsley

3-in (7½-cm) piece fresh horseradish root, peeled and finely grated

zest of 1 lemon

2 tbsp (30 ml) extra virgin olive oil

handful of croutons, fully cooled (see above)

flaky sea salt

CROUTONS

Take a large fry pan and heat to medium hot. Add the olive oil then the bread and toss constantly for 4 to 5 minutes until golden in colour all over and crispy; season with sea salt. Transfer to paper towels and allow to cool.

GREMOLATA

In a small bowl, combine the parsley, horseradish root, lemon zest, and olive oil together. Place the croutons on a work surface and, using a rolling pin or a chef's knife, crush into coarse crumbs. Add the crumbs to the bowl, stir to combine, and season with salt. This is best made just before using.

INGREDIENTS

6 oz/1½ sticks (175 g)
unsalted butter

4 onions (2 lb/900 g),
peeled and cut into
¼-in (½-cm) dice

16 stalks celery, cut into
¼-in (½-cm) dice

10 large fresh sage
leaves, chopped, or
2 tsp crushed dried sage

6 cups (1½ litres)
homemade (p. 482)
or low-sodium canned
chicken stock

2 loaves stale white
bread (about 36 slices),
crust on, cut into 1-in
(2½-cm) cubes

2 tsp salt

4 tsp freshly ground
black pepper

3 cups (about 60 g)
coarsely chopped
flat-leaf parsley leaves
(about 2 bunches)

2 cups (220 g) pecans,
toasted and chopped
(optional)

2 cups (about 200 g)
dried cherries (optional)

This recipe accompanies
Martha Stewart's Perfect
Roast Turkey recipe,
p. 218.

Classic Turkey Stuffing

Martha Stewart

COMPLEXITY: EASY | PREP TIME: 35 MINUTES | COOK TIME: 20 MINUTES
MAKES: 12 CUPS (ABOUT 2 KG)

METHOD

Melt butter in a large skillet or frying pan. Add onions and celery
and cook over a medium heat until onions are translucent, about
10 minutes. Add sage, stir to combine, and cook for 3 to 4 minutes.
Add ½ cup (120 ml) stock and stir well. Cook for about 5 minutes,
until liquid has reduced by half.

Transfer onion mixture to a large mixing bowl. Add all remaining
ingredients, including the remaining stock; mix to combine.

"The terms stuffing and dressing are often used interchangeably,
but they do have different meanings: stuffing is cooked inside
the bird, dressing on its own."

– MARTHA STEWART

Kohlrabi Kimchi

Andrew McConnell

COMPLEXITY: MODERATE | PREP TIME: 1 HOUR, PLUS MARINATING TIME | SERVES: 8 TO 10

INGREDIENTS

KIMCHI BASE

½ cup plus 1 tsp
(125 ml) light soy sauce

½ cup plus 1 tsp
(125 ml) Korean fish
sauce

½ cup plus 1 tsp
(125 ml) sesame oil

3 tbsp superfine/caster
sugar

3 cloves garlic,
finely chopped

1½-in (4-cm) piece
ginger, peeled and
shredded

2 green onions/spring
onions, finely sliced

8 tbsp Korean chilli
powder

KOHLRABI

3 kohlrabi, peeled and
cut into batons ½ in
(1 cm) thick

1 tbsp sea salt

7 oz (200 g) kimchi base
(see below)

½ bunch garlic chives,
cut into 2-in (5-cm)
lengths

JOSH'S NOTES

Preparation: This can be
made days in advance.

Key element: Salting
for the correct length
of time.

METHOD

First make the kimchi base. Combine the soy sauce, fish sauce, sesame oil, and sugar in a bowl, stirring until the sugar has dissolved. Add the garlic, ginger, green onion/spring onion, and chilli powder and mix well. Set aside.

Toss the kohlrabi and salt together in a bowl. Transfer to a colander set over a bowl and leave to drain for 30 minutes.

Wash the kohlrabi in plenty of cold water and drain well. In a large bowl, combine the salted kohlrabi, kimchi base, and garlic chives. Wearing disposable gloves, mix the kimchi thoroughly through the kohlrabi. Cover and leave in the fridge to marinate for 3 hours before eating.

———

"This is one of my favourite vegetables. I serve this at home when we are eating dumplings. It's especially good served with a cold beer."

– ANDREW MCCONNELL

Sauerkraut

Skye Gyngell

COMPLEXITY: EASY | PREP TIME: 15 MINUTES, PLUS FERMENTING TIME
MAKES: ABOUT 2½ CUPS (600 G)

INGREDIENTS

1 red cabbage

1½ tbsp coarse salt

1 tbsp caraway seeds

METHOD

Using a sharp knife, slice the cabbage in half, remove the outer leaves and set aside. Cut out and discard the core from the cabbage. Lay the cabbage halves cut side down on a board and slice each half as finely as possible.

Put the shredded cabbage in a bowl and sprinkle over the salt and caraway seeds. Using very clean hands, massage the cabbage vigorously – this will help it soften and release its natural juice.

When the cabbage is almost wet, transfer it to a sterilized 6-cup (1½-litre) Kilner jar (with a screw-top lid), packing it in tightly until it reaches the top of the jar. Place one of the discarded outer leaves on top to help seal the cabbage, and screw the lid of the jar on tightly.

Store in a cool, dark cupboard – the cabbage will be ready to eat after 2 to 3 days, but it can be kept for 2 to 3 months. Once opened, refrigerate and use within a few days.

"Real homemade sauerkraut is a world away from the sharp, astringent shop-bought variety. Delightfully crunchy and sour, it is easy to make and addictive to eat. If you are new to fermentation, sauerkraut is a perfect first thing to try."

– SKYE GYNGELL

JOSH'S NOTES

Preparation: Take time to ensure the cabbage is finely shredded.

Key element: Use the right sized jar and pack it tightly.

Tip: Discard chunky pieces of cabbage after slicing so that the sauerkraut is uniform.

Pickled Vegetables

Colin Fassnidge

COMPLEXITY: EASY | PREP TIME: 20 MINUTES
COOK TIME: 5 MINUTES, PLUS PICKLING TIME | MAKES: 2 MEDIUM-SIZED JARS

INGREDIENTS

PICKLING LIQUOR

1 stick cinnamon

3 star anise

1¼ cups (300 ml) white wine vinegar

1¾ cups plus 2 tbsp (450 ml) water

¾ cup (150 g) granulated sugar

2 bay leaves

¼ bunch thyme

3⅓ tsp salt

VEGETABLES

1 cucumber, seeded and cut into batons on an angle

1 bunch baby carrots, peeled and halved

1 bunch baby turnips, thickly sliced

1 bunch radishes, thickly sliced

¼ cauliflower, broken into small florets

1 bunch green onions/ spring onions, trimmed and halved

METHOD

To make the pickling liquor, place the cinnamon and star anise in a saucepan and dry-roast over a medium heat for about 1 minute, or until fragrant. Add the remaining ingredients together with the water and bring to the boil.

Combine the vegetables in a large, non-metallic bowl. Pour the hot pickling liquor over the vegetables (it needs to cover them), and leave for 6 hours.

To store, transfer to sterilized jars, seal tightly and keep in the refrigerator for up to 4 weeks.

JOSH'S NOTES

Preparation: Allow 6 hours for the pickling.

Key element: Keep the vegetables the same thickness so that they pickle evenly.

Fermented Cucumbers

Lennox Hastie

COMPLEXITY: EASY | PREP TIME: 30 MINUTES, PLUS FERMENTING TIME
COOK TIME: 2 TO 3 MINUTES | SERVES: 4

INGREDIENTS

½ bunch dill, chopped

3½ oz (100 g) crème fraîche

4 baby cucumbers, halved longways

fruity, mild extra virgin olive oil, such as Arbequina or Koroneiki

1 lemon or apple cucumber, cut into eighths

3 lemon balm leaves, chopped

1 bunch watercress, leaves picked

½ oz (15 g) fresh horseradish root, peeled

FERMENTED CUCUMBERS

4 baby cucumbers, trimmed to remove the blossom end, halved longways

⅓ oz (10 g) horseradish root, peeled and sliced

½ bunch dill, chopped

2 cups plus 1¼ tbsp (500 ml) 5% salt brine, chilled (see tips)

3 tbsp plus 1 tsp (50 ml) whey (see tips)

METHOD

To ferment the cucumbers, place them in a sterilized glass jar 16-oz (500-ml) capacity, adding the sliced horseradish and dill and submerging in the cold salt brine and whey. Seal tightly and leave to ferment in a cool place out of direct light for 3 days. The cucumbers will break down naturally and develop lactic acid. Once fermented, refrigerate for up to 8 months, until ready to use.

Prepare your embers and arrange a grill directly on the embers.

Remove the fermented cucumber from the brine and drain, reserving the fermented liquid.

In a bowl, mix the dill through the crème fraîche together with ¼ cup (60 ml) of the fermented cucumber liquid.

Grill the raw and fermented cucumbers over direct heat for approximately 2 minutes, until lightly charred. Remove, drizzle with the olive oil and toss through the lemon or apple cucumber, lemon balm leaves and watercress.

Arrange the cucumbers on top of the dill crème fraîche and grate over the fresh horseradish to finish. Serve immediately.

TIPS

- Make up 5 per cent salt brine by dissolving 1½ tablespoons (25 g) salt in 2 cups plus 1¼ tablespoons (500 ml) of water.

- Whey is the reserved liquid left over from making ricotta or butter. Alternatively, substitute the whey with 2 tablespoons (30 ml) of buttermilk mixed with 4 teaspoons of filtered water.

"The combination of fermented and grilled cucumber, and the bracing nature of the raw cucumber, results in notes of complex char, briny tang, and unadulterated rawness in the same mouthful. The dill crème fraîche binds the cucumbers into a heavenly threesome."

– LENNOX HASTIE

Preserved Lemons

Bruno Loubet

COMPLEXITY: EASY | PREP TIME: 15 MINUTES, PLUS FREEZING TIME
COOK TIME: 1 HOUR 30 MINUTES | MAKES: TWO 10½-FL-OZ (300-ML) JARS

INGREDIENTS

5 lemons, unwaxed if possible, finely sliced and pips removed

4 tbsp sea salt

5 cloves garlic

½ stick cinnamon

1 star anise

1 red chilli

1 bay leaf

½ tsp cumin seeds, toasted

½ cup plus 2 tbsp (150 ml) olive oil, plus extra to layer

2 tbsp superfine/caster sugar

METHOD

Lay the lemon slices on a tray or trays lined with plastic wrap and sprinkle with the salt. Place in the freezer and leave for 24 hours.

The next day, allow the lemons to defrost for about 10 minutes. Put the lemon, any juices from the defrosting, and all the remaining ingredients in a pan set over a medium heat. Bring to a simmer, mix well and cover with a lid. Lower the heat to a very gentle simmer, then leave to stew for about 45 minutes. Remove from the heat and leave to rest for 30 minutes.

Remove the cinnamon. There are now two ways to proceed depending on your taste:

- Purée the mixture in a food processor then transfer to sterilized jars.

- Whisk the mixture firmly to break all the pieces down, then fill the sterilized jars.

When each jar is full, pour a small layer of olive oil over the top. Leave to cool completely, then store in the fridge for up to 2 months.

"I love the flavour of preserved lemons, but not biting into whole pieces – that got me thinking. The result is something I have called 'user-friendly preserved lemons' ... there won't be any lemony surprises. I always have a jar in my fridge."

– BRUNO LOUBET

Pickled Red Onion

Josh Emett

COMPLEXITY: EASY | PREP TIME: 5 MINUTES | COOK TIME: 5 MINUTES
MAKES: ABOUT ½ CUP (75 G)

INGREDIENTS

1 red onion

¾ cup plus 1¼ tbsp (200 ml) Cabernet Sauvignon vinegar

¼ cup (50 g) sugar

pinch of salt

sprig of thyme

Peel, quarter, and then finely slice the red onion across the grain, keeping all the lengths similar. Place in a small, non-metallic bowl.

In a small saucepan, bring the vinegar, sugar, and salt to the boil to dissolve the sugar, then allow to cool. Pour over the sliced onion, add the thyme, stir, cover and allow to sit in the fridge for at least a day. It will keep in the fridge for up to 2 weeks.

Green Tomato Chutney

Daniel Puskas

COMPLEXITY: EASY | PREP TIME: 15 MINUTES | COOK TIME: 4 HOURS
MAKES: ABOUT 5 LB (2¼ KG)

INGREDIENTS

10 lb (4½ kg) green (unripe) tomatoes

sugar, ⅓ of the roasted and passed tomato weight

apple cider vinegar, ⅙ of same tomato weight

½ onion, chopped

1 clove garlic, chopped

1 tbsp (15 ml) vegetable oil

salt, to taste

———————

This recipe accompanies Daniel Puskas's Gouda & Sweet Chutney Gougères recipe, p. 306.

Pre-heat the oven to 265°F (130°C). Place the whole tomatoes in a large roasting tray and roast until nice and soft, this takes about 1 hour.

Pass the tomatoes, with skin remaining, through a Mouli into a large bowl, tared off to zero. Note the weight. Work out the weight in sugar and vinegar, and add to the roasted tomato.

Over a medium heat, sweat the onion and garlic in a little oil until soft but not coloured, then add the tomato mix. Cook out over a medium to high heat until it resembles marmalade – this takes about 3 hours.

When it has finished reducing, you should have about 5 lb (2¼ kg) of unseasoned chutney. Season to taste with salt and soft herbs, such as chervil, chives, and tarragon.

INGREDIENTS

3 lb (1.4 kg) tomatoes, such as Roma or Early Girl

kosher/flaky salt

10 garlic cloves, smashed

10 fresh thyme sprigs

1 tbsp dried oregano

pinch of crushed red pepper flakes

2 cups (480 ml) extra-virgin olive oil, plus more as needed

This recipe accompanies Trevis Lett's Pizza Pomodoro recipe, p. 310.

Confit Tomatoes

Travis Lett

COMPLEXITY: EASY | PREP TIME: 30 MINUTES | COOK TIME: 4 HOURS
MAKES: 2 CUPS (520 G)

METHOD

Preheat the oven to 250°F (120°C). Bring a large pot of water to boil over high heat. Prepare an ice-water bath by filling a large bowl with ice water.

Use a paring knife to score a small 'X' in the bottom of each tomato. Plunge the tomatoes into the boiling water for 20 seconds, and immediately transfer them to the ice-water bath. Work in batches, if necessary, until all of the tomatoes have been blanched.

When the tomatoes are cool, remove them from the water. With a sharp paring knife, peel the skin from the tomatoes; it should slip off easily. Cut the tomatoes into halves or quarters, depending on size, and gently pull the seeds out with your fingers. The tomatoes do not need to be perfectly seedless, but do your best to clean them so that just the tomato flesh remains.

Place the tomatoes in a shallow baking dish or roasting pan and season with salt. Scatter the garlic, thyme, oregano, and red pepper flakes over the tomatoes. Pour the olive oil over all. Bake until the tomatoes are shrivelled and browned around the edges, about 3 to 4 hours. Turn them and move them around occasionally while baking so that the tomatoes closest to the edge of the pan don't burn. Remove from the oven and allow to cool to room temperature.

Store in an airtight container in the refrigerator for up to 1 month, completely covered with olive oil to prevent air from reaching them.

"These preserved tomatoes are amazingly versatile. We cook with them all year round. Be sure to use the tomato oil on anything that tastes better with a little olive oil and tomato – which is just about everything."

– TRAVIS LETT

Basic Barbecue Sauce

Ben O'Donoghue

COMPLEXITY: EASY | PREP TIME: 10 MINUTES | COOK TIME: 30 MINUTES
MAKES: ABOUT 2 CUPS (480 ML)

INGREDIENTS

1 cup (200 g) dark brown sugar

1 cup plus 2 tsp (250 ml) sherry vinegar (preferably aged)

1 onion, chopped

1 tsp ground cumin

½ tsp ground cinnamon

1 star anise

1 jalapeño, halved

2 tsp smoked paprika

4 tbsp tomato ketchup

7 oz (200 g) canned chopped tomatoes

1 tbsp salt

METHOD

Place all the ingredients in a heavy-bottomed saucepan. Bring to the boil, stirring to dissolve the sugar, then reduce to a low simmer and cook, uncovered, for 30 minutes.

Use a stick blender to purée until the sauce is smooth. If the sauce is still thin, continue to simmer it until it coats the back of a wooden spoon well.

Serve at room temperature. The sauce will keep for up to 3 months in the refrigerator if stored in an airtight container.

"This barbecue sauce is both a sauce and a glaze. This basic recipe combines sweet and sour components that work really well together. For something a little different, experiment with fruit juices and other spices."

– BEN O'DONOGHUE

JOSH'S NOTES

Tip: Use a sweet smoked paprika if you prefer a less spicy sauce.

Peanut Sauce Four Ways

Mark Bittman

COMPLEXITY: EASY | PREP TIME: 15 MINUTES | COOK TIME: 20 MINUTES | MAKES: 2 CUPS (480 ML)

INGREDIENTS

3 hot fresh red chillies, seeded, or cayenne or red chilli flakes to taste

3 cloves garlic, peeled

2 shallots, peeled

1 stalk lemongrass, white part only, thinly sliced (optional)

2 tsp ground turmeric

1 tbsp (15 ml) groundnut/peanut or grapeseed oil

1 cup (240 ml) coconut milk

2 tbsp (30 ml) soy sauce, plus more to taste

2 tbsp (30 ml) fresh lime juice

1 tbsp brown sugar

½ cup (35 g) chopped roasted groundnuts/ peanuts or crunchy peanut butter

salt

METHOD

Put the chillies, garlic, shallots, lemongrass if you're using it, and turmeric in a food processor and grind until fairly smooth; scrape down the sides of the bowl once or twice if necessary.

Put the oil in a medium saucepan or frying pan over a medium heat. When it's hot, add the chilli garlic mixture and cook until fragrant, about 1 minute. Add the coconut milk, soy sauce, lime juice, sugar, and groundnuts/peanuts, and whisk until fully combined. Simmer, stirring occasionally, until the sauce thickens, about 15 minutes. Taste and add a sprinkle of salt or a little more soy sauce if necessary.

Serve straight away or cool, cover, and refrigerate for up to 1 week. Gently rewarm before using.

CURRY PEANUT SAUCE

Another layer of flavour: Omit the chillies, lemongrass, and turmeric. Instead, put a 2-in (5-cm) piece of fresh ginger and 2 tablespoons of curry powder in the food processor along with the garlic and shallots.

SWEET PEANUT SAUCE

Indonesian in spirit: Add ¼ cup (60 g) ketchup along with the coconut milk.

SIMPLER PEANUT SAUCE

More 'peanutty' (and makes less): Use only the chillies, sugar, soy sauce, and groundnuts/peanuts. Blend in a food processor, adding a little water or more soy sauce to get the consistency you like. Gently heat the sauce in a small saucepan over a low heat, or in the microwave in bursts of 20 seconds on high, stirring in between bursts. Stir in ¼ cup (25 g) sliced scallions/spring onion and ¼ cup (5 g) minced fresh cilantro/coriander, and serve.

"Best tossed with Chinese egg noodles or pooled on the bottom of a plate and topped with slices of grilled or fried vegetables or tofu. If you want a smooth sauce, use peanut butter instead of chopped peanuts."

– MARK BITTMAN

Sweet Chilli Sauce

Peter Gordon

COMPLEXITY: EASY | PREP TIME: 25 MINUTES | COOK TIME: 10 MINUTES
MAKES: 2 CUPS, PLUS 1¼ TBSP (500 ML)

INGREDIENTS

3 lemongrass stems

10 cloves garlic, peeled

4 large red chillies, stems off, roughly chopped

3½ oz (100 g) ginger, peeled and sliced against the grain

1½ oz (40 g) galangal, peeled and sliced against the grain

1 medium-sized red beet/beetroot, peeled, halved and sliced

10 *makrut* (kaffir) lime leaves, central vein removed

1 bunch cilantro/coriander, washed and shredded

¾ cup (180 g) superfine/caster sugar

3 tbsp plus 1 tsp (50 ml) cider vinegar

3 tbsp plus 1 tsp (50 ml) Thai fish sauce

3 tbsp plus 1 tsp (50 ml) tamari (wheat-free soy sauce)

———————

This recipe accompanies Peter Gordon's Grilled Scallops with Sweet Chilli Sauce & Crème Fraîche recipe, p. 154.

METHOD

Remove the two outside leaves from the lemongrass, cut ½ in (1 cm) away from the base, then slice 4 in (10 cm) of the inside thinly. Place in a food processor along with garlic, chillies, ginger, galangal, beet/beetroot, lime leaves, and cilantro/coriander, and blend to a coarse paste.

Place sugar in a heavy-based pot and cook over a medium-low heat until it has turned a dark caramel colour. Swirl the pan from time to time but do not stir it. Carefully stir in the paste (it may spit), then bring back to the boil. Add the vinegar, fish sauce, and tamari, then bring back to the boil and simmer for 1 minute. Leave to cool before using.

———————

"The recipe makes much more than you normally need, but it's very hard to make it in a smaller quantity, and it keeps for a month in the fridge in a sealed jar."

– PETER GORDON

Fermented Chilli Paste

Lennox Hastie

COMPLEXITY: EASY | PREP TIME: 5 MINUTES | COOK TIME: 5 DAY FERMENT
MAKES: 18 OZ (500 G)

INGREDIENTS

18 oz (500 g) chilli peppers, stems removed and green caps retained (see tip)

2 cloves garlic, peeled and minced

1 tbsp sugar

½ tsp sea salt

5 tsp liquid from fermented cucumber (p. 452), or 1 tbsp (15 ml) buttermilk mixed with 2 tsp filtered water

This recipe accompanies Lennox Hastie's Bone Marrow with Sea Urchin & Purslane recipe, p. 290.

METHOD

Place all the ingredients in a food processor and blend to form a fairly smooth paste. Pour into a sterilized jar and seal tightly. Leave to ferment, out of direct light, in a cool place for 5 days, by which time the paste should be gently bubbling with life.

Once fermented, refrigerate until needed. It can be kept in the refrigerator for up to 6 months.

TIP

Like tomatoes, chilli peppers have a lot of flavour in their green tops or calyx, so these are best kept on the fruit when fermenting.

"Making fermented chilli paste is a great way to use the liquid from fermented cucumber [p. 452], along with any chilli trimmings. The simple process of lactic fermentation results in a rich, complex paste with an amazing aroma and a fiery flavour. You can use whatever chillies you like, depending on how hot you can handle it."

– LENNOX HASTIE

Green Curry Paste
Nam Phrik Kaeng Kheaw-wan

Ian Kittichai

COMPLEXITY: EASY | PREP TIME: 25 MINUTES | COOK TIME: 10 MINUTES
MAKES: 9 OZ (250 G)

INGREDIENTS

1 tsp coriander seeds

1 tsp cumin seeds

1 tsp coarse sea salt

1 tsp white peppercorns

⅓ oz (10 g) green bird's-eye chilli peppers

2 oz (60 g) long green chilli peppers

3 oz (80 g) lemongrass, finely sliced

¾ cup (20 g) shallots, finely sliced

⅓ oz (10 g) garlic, finely sliced

⅓ oz (10 g) galangal, finely sliced

1 tsp kaffir lime zest

½ tsp kaffir lime leaves, finely chopped (veins removed first)

15 Thai basil leaves

3½ oz (100 g) cilantro/coriander roots, chopped

¾ oz (20 g) Thai shrimp paste

1 section banana leaf (substitution: aluminium foil)

This recipe accompanies Ian Kittichai's Beef Green Curry recipe, p. 248.

METHOD

In a dry pan, combine the coriander seeds, cumin seeds, salt, and peppercorns and cook over a moderate heat for 2 to 3 minutes, until fragrant. Place the spices in a mortar and grind finely, or use a food processor and blend until smooth.

Add the bird's-eye and green chilli peppers, lemongrass, shallots, garlic, galangal, kaffir lime zest, kaffir lime leaves, Thai basil leaves, and cilantro/coriander roots and grind finely.

Wrap the shrimp paste in the section of banana leaf and roast the parcel in a dry frying pan for 1 minute on each side. Remove paste from the parcel and set aside to cool. (Aluminium foil can be used instead of the banana leaf.)

Place the shrimp paste with other ingredients in a mortar or food processor and grind finely until smooth.

The curry paste can be stored in an airtight container in the refrigerator for up to 5 days.

Salsa Romesco

Carme Ruscalleda

COMPLEXITY: EASY | PREP TIME: 20 MINUTES | COOK TIME: 35 MINUTES
MAKES: ABOUT 18 OZ (500 G)

INGREDIENTS

14 oz (400 g) ripe tomatoes

1 fresh whole garlic head, un-skinned and halved

pulp of 4 *ñora* peppers

1½ oz (40 g) toasted almonds, peeled

1½ oz (40 g) toasted hazelnuts, peeled

½ cup plus 1 tsp (125 ml) extra virgin olive oil

1 tbsp (15 ml) sherry vinegar

salt and freshly ground black pepper

METHOD

Preheat the oven to 350°F (180°C).

Place whole tomatoes and garlic in a roasting tray and roast for 30 minutes. Remove garlic and return tomatoes to the oven for a further 5 minutes. Allow to cool slightly, then peel tomatoes and remove the seeds, catching the juices in the roasting tray. Squeeze garlic out of its skins into the tray.

Place roasted tomato flesh and juices, roasted garlic, *ñora* pepper pulp, almonds, hazelnuts, olive oil, and vinegar in a blender and blend until smooth. Season to taste with salt and pepper.

TIP

Ñoras are a type of pepper from the '*Capsicum annum*' family, used in the Mediterranean. They are always sold dried, and are available in specialist stores or online.

JOSH'S NOTES

Preparation: Allow time to roast and cool the tomatoes before you peel them.

Tip: Once peeled, you can pass the tomato seeds through a rough sieve to save time.

Complements: Classically, this is served with *calçots* (Catalan green onions), but it also works well as a dip.

Image on p. 426

Tasha's
Napolitana Sauce
Natasha Sideris

COMPLEXITY: EASY | PREP TIME: 5 MINUTES | COOK TIME: 1 HOUR
MAKES: 2 CUPS, PLUS 1¼ TBSP (500 ML)

INGREDIENTS

½ cup/1 stick (120 g) butter

2 onions, chopped

2 pinches of dried oregano

salt

5 x 14 oz (400 g) cans tomatoes, crushed

2 tsp granulated sugar

METHOD

Melt half the butter in a large saucepan over a medium heat, add the onion and fry, stirring, until soft but not coloured.

Add the oregano and salt, then the tomatoes, and bring to the boil before adding the sugar. Stir well to dissolve the sugar. Add the remaining butter and stir until it has melted, then turn down the heat and simmer, uncovered, for about 45 minutes, until reduced to half of the original quantity.

_____

"This classic sauce is so versatile and such an important staple in so many dishes. You can make it in bulk and freeze it for use in other recipes."

– NATASHA SIDERIS

JOSH'S NOTES

Preparation: Cook the sauce gently to avoid splashing, or use a splash guard if you have one.

Tip: The more you cook the sauce down, the better it will taste.

Image on p. 426

Pomodoro Sauce

Travis Lett

INGREDIENTS

8 lb (3.6 kg) tomatoes, such as Early Girl or San Marzano, quartered

½ cup (120 ml) extra-virgin olive oil

3 tbsp flaky sea salt

½ cup (15 g) basil leaves

1 to 2 tsp sugar (optional)

This recipe accompanies Trevis Lett's Pizza Pomodoro recipe, p. 310.

COMPLEXITY: EASY | PREP TIME: 10 MINUTES | COOK TIME: 30 MINUTES
MAKES: ABOUT 6½ CUPS (1½ LITRES)

In a large stockpot over low heat, combine the tomatoes, olive oil, and salt. Cook, stirring occasionally, until the tomatoes have lost most of their acidity and the sauce begins to sweeten and thicken slightly, about 30 minutes. The sauce should be thick enough to coat a spoon, but not too dense or pasty.

Add the basil and taste; if the sauce seems too acidic, add the sugar 1 teaspoon at a time until the flavour is well-balanced. Pass the sauce through a food mill and let it cool completely.

Store in an airtight container in the refrigerator for up to 1 week, or in the freezer for up to 3 months.

Butter & Sage Sauce
Salsa al Burro e Salvia

Lidia Bastianich

INGREDIENTS

6 oz/1½ sticks (170 g) unsalted butter

10 fresh sage leaves

1 cup (240 ml) hot water from the cooking pot of your pasta of choice

¼ tsp freshly ground black pepper, or to taste

1 cup (100 g) freshly grated Grana Padano

This recipe accompanies Lidia Bastianich's Butternut Squash Gnocchi recipe, p. 66.

COMPLEXITY: EASY | PREP TIME: 5 MINUTES | COOK TIME: 5 MINUTES
MAKES: ABOUT 1 CUP (240 ML), ENOUGH TO DRESS 1 LB (450 G) COOKED PASTA

Heat the butter in a large frying pan over a medium heat until melted and just foaming. Gently lay the sage leaves in the pan, and heat until they crisp up, about 1 minute.

Ladle in 1 cup (240 ml) of boiling pasta water, stir the sauce, and simmer for about 2 minutes, to reduce the liquid by half. Grind the black pepper directly into the sauce.

Keep the sauce hot over a very low heat, then return it to a simmer just before adding the drained pasta. Toss the pasta in the sauce until well coated. Remove from the heat and toss in the cheese just before serving.

INGREDIENTS

3 banana shallots, sliced

4 cloves garlic, crushed

15 whole peppercorns

1¼ cups (300 ml) Noilly Prat or white wine

2½ cups (600 ml) fish stock (p. 483)

1⅓ cups plus 2 tbsp (350 ml) heavy/double cream

Fish Velouté

Josh Emett

COMPLEXITY: EASY | PREP TIME: 10 MINUTES | COOK TIME: 20 MINUTES
MAKES: 1 CUP, PLUS 2 TSP (250 ML)

Place the shallots, garlic, peppercorns, and Noilly Prat or white wine in a saucepan, bring to a simmer over a medium heat, and simmer, uncovered, for 4 to 5 minutes to reduce to a glaze.

Add the fish stock and again simmer, uncovered, for 4 to 5 minutes until reduced by half.

Add the cream and reduce for 3 to 4 minutes, until it thickens slightly and coats the back of a spoon.

Pass the sauce through a fine chinois, discarding the solids. Cover and keep chilled until needed; up to 2 to 3 days.

INGREDIENTS

1 clove

1 bay leaf

½ onion

1⅔ cups (400 ml) milk, plus extra if needed for reheating

freshly grated nutmeg to taste

3½ oz (100 g) fresh white bread, crusts removed, diced

2 tbsp (30 g) butter

This recipe accompanies Tom Kitchin's Roast Grouse with Game Chips & Bread Sauce recipe, p. 214.

Bread Sauce

Tom Kitchin

COMPLEXITY: EASY | PREP TIME: 5 MINUTES | COOK TIME: 20 MINUTES | SERVES: 8

Use the clove to secure the bay leaf to the onion half; set aside.

Bring the milk to a simmer in a small saucepan, then add the onion and nutmeg. Cover and leave to infuse for 8 to 10 minutes off the heat.

Strain the milk into another pan, add the bread and butter and bring to the boil, whisking constantly to break up the bread. Season with salt and pepper.

If not serving immediately, press a piece of plastic wrap on the surface to prevent a skin from forming. The sauce can be made a day ahead and stored in an airtight container in the fridge for reheating just before serving. You may need to add a little more milk.

Homemade Apple Sauce

Curtis Stone

COMPLEXITY: EASY | PREP TIME: 10 MINUTES | COOK TIME: 45 MINUTES
MAKES: 4 CUPS (960 ML)

INGREDIENTS

3 tbsp (45 ml) Calvados or other apple brandy

2 tbsp (30 g) unsalted butter

1 tbsp sugar

½ tsp kosher/flaky salt

1 whole star anise

1 whole clove

2½ lb (1.15 kg) Fuji apples (about 5 large or 7 small), cored and cut into quarters

This recipe accompanies Curtis Stone's Roasted Pork Belly with Homemade Apple Sauce recipe, p. 275.

METHOD

Pre-heat the oven to 400°F (200°C).

In a small, heavy saucepan, stir the Calvados, butter, sugar, salt, star anise, and clove over a medium heat until the butter melts.

In a medium bowl, toss the apples with the melted butter mixture to coat. Place the apples cut side down in a 9-in (23-cm) square baking dish. Roast for about 45 minutes, or until the apples are soft. Set aside until the apples are cool enough to handle.

Using a spoon, scoop the flesh from the apple peels and discard the peels. Remove and discard the star anise and clove. Using a potato masher, carefully mash the apples to a chunky consistency, in the baking dish, with the juices.

Serve the apple sauce warm, at room temperature, or cold. It will keep, cooled, covered, and refrigerated, for up to 3 days. If desired, re-warm, covered, over a medium-low heat before serving.

Apple-onion Soubise

Monique Fiso

COMPLEXITY: EASY | PREP TIME: 10 MINUTES | COOK TIME: 30 MINUTES
MAKES: ABOUT 3 CUPS, PLUS 2 TBSP (750 ML)

INGREDIENTS

3½ oz/7 tbsp (100 g) unsalted butter

3½ oz (100 g) Granny Smith apples, peeled, cored, and julienned

14 oz (400 g) onions, peeled and diced

1 fresh bay leaf

6½ tbsp (50 g) all-purpose/plain flour

2 cups plus 1¼ tbsp (500 ml) full-fat milk

salt and white pepper to taste

METHOD

Melt half of the butter in a heavy-based saucepan and add the apples and onions. Gently cook the apples and onions at a low to moderate heat until soft and translucent. Most soubise recipes call for 'no colour', but for this recipe an amber colour is preferred.

In a separate saucepan, melt the remaining butter along with the bay leaf over a medium heat. Once the butter is melted, add the flour and continue cooking over a medium heat until the mixture becomes sandy and smells nutty.

Add ½ cup plus 1 teaspoon (125 ml) of the milk to the butter and flour, stirring the entire time to ensure that the mixture comes out smooth. Add the remaining milk in stages until all has been incorporated and you have a smooth white sauce.

Add the white sauce to the cooked apples and onions. Stir thoroughly to combine. Transfer the mixture (in batches if necessary) to a high-speed blender and blend until smooth. While the mixture is still hot, pass it through a fine chinois to remove any possible lumps.

When all the soubise has been blended and passed, season with salt and white pepper. Serve hot.

Red Wine Sauce

Clare Smyth

COMPLEXITY: MODERATE | PREP TIME: 10 MINUTES | COOK TIME: 2 HOURS
MAKES: ABOUT 1½ QT (1½ LITRES)

INGREDIENTS

6⅔ lb (3 kg) beef trimmings (brisket)

3½ oz (100 g) beef fat

3½ oz/7 tbsp (100 g) butter

1½ lb (700 g) shallots

3½ oz (100 g) garlic

1 bay leaf

3 tbsp thyme leaves

2 tsp white peppercorns

3 tbsp plus 1 tsp (50 ml) Cabernet Sauvignon vinegar

2 bottles red wine

5 qt (5 litres) reduced beef stock (p. 484)

salt to taste

METHOD

In a large pan (or cocotte), roast the beef trimmings in the beef fat for about 20 minutes, making sure that the meat is well caramelized. Drain off the excess fat and set the trimmings aside.

To the same pan, add the butter, shallots, and garlic and caramelize for 15 minutes. Add the herbs and peppercorns.

As soon as the shallots are translucent, return the roasted trimmings to the pan and deglaze with the vinegar. Reduce to glaze. Add the wine, bring to a simmer, and let it reduce to a really thin glaze, about 20 to 30 minutes.

Add the reduced beef stock and continue to simmer until it coats the back of a spoon. Adjust with salt only. Pass through a fine chinois lined with muslin (cheesecloth).

To serve, emulsify in some of the reserved roasting fat and add a bit of salt if needed.

Pepper Sauce

Clare Smyth

COMPLEXITY: MODERATE | PREP TIME: 25 MINUTES | COOK TIME: 3 HOURS
MAKES: 3 QUARTS (3 LITRES)

INGREDIENTS

6⅔ lb (3 kg) beef trimmings (brisket)

3½ oz (100 g) beef fat

3½ oz/7 tbsp (100 g) butter

1½ lb (700 g) shallots, sliced

3½ oz (100 g) garlic, crushed

1 bay leaf

3 tbsp thyme

2 tsp white peppercorns

3 tbsp plus 1 tsp (50 ml) cabernet sauvignon vinegar

½ bottle (about 1½ cups/350 ml) brandy, plus 6¾ tbsp (100 ml)

¼ bottle (about 1½ cups/350 ml) port

1 bottle (about 3 cups plus 2 tbsp/750 ml) red wine

4 qt (4 litres) reduced beef stock (p. 484)

2 qt (2 kg) double cream

3½ oz (100 g) mignonette black pepper

JOSH'S NOTES

Tip: Use a large pan and a fat guard for the roasting.

Add cream each time you require the sauce to make it keep longer.

METHOD

In a large pan (or cocotte), brown the beef trimmings in the beef fat, making sure that the meat is well caramelized. When it is well caramelized, drain off the fat and discard. Reserve the beef trimmings.

To the same pan, add the butter, shallots, and garlic, cook, stirring occasionally, until caramelized. Add the herbs and spices, then the roasted beef trimmings, and deglaze with the vinegar. Let this reduce to a glaze, add the brandy and let it reduce by half, then add the port and let it reduce by half. Finally, add the red wine and let it reduce to a really thin glaze, about 1⅔ cups (400 ml).

Add the reduced beef stock and simmer for about 2 hours until it reaches a nice viscosity. Check and adjust the seasoning. Pass through a fine chinois lined with muslin and reduce further if required (it should have reduced by approximately two-thirds). Add the cream, additional brandy and the mignonette pepper, and allow to reduce until it coats the back of a spoon.

Béchamel Sauce

Lidia Bastianich

COMPLEXITY: EASY | PREP TIME: 10 MINUTES | COOK TIME: 10 MINUTES
MAKES: ABOUT 2 CUPS (480 ML)

INGREDIENTS

2 cups (480 ml) milk

salt and freshly
ground pepper
(preferably white)

2 large pinches of
nutmeg, preferably
freshly grated

1 bay leaf

3 tbsp (40 g) unsalted
butter

¼ cup (30 g) all-
purpose/plain flour

⅓ cup (30 g) freshly
grated Parmigiano
Reggiano cheese

───────────

This recipe accompanies
Lidia Bastianich's Meat
& Spinach Cannelloni
recipe, p. 62.

METHOD

Pour the milk into a medium-sized saucepan, season lightly with salt
and pepper, add the nutmeg, and toss in the bay leaf. Heat over a
medium-low heat until bubbles form around the edge. Remove and
keep hot.

Melt the butter in a separate medium-sized saucepan over a
medium heat. When it starts to foam, dump in the flour and whisk
until smooth. Continue cooking, whisking constantly, until the flour
mixture changes colour, 3 to 4 minutes.

Pour the seasoned hot milk into the flour mixture in a steady stream,
whisking constantly. Cook the sauce, whisking constantly and paying
special attention to the bottom and corners of the pan, until the
sauce comes to a simmer. Adjust the heat to a slow boil and cook,
whisking constantly, until the sauce is thickened, about 3 minutes.
Remove from the heat and whisk in the grated cheese.

Strain the sauce through a fine sieve into a clean bowl. The sauce
will keep at room temperature for up to a few hours.

───────────

"Stand by the pot as the sauce cooks – once it starts to thicken, it
will stick to the bottom of the pan if you don't stir it constantly."

– LIDIA BASTIANICH

Fennel Sabayon

Alla Wolf-Tasker

COMPLEXITY: MODERATE | PREP TIME: 10 MINUTES | COOK TIME: 30 MINUTES | SERVES: 8

INGREDIENTS

2 heads fennel, trimmed of sprigs and diced

2 tbsp (30 ml) Pernod (or pastis)

1 oz (30 g) spinach leaves

salt and freshly ground black pepper

1 free-range egg yolk

3 tbsp plus 1 tsp (50 ml) lemon juice

METHOD

Vacuum-pack the fennel and Pernod. Place in a saucepan of boiling water and cook at a high simmer for 20 minutes, or until the fennel is tender. Drain off the excess liquid, put in a blender together with the spinach and blend to a purée. Season with salt and freshly ground black pepper and allow to cool.

Place the mixture in a heatproof bowl together with the egg yolk and lemon juice, set over a pot of simmering water and whisk to make a sabayon. The mixture should be the same texture as soft whipped cream. Place in the canister of a siphon (foam gun), charge with two charges and keep warm by placing the canister in a water bath at 115°F (45°C).

"A favourite accompaniment to fish. Wonderful with confit ocean trout, scattered with some hand-milked trout roe and garnished with fennel sprigs and pollen."

– ALLA WOLF-TASKER

Béarnaise Sauce

Michael Caines

COMPLEXITY: EASY | PREP TIME: 10 MINUTES | COOK TIME: 35 MINUTES | SERVES: 8

INGREDIENTS

3 tbsp (45 ml) white wine vinegar

6 peppercorns, lightly crushed

sprig of tarragon

1 tsp roughly chopped shallot

1 bay leaf

3 tbsp (45 ml) water

4 egg yolks

9 oz/2¼ sticks (250 g) butter

3 tbsp chopped fresh tarragon leaves

METHOD

Put the vinegar, peppercorns, tarragon sprig, and shallot into a pan set over a medium heat, bring to a simmer and reduce to 1 teaspoon. Add the water to make a reduction.

Put the egg yolks into a round-bottomed, heatproof bowl. Strain in the reduction from the pan, then place the bowl over a pan of barely simmering water and whisk continuously to make a sabayon. Cook out the sabayon to a peak, where it stands alone without deflating.

Gently heat the butter in a small pan so that the solids fall to the bottom, then gradually whisk it into the egg yolks, adding the buttermilk at the bottom too. Season with salt and pepper. Put the sauce in a blender and blend it to a smooth finish.

Add the chopped, fresh tarragon and stir through. Keep warm and use immediately.

Hollandaise Sauce

Josh Emett

COMPLEXITY: EASY | PREP TIME: 10 MINUTES | COOK TIME: 35 MINUTES | SERVES: 8

INGREDIENTS

¼ cup plus 2½ tbsp (100 ml) white wine vinegar

6 peppercorns

1 dried bay leaf

yolks of 4 eggs

9 oz/2¼ sticks (250 g) butter

sea salt and freshly ground black pepper

lemon juice to taste

METHOD

Put the vinegar in a small pan with the peppercorns and bay leaf. Over a high heat, reduce the vinegar until there is only about 1 tablespoon (15 ml) left. Strain the peppercorns and the bay leaf from this reduction.

Allow the vinegar reduction to cool then place in a food processor together with the egg yolks. Blend for 30 seconds until the mixture thickens.

Gently melt the butter in a small saucepan over a low heat so that the butter solids fall to the bottom of the pan, pour off the clear clarified butter into a jug; this can be done ahead of time but must be added warm.

Turn the food processor on and with the motor running, slowly pour the butter onto the egg yolks/reduction. The sauce will start to thicken. Once it is completely emulsified, stop blending. If the sauce is too thick, add a little hot water while blending.

Season to taste with salt, pepper and a little lemon juice.

JOSH'S NOTES

Preparation: Melt the butter gently when clarifying.

Key element: Whisk the egg yolk mixture until it thickens before adding the butter.

Tip: If whisking by hand, ask a second person to pour the butter.

INGREDIENTS

2 pasteurized egg yolks

1 tsp fine salt

3 tbsp plus 1 tsp (50 ml) white wine vinegar

1¼ cups (300 ml) sunflower oil

Mayonnaise

Sat Bains

COMPLEXITY: EASY | PREP TIME: 10 MINUTES | MAKES: 1½ CUPS, PLUS 1 TBSP (375 G)

Allow all the ingredients to come to room temperature. This makes the emulsification process easier.

Start whisking the egg yolks with the salt and vinegar. Add the oil in a slow, steady stream, while continuing to whisk, until fully emulsified. Correct the seasoning if necessary.

You can thin the mayonnaise down by adding a little hot water if needed.

Store in an airtight container for up to 7 days.

INGREDIENTS

3½ oz (100 g) shallots

1 tbsp tarragon leaves

3½ oz (100 g) truffle paste

2¾ tbsp (40 ml) truffle oil

About 3 cups (730 ml) mayonnaise (see recipe above)

sea salt and freshly ground black pepper

Truffle Mayonnaise

Luke Mangan

COMPLEXITY: EASY | PREP TIME: 10 MINUTES | MAKES: ABOUT 4 CUPS (980 G)

Chop the shallots and tarragon very finely. Mix this through with the remaining ingredients. Season to taste with salt and freshly ground black pepper.

The mayo can be kept in a sealed jar in the fridge for up to 4 to 5 days.

"This truffle mayo is an ideal dip for fresh, cold prawns. It also makes a great spread for steak sandwiches or tossed through a potato salad."

– LUKE MANGAN

INGREDIENTS

2 small cloves garlic

pinch of salt

1 organic egg yolk,
at room temperature

½ tsp water

1 cup (240 ml) extra
virgin olive oil

JOSH'S NOTES

Tip: Use an olive oil that
is rich and well-rounded
in flavour.

Preparation: This can
be made up to 5 days
in advance.

Key element: Start
adding oil in a very thin
stream to avoid splitting.

Aïoli

Alice Waters

COMPLEXITY: EASY | PREP TIME: 10 MINUTES | MAKES: ABOUT 1 CUP (240 G)

Peel the garlic. Pound, along with the salt, with a mortar and pestle
until smooth.

Place the egg yolk in a mixing bowl. Add about half the garlic mix,
and the water. Mix well with a whisk. While whisking constantly,
slowly dribble the oil into the egg yolk mixture. As the egg yolk
absorbs the oil, the sauce will thicken, lighten in colour, and become
opaque. This will happen rather quickly. Then you can add the oil a
little faster, whisking all the while.

If the sauce is thicker than you like, thin it with a few drops of water.
Taste and add more salt and garlic, as desired.

Image on p. 426

INGREDIENTS

6 anchovy fillets

5 cloves garlic

1 whole egg plus 2 yolks

juice of 1 lemon

1 tbsp Dijon mustard

1 cup (240 ml)
grapeseed or canola oil

1 tbsp (15 ml) extra
virgin olive oil

¼ cup (25 g) grated
Parmesan

sea salt or kosher/flaky
salt and freshly ground
black pepper

This recipe accompanies
Tyler Florence's Caesar
Salad with Potato
Croutons recipe, p. 110.

Caesar Dressing

Tyler Florence

COMPLEXITY: EASY | PREP TIME: 15 MINUTES | MAKES: ABOUT 2 CUPS (480 ML)

Place the anchovies, garlic, egg and yolks, lemon juice, mustard,
and a splash of water in a blender and mix.

With the blender running, slowly pour in the oil to make a thick
dressing. Add the olive oil, Parmesan, and salt and pepper to taste,
and blend.

Refrigerate the dressing if you will not be using it right away.

Classic Vinaigrette

Skye Gyngell

COMPLEXITY: EASY | PREP TIME: 10 MINUTES | MAKES: 1 CUP (240 ML)

INGREDIENTS

1 tbsp Dijon mustard

1 tbsp (15 ml) sherry vinegar

sea salt and freshly ground black pepper

generous ¾ cup plus 1¼ tbsp (200 ml) extra virgin olive oil

juice of ½ lemon

METHOD

Put the mustard and vinegar into a bowl and add a generous pinch each of salt and pepper. Stand the bowl on a cloth to keep it steady, then gradually whisk in the extra virgin olive oil to emulsify. Lastly, squeeze in the lemon juice and whisk to combine. Check the seasoning and set aside until ready to use.

If the vinaigrette separates before you are ready to use it, give it a vigorous whisk and it will re-emulsify.

It is important to understand that when flavours are put together, they need a little time to become acquainted. This certainly applies to sauces, mayonnaises, and vinaigrettes. So, wait about 10 minutes before tasting and adjusting the seasoning. Once the ingredients have married, you may find that you need something quite different from what you first suspected, or indeed nothing at all.

"I vary vinaigrettes according to the season and the food I am dressing. This is a simple, versatile vinaigrette; you can use a different vinegar and/or oil as you like, to alter its character."

– SKYE GYNGELL

INGREDIENTS

pinch of sea salt and
freshly ground black
pepper

1 tsp Dijon mustard

1 tsp honey

2 tbsp (30 ml) good
Chardonnay vinegar

2 tbsp (30 ml) vegetable
oil

4 tbsp (60 ml) extra
virgin olive oil

JOSH'S NOTES

Key element: Good-
quality vinegar is the
key.

Tip: Quick and easy to
make in a glass jar.

French Vinaigrette

Josh Emett

COMPLEXITY: EASY | PREP TIME: 10 MINUTES | MAKES: ½ CUP, PLUS 1 TSP (125 ML)

Put the salt and pepper, mustard, and honey in a jar, and shake
together into a paste. Add the vinegar and stir to combine.

Pour in the oils, screw the lid on tightly, and shake until
it emulsifies. Add a touch of warm water if it's too thick.

Use straight away or store in the fridge.

INGREDIENTS

½ tsp Dijon mustard

1 tsp sugar or honey

finely grated zest of
1 lemon

5 tsp freshly squeezed
lemon juice

3 tbsp plus 1 tsp (50 ml)
extra virgin olive oil

3 tbsp plus 1 tsp (50 ml)
vegetable oil

sea salt and freshly
ground black pepper

JOSH'S NOTES

Tip: The sugar is
included to balance
the acidity, so taste and
adjust if necessary.

Lemon Vinaigrette

Josh Emett

COMPLEXITY: EASY | PREP TIME: 10 MINUTES | MAKES: ½ CUP, PLUS 1 TSP (125 ML)

Mix together the mustard, sugar, lemon zest, and lemon juice.
Whisk in the olive oil and the vegetable oil, then season to taste
with salt and pepper. Store in the fridge until needed.

INGREDIENTS

1 cup plus 2 tsp (250 g)
mayonnaise (p. 474)

5 oz (150 g) sour cream

1 clove garlic

¾ oz (20 g)
parsley, picked

½ oz (15 g)
tarragon, picked

½ oz (15 g) chives

1 mild green chilli,
de-seeded

sea salt

lemon juice

Green Goddess Dressing

Dave Verheul

COMPLEXITY: EASY | PREP TIME: 10 MINUTES | SERVES: 1½ CUPS, PLUS 1 TBSP (375 ML)

Using an upright blender, blend the mayo, sour cream, garlic, and herbs until smooth. Season to taste with salt and a touch of lemon juice.

INGREDIENTS

4 cups (1 litre) boiling
water

2 x 4-in (10-cm) pieces
konbu

¾ to 1 oz (20 to 30 g)
dried, shaved bonito

Dashi

Tetsuya Wakuda

COMPLEXITY: EASY | PREP TIME: 5 MINUTES | COOK TIME: 10 MINUTES
MAKES: 4 CUPS (1 LITRE)

Put the water and *konbu* in a saucepan and bring to the boil. When the water begins to boil, take out the *konbu* and add the bonito. Turn off the heat and allow to sit for 1 to 2 minutes, then strain.

For a stronger stock, increase the quantities of *konbu* and bonito.

Ponzu Sauce

Al Brown

COMPLEXITY: EASY | PREP TIME: 5 MINUTES | COOK TIME: 40 MINUTES, PLUS COOLING TIME
MAKES: 1½ CUPS, PLUS 1 TBSP (375 ML)

INGREDIENTS

½ cup plus 1 tsp
(125 ml) rice wine
vinegar

½ cup plus 1 tsp
(125 ml) soy sauce

¼ cup plus 1 tsp (65 ml)
red wine

1½ tbsp dried bonito
flakes

2 pickled plums
(available at most
Asian stores)

1 lime, quartered

This recipe accompanies
Al Brown's Pan-fried
Crispy Skate with Ponzu
Sauce recipe, p. 174.

Place all the ingredients in a small saucepan over a medium-low heat. Bring up to a very slight simmer.

Simmer for a couple of minutes, then remove from the heat to let the flavours infuse for 30 minutes or so. Strain through a fine sieve lined with a muslin cloth, and discard the solids.

Cool the sauce to room temperature, then refrigerate. It will keep in the refrigerator for a few weeks.

Meat Brine

Josh Emett

COMPLEXITY: EASY | PREP TIME: 5 MINUTES | COOK TIME: 5 MINUTES, PLUS CHILLING TIME
MAKES: 1 QT (1 LITRE)

INGREDIENTS

1 qt (1 litre) water

4 tbsp salt

sprig thyme

sprig rosemary

1 tsp white peppercorns

1 tsp coriander seeds

1 tsp fennel seeds

1 tsp juniper berries

1 bay leaves

Place all ingredients in a large pan. Add half of the water and bring to the boil. Remove from the heat and add the remaining water, then cover and chill.

Chinese Master Stock

Teage Ezard

COMPLEXITY: EASY | PREP TIME: 15 MINUTES, PLUS COOLING TIME
COOK TIME: 25 MINUTES | MAKES: 3 QUARTS (3 LITRES)

INGREDIENTS

3 qt (3 litres) water

2 cups plus 1¼ tbsp (500 ml) Shaoxing rice wine

1¼ cups (300 ml) light soy sauce

7 oz (200 g) yellow rock sugar

6 cloves garlic, bruised with the back of a knife and peeled

1¾ oz (50 g) fresh ginger, peeled and roughly chopped

7 whole star anise, lightly toasted

4 sticks cinnamon, lightly toasted

5 cardamom pods, lightly toasted

1 tsp fennel seeds, lightly toasted

1 tsp Sichuan peppercorns, lightly toasted

3 whole cloves, lightly toasted

6 black peppercorns

METHOD

Place all of the ingredients in a stockpot or large saucepan, bring to the boil and simmer, uncovered, for 25 minutes. Set aside to cool completely.

When using the stock, after braising meat, usually poultry or pork, bring the master stock back to the boil, skim away any impurities and strain into a clean, airtight container. When cool, store in the refrigerator for up to 7 days. If you are not using the master stock all the time, store it in the freezer, then thaw it and bring it to the boil when you wish to use it.

Every second time you use it, add about half the quantity of rock sugar, garlic, ginger, star anise, cinnamon, cardamom pods, fennel, Sichuan peppercorns, cloves, and peppercorns and one-third the quantity of the liquids (4 cups/1 litre water, ⅔ cup/165 ml Shaoxing rice wine, 7 tablespoons/100 ml light soy sauce). You want to retain the balance of flavours in the aromatic, glossy stock. If it starts to get too strong, add more water. It needs to be brought to the boil every time you use it, and adding some more Shaoxing wine will help it keep.

"This is the key ingredient in Chinese red-cooking. Meats braised in master stock take on a deep red colour and a sweet, aromatic flavour. The stock can live forever if you treat it correctly, and it will become richer over time."

– TEAGE EZARD

JOSH'S NOTES

Preparation: Make ahead of time for the first use to allow enough time to cool completely.

Key element: Good-quality and very fresh spices.

Chicken Stock
White & Brown

Adam Byatt

COMPLEXITY: EASY | PREP TIME: 10 MINUTES | COOK TIME: 4 HOURS (WHITE),
5 HOURS 20 MINUTES (BROWN), PLUS COOLING TIME | MAKES: 5¼ QUARTS (5 LITRES)

INGREDIENTS

3½ lb (1½ kg)
chicken wings

1 carrot, peeled and
roughly chopped

1 onion, peeled
and sliced

1 stick celery, peeled
and roughly chopped

½ leek (white part only),
roughly chopped

1 whole head garlic,
cut crossways in half

6 qt (6 litres) cold water

½ bunch thyme

2 bay leaves

1 tsp peppercorns

METHOD

WHITE CHICKEN STOCK

Put the chicken wings, vegetables, and garlic in a tall pan. Pour in the water and bring to the boil. Simmer, uncovered, for 4 hours, adding the thyme, bay leaves, and peppercorns after 3 hours.

BROWN CHICKEN STOCK

Pre-heat the oven to 425°F (220°C). Put the chicken wings in a roasting tray and roast for 50 minutes, until browned. Add the vegetables, garlic, thyme, bay leaves, and peppercorns and roast for a further 30 minutes.

Drain off the excess fat and oil from the roasting tray, then transfer the chicken and vegetable mixture to a tall pan. Pour in the water and bring to the boil. Simmer, uncovered, for 4 hours.

BOTH STOCKS

During the simmering process you will need to be on hand with a ladle to skim away any excess fat that rises to the surface of the stock.

Strain the stock into a large container, cover, and allow to cool. Store in the fridge once cooled (it will keep for up to 5 days).

Fish Stock

Marcus Wareing

COMPLEXITY: EASY | PREP TIME: 15 MINUTES | COOK TIME: 45 MINUTES TO 1 HOUR
MAKES: ABOUT 1½ QUARTS (1½ LITRES)

INGREDIENTS

3½ lb (1½ kg) fish bones, with heads, but eyes and gills removed

5 tbsp (75 ml) olive oil

1 onion, chopped

1 leek, white part only, chopped

2 stalks celery, chopped

1 whole head garlic, unpeeled and halved horizontally

1 bay leaf

a few parsley stalks

10 coriander seeds

5 white peppercorns

1 star anise

1¼ cups (300 ml) dry white wine

2 qt (2 litres) water

METHOD

Roughly chop the fish bones and put them in a bowl or pan of cold water to soak for about 10 minutes. Drain and set aside.

Heat the olive oil in a large stockpot. Add the onion, leek, celery, garlic, bay leaf, parsley stalks, coriander seeds, peppercorns, and star anise. Bring to a simmer and cook over a low heat for about 5 minutes, until the vegetables start to soften.

Increase the heat, pour in the wine and boil until the wine has reduced by half. Stir in the fish bones and 2 quarts (2 litres) of water. Bring back to the boil, skim any discoloured foam/scum from the surface, reduce the heat to low and simmer gently, uncovered, for 30 minutes, skimming occasionally.

Strain the stock through a colander and then through a fine sieve. Use the stock straight away, or cool and chill in the fridge for 3 to 4 days. Alternatively, freeze and use within 4 months.

Beef Stock

Daniel Boulud

COMPLEXITY: EASY | PREP TIME: 20 MINUTES | COOK TIME: 3 HOURS, PLUS COOLING TIME
MAKES: ABOUT 5 QUARTS (4½ LITRES)

INGREDIENTS

1 large onion, peeled and halved crosswise

2 whole cloves

1 x 6 lb (2½ kg) bone-in beef shank, cut crosswise into slices 2 in (5 cm) thick and trimmed of excess fat (ask your butcher to do this for you)

coarse sea salt or kosher/flaky salt and freshly ground black pepper

6 qt (6 litres) water

2 tbsp (30 ml) vegetable oil

6 large white mushrooms, trimmed, cleaned and halved

4 stalks celery, trimmed, and cut into 2-in (5-cm) pieces

3 carrots, peeled, trimmed, and cut into 1-in (2½-cm) pieces

6 cloves garlic, peeled and crushed

5 sprigs fresh flat-leaf parsley

2 sprigs fresh thyme

2 bay leaves

1 tsp coriander seeds, toasted

METHOD

Heat a griddle pan or small cast-iron frying pan over a high heat. Place the onion halves in the pan, cut side down, and cook until blackened (they should be as dark as you can get them). Transfer the onion to a plate and stick 1 whole clove in each half.

Season the beef with salt and pepper. Heat the oil in a large non-stick frying pan over a high heat. Working in batches, sear the beef until well browned on all sides, about 20 minutes per batch. As the pieces of meat are browned, transfer them to a large stockpot.

When all the meat is browned and in the stockpot, pour in 6 quarts (6 litres) water. Add the remaining ingredients and bring the liquid to a boil. Lower the heat to a simmer and cook, uncovered, for 2 hours, frequently skimming off the foam and fat that bubble to the surface.

Strain the stock through a colander and then pass it through a chinois or fine-meshed sieve. Let cool to room temperature, then cover and refrigerate. When the stock is chilled, the fat will rise to the top. Before reheating, spoon off and discard the fat.

The stock can be kept tightly covered in the refrigerator for up to 4 days or in the freezer for up to 1 month.

Veal Stock

Gary Rhodes

COMPLEXITY: EASY | PREP TIME: 25 MINUTES | COOK TIME: 10 HOURS
MAKES: 4¾ TO 6 QUARTS (4½ TO 6 LITRES) STOCK OR 2½ TO 5 CUPS (600 TO 1,200 ML) JUS/GRAVY

INGREDIENTS

3 onions, halved

2 to 3 tbsp (30 to 45 ml) oil

5 lb (2¼ kg) veal or beef bones and trimmings (from the butcher, in equal amounts)

8 oz (225 g) carrots, coarsely chopped

2 sticks celery, coarsely chopped

1 leek, chopped

3 to 4 tomatoes, chopped

1 clove garlic, halved

1 bay leaf

sprig of thyme

salt

6 to 7 qt (6 to 7 litres) water

1 tsp cornstarch/ cornflour

METHOD

Pre-heat the oven to 250°F (120°C). Lay the onion halves flat in a roasting tray and add the oil. Place the tray in the oven and allow the onions to caramelize slowly until they have totally softened and coloured. This process will take 1 to 2 hours. The sugars in the onions will cook slowly and give a wonderful taste. Pop the onions into a large stockpot and leave on one side.

Increase the oven temperature to 400°F (200°C). Place all the bones and trimmings in the roasting tray and roast for about 30 minutes, until well coloured. In another roasting tray, roast the chopped carrots and celery (without adding any oil) for about 20 minutes, until lightly coloured.

When ready, add the roasted bones, trimmings, and vegetables to the onions in the pot, along with the leek, tomatoes, garlic, bay leaf and thyme. Fill the pot with cold water – you'll need 6 to 7 quarts (6 to 7 litres). Bring to a simmer, season with salt and skim off any impurities. Allow to cook, uncovered, for 6 to 8 hours for the maximum flavour. If it seems to be reducing too quickly, top up with cold water.

When ready, drain and discard the bones and vegetables. The liquid now remaining is your veal stock, and you can cool it and freeze it in convenient quantities.

Alternatively, make a veal or beef jus/gravy with the stock. Allow the liquid to boil, uncovered, and reduce to 2½ to 5 cups (600 to 1,200 ml), skimming all the time. The stock should be thick and of a sauce-like consistency. Make sure that you taste all the time during reduction. If the sauce tastes right but is not thick enough, thicken it slightly with cornstarch/cornflour. Start with 1 teaspoon cornstarch/ cornflour mixed with 1 teaspoon water. You now have a veal or beef jus/gravy, a classic sauce.

––––––––––

"This brown stock is the basis of many dishes and sauces, and often contributes the defining flavour and richness – the essence – of a good dish. The stock is best started in the morning so that you can allow it to cook throughout the day."

– GARY RHODES

Crème Pâtissière

Philippa Sibley

COMPLEXITY: EASY I PREP TIME: 10 MINUTES I COOK TIME: 20 MINUTES
MAKES: ABOUT 1⅔ LB (750 G)

INGREDIENTS

1¼ cups (300 ml) milk

¾ cup plus 3 tbsp
(225 ml) thickened
cream (35% milk fat)

½ cup (100 g) superfine/
caster sugar

½ vanilla bean, halved
and seeds scraped
(optional)

2 tbsp cornstarch/
cornflour

2⅛ oz (60 g) egg yolks
(about 3)

METHOD

Combine the milk and cream in a saucepan. Add half the sugar
and the vanilla bean and seeds, and bring to a simmer over a
medium heat.

In a large bowl, whisk the remaining sugar with the cornstarch/
cornflour into the egg yolks until pale and thick.

Strain a little of the hot milk mixture through a sieve into the egg
yolk mixture, whisking constantly. Continue straining in the milk
mixture, bit by bit, and whisking it in. The cornstarch/cornflour
prevents the egg yolk from scrambling, so there's no need to
worry about over-cooking.

When all the hot milk mixture is whisked in, pour the mixture back
into the pan. Place over a medium heat and bring to a simmer,
whisking all the time until it is thick and shiny. Remove from the heat
and keep whisking until it cools slightly (a few minutes). It is now
ready to use. If not using immediately, place a piece of plastic wrap
directly onto the surface or dust with powdered sugar/icing sugar
to prevent a skin forming. You can store the crème pâtissière in the
fridge for up to 1 week.

"A delicious, unctuous cream thickened with cornflour to add
more body than crème anglaise. Also known as pastry cream,
its extra heft means that it holds up well as a filling in cakes,
eclairs, and profiteroles."

– PHILIPPA SIBLEY

JOSH'S NOTES

Tips: Don't leave
unattended during
cooking, or you
won't achieve the
correct consistency.
Once cooked, cover
so skin does not form.

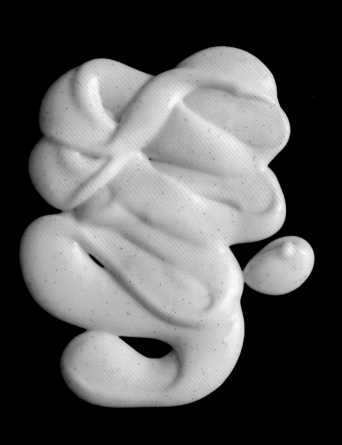

Crème Anglaise

Dorie Greenspan

COMPLEXITY: EASY | PREP TIME: 10 MINUTES
COOK TIME: 20 MINUTES, PLUS REFRIGERATION TIME | SERVES: 2½ CUPS (600 ML)

INGREDIENTS

1 cup (240 ml) whole milk

1 cup (240 ml) heavy cream

6 large egg yolks

½ cup (100 g) sugar

2 tsp pure vanilla extract

METHOD

Fill a large bowl with ice cubes and set out a smaller bowl that can hold the finished crème anglaise. Bring the milk and cream to a boil in a small saucepan.

In a medium-sized heavy-bottomed saucepan, whisk the yolks and sugar together until very well blended and just slightly thickened. Still whisking, drizzle in about one-quarter of the hot liquid – this will temper, or warm, the yolks so they don't curdle. Whisking all the while, slowly pour in the remaining liquid.

Put the pan over a medium heat and stir without stopping, until the custard thickens slightly and coats the back of a spoon. If you run your fingers down the bowl of the spoon, the custard should not run into the track. The custard should reach at least 170°F (77°C), but no more than 180°F (82°C), on an instant-read thermometer. Immediately remove the pan from the heat and pour the custard into a large jug or a clean heatproof bowl. Stir in the vanilla extract.

Refrigerate the crème anglaise until it is very cold, then cover it tightly. If possible, refrigerate for 24 hours before using it – the extra chilling time will intensify the flavour and allow it to thicken a bit more.

Meyer Lemon Curd

Monique Fiso

COMPLEXITY: EASY | PREP TIME: 15 MINUTES
COOK TIME: 20 MINUTES, PLUS COOLING TIME | MAKES: 2¼ LB (1 KG)

INGREDIENTS

9 oz (250 g) whole eggs

1⅓ cups (300 g) superfine/caster sugar

13¼ oz/3⅓ sticks (375 g) unsalted butter, melted

zest of 8 Meyer lemons

¾ cup plus 1¼ tbsp (200 g) fresh Meyer lemon juice

2 sheets (5 g) gelatine

METHOD

Halfway fill a pot with water, place on the stovetop and bring up to a simmer to use as the base of a bain marie to cook your curd. Find a heatproof bowl that fits snugly over your simmering pot of water but without the base of the bowl touching the water. If it does touch the water, remove some of the water until it no longer touches.

Off the heat, place the whole eggs, sugar, butter, and lemon zest and juice in the bowl and blend together using an immersion hand blender.

Place the bowl over the simmering pot of water to cook the curd. It is ready when the temperature of the mix reaches 180°F (82°C). This will take approximately 15 to 20 minutes and you will need to occasionally whisk the mixture as it thickens.

While the curd is cooking, bloom (soften) your gelatine in ice-cold water. When the gelatine is fully bloomed, squeeze out the excess water and set aside.

When the curd has thickened and reached temperature, add the bloomed gelatine and blend smooth using an immersion hand blender.

While still warm, pass the curd through a fine chinois, then place in the refrigerator to cool. Once cool, whisk the mixture until it's smooth and lightly aerated, then serve.

The curd can be stored in an airtight container in the refrigerator for up to 1 week.

INGREDIENTS

½ cup (120 ml) crème fraîche

⅓ cup (40 g) powdered sugar/icing sugar

1½ tbsp (22½ ml) Calvados

———————

This recipe accompanies Chris & Jeff Galvin's Apple Tarte Tatin with Crème Normande recipe, p. 394.

Crème Normande

Chris & Jeff Galvin

COMPLEXITY: EASY | PREP TIME: 5 MINUTES, PLUS REFRIGERATION TIME | SERVES: 6

Mix all the ingredients together in a bowl, then cover with plastic wrap and refrigerate for 1 hour.

INGREDIENTS

5¼ oz (150 g) dark chocolate

2 tbsp (30 ml) rum or strong coffee

1 oz/¼ stick (30 g) unsalted butter

———————

This recipe accompanies Diane Holuigue's Chocolate Profiteroles recipe, p. 412.

Chocolate Sauce with Rum or Coffee

Diane Holuigue

COMPLEXITY: EASY | PREP TIME: 10 MINUTES | COOK TIME: 10 MINUTES | SERVES: 10

Break up the chocolate and melt it in a heatproof bowl set over a pan of just-simmering water. Add the rum or coffee (you can also use 2 tablespoons/30 ml) of water or milk). Then add the butter, stirring until it melts. The chocolate must never boil or its sugar will crystallize.

Use the chocolate sauce as it is for dipping, or thin with a little water and serve in a sauceboat.

INGREDIENTS

INGREDIENTS

5¼ oz (150 g) light palm sugar

1½ cups (360 ml) coconut cream (I use Kara brand)

1 oz/¼ stick (30 g) unsalted butter

juice of 1 lime

pinch of flaky salt

JOSH'S NOTES

Preparation: You can make ahead, as it will keep for 3 days in the fridge.

Tip: Grate the palm sugar, as this helps it to melt evenly.

Salted Coconut Caramel

Michael Meredith

COMPLEXITY: EASY | PREP TIME: 10 MINUTES | COOK TIME: 20 MINUTES | SERVES: 4

Place sugar in a large, deep-sided pot over a medium heat and cook, stirring occasionally, until golden and melted. Add coconut milk (the caramel will spit, so be careful), stir to combine, and cook for 8 to 10 minutes, until a thick and syrupy consistency. Add salt and taste; adjust as necessary.

Set aside to cool a little. While still warm, stir in the butter and lime juice and set aside to cool completely.

Bagels

Peter Reinhart

COMPLEXITY: DIFFICULT | PREP TIME: 1 HOUR, PLUS PROVING AND REFRIGERATION TIME
COOK TIME: 30 MINUTES | MAKES: 12 LARGE OR 24 MINI BAGELS

INGREDIENTS

SPONGE

1 tsp instant dried yeast

4 cups (510 g) unbleached high-gluten or strong/bread flour

2½ cups (600 ml) water, at room temperature

DOUGH

½ tsp instant dried yeast

3¾ cups (480 g) unbleached high-gluten or strong/bread flour

2¾ tsp salt

2 tsp malt powder, or 1 tbsp dark or light malt syrup, honey, or brown sugar

TO FINISH

spray oil

1 tbsp baking soda, added to the boiling water (optional; or substitute 1 tbsp honey or malt syrup)

maize meal/cornmeal or semolina for dusting

TOPPINGS

sesame seeds, poppy seeds, kosher/flaky salt, rehydrated dried minced garlic or onion, or chopped fresh onion tossed in oil (optional)

METHOD

To make the sponge, stir the yeast into the flour in a 4-quart (4-litre) mixing bowl. Add the water, whisking or stirring just until a smooth, sticky batter (like pancake batter) forms. Cover bowl with plastic wrap and leave at room temperature for 2 hours, or until the mixture becomes very foamy and bubbly. It should swell to nearly double in size and collapse when the bowl is tapped on the countertop.

To make the dough, in the same mixing bowl (or in the bowl of an electric mixer), add the additional yeast to the sponge and stir. Then add 3 cups (380 g) of the flour and all of the salt and malt. Stir (or mix on low speed with the dough hook for about 3 minutes) until the ingredients form a ball, slowly working in the remaining ¾ cup (100 g) flour to stiffen the dough.

Transfer the dough to a work surface and knead for at least 8 to 10 minutes (or for about 6 minutes on low speed with the dough hook). The dough should be firm, but still pliable and smooth. There should be no raw flour and all the ingredients should be hydrated. The dough should pass the windowpane test (stretch a small piece of dough into a thin, translucent membrane, indicating the gluten has developed enough) and register 77 to 81°F (25 to 27°C). If the dough seems too dry and rips, add a few drops of water and continue kneading. If the dough seems tacky or sticky, add more flour to achieve the stiffness required. The kneaded dough should feel satiny and pliable, but should not be tacky.

Immediately divide the dough into 4½ oz (130 g) pieces for standard bagels, or 2½ oz (70 g) pieces for mini bagels. Form into balls. Cover with a damp tea towel and allow to rest for approximately 20 minutes.

Line 2 baking trays with baking parchment and mist lightly with spray oil. Proceed with one of the following shaping methods.

SHAPING BAGELS

With your thumb, poke a hole in a ball of bagel dough and gently rotate your thumb around the inside of the hole to widen it to approximately 2½ inches (6 cm) inner diameter (1½ in/4 cm for mini bagels). The dough should be as evenly stretched as possible (try to avoid thick and thin spots).

PROVING AND COOKING

Place the shaped pieces 2 inches (5 cm) apart on the prepared baking trays. Mist the bagels very lightly with spray oil and slip each tray into a food-grade plastic bag, or cover loosely with plastic wrap. Immediately place the trays in the refrigerator to chill overnight. They can remain in there for up to 3 days, but are best used the following day.

When you are ready to bake the bagels, pre-heat the oven to 500°F (260°C) with 2 racks set on the middle shelves. Put a large pot of water on to boil (the wider the pot, the better) and add the baking soda. Have a slotted spoon or skimmer nearby.

Remove the trays from the refrigerator and check the bagels are ready by using the 'float test'. Fill a small bowl with cool or room-temperature water. The bagels are ready to be boiled when they float within 10 seconds of being dropped into the water. Take 1 bagel and test it. If it floats, immediately return the tester bagel to the tray, pat it dry, cover the tray, and return it to the refrigerator until the water is boiling. If the bagel does not float, return it to the tray, pat it dry, and continue to prove the dough at room temperature, checking back every 10 to 20 minutes or so until a tester floats. The time needed to accomplish the float will vary depending on the ambient temperature and stiffness of the dough.

When the bagels are ready, gently drop them into the water, boiling only as many as will fit comfortably (they should float within 10 seconds). After 30 seconds, flip them over and boil for another 30 seconds. If you like very chewy bagels, extend the boiling time to 1 minute per side. While the bagels are boiling, sprinkle the same baking trays with maize meal/cornmeal or semolina (if you decide to replace the paper, spray the new paper lightly with spray oil to prevent the bagels from sticking to the surface). If you want to top the bagels, do so as soon as they come out of the water, while still wet. Place the boiled bagels on a cooling rack, placed over a pan to catch the drips, until all the bagels are boiled and topped (try any of the suggestions in the ingredients list, or a combination. I usually use a seed-and-salt blend). Then, transfer to the baking pan/tin and bake for 8 minutes. Rotate the pan and continue baking another 5 to 9 minutes, or until golden brown on the top and bottom. (Note: If the underside of the bagels become too dark, before the tops are brown, place a second baking pan/tin underneath to delay the underside browning.) Transfer the baked bagels to a cooling rack for at least 10 minutes before serving.

"Having grown up on the East Coast in a predominantly Jewish neighbourhood, I am naturally inclined towards what I think of as the true bagel, the thick-crusted, dense, boiled version, called the water bagel because it is poached in a kettle of boiling, alkalized water."

– PETER REINHART

Multi-seeded Fennel-flavoured Challah

Joan Nathan

COMPLEXITY: MODERATE | PREP TIME: 20 MINUTES, PLUS PROVING TIME
COOK TIME: 40 MINUTES | MAKES: 2

INGREDIENTS

1½ tbsp active dry yeast

1 tbsp plus ⅓ cup (70 g) sugar

⅓ cup (80 ml) vegetable or rapeseed/canola oil

3 large eggs, plus 1 egg yolk

1 tbsp salt

1 tbsp fennel seeds, divided

6 to 7½ cups (750 to 940 g) unbleached all-purpose/plain flour, plus more as needed

2 tsp poppy seeds

2 tsp roasted sesame seeds

JOSH'S NOTES

Key element: Work on getting the proving right; have a nice warm room or set your oven to prove if it has that feature.

Tip: Add enough flour so that it just comes away from the bowl.

METHOD

In the bowl of a stand mixer, dissolve the yeast and 1 tablespoon sugar in 1½ cups (360 ml) lukewarm water. Using the paddle attachment, stir the oil into the yeast mixture, then add 2 eggs, one at a time, the remaining sugar, the salt, and 2 teaspoons fennel seeds. Switch to the dough hook and gradually add 6 cups (750 g) flour, kneading for about 5 minutes and adding more flour as needed to make a slightly sticky, smooth and elastic dough.

Grease a large bowl, turn the dough into it and put the greased side up. Cover with plastic wrap and let rise in a warm place for 1 hour, or refrigerate for a few hours overnight.

When the dough has almost doubled, punch it down, remove it to a lightly floured counter, knead it briefly until smooth, and divide it in half. Roll each piece into a cylinder about 27 in (70 cm) long, making sure there are no seams in the dough, and cut each into 3 pieces. Braid each loaf, and put on a parchment-lined baking sheet at least 4 in (10 cm) apart. You can also twist the loaves into a circle if you like; the dough is very malleable.

Beat the remaining egg and egg yolk together and brush about half the mixture on the loaves, reserving the rest. Let the dough rise, uncovered, for another 30 minutes, or overnight in the refrigerator.

If dough has been refrigerated, bring it to room temperature. Heat the oven to 350°F (180°C) and either combine in a small bowl or keep separate the remaining fennel seeds and the poppy and sesame seeds. Brush the loaves with egg again and sprinkle with seeds, making your own design.

Bake for 35 to 40 minutes, or until golden and firm when tapped with a spatula. Cool on a rack.

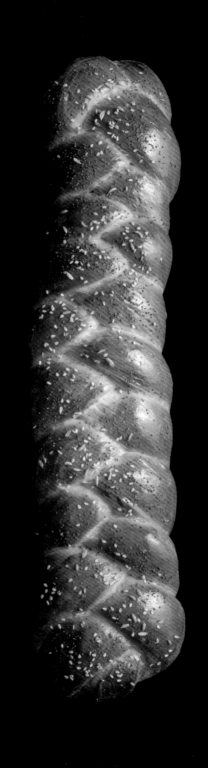

Potato Foccacia

Casey McDonald

COMPLEXITY: MODERATE | PREP TIME: 30 MINUTES, PLUS PROVING TIME
COOK TIME: 35 MINUTES | MAKES: 2 LOAVES

INGREDIENTS

28½ oz (800 g) potato

2 qt (2 litres) water

4½ lb (2 kg) 00 flour

1⅓ oz (40 g) dried yeast

2 tbsp plus 2½ tsp sugar

4 tsp salt, plus extra for
the tops

olive oil

METHOD

Place the potatoes in a large saucepan, cover with cold water, bring to the boil and boil gently for 20 minutes, or until just tender. Drain, reserving the water, and transfer the potatoes to a blender. Blend to a purée.

Pour the 2 quarts (2 litres) water into a microwave-safe bowl and warm in the microwave to about 110°F (45°C). Add the flour and potato and combine, using your hand or a spatula. Add the sugar and yeast, then the salt, mixing to combine each time.

Divide the dough into 28½ oz (800 g) portions, shape neatly and place in very well oiled and salted heavy black pans. Cover and prove for about 1 hour. Using a spatula, 'turn' the edges of the dough over, back into the middle of the dough, to allow oil to slip down the edge, and prevent the dough sticking to the pan.

Pre-heat the oven to 410°F (210°C) fan-forced. Brush the proved loaves with more olive oil, sprinkle with salt and bake 20 minutes. Drop the oven temperature to 375°F (190°C) and bake for another 15 minutes. Flip out onto cake racks to cool.

JOSH'S NOTES

Key element: Heavy pans that are well seasoned and won't stick.

Tip: Ensure the loaves have great colour and are cooked through. Fry slices of bread to reheat them and get them crispy and golden around the outside.

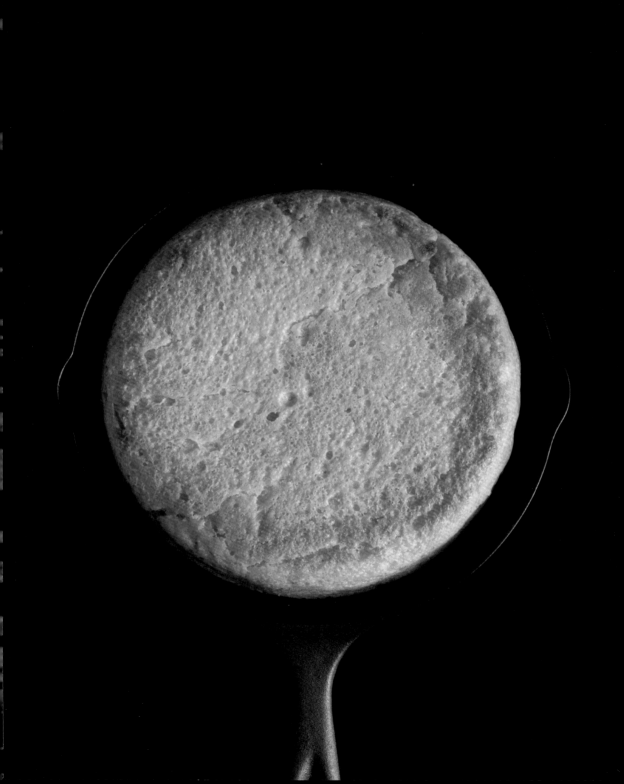

Sourdough Bread

Sat Bains

COMPLEXITY: MODERATE | PREP TIME: 30 MINUTES, PLUS 2 DAYS FOR SOURDOUGH STARTER AND PROVING TIME | COOK TIME: 1 HOUR | SERVES: 10

INGREDIENTS

SOURDOUGH STARTER

1 cup plus 2½ tbsp (150 g) wholewheat or spelt flour

1 cup plus 3 tbsp (150 g) strong (bread) flour

1¾ cups plus 2 tbsp (450 ml) water

1¾ oz (50 g) live yoghurt

2 tsp sugar

FINAL DOUGH

½ tbsp salt

½ cup (120 ml) water, at room temperature

3½ oz (100 g) sourdough starter

1½ cups (200 g) strong (bread) flour

⅓ cup (50 g) whole wheat or spelt flour

METHOD

Mix all the ingredients for the sourdough starter in a bowl. Cover and keep at room temperature for 2 days, making sure it is stirred every 12 hours. The mix is ready when it has trebled in size and has live pockets of air across the surface.

For the dough, dissolve the salt in the water, in the bowl of a stand mixer fitted with the dough hook attachment. Add both flours and mix for 4 minutes. Blend with the sourdough starter and mix for 10 minutes, until completely smooth and elastic. Transfer to a clean bowl. Cover and leave to rise at room temperature until doubled in size, 4 to 6 hours depending on temperature and humidity.

When ready, tip the dough onto a floured surface and leave for 10 minutes to settle.

Separate the dough into 2 pieces and place in proving baskets. Leave at room temperature again until they have doubled in size.

Pre-heat the oven to 475°F (240°C). Tip the two doughs into two Le Creuset (or a Dutch oven) pots. Make a few slits along the top of the loaves and place the lids on the pots. Bake for 20 minutes, then remove the lids and bake for a further 10 minutes. Turn the oven down to 425°F (220°C) and bake for a further 10 minutes.

Remove the bread from the oven and leave in the pots for 10 minutes, then remove from the pots and allow to cool on a wire rack.

JOSH'S NOTES

Preparation: Make the starter at least 2 days in advance, and mix regularly.

Key element: If you can't source live yoghurt, add 1½ tsp fresh yeast to the starter to help activate it.

Milk Bread

Ron Paprocki

COMPLEXITY: MODERATE | PREP TIME: 30 MINUTES, PLUS PROVING TIME
COOK TIME: 12 MINUTES | MAKES: 15 TO 20 MINI LOAVES

INGREDIENTS

3 tbsp plus 1 tsp (50 ml) milk

¾ oz (20 g) fresh yeast

¼ cup plus 2 tsp (65 g) sugar

4 cups plus 2 tbsp (525 g) strong/bread flour (T55)

½ oz (12 g) milk powder

½ oz (12 g) salt

4 oz (112 g) eggs

½ cup plus 2 tbsp (150 ml) water

3½ tbsp (70 g) butter, at room temperature

EGG WASH

1 egg yolk

1 tbsp (15 ml) milk

METHOD

Warm the milk and add it to the yeast and sugar, stir to combine and leave to activate for a few minutes.

Place the flour, milk powder, and salt in the bowl of a stand mixer with a dough hook attached. Add the eggs and water, and mix on speed 2 for 2 minutes, then on speed 3 for 3 minutes. Add the butter and continue mixing on speed 3 for 4 minutes. You should have a smooth dough that comes away from the sides of the bowl.

Transfer the dough to a clean bowl and cover with a tea towel. Leave to proof in a warm place until doubled in size, about 1 hour.

Knock the dough back and divide and shape into the desired shapes. Proof again for a further 20 minutes, or until they have doubled in size.

Pre-heat the oven to 400°F (200°C). Mix the egg yolk and milk to form an egg wash. Brush the proofed loaves with the egg wash and bake for about 12 minutes, depending on the size of the loaves. They are ready when golden brown and sound hollow when tapped on the bottom. Remove from the oven and cool on a wire rack.

JOSH'S NOTES

Key element: When shaping, try to achieve just one seam on the bottom of the loaves so they bake evenly.

Tip: Add a touch more flour if necessary when mixing the dough.

Naan

Sid Sahrawat

COMPLEXITY: EASY | PREP TIME: 5 MINUTES, PLUS RESTING TIME
COOK TIME: 5 MINUTES | MAKES: 8 TO 10

INGREDIENTS

2½ lb (1 kg) strong/bread flour

6¾ tbsp (100 ml) milk

1 oz (28 g) sugar

3 tsp salt

2⅕ tbsp baking powder

2⅓ cups plus 2 tsp (570 ml) water

Place all the ingredients in the bowl of a stand mixer fitted with a dough kneading attachment and knead for 3 to 4 minutes until a smooth dough forms.

Rest the dough for 2 hours covered with a thin film of oil to prevent it from drying out and forming a crust. Keep covered with a wet tea towel or cling wrap.

Firm into 8-10 round mounds/balls and flatten with the oiled palm of your hand, then using a rolling pin dusted with flour, shape into ovals.

Cook the naan on high heat, 425°F to 450°F (220 to 230°C), on a flat griddle in the oven. Brush with melted butter and serve.

Chapati

Christine Manfield

COMPLEXITY: EASY | PREP TIME: 5 MINUTES, PLUS RESTING TIME
COOK TIME: 10 MINUTES | MAKES: 12

INGREDIENTS

4 cups (500 g) wholemeal flour

1 tsp salt

1¼ cups (300 ml) water

Mix the flour and salt in a bowl, make a well in the centre and add the water. Using your fingers, mix to make a dough, adding a little extra water if it seems too stiff. Roll the dough into a ball, cover with a cloth and leave to rest for 30 minutes.

Divide the dough into 12 pieces. On a floured surface, roll each piece into a round about ⅛ in (3 mm) thick and 5 in (12 cm) in diameter. Heat a tawa or heavy-based frying pan over a medium heat and cook each chapati until it starts to turn golden brown, then flip over and cook the other side until browned.

Set aside, covered with a cloth to keep warm, stacking the chapatis as they are cooked.

JOSH'S NOTES

Tip: Make sure your pan is very hot before starting to cook.

Gjelina
Pizza Dough
Travis Lett

COMPLEXITY: EASY | PREP TIME: 30 MINUTES, PLUS PROVING TIME
MAKES: THREE 6½ OZ (185 G) PORTIONS

INGREDIENTS

1 cup plus 2 tbsp
(270 ml) warm water
(87°F/30°C)

1 tsp fresh yeast (baker's
compressed fresh yeast)

1½ cups (170 g) 00 flour

1½ cups (180 g) strong/
bread flour, plus more
for dusting

3 tsp fine sea salt

2 tbsp (30 ml) extra-
virgin olive oil, plus
more for brushing

semolina flour for
dusting

all-purpose/plain flour
for dusting

_____

This recipe accompanies
Trevis Lett's Pizza
Pomodoro recipe,
p. 310.

JOSH'S NOTES

Preparation: Make a
few days in advance,
to allow the dough to
develop correctly.

Key element: Using
the correct stretching
technique to allow air
pockets to work their
way to the perimeter.

Tip: Don't go near a
rolling pin – using your
hands will give you the
perfect aerated result.

METHOD

In a small bowl, combine the water and yeast, stirring until the
yeast dissolves.

In the bowl of a stand mixer fitted with the dough hook attachment,
combine the 00 flour and strong/bread flour. Add the dissolved yeast
to the flours and mix at medium speed just until the dough comes
together, about 3 minutes. Drape a clean kitchen towel over the
dough and let it rest for 15 minutes. Add the salt and mix at medium-
high speed for 5 to 7 minutes, until smooth and very elastic.

Coat a large glass or metal bowl with olive oil. Fold the dough into
thirds like a giant letter and put it in the bowl, turning it over several
times to coat it with oil. Cover the bowl with plastic wrap and let
the dough rise at warm room temperature until it has increased its
volume by 50 to 70 per cent, about 3 hours.

Punch the dough down, fold in thirds, and rotate it 90 degrees, then
fold in thirds again. Cover the bowl with plastic wrap and refrigerate
for 1 to 2½ days. If the dough grows larger than the bowl, punch it
down and return it to the refrigerator.

Divide the dough into three 6½ oz (185 g) pieces. Dust a little
strong/bread flour on your work surface, put the dough on the work
surface and, pressing down on it lightly with the palm of your hand,
roll it in a circular motion, forming a boule (dough ball). If the dough
is sliding around, there is too much flour on the work surface. Wipe
some away if necessary.

Once the dough gathers into a tight ball and the outer layer is pulled
taut over the surface, check the bottom of the dough to see that the
seam has sealed. If there is an opening on the bottom, you need
to roll the dough more tightly or it will tear easily when stretched.
Repeat with the remaining pieces of dough.

Transfer the dough balls to a baking sheet brushed with a bit of olive
oil, leaving plenty of space between the balls so they have room to
rise and expand. (The boule shape encourages an even, round, and
more vertical rise, as opposed to a flatter, more irregular shape.)

Brush the tops with a bit of olive oil, loosely cover with plastic wrap, and let it rise at room temperature until doubled in size, 1½ to 3 hours.

In a small bowl, combine 2 to 3 tablespoons semolina flour and an equal amount of all-purpose/plain flour and then mound the blended flours on your work surface. Put another 2 to 3 tablespoons all-purpose/plain flour in a medium-sized bowl. Put one of the dough balls in the bowl of all-purpose/plain flour and turn to coat with the flour on all sides, handling the dough gently so as not to force out the air or misshape it.

Put the floured dough ball on top of the mound of flour on your work surface. With your fingertips, punch the air out of the dough and press your fingers into the centre and extend outwards to shape the mass into a small disc. Continue to press your fingers and palm down onto the centre of the dough, while turning the dough with your other hand, pushing out the dough from the centre but maintaining an airy rim around the perimeter. Continue stretching out the dough on the work surface with your hand by spreading your fingers as far as you can turn the dough.

Some of my guys with smaller hands use two hands to stretch the dough as it grows larger, using this technique: With the palms of your hands facing down, slip your hands under the dough, lift it up, and use the backs of both hands to gently pull on the dough while continuing to turn it. The dough should stretch easily, resting on the backs of your wrists and forearms, so do not pull on it too much. If it is super-elastic, then the dough probably has not proved enough. If the dough is super-soft and tears easily, it has proved too much. You are done stretching out the dough when it is 10 to 12 in (25 to 30 cm) in diameter and thin enough so that you can read a newspaper through it. This takes a bit of practice so be patient, but under no circumstances should you resort to a rolling pin.

Follow the topping and baking instructions as directed in the pizza recipe, p. 310, repeat the stretching process for the remaining dough balls while the pizza you stretched and just topped cooks.

Egg Yolk Pasta Dough

Marc Vetri

COMPLEXITY: EASY | PREP TIME: 30 MINUTES, PLUS RESTING TIME
MAKES: ABOUT 1 LB (455 G)

INGREDIENTS

1⅓ cups (170 g) 00 or all-purpose/plain flour, plus some for dusting

7 tbsp (55 g) durum flour

9 egg yolks

1 tbsp (15 ml) extra virgin olive oil

3 tbsp (45 ml) water, plus more as needed

METHOD

Combine both flours in the bowl of a stand mixer fitted with the paddle attachment, or mix the flours together on a work surface and make a well in the centre. On medium speed, or with your fingers, add the egg yolks, oil, and water, adding them one ingredient at a time and mixing just until the dough comes together, about 2 to 3 minutes. If necessary, add a little more water, 1 tablespoon (15 ml) at a time, for the dough to come together.

Turn the dough out onto a lightly floured work surface and knead it until it feels silky and smooth, about 5 minutes, kneading in a little extra flour if necessary to keep the dough from sticking. The dough is ready if when you stretch it with your hands, it gently pulls back into place.

Shape the dough into a ball, then flatten the ball into a disc. Cover the dough and set it aside for at least 30 minutes, or wrap it in plastic wrap and refrigerate it for up to 3 days. (You can also freeze the dough for up to 3 months. Thaw the dough overnight in the refrigerator before using it. Alternatively, thaw it quickly in a microwave oven on 50 per cent power in 5-second increments, just until cool to the touch.)

To roll out the dough, cut it into 4 equal pieces. If you have a very long work surface, you can cut the dough into fewer pieces. If the dough was chilled, let the pieces sit, covered, at room temperature for 10 minutes. The dough should be cool but not cold.

Shape each piece into an oval wide enough to fit the width of your pasta roller. Lightly flour your work surface and set the pasta roller to its widest setting. Lightly flour one piece of dough, pass it through the roller and then lightly dust the rolled dough with flour, brushing off the excess with your hands. Pass the dusted dough through the widest setting again.

Set the roller to the next narrowest setting and pass the dough through, dusting again with flour and brushing off the excess. Pass once again through the roller. Fold the dough in half lengthwise over itself and cut about ¼ in (6 mm) off both corners at the fold. This folding and cutting helps to create an evenly wide sheet of dough.

Continue passing the dough once or twice through each progressively narrower setting.

For thicker pasta like corzetti, chitarra, pappardelle, fettuccine, and tagliatelle, you want to roll the dough about ⅛ in (3 mm) thick – setting 2 or 3 on a KitchenAid attachment – or about as thick as a thick cotton bedsheet. For sheet pastas like lasagne and cannelloni, you want to roll it a little thinner, just under ⅛ in (3 mm) thick, and for rotolo thinner still, about 1/16 in (1½ mm) thick – setting 4 or 5 on a KitchenAid attachment, or about as thick as a thin cotton bedsheet. For ravioli, you want to roll the pasta even thinner, to about 1/22 inch (0.8 mm) thick or setting 6 or 7 on a KitchenAid; ravioli sheets should generally be thin enough to read a newspaper through.

As you roll and each sheet gets longer and more delicate, drape the sheet over the backs of your hands to easily feed it through the roller. You should end up with a sheet 2 to 5 feet (61 cm to 1½ m) long, 5 to 6 in (12½ to 15 cm) wide, and ⅛ to 1/32 in (3 to 0.8 mm) thick, depending on your roller and the pasta you are making.

To cut the pasta sheet into the right shape for the dish you are making, lay it on a lightly floured work surface and use a cutting wheel or knife, or the cutter attachment on the pasta machine. If you want to hold the pasta after cutting it, dust it with flour, cover it, and refrigerate it for a few hours; or freeze it in a single layer, transfer the frozen pasta to a zip-lock bag, and freeze it for up to 1 month. Take the pasta straight from the freezer to the boiling pasta water. That's what I usually do.

Semolina Pasta Dough

Alfred Portale

COMPLEXITY: EASY | PREP TIME: 30 MINUTES | MAKES: 1¾ LB (800 G)

INGREDIENTS

1¼ cups (175 g) unbleached flour, plus extra for dusting the pasta dough

1¼ cups (210 g) durum semolina (also called pasta flour)

4 large eggs, at room temperature

½ tsp olive oil

2 tbsp (30 ml) water, or as needed

This recipe accompanies Alfred Portale's Goat Cheese Ravioli in Pancetta & Shallot Sauce recipe, p. 56.

"This pasta can be made up to 8 hours in advance and stored at room temperature, although it will begin to dry out and will take slightly longer to cook."

– ALFRED PORTALE

METHOD

In a food processor fitted with the metal blade, pulse the flour and semolina for about 40 seconds to combine. In a small measuring cup, mix the eggs and olive oil. With the machine running, pour the egg mixture through the feed tube, then add water just until the dough comes together into a mass, about 1 minute. Check the consistency of the dough. If it feels too soft and sticky, add a tablespoon or so of flour. If it is dry and crumbly, add a tablespoon or so of water. Process the dough for 30 seconds and check again. Remove the dough and knead it on a lightly floured surface until smooth and resilient, 5 to 10 minutes. Wrap the dough in plastic wrap.

Attach the pasta machine to a work surface. Set the rollers to the widest setting. Place a bowl of flour near the machine.

Cut the dough into 4 equal portions and work with one portion at a time, keeping the rest covered. Pat the dough to form a thick oblong and run it through the machine, turning the crank with one hand while supporting the rolled dough with the other. Fold the dough into thirds and repeat until the dough has straight, even sides approximately the width of the rollers. Dust with flour as needed. Continue to roll and reduce the width of the rollers until the dough has passed through the second-to-last setting and is about ¹⁄₁₆ in (1½ mm) thick. Lay the pasta sheets on a lightly floured work surface. Repeat the procedure with the remaining dough.

Let the pasta sheets dry, turning occasionally, until they are slightly leathery but still pliable. Depending on the temperature and humidity, this will take anywhere from 15 to 60 minutes.

To make fettuccine, roll each pasta sheet through the wide cutters. To make linguine, roll through the narrow cutters. To make pappardelle, cut each pasta sheet into 16-in (40-cm) lengths and roll them into short cylinders.

Using a sharp knife, cut each cylinder into ½-in (1-cm), or wider, strips. Unravel each portion, twist it into a spiral, and place it on a lightly floured baking sheet. Cover loosely with plastic wrap and let it stand at room temperature until ready to cook.

Traditional Pie Dough

Kate McDermott

COMPLEXITY: EASY | PREP TIME: 20 MINUTES, PLUS REFRIGERATION TIME
MAKES: ENOUGH FOR ONE DOUBLE-CRUST 9-IN (23-CM) DEEP-DISH PIE

INGREDIENTS

3 cups (375 g) unbleached all-purpose/plain flour (use the 'dip and sweep' method; see tips)

½ tsp salt

4 oz/1 stick (112 g) salted or unsalted butter, cut into tablespoon-sized pieces

8 tbsp rendered leaf lard, cut into tablespoon-sized pieces

½ cup (120 ml) ice-cold water, plus 1 to 2 tbsp (15 to 30 ml) more as needed

———————

This recipe accompanies Kate McDermott's Quintessential Apple Pie recipe, p. 362.

JOSH'S NOTES

Preparation: This can be made a day in advance.

Key element: Achieving the correct texture with the butter and leaf lard.

Tip: Moulding the dough into a round, flat shape makes it easier to roll out after chilling.

Comment: This is an outstanding flaky pastry with great flavour.

METHOD

Put the flour, salt, butter, and lard in a large bowl. With clean hands, quickly smoosh the mixture together, or use a pastry blender with an up-and-down motion, until the ingredients look like cracker crumbs with lumps the size of peas and almonds. These lumps will make your crust flaky.

Sprinkle the ½ cup (120 ml) ice-cold water over the mixture and stir lightly with a fork. Squeeze a handful of dough to see if it holds together. If not, mix in more water as needed. Divide the dough in half and make two chubby discs each about 5 in (13 cm) across. Wrap the discs separately in plastic wrap and place in the refrigerator to chill for about 1 hour before rolling out and using.

TIPS

Exact measuring is needed for cakes, but pie dough – at least mine – is pretty forgiving. A bit extra here or there, and it will still turn out fine. But if you measure way over or under the rim of your cup when measuring out the flour, your results may vary from mine. So, I recommend using the 'dip and sweep' method: Dip the measuring cup into the flour, overfilling it, then sweep the top of the cup level with the flat edge of a knife. For those who like to be precise, I have supplied gram measures as an alternative.

For an all-butter crust, use 7 oz/1¾ sticks (200 g) salted or unsalted butter.

Brioche Dough

Philippa Sibley

COMPLEXITY: DIFFICULT | PREP TIME: 30 MINUTES, PLUS PROVING TIME
COOK TIME: 40 MINUTES | MAKES: 1 LARGE DOUBLE LOAF OR 4 SMALL SINGLE LOAVES

INGREDIENTS

3¼ tsp fresh yeast

¼ cup plus 2 tsp (70 ml) milk, warmed slightly

6 eggs, at room temperature

4 cups (500 g) all-purpose/plain flour, plus extra for dusting

1 tbsp cooking salt

2 tbsp superfine/caster sugar

1½ cups/3 sticks (350 g) unsalted butter, softened

1 egg yolk

1 tbsp (15 ml) milk

JOSH'S NOTES

Preparation: Pay attention to proper preparation and planning to get this just right.

Key element: The resting time is key, but also folding the dough and knocking it down in the mould will make sure there are no air pockets.

Tip: In general, making great brioche (and bread) is all about taking the time needed to complete each step properly.

METHOD

To make the dough, put the yeast and milk in a bowl and lightly whisk to combine. Add the eggs and whisk in lightly.

Sift the flour and salt into the bowl of an electric mixer fitted with a dough hook. Pour the yeast mixture into the flour and knead on medium speed until the dough becomes smooth and elastic. This will take about 10 minutes.

Meanwhile, in a separate bowl, work the sugar into the softened butter until pale and creamy.

When the dough starts to come together as a lump on the hook, tearing away from the side of the bowl, it's time to add the butter mixture. Start adding it about 2 tablespoons at a time, making sure that each addition is completely combined before adding more. Once all the butter has been added, continue to mix for 5 minutes or until the dough is shiny and elastic. Transfer to a clean bowl, cover with plastic wrap and leave at about 74°F (24°C) for 2 hours. It should double in volume; if it doesn't, leave it to rise for a bit longer.

When risen, flip the dough over your fingertips a couple of times and then put it back into the bowl. Cover with plastic wrap and refrigerate for several hours, but not more than 24 hours. This second proving is important, as it firms the butter and makes the dough workable.

To make four small single loaves, lightly spray four 6 x 3½ in (15 x 8 cm) loaf tins or one 10 x 5 in (25 x 12 cm) loaf tin with cooking oil spray. In a small bowl, mix the egg yolk and milk together to make an egg wash, and set aside.

Place the dough on a work surface, dust lightly with flour and divide into four equal pieces (for small loaves). Work with one piece at a time, keeping the other pieces covered with a clean tea towel. Using your fist, punch down the piece of dough, then form it into a rectangular shape, about ¾ in (2 cm) thick and measuring 8 x 6 in (20 x 15 cm). With one of the short edges closest to you, begin rolling up the dough to make a neat cylinder. Tuck in the edges as you go to prevent the pastry from blooming out when it proves. Pinch the seam together to seal it. This is your completed loaf.

Place the loaf, seam side down, in the prepared tin. Press the dough down firmly with your fist. Then, using your fingertips dipped in flour, push the edges of the loaf downwards. This ensures that the dough rises evenly and that there are no air pockets. Lightly brush the loaf with egg wash.

Repeat for all the loaves, then cover with a clean tea towel and leave at about 75°F (24°C) until doubled in volume. This will take about 40 minutes at this temperature, but longer if cooler. Don't be tempted to place the loaves somewhere warm to speed up the process, as the butter may begin to soften or even melt and this could ruin the final result.

To bake, preheat the oven to 425°F (220°C). Lightly brush loaves again with egg wash. Bake for 20 minutes, then reduce the oven temperature to 375°F (190°C) and bake for a further 20 minutes. Cool in the tin briefly, then turn out onto a rack to cool fully.

TIP

Fresh yeast is available from bakeries and health food stores. You can substitute 2½ teaspoons (10 g) dried active yeast, mixed with the flour before the milk mix is added.

"Brioche is a rich, buttery yeasted bread. I like to make the most of its buttery nature as a base in bread and butter pudding (where it transforms a classic comfort food from my childhood into an elegant dessert) or in *pain perdu*."

– PHILIPPA SIBLEY

Sweet Pastry
Pâté Sucrée

Philippa Sibley

COMPLEXITY: MODERATE | PREP TIME: 45 MINUTES, PLUS REFRIGERATION TIME
COOK TIME: 20 TO 30 MINUTES | MAKES: ENOUGH FOR 1 TO 2 TARTS

INGREDIENTS

12½ oz/3 sticks plus
1⅓ tbsp (360 g)
unsalted butter,
softened

1¼ cups (150 g) pure
powdered sugar/icing
sugar, sifted

4 egg yolks

3 tbsp plus 1 tsp (50 ml)
cold water

4 cups (500 g) all-
purpose/plain flour,
sifted, plus extra for
dusting

pinch of cooking salt

TO FINISH

1 egg yolk,
lightly beaten

JOSH'S NOTES

Key element: Work
quickly when rolling out
the dough, to ensure it
doesn't get too warm.

Tip: Have enough
flour on your bench to
prevent the pastry from
sticking.

METHOD

MAKING THE DOUGH

Place the butter in the bowl of an electric mixer fitted with the paddle attachment. Work the butter on low speed until smooth and the same texture throughout.

Add the powdered sugar/icing sugar and mix together on medium speed until combined, taking care not to aerate too much – you don't want it to be pale and fluffy.

In a separate bowl, combine the egg yolks and cold water. While still mixing, add to the butter mixture bit by bit. At this stage the mixture may look as though it has separated, but once the flour is added this will be rectified.

Now turn off the mixer, then tip in the flour and salt. On low speed, work in the flour and salt until the mixture comes together and is crumbly. Do not overwork at this stage, as the gluten in the flour will activate and the pastry could become tough.

Tip the contents of the bowl onto a work surface and, using the heel of your hand, smear the mixture away from you until it looks smooth and no patches of butter remain.

Using a palette knife or scraper, scrape the pastry together into a mound. Divide the mound of pastry in half and pat each half into a round about 1¼ in (3 cm) high – you don't want a big boulder, otherwise it will make it harder later to achieve the right temperature to work the dough. Wrap in plastic wrap and refrigerate until chilled all the way through, about 1 hour.

WORKING THE DOUGH

Once the dough has chilled, remove it from the fridge and place on a work surface lightly dusted with flour. Chop the dough into manageable bits and smear each bit with the heel of your hand to get the dough going. If you missed any bits of butter before, make sure you smear them out this time.

Once the pastry is all the same texture, bring it all together again. Shape it back into a ball, ready to roll out.

Gently but firmly tap the pastry out slightly with your rolling pin to get things going. Then roll the pastry out quickly so it doesn't warm up too much and become soft and unmanageable. Roll evenly and make a quarter-turn every couple of rolls to keep the shape even.

LINING A TART RING

Line a baking tray with baking paper and place a tart ring on top.

Roll the pastry out to a thickness of about ¼ in (5 mm). The pastry should feel supple and roll out easily without cracking. Now roll up the pastry loosely onto the rolling pin and gently unroll over the tart ring.

Ease the pastry into the tin, taking care that there are no creases or cracks. Just smooth out any cracks or creases with your fingertips. Do not trim the excess pastry, but leave it overhanging. This ensures that the edge of the pastry will be still perfectly flush with the ring even if the shell shrinks. Reserve a few of the dough scraps for patching up the shell later.

Freeze the tart shell until very firm, about 1 to 2 hours.

TO BLIND-BAKE

Preheat the oven to 350°F (180°C).

Carefully line the chilled tart shell with foil, smoothing out any wrinkles and pressing the foil over the edges. Fill with uncooked rice all the way to the top. I prefer to use rice instead of dried beans or baking weights because the rice creates a uniform mass that doesn't have any gaps.

Bake for 20 minutes for a large tart (or less for smaller tarts), or until the tart shell is golden brown all over. Remove from the oven, tip out the rice (allow to cool and use again as baking weights), and remove the foil. Return to the oven for 5 minutes to dry the pastry completely.

Remove from the oven and while the tart shell is still hot, patch up any holes or cracks with a smear of the reserved pastry scraps. You will only need to do this for large tart shells as they tend to crack.

While still hot, very lightly brush the potentially leaky parts of the shell or miniscule holes with the beaten egg yolk to seal. This is an important step if you are filling the tart with a liquid mixture. The tart shell is now ready to use.

"This sweet pastry is your dessert workhorse. The pastry is not too 'short', [and] so easy to work with. Make the full quantity because you can always freeze the portion you don't use."

– PHILIPPA SIBLEY

Chou Pastry
Pate à Chou

Diane Holuigue

COMPLEXITY: MODERATE | PREP TIME: 10 MINUTES | COOK TIME: 45 MINUTES
MAKES: 10 OR MORE (AS PUFFS)

INGREDIENTS

1 cup plus 2 tsp (250 ml) cold water

1 tbsp sugar

pinch of sea salt

3½ oz/7 tbsp (100 g) unsalted butter

1 cup plus 1 tbsp (130 g) all-purpose/plain flour, sifted

4 eggs

GLAZE

1 egg

1 tbsp (15 ml) milk

This recipe accompanies Diane Holuigue's Chocolate Profiteroles recipe, p. 412.

JOSH'S NOTES

Preparation: Have everything ready before you start, in order to work smoothly through the process.

Key element: Go carefully when you reach the ball-around-the-spoon stage.

Tip: Have someone else on hand to help with the stirring; you do need to work the pastry well.

METHOD

Place the cold water in a saucepan together with the sugar, salt, and butter (cut into pieces). Bring to the boil, stirring occasionally with a wooden spatula to make sure that the butter is fully melted by the time the water boils. Note: Any further boiling will evaporate water and disturb the water–flour ratio.

Lift from the stove and add the sifted flour, all at once. Stir well, then return to the stove and stir for the count of 20, or until the flour rolls off the edges of the saucepan and clings, in a ball, around the spatula. Remove from the heat. Note: This stage is the making or breaking of your pastry, but a careful eye can counteract any faults so far. If the mixture is too sloppy, simply dry it out a little more over the heat. If the water was under-measured or evaporated, you will reach the 'ball-around-the-spoon' stage quicker.

Off the heat, add 2 eggs and stir briskly until mixture seems to roll off the sides of the saucepan again. Then add the other 2 eggs and blend in the same way. It is possible to transfer the dough to a food processor to mix in the eggs, but it seems hardly worth the while.

Shape the mixture while still warm. If making puffs, transfer it to a bag with a ½ in (1 cm) nozzle and pipe onto a greased baking tray in dollops measuring ½ to ¾ in (1½ to 2 cm) across. The dough may also be formed by dropping it from a teaspoon.

Before baking, beat the egg and milk together in a cup and glaze the pastry with a pastry brush.

"Basic to success with these desserts is an understanding of making and baking the pastry. Follow the step-by-step procedure, then try your hand at varying it. Remove sugar and add salt and pepper. Try adding chopped anchovy, diced cheese and ham to the raw mixture and either baking or deep-frying for tasty little puffs."

– DIANE HOLUIGUE

Puff Pastry

Jean-André Charial

COMPLEXITY: MODERATE | PREP TIME: 3- MINUTES, PLUS REFRIGERATION TIME | SERVES: 10

INGREDIENTS

2 cups (250 g) flour

1 generous tsp salt

1 tbsp (15 g) butter, softened

scant ½ cup (100 ml) cold water

FOR ROLLING

7 oz/1¾ sticks (200 g) butter

_____

This recipe accompanies Jean-André Charial's Millefeuille à la Baumanière recipe, p. 322.

METHOD

Mix the flour, salt, and softened butter, add the cold water, then mix with your fingers until the dough is firm and smooth. Cover in plastic wrap and refrigerate for 4 hours.

Roll the butter out between two pieces of plastic wrap. Roll the dough into a rectangle and place the butter in the centre. Fold in the corners so that the butter is wrapped in dough, then roll out again until 1¼ in (3 cm) thick. Fold in thirds and refrigerate for a further 2 hours. Repeat this a total of four times – each time you will roll it out again and fold it in thirds.

Croissants

Jean Michel Raynaud

COMPLEXITY: DIFFICULT | PREP TIME: 2 HOURS, PLUS PROVING AND REFRIGERATION TIME
COOK TIME: 25 MINUTES | MAKES: 10 TO 12

INGREDIENTS

CROISSANT DOUGH

4 cups (500 g) all-purpose/plain flour, plus extra for dusting

¼ cup (60 g) superfine/caster sugar

2 tsp fine salt

2½ tsp dried yeast

1¼ cups (300 ml) full-fat milk

9½ oz/1¼ cups (270 g) block cold unsalted butter

CROISSANTS

1 recipe cold croissant dough, 1 single and 1 double turn

3 eggs

pinch of fine salt

METHOD

MIXING THE DOUGH

Using an electric mixer fitted with a dough hook attachment, mix the flour, sugar, salt, and yeast on low speed until well combined. Gradually add the milk and mix for 5 minutes. At this stage the dough should be firm but not dry. If the mixture looks too hard or your mixer finds it hard to mix properly, add 1 to 2 tablespoons (15 to 30 ml) extra milk to soften it up. Some types of flour, or flours made from different types of wheat, have different rates of absorption.

After 5 minutes, increase the speed slightly and mix for another 10 minutes, or until the dough is smooth and comes away from the side of the bowl. Be careful when increasing the speed of your mixer; this dough can be hard on small mixers so if you feel like your mixer is struggling, reduce the speed and mix for a few minutes longer.

Stop the mixer, remove the dough and place in a bowl. Lightly dust with flour and cover with a clean cloth. Set aside in a warm place for the first prove (*pointage*), for 1 hour or until increased in size by half. Always check how fast your dough is proofing. The first prove is meant to stimulate the yeast only, so as soon as the dough increases by roughly half of its original size, transfer it to a tray lined with baking paper. Flatten the dough over the tray as much as you can to remove as many gas bubbles as possible. Cover the tray with plastic wrap and refrigerate on the top shelf for at least 1 hour.

PREPARING THE BUTTER

When the dough (*détrempe*) is cold, you will need to prepare the butter for the laminating (layering) process. This involves pounding the cold butter into a rectangle roughly half the size of your dough. To do this, place the block of cold butter on a piece of baking paper, cover with another piece of baking paper and use a rolling pin to pound the butter, regularly turning it by 90 degrees, into a rectangle about 7 x 8 in (18 x 20 cm). Cover the butter in the plastic wrap and set aside.

LAMINATING

Place the dough on a lightly floured work surface and dust the top with flour. Roll the dough from the middle all the way to the edges into a rectangle measuring 8 x 14 in (20 x 35 cm). Keep moving the dough and dusting with a little extra flour to stop it sticking (however, be frugal with the flour you use during this process). If you can't roll your dough out to the exact dimensions, use your hands to stretch it into shape. Rotate the dough 90 degrees.

Unwrap the butter and place it in the centre of the dough rectangle. Fold both ends of the dough over the top so they meet in the middle of the butter and pinch the ends together. You should end up with a rectangle measuring about 8 x 7 in (20 x 18 cm), with the butter exposed at two ends and a tightly sealed seam over the top.

With one short end facing you, begin rolling the dough from the middle to the top, flouring as needed. Rotate the block 180 degrees and repeat the process until you have a rectangle that measures 8 x 25½ in (20 x 65 cm). Fold one-third of the rectangle over the middle of the block, then fold the other end over the top. This will give you a single turn. During the process of turning, make sure that you maintain your original rectangular shape by either gently rolling or stretching the dough into shape, as this will ensure an even distribution of butter throughout the croissants.

Use your finger to mark a dot in the dough, as a reminder that this is the first turn. (Increase the number of dots for subsequent turns.) Cover the dough in plastic wrap and refrigerate for 1 hour, or until the butter is firm.

The next and final turn is a double turn, or book turn, and for this the dough will need to be rolled out thinner to accommodate an additional fold. Repeat the process as for the first turn but continue rolling until you get a larger rectangle measuring 8 x 35½ in (20 x 90 cm). Once you have rolled and stretched the dough to the correct dimension, fold both ends to meet in the middle of the rectangle, then fold it in half again to end up with a block roughly the original size of the butter.

Wrap the croissant dough (*pâton*) in plastic wrap and refrigerate for 2 hours. Resting the dough in the fridge enables the gluten (protein in the flour) to relax and also helps the butter to harden. This not only makes it a lot easier to work with the dough, but also ensures that the butter isn't absorbed into the thin layers of the dough, which would effectively negate most of the work you have just done.

CUTTING THE CROISSANTS

Line two baking trays with baking paper. Remove the croissant dough from the fridge and place on a lightly floured work surface with one short, open side facing you. Dust the top with a little extra flour and begin rolling lengthwise, regularly moving the dough and dusting with flour to ensure that it doesn't stick to the work surface.

Continued overleaf

Croissants cont.

This final process is the most demanding one. If you're getting tired or if the dough softens up too much, simply sprinkle the top of the dough with flour, fold it gently over itself and refrigerate until it sets again. Continue the rolling process until you get a long rectangle that measures about 8 x 24 in (20 x 60 cm) and is about ¼ in (5 mm) thick.

Before you begin cutting your rolled-out dough (*abaisse*), fluff it up by running your hand underneath it and lifting it up gently on all sides. This allows the gluten time to relax, and stops your cut pieces from shrinking and losing their shape during the cutting process.

Use a large knife to cut the dough into alternating triangles with a 4-in (10-cm) base. Gently lift each triangle and stretch it with your hands until it is lengthened by about 10 per cent, to roughly 8½ in (22 cm) long. Remove any excess flour from the work surface, as the dough needs to adhere to the surface for the croissants to be rolled properly. Place one triangle on the work surface with the pointed end facing you. Using both palms, roll the wide end (the base) of the croissant towards you, all the way to the tip of the triangle. When the croissant is rolled, simply bend it in the shape of a crescent and place it on a lined baking tray, leaving a 2 in (5 cm) gap between croissants.

Cover the croissants with a damp cloth and place in a warm place to proof for 2 hours, or until doubled in size. To check if your pastries are ready to bake, poke them with your index finger; they should feel soft but still elastic. If the pastry doesn't bounce back after being poked, they are probably slightly overproofed, so occasionally check their progress towards the end of the recommended proofing time.

BAKING THE CROISSANTS

To make an egg wash, lightly beat the eggs and salt together in a small bowl, then set aside for 5 minutes.

Pre-heat the oven to 365°F (185°C). When the croissants have proved, brush them generously with the egg wash and bake for 25 minutes, or until golden brown. Unlike puff pastry, croissant dough has a leavening agent (yeast), so does not rely solely on the steam created by water evaporation during the baking process to develop. Croissants should have a flaky skin and a soft, fleshy centre, so they need to be cooked at a much lower temperature for a shorter period – don't be tempted to leave them for too long in the oven. Generally speaking, if you respect the cooking temperature then the colour will be a great indicator of whether the croissants are ready or not.

Reference

As a recipe book for home cooks around the world, consisting of recipes from around the world, there is a wide variety of ingredients, measures, and terminology which differ according to location. In all the recipes contained here, we have provided both imperial and metric measurements in each recipe, with imperial listed first and metric following in parenthesis. (It is important to note that the imperial cup (240 ml) is a different size to the metric cup (250 ml), so if you are using metric measurements make sure you follow the millilitre measurements in parenthesis after all cup measurements.) Refer to our detailed conversion charts on pp. 518–521 if you are unsure of a measurement. Most importantly, remember to taste as you go – ultimately your own palate will guide you.

Other things you need to know:

Each country has different minimal legal weights for eggs and the ones used in this book are typically medium size (approximately 50 g). You can find equivalent sizes listed on p. 520.

The fat content in cream differs widely around the world, and we have provided the different terms and their approximate conversions on p. 521.

Just as measurements differ from country to country, so do terms, and a comprehensive glossary of terms, ingredients, and equivalent words on pp. 522–526 attempts to cover the varying references contained in the recipes. American words and terms are listed first throughout the book where applicable, with Commonwealth English alternatives following, separated by a solidus.

The list of kitchen equipment on pp. 527–528 provides guidance on the essential items you'll need to prepare your kitchen ready for battle, together with optional equipment used by some of the chefs.

Lastly, a detailed index by recipe name, ingredient, and chef or cook will help you quickly find what you're looking for.

Conversion Tables

Abbreviations

g	gram
kg	kilogram
oz	ounce
qt	quart
lb	pound
mm	millimetre
cm	centimetre
in	inch
ml	millilitre
L	litre
fl oz	fluid ounce
tsp	teaspoon
tbsp	tablespoon
°C	degrees Celsius
°F	degrees Fahrenheit

Weight Conversions

Metric	Imperial/US
15 g	½ oz
30 g	1 oz
60 g	2 oz
90 g	3 oz
100 g	3½ oz
125 g	4½ oz
150 g	5 oz
175 g	6 oz
200 g	7 oz
225 g	8 oz
250 g	9 oz
300 g	10½ oz
325 g	11½ oz
350 g	12½ oz
375 g	13 oz
400 g	14 oz
450 g	16 oz (1 lb)
500 g	18 oz
1 kg	36 oz (2¼ lb)

Note: 1 stick butter = 4 oz (112 g).

Liquid Conversions

Metric	Imperial/US
5 ml	⅙ fl oz
15 ml	½ fl oz
30 ml	1 fl oz (28 ml)
60 ml	2 fl oz
90 ml	3 fl oz
100 ml	3½ fl oz
125 ml	4 fl oz (¼ pint US)
150 ml	5 fl oz (¼ pint imperial)
175 ml	6 fl oz
200 ml	7 fl oz
225 ml	8 fl oz (½ pint US)
250 ml	9 fl oz
280 ml	10 fl oz (½ pint imperial)
340 ml	12 fl oz (¾ pint US)
420 ml	15 fl oz (¾ pint imperial)
450 ml	16 fl oz (1 pint US)
500 ml	18 fl oz
560 ml	20 fl oz (1 pint imperial)
1 L	36 fl oz (1¾ pint imperial, 2¼ pint US)

Length Conversions

Metric	Imperial/US
0.5 cm (5 mm)	¼ in
1 cm	½ in
2.5 cm	1 in
5 cm	2 in
7.5 cm	3 in
10 cm	4 in
12.5 cm	5 in
15 cm	6 in
18 cm	7 in
20 cm	8 in
23 cm	9 in
25.5 cm	10 in
28 cm	11 in
30 cm	12 in (1 foot)
40 cm	16 in

Conversion Tables cont.

Cup & Spoon Conversions

Spoon/cup	Metric	US metric
½ tsp	2.5 ml	2.5 ml
1 tsp	5 ml	5 ml
1 dsp	10 ml	–
1 tbsp	15 ml	15 ml
1 tbsp (Australia)	20 ml	–
⅛ cup	30 ml	30 ml
¼ cup	65 ml	60 ml
⅓ cup	85 ml	80 ml
½ cup	125 ml	120 ml
⅔ cup	170 ml	160 ml
¾ cup	190 ml	180 ml
1 cup	250 ml	240 ml
1½ cups	375 ml	360 ml
2 cups	500 ml	480 ml
4 cups	1 L	960 ml

Egg Sizes (minimum weights)

Each country has different minimal legal weights; the following weights are approximated for the purposes of conversion.

	Australia	NZ	South Africa	UK/Europe	US
around 35 g	–	Pullet (4)	Small	–	Peewee
around 43 g	Medium	Small (5)	Medium	Small	Small
around 53 g	Large	Standard (6)	Large	Medium	Medium
around 60 g	Extra Large	Large (7)	Very Large	Large	Large
around 70 g	Jumbo	Jumbo (8)	Jumbo	Very Large	Extra Large
around 75 g	King Size	–	Super Jumbo	–	Jumbo

Oven Temperatures

Celsius	Fahrenheit	Gas mark	Description
110°C	225°F	¼	very low/cool
120°C	250°F	½	
140°C	275°F	1	low/cool
150°C	300°F	2	
170°C	325°F	3	medium/moderate
180°C	350°F	4	
190°C	375°F	5	moderate/hot
200°C	400°F	6	
220°C	425°F	7	high/hot
230°C	450°F	8	
240°C	475°F	9	very hot
260°C	500°F	10	

Cream Equivalents

The fat content in cream differs widely, but approximate conversions are listed below. Both single and double cream are now widely available in most countries, though in countries like New Zealand where there is only one main type of cream, you can adjust recipes that call for double cream through methods such as simmering cream sauces for longer.

Australia	NZ	South Africa	UK/Europe	US
Light	Lite	Pouring	Single	Light
Single	Cream	Pouring	Single	Light
Thickened	Thickened	Whipping	Whipping	Light Whipping
Double	Cream	Double Thick	Double	Heavy

Glossary

All of the terms listed below appear in *The Recipe*. Here you will find definitions for specific ingredients, items, cooking terms and methods, together with alternate words for particular terms.

abaisse: a thin rolled-out pastry
amaretto: an almond-flavoured Italian liquor
amazu: a Japanese sauce made from rice vinegar
ancho chilli powder: a hot spice made from ground ancho peppers
Arbequina: Spanish olive oil
arugula: an edible plant with a peppery flavour
aubergine: *see* eggplant
baking beans: any form of dried or ceramic beans used to blind-bake pastry; rice may be used as a substitute
banana shallot: a cross between an onion and a regular shallot (*see* shallot)
banno soy sauce: a soy sauce flavoured with *konbu* seaweed and mirin, often used in Japanese cuisine
bash: *see* mash
batons: a style of cutting vegetables where each item is sliced into slim rectangles
bavette: a cut of meat similar to a flank steak
Bayonne ham: speciality French ham cured with wine
béchamel: commonly known as white sauce, béchamel is made from milk and a white roux
beetroot: *see* beets
beets: a hard, purple-red vegetable
beurre blanc: an emulsified butter sauce
biscuit: a round soft, flour-based food served sweet or savoury depending on toppings; also
biscuit: *see* cookie
black pudding: *see* blood sausage
blanch: a cooking method where food is placed first in boiling water then in iced water, typically used for vegetables
blind-bake: to bake a pastry without its filling, usually by covering in baking paper/parchment paper and weighing down with baking beans or rice
blood sausage: a sausage filled with blood that is dried or cooked then mixed with a filler
bloom: to soften gelatine in cool liquid
bonito: a medium-sized fish from the same family as the mackerel and tuna
bonito flakes: flakes of dried, smoked bonito fish
borlotti beans: a plump pinkish-brown bean with dark streaks, used widely in Italian cuisine
bouillon cube: dehydrated bouillon (broth) formed into a small cube
boule: a dough ball
bouquet garni: a bunch of herbs, usually encased in a muslin bag or tied together with string, used for flavouring soups or stews
braise: to lightly fry food then stew slowly in a sealed container
brunoise: a mixture of finely diced vegetables fried in butter and used to flavour sauces and soups

butternut squash: an orange-yellow winter squash with a nutty, sweet taste
Calvados: a pear or apple brandy from France's Normandy region
canelé: a French pastry with a soft custard centre, flavoured with vanilla and rum
candlenuts: a large waxy, pale nut
candy: confectionery
cane sugar syrup: *see* corn syrup
cannellini beans: a soft creamy bean that has a fluffy texture when cooked
canola oil: *see* rapeseed oil
Cantábrico anchovies: anchovies fished off the Cantábrico coast, carrying a mild, creamy taste
capon: a rooster that has been chemically castrated to improve the quality of its meat
capsicum: *see* pepper / bell pepper
celeriac: *see* celery root
celery root: a variety of celery with a sharp flavour
ceviche: a dish made from fresh raw fish cured in citrus juice and spiced
Champagne vinegar: a wine vinegar with a more mild flavour than other types of vinegar
chana dal: a dried legume also known as split chickpeas
chawanmushi: a savoury egg custard dish originating from Japan
cheese;
    Comté: a creamy, nutty-flavoured French cheese made from unpasteurized cow's milk
    buffalo mozzarella: mozzarella made from the milk of Italian Mediterranean buffalo
    Emmental: a yellow Swiss cheese with a mild, savoury taste, characterized by shallow holes
    fromage blanc: a soft, creamy French cheese made from cow's milk, with a sour taste
    Grana Padano: a hard cow's milk cheese from Italy that becomes crumbly with age
    Gruyère: a hard, nutty cheese from Switzerland
    Kefalograviera: a hard table cheese made from sheep's or goat's milk
    mascarpone: an Italian cream cheese mild in flavour
    Parmesan: a hard, dry cheese with a mild flavour, typically grated and served with pasta dishes and risotto
    Parmigiano Reggiano: a hard Italian cheese from Italian provinces of Parma, Reggio Emilia, Bologna, Modena, and Mantua
    pecorino: a hard Italian cheese made from sheep's milk with a sharp smoky flavour
    pecorino Romano: a hard, salty Italian cheese made from sheep's milk
chermoula paste: a North African spice paste typically used to marinate fish and poultry
chickpeas: *see* Garbanzo beans
chiffonade: a slicing technique used to cut herbs and leafy greens into long, thin strips
chile: *see* chilli
chilli;
    ají limon chilli: a bright yellow chilli also known as the lemon drop chilli
    bird's-eye chilli: an extremely hot chilli pepper popular in Thai cuisine
    jalapeño: a common green medium-sized chilli which varies in heat

mouse shit chilli: a small, hot red chilli from Thailand

peperoncino: the Italian name for hot chilli peppers

poblano pepper: a mild, wide chilli pepper from Mexico

serrano chilli: a small, thick Mexican chilli pepper with a sharp flavour

chilly bin: see cool-box

Chinese five spice: a blend of five powdered spices, typically cloves, star anise, fennel seeds, cinnamon, and peppercorns

Chinese white rice vinegar: a colourless liquid with a high vinegar content, similar in flavour to standard vinegar

chorizo: a small spicy Spanish pork sausage

cilantro: a strong-tasting herb with soft leaves, often used in Mexican cuisine

Ciliegini tomatoes: cherry tomatoes

clarified butter: butter with all milk solids removed

coarse oatmeal: see pinhead oatmeal

cockerel: a young domestic rooster

cookie: a small, round baked sweet such as a chocolate chip

cool-box: an insulated box for keeping food and drink cold

coriander: see cilantro

corn syrup: a food syrup made from the starch of corn and used to soften the texture and enhance the flavour of foods

cornmeal: see maize meal

cos lettuce: see romaine lettuce

courgette: see zucchini

cream;

Chantilly cream: flavoured or sweetened whipped cream

crema agria: the Spanish term for sour cream

crème fraîche: a dairy product made from double cream that is sweeter and more fluid than sour cream

heavy cream / double cream: thick cream containing plenty of milk fat

cream stiffener / stabilizer: a combination of starch, glucose, and separating agent used to ensure whipped cream remains stiff

cultured butter: a slightly tangy-tasting butter made from cream that is cultured with active bacteria

daikon / mooli / Japanese white radish: a mild-flavoured winter radish with a large white root

deglaze: to make a sauce or gravy by adding liquid to a pan containing cooking juices from meat

demi-glace: a rich brown sauce from which the liquid has been partly evaporated, usually flavoured with wine and served with meat

dessicated coconut: see shredded coconut

détrempe: soaked, or softened

digestive biscuits: see Graham cracker

Dijon mustard: a French mustard typically made with white wine, with a medium-hot flavour

eggplant: a deep purple fruit with soft flesh

endive: a leafy vegetable with a nutty, bitter flavour

English mustard: a vibrant yellow mustard made with turmeric, with a sharp flavour

escarole: a leafy vegetable with broad leaves, similar in appearance to a cross between lettuce and bok choy

filé powder: a hot spice made from ground dried leaves of the sassafras tree, typically used when making gumbo

filo pastry: see phyllo pastry

fishcake: a patty made from mashed potato and shredded fish then coated in breadcrumbs and fried

flaked almonds: see slivered almonds

flaky salt: flaked sea salt in dry, flat crystals

flat rice noodle: a rice noodle with a wide, flat shape

fleur de sel: a delicate sea salt formed on the surface of seawater as it evaporates

flour:

all-purpose / standard flour: a standard white flour

bread flour: see strong flour

cake flour (T45 and T55): see soft flour

cornflour: see cornstarch

cornstarch: starch derived from the corn grain, typically used to thicken soups and sauces

durum flour: an unbleached flour made from durum wheat, similar to semolina

maize meal: a coarse flour made from maize

plain flour: see all-purpose / standard flour

self-rising flour / self-raising flour: all-purpose / standard flour with baking powder and salt added

soft flour: finely-milled, delicate flour typically used in cakes

strong flour: high-grade flour, hard flour

fond: refers to the caramelized drippings of food that stick to the bottom of a pan after roasting or sautéing

fondant: a stiff, edible icing used on decorative cakes and pastries

French bean: a narrow green bean

French breakfast radish: a vibrant red radish with edible green leaves and a sharp, crisp flavour

French shallot: similar in appearance to a small onion, with a mild flavour

fried tofu puff: bite-sized pieces of tofu fried in a wok until golden brown all over

frisée: curly endive (see endive)

frosting: a sweet, creamy substance spread over cakes, pastries and more

galangal: a spice similar in appearance to ginger, with a sharp, citrus flavour

gammon: cured meat from the hind legs of a pig

Garbanzo beans: small golden legumes high in protein and dietary fibre

ghee: a type of clarified butter from India, typically used in Middle Eastern cuisine

giblet: the edible offal of a fowl

gizzard: the muscular stomach of certain birds, fish, and, insects, considered a delicacy in certain parts of the world

glucose syrup: a sugary syrup made from the hydrolysis of starch

goat's cheese crottins: a famous goat's cheese with a subtle, nutty flavour, produced in France's Loire Valley

golden raisins: a small, brown seedless raisin used in desserts and cakes

golden syrup: see corn syrup

Graham cracker: a type of thin, dry brown cracker used to make cheesecake crusts and more

greaseproof paper: see waxed paper

green bean: long, thin green vegetables that can be eaten raw or cooked

green onion: a small onion pulled from the ground before the bulb has formed

ground beef: beef that has been very finely chopped with a meat grinder or mincing machine

groundnut: a small nut with a dimpled large shell

guanciale: an Italian cured meat made from pork cheek

hajikami: ginger shoots pickled in vinegar

haricot beans: *see* navy beans

harissa paste: a rich, red paste made from roasted peppers, chilli peppers, and various herbs

Himalayan salt: a pink rock salt from Pakistan

hob / range: the flat top of a cooker with burners and hotplates

hoisin sauce: a rich brown sauce with a sweet flavour, typically used in Chinese cuisine

holy basil: a bright green herb similar in appearance to basil, with a sharp, peppery flavour

Ibérico ham: a type of cured ham produced in Portugal and Spain

ichiban dashi: a broth made with dried bonito flakes and dried kelp

icing: *see* frosting

Iranian sumac: a fragrant red spice with a tangy citrus flavour

Irish butter: a soft, rich butter made from the milk of Irish grass-fed cows

Italian parsley: a bright green flat-leaf parsley with a mild flavour

jam: *see* jelly

jamón: the Spanish word for ham

julienne: to slice food (usually vegetables) into long, very thin strips

jus: a thin, flavoursome sauce made from meat juices

kecap manis: Indonesian sweet soy sauce

kerisik: fried coconut paste typically used in Malaysian and Singaporean cuisine

khoa / mawa: a dairy product made from milk thickened by heating or drying whole milk

kokotxas: the flesh under a fish's jaw

konbu: kelp

Korean chilli powder: a smoky, sweet chilli powder with a moderate-high heat

Korean fish sauce: a type of fish sauce made from fermented anchovies or sand lance or salted shrimp

Koroneiki olive oil: a robust olive oil from Greece

kosher salt: coarse salt free of common additives such as iodine

La Viette butter: sweet butter produced in France

ladyfingers: sweet sponge shaped into long, slim pieces

laminate: to layer dough, separated by butter

lap cheong: Chinese sausage

lard: the fat from a pig

lardo: a type of salami made with rosemary and other herbs

lardons: a chunk of fatty bacon or pork used to lard meat (thread with a needle into meat that is to be braised or roasted) or to flavour savoury foods

lingot beans: white oval beans often used in French cuisine

lollies: *see* candy

macerate: to soften by soaking in liquid

magatello: a cut of meat from the bovine thigh

makrut: kaffir lime

Maldon salt: a sea salt from the UK featuring soft sea salt flakes with a crunch

mam ruoc: a Vietnamese fermented shrimp paste

mange tout: *see* snow pea

Marie biscuits: a round brown cookie/biscuit of plain flavour

mash: the act of reducing food to a uniform mash by crushing it

Medjool date: a sweet, succulent variety of date from Morocco

Meyer lemon: a hybrid citrus fruit from China, similar to both mandarin and lemon

minced beef: *see* ground beef

mirin: a tangy, sweet rice wine typically used in Japanese cuisine

mixed spice: a spice mix typically consisting of ground nutmeg, cloves, ginger, cinnamon, and allspice

morcilla: *see* blood sausage

mortadella: a thick Italian pork sausage

Morteau sausage: a dense smoked sausage with a strong smoky flavour

mushrooms;

    champignons: an edible mushroom

    chanterelles: the common name of a group of popular edible fungi

    chestnut mushroom: a small edible fungus, white or brown in colour

    enoki mushroom: a long, thin white mushroom with a delicate mild flavour

    girolle: a chanterelle mushroom

    morel: an elongated edible fungi with a honeycomb appearance

    nameko mushroom: a small, golden brown mushroom, typically used in miso soup

    porcini: a rounded mushroom with a nutty flavour

    shiitake: a common type of mushroom with a thick texture and an earthy flavour

nam phrik: a hot, spicy chilli-based sauce, typically used in Thai cuisine

navy beans: a small, dry white bean

nori: edible seaweed

olives;

    Kalamata: a large brown or black olive with a smooth, thick texture

    Moroccan: a green olive from Morocco

    Niçoise: a dark brown olive with a deep, savoury flavour

pancetta: an Italian cured bacon made from pork belly meat

pandan leaf: a leaf used to add aroma to drinks, desserts, and savoury dishes

pasta: a staple food of Italian cuisine;

    cannelloni: a cylindrical pasta typically served with a filling and baked in the oven

    chitarra: a type of pasta similar to spaghetti

    corzetti: circular, flat pieces of pasta

    fettuccine: a long, flat, thick type of pasta

    lasagne: a wide, flat type of pasta usually layered with meat and cheese

    linguine fine: fine linguine, slender ribbons of pasta

    pappardelle: wide, flat strips of pasta

    ravioli: envelopes of pasta filled with minced / ground meat or vegetables

    rotolo: a type of pasta rolled into small wheels with filling

    spaghetti: a staple of Italian cuisine in the form of long, thin, rounded ribbons

    stortini bucati: small, thin curved pieces of pasta

    tagliatelle: a traditional pasta in long, flat ribbons

pasty: *see* turnover / hand pie

pâte à croissant: croissant dough

pâte brisée: pie / tart pastry

pâton: softened base dough that has been combined with butter

peanut: a small nut with a dimpled large shell

pepitoria: a Spanish powder made from grinding roast squash seeds

pepper / bell pepper;
  choricero pepper: a dried smoky pepper with a slight spice
  Espelette pepper: a smoky pepper with a subtle heat produced in the Basque country of Southern France
  ñora pepper: a round dried pepper from Spain
  Padrón pepper: a small pepper, usually green, with a sweet, earthy flavour
  piment d'espelette: Espelette pepper, a small variety of pepper / bell pepper
  pimiento picante: a spicy pepper / bell pepper

Pernod / pastis: a French spirit with an aniseed flavour

phyllo pastry: a thin, light, and flaky pastry

picada: a Spanish sauce used in cooking, typically made of crushed almonds, bread, and liquid

pickled jalapeño: jalapeño that has been preserved in vinegar or brine

pickled plums: plums preserved in vinegar or brine

pinhead oatmeal: whole oats that have been chopped into multiple pinhead-sized pieces

plum tomato: a large Italian tomato shaped like a plum, often bred for purée / paste

pointage: the first proof of a dough

ponzu: a tart, citrus-based brown sauce with a thin consistency

porcini powder: a light brown powder made from dried, ground porcini

poussin: a chicken less than twenty-eight days old

potato;
  Agria: a common type of potato high in starch and low in water content
  Belle de Fontenay: a long, yellow-skinned type of potato
  Charlotte: a popular salad variety of potato with yellow skin and an oval shape
  Chippies Choice potatoes: a medium-sized specialist type of potato from the UK
  Desiree: a round, red-skinned potato with a creamy-tasting yellow flesh
  fingerling: a small potato with a yellow, pink, or blue skin
  Golden Wonder: a large potato with yellow-brown skin and a floury, dry texture
  Kerr's Pinks: a round potato with pink-brown skin produced in the UK
  King Edward: a small potato from the UK with yellow-pink skin
  Kipfler: an elongated potato with yellow skin and flesh originating from Germany
  Maris Piper: a common potato grown in the UK, with an oval shape
  royal blue: oval potatoes with purple skin and yellow flesh
  russet: a large, dark-skinned potato with dry, white flesh
  Yukon Gold: a large, smooth-skinned potato with yellow flesh

prawns: *see* shrimp

prosciutto: a thin, salty dry-cured Italian ham

prove / proving: to rise dough before baking; also called proof / proofing

Provençal herbs: a mixture of dried herbs considered typical to France's Provence region, usually consisting of thyme, rosemary, mint, marjoram, sage, fennel seeds, summer savoury, and lavender

pumpkin: *see* butternut squash

pumpkin pie spice: an American spice mix typically consisting of ground nutmeg, cloves, ginger, cinnamon, and allspice

purslane: an edible succulent with small green leaves, used in cooking or as a garnish

quark: a fresh dairy product made from soured milk that is curdled then strained

quenelle: an ingredient or mixture of ingredients served in a smooth oval shape

ragú: an Italian meat-based sauce typically served with pasta

rapeseed oil: a plant-based oil extracted from the seeds of the rapeseed plant

rashers: *see* slices

red Asian shallot: a small, plump shallot with red-pink skin

rice;
  Arborio rice: a short-grain Italian rice, typically used in risotto
  Callasparra rice: a short-grain rice used to make paella
  Carnoroli rice: a medium-grain rice used as an alternative to arborio rice when making risotto
  basmati rice: a long-grain aromatic rice
  Japanese rice: short, translucent grains of white rice
  jasmine rice: a fragrant long-grain white rice
  paella rice: a short, rounded Spanish rice that absorbs flavour easily

rice stick noodles: a delicate noodle made with rice flour in very thin, long pieces

rice wine vinegar: a mild-flavoured vinegar with a less acidic flavour than white distilled vinegar

roasted shrimp paste: a salty condiment made from ground shrimps which have been fermented in the sun, and roasted in the oven wrapped in foil

rocket: *see* arugula

Roma tomato: a mild-tasting plum tomato, often bred for purée / paste

romaine lettuce: a variety of lettuce with tall, firm leaves that feature a hard central rib

rouille: a French sauce made from garlic, chilli, breadcrumbs, and other ingredients, typically used in a bouillabaisse

roux: a mixture of fat (usually butter) and flour used to thicken soups and sauces

runner bean: *see* green bean

rutabaga / yellow turnip: a large, yellow round root vegetable similar to the turnip

sabayon: an Italian dessert featuring a light, whipped custard

sack: fortified white Spanish wine

saikyo miso: sweet white miso

sake: a Japanese rice wine

salo: a type of underskin pig fat

saltpetre: another form of potassium nitrate (salt), often used as a thickening agent in stews and soups

sambal oelek paste: a hot, sweet red paste traditionally used in Malaysian and Thai cuisines

Savora mustard: a deep yellow, aromatic French mustard with a vibrant flavour

scone: *see* biscuit

shallot: a type of onion smaller in size than a regular onion

Shaoxing rice wine: a traditional Chinese rice wine

sherbet: a frozen dessert containing dairy

sherbet / sorbet stabilizer: a powder that reduces the size of the ice crystals in sherbet, improving its creamy texture

sherry: *see* sack

shredded coconut: dried coconut that has been shredded into tiny pieces

shrimp: a small, juicy shellfish often served with its tail attached

silicone paper: parchment / baking paper coated with silicone to give a non-stick effect

slivered almonds: almonds that have been sliced into narrow pieces

snow pea: a type of pea eaten in its pod while young

socarrat: the crust that forms on the bottom of a paella pan while cooking

sofrito: fried onion and garlic, often mixed with tomato and other vegetables, used as a stew or soup base in Spanish and Italian cuisine

sorbet: *see* sherbet

soy: *see* soya

soya: a protein derived from the soybean, an Asian species of legume

Spanish Fino sherry: the driest variety of traditional sack / sherry (*see* sack)

Spanish onion: a round onion with papery yellow-brown skin, common in the United States

spatchcock: poultry that has been split open and grilled

speck: cured, smoked Italian pork

spring onion: *see* green onion

sriracha: a spicy red sauce made with garlic and red chilli

stock cube: *see* bouillion cube

stovetop: *see* hob / range

string bean: a long, narrow green bean

suet: a hard, raw fat of mutton or beef from the area around the kidneys or loins

sugar:
- caster sugar: *see* superfine sugar
- dark coconut sugar: a subtly sweet dark palm sugar similar in flavour to brown sugar
- Demerara sugar: a light-brown cane sugar
- granulated sugar: standard white sugar
- icing sugar: *see* powdered sugar
- maltose: a sugar produced by the breakdown of starch
- muscovado sugar: a dark brown unrefined sugar with a high molasses content
- palm sugar: a sweetener derived from the sap of palm trees
- powdered sugar: a fine white sugar with a powdery consistency, typically used to make frosting
- superfine sugar: fine granulated white sugar
- unpolished sugar: unrefined sugar; sugar that has not been processed
- yellow rock sugar: lumps of yellow crystallized sugar made from unprocessed cane sugar

sultanas: *see* golden raisins

sumac: a red-brown spice with a tangy flavour

swede: *see* rutabaga / yellow turnip

Szechuan peppercorn: an aromatic peppercorn with citrus notes

tahini: a condiment made from toasted ground hulled sesame and cooking oil

tamari: a soy sauce with a thicker consistency than regular soy sauce, usually gluten-free

tamarind concentrate: a thick, dark paste with a sweet flavour, made from the tamarind fruit

Tarbais bean: a plump, white bean similar in texture and appearance to the cannellini bean

tare: a concentrated liquid typically used in Japanese dishes such as ramen

tataki: a Japanese method of preparing meat or fish whereby the product is either pounded into pieces and served with garnishes, or seared, marinated in vinegar, then thinly sliced and seasoned with ginger that has been pounded into a paste

Thai fish sauce: an amber-coloured fish sauce with a strong, salty flavour

Thai shallot: small red-skinned onion with a sharp, zesty flavour

Thai shrimp paste: a brown paste made from fresh shrimp and salt, darker in colour than Vietnamese paste

tomatillo: a small, green fruit from Mexico with a tart flavour

tomato passata: uncooked purée sieved to remove seeds and skin

tomato paste: a rich, thick paste made from cooked tomato

tomato purée: a thick, condensed purée

Toulouse sausage: a deep red French pork sausage, typically used to make cassoulet

treacle: a sticky, thick golden-brown syrup made from partially refined sugar

turnover / hand pie: a pastry with filling in a semicircular shape, that is crimped on the curve

upland cress: an edible green plant with a peppery flavour, often used in salads and sandwiches or as a garnish

usukuchi: a light soy sauce with a salty flavour

velouté: a white sauce made from a roux of flour and butter with veal, chicken, or pork stock

vermicelli noodles: a long, thin, rounded rice noodle

Vietnamese mint: a herb with pointed leaves and a spicy, peppery flavour

wasabi: a strong-smelling, bright green paste with a hot, sharp flavour

waxed paper: moisture-proof paper

whey: the liquid remaining after milk has been curdled then strained

white soy sauce: a pale, mild-tasting soy sauce brewed with added wheat

wide rice noodles: broad noodles made from rice flour

zucchini: a versatile dark green summer squash with a mild flavour

Kitchen Equipment

All of the kitchen equipment listed here is used throughout *The Recipe*. Most home kitchens will have the necessary items required for the majority of recipes in this book, but read each recipe before you begin, to find out if you need any additional equipment.

aluminium foil: *see* tinfoil
bain-marie: *see* double boiler
baking pan: an open metal container used for baking doughs, cakes and more
baking paper: *see* parchment paper
baking tin: *see* baking pan
baking tray: *see* cookie sheet
barbecue: a cooking method that cooks food using heat from below, typically fuelled by charcoal or gas
bench: *see* counter
blender: *see* liquidizer
blini pancake pan: a small pan approximately 4½ in (12 cm) in diameter made for cooking blini (Russian pancakes made from buckwheat flour or wheat)
blow torch: *see* chef's torch
brioche mould: a round, fluted mould with a wide top specifically designed for making brioche
braai: *see* barbecue
brandy snap roller: a long, narrow cylindrical instrument used to roll flat brandy snap mixture into a cigar shape
broil: *see* barbecue; also, to grill food under heat in an oven
brûlée dish: an oval ovensafe dish with a flat surface, used to make crème brûlée
bundt cake tin / pan: a baking tin / pan of a circular shape with a cylindrical hole in the centre, often featuring grooved sides
butcher's string: *see* butcher's twine
butcher's twine: a type of cotton string typically used for trussing meats and poultry
butchery scissors: *see* kitchen scissors
cake rack: a raised wire rack used for cooling baking
cake tin: a baking pan / baking tin
canelé mould: a round, fluted mould used to make canelés, traditionally made of copper
cartouche: a round piece of greaseproof paper / wax paper to cover sauces, stews, and soups to reduce evaporation
casserole dish: *see* casserole pan
casserole pan: a large, deep, heavy ovenproof dish in which food is cooked and served
cheesecloth: *see* muslin
chef's torch: a portable tool used to apply flame and heat to specific ingredients, such as crème brûlée
chinois: a cone-shaped sieve for straining sauces
cling film: thin plastic film used to cover food to keep it fresh
cocotte: a small, round heatproof dish in which food is cooked and served
colander: a round utensil featuring multiple holes, used for rinsing vegetables or draining food such as pasta

conical strainer: similar to a chinois, but with larger holes
cookie sheet: a metal tray on which food is cooked in an oven
counter: a flat surface, typically in a kitchen, on which to prepare food
cream gun: *see* foam gun
crock-pot: *see* slow cooker
dariole mould: small stainless steel moulds used to make desserts such as crème caramel
Dutch oven: a large, deep, heavy ovenproof dish in which food is cooked and served, made of cast-iron and coated with enamel
double boiler: a pan containing hot water in which food placed in smaller cooking containers is cooked
dough hook: a stand mixer attachment typically shaped like a hook or corkscrew
drum sieve: a cylindrical kitchen utensil used for straining, grating, or sieving
electric beater: *see* hand blender
fish scaler: a utensil designed to easily remove the scales from a fish
flame diffuser: *see* heat diffuser
flan tin with a removable base: a non-stick fluted tin with a removable base, to make serving flan simpler
foam gun: a utensil used to turn foods into foam
food processor: an electric appliance used to blend, mix, chop, and purée foods
frying pan: *see* skillet
funnel: a narrow tube with a wide top, used to pour liquid into a small opening
greaseproof paper: *see* wax paper / waxed paper
griddle pan: a heavy pan with a flat, ribbed base
grill: *see* barbecue; also, to grill food under a heat in an oven
hand blender: an appliance with removable whisk-like attachments used to beat, mix, knead, and whip foods
heat diffuser: a flat, circular tool placed over stovetop elements to control the flame and distribute heat evenly
ice cream machine: *see* ice cream maker
ice cream maker: an electric appliance used to make small amounts of ice cream at home
immersion blender: a handheld electric vertical blender used to blend smoothies, soups and more; *see also* Mouli
iSi Whip: *see* foam gun
Japanese mandolin: *see* mandolin
Kenwood: *see* stand mixer
KitchenAid: *see* stand mixer
kitchen paper: an absorbent disposable towel made from tissue paper
kitchen scissors: a special pair of cooking scissors designed for cutting meat, poultry, fish, and bone
kitchen spatula: *see* palette knife
kitchen tongs: a metal utensil with two movable arms joined at one end, used to lift, toss, and serve foods
kitchen towel: a small rectangular cloth used to dry dishes
kitchen tweezers: slim metal tweezers used to debone fish and plate food
kitchen twine: *see* butcher's twine
Le Creuset / enamel cast-iron casserole dish: *see* Dutch oven
liquidizer: an electric machine for liquidizing, puréeing, and blending food, predominantly used for liquids
loaf tin: a rectangular tin with high sides used for baking breads, loafs, and cakes

madeleine mould: a shallow, ribbed mould shaped like a shell, designed for making madeleines

mandolin: a utensil with multiple attachments used to cut juliennes and slice vegetables

meat bat: *see* meat mallet

meat mallet: a handheld tool similar in shape to a hammer, used to tenderize slabs of meat ahead of cooking

meat thermometer: a cooking thermometer with a skewer-like point, used to measure the internal temperature of meat

melon baller: a spoon-shaped utensil used to cut circular portions of flesh from fruit

metal skewers: stainless steel skewers primarily used to stack foods or check that baked goods are adequately cooked

microplane: a long utensil shaped like a rasp, used to grate and zest food

microwave oven: a small electric benchtop oven used to cook food quickly

mortar and pestle: an ancient utensil set consisting of a hard bowl (mortar) and blunt tool with a rounded end (pestle) used to grind and crush ingredients into powders and pastes

Mouli: a kitchen utensil used for puréeing or grinding food

muffin pan: a rectangular tray typically containing 12 small circular moulds in which muffins and cupcakes are baked

muffin tray: *see* muffin pan

muslin: finely woven cotton material that is used to filter consommés and stocks and strain cheeses and jellies.

oven thermometer: a cooking thermometer with a dial that is used to measure an oven's internal temperature

ovenproof pan: a metal tray with raised sides used for baking foods in an oven

ovenproof tray: *see* ovenproof pan

Paco jet: an appliance that micro-purées frozen foods into fine consistencies such as a mousse or sauce, without thawing the food

paddle attachment: a rounded triangle attachment for a stand mixer, typically the default attachment for most mixers

paella pan: a wide, deep pan with handles and a lid, traditionally used to cook paella

palette knife: also known as a kitchen spatula, palette knives feature a long, rounded, flexible blade and are typically used for spreading substances onto flat items, such as frosting onto a cake, or lifting baked goods

paper towel: *see* kitchen paper

parchment paper: disposable non-stick paper used in baking

pasta machine: a hand-cranked or electric machine used to roll out and cut pasta dough

pastry brush: a utensil, shaped like a small paint brush, used to spread glaze, oil, and butter on foods

pastry wheel: a handheld utensil with a sharp-edged wheel used to mark and cut dough

pie dish: a pan / tin in which the filling and dough of a pie is shaped and cooked

piping bag and nozzles: a cone-shaped cloth, paper, or plastic bag with a small opening at the bottom. Nozzles of varying diameters and shapes are affixed to the opening. The bag is then used to pipe semi-soft foods onto other items, such as frosting onto a cupcake

pizza peel: a wide, flat metal utensil used to transfer pizza from its cooking tray to a different surface

pizza stone: a circular stone slab placed in the oven and used to cook pizza and breads

plastic wrap: *see* cling film

ricer: a metal utensil with small holes used to turn soft foods such as boiled potatoes into rice-sized pieces

ring cutter: *see* ring mould

ring mould: a stainless steel ring with an adjustable diameter, used to shape cakes and more

rolling pin: a cylindrical tool with small handles used to roll out dough, pastry and more

Saran wrap: *see* cling film

sieve: a utensil with mesh through which food is passed to separate coarse foods from fine foods

silicone mat: a non-stick silicone baking mat used to line baking trays or pans as an alternative to paper

Silpat sheet: *see* silicone mat

siphon: *see* foam gun

skillet: flat-bottomed pan used to fry and sear foods

slow cooker: an electrical benchtop / countertop / worktop appliance used to slow cook food

soufflé dish: a small, round dish used to bake soufflés

sous vide: a method of preserving food by partial cooking, then vacuum sealing and chilling

speed peeler: a wide-handled peeler designed to accelerate the peeling process with minimal wastage. It can also be used to shave hard foods such as cheese and chocolate

spice grinder: an electric utensil used to grind dried spices into coarse flakes or a fine powder

spider: *see* wire skimmer

springform tin: a cake tin / baking tin with removable sides

stand mixer: a stationary mixer used to beat, mix, knead, and whip various foods

steamer: type of double-layered pot, where the first layer contains small holes, used for steaming food

steamer basket: a round double-layered bamboo basket, where the first layer contains slits, used for steaming food

steel or knife sharpener: a steel rod with a flat or round cross-section, used for sharpening knife blades

step palette knife: similar to the palette knife, with the addition of a step in it to allow easier movement and decoration, also called an offset spatula

stick blender: *see* immersion blender

stock pot: a large, tall pot, typically with handles, used to make stocks, broths and more

sugar thermometer: a cooking thermometer larger than a meat thermometer, used to measure the temperature of a cooking sugar solution or hot oil

tamis sieve: *see* drum sieve

tart tin: a round shallow, fluted tin used for baking tarts, flans, quiches, and more

tawa: a flat, heavy-based frying pan/skillet made from metal

tea towel: *see* kitchen towel

tinfoil: thin flexible sheets of aluminium used for wrapping and covering food

vacuum packing / sealing: a method of food packaging that removes air from the package before sealing

wax paper / waxed paper: thin, water-resistant paper used in cooking and to wrap food

wire skimmer: a utensil used to retrieve food from pans and pots of hot liquid or skim foam from the surface of a broth

wok: a large round-bottomed pan with deep sides, originating from China

Yorkshire pudding pan / tray: a tray, typically containing 4 circular moulds, used for baking Yorkshire puddings

Index

Recipe names are denoted in bold; main ingredients are denoted in grey, with corresponding recipes listed underneath.

Contributor Index

Contributing chefs and cooks are listed alphabetically by surname, along with their relevant contact details.

Bread with Tomato (Pan con Tomate) from *Barrafina* by Nieves Barragán Mohacho (Penguin Books, 2011). | St George's Mushrooms, Garlic & Parsley on Sourdough Toast from *Tom Kerridge's Proper Pub Food* by Tom Kerridge (Bloomsbury Publishing Plc, 2013). | Roasted Vegetables, Catalan-style (Escalivada Catalana) from *Tapas: A Taste of Spain in America* by José Andrés (Clarkson Potter Publishers, an imprint of the Crown Publishing Group, a division of Penguin Random House LLC, 2005). All rights reserved; and (Clarkson Potter Publishers, an imprint of the Crown Publishing Group, a division of Penguin Random House LLC, and ICM Partners 2005). All rights reserved. | Caponata from *The Agrarian Kitchen* by Rodney Dunn (Penguin Books Australia, Penguin Random House Australia Pty Ltd, 2013). | Colcannon © Darina Allen, Ballymaloe Cookery School | Potato Puffs (Pommes Dauphine) from *Scook – The Complete Cookery Guide* by Anne-Sophie Pic (Jacqui Small, Quarto Group, 2013); and (Hachette Pratique, 2013).

SEAFOOD – SHELLFISH: Mussels in White Wine (Moules Marinière) from *Fish & Shellfish* by Rick Stein (BBC Books, The Random House Group Ltd, 2014). | Scallop & Tomato Ceviche (Ceviche de Conchas y Tomates) from *LIMA The Cookbook* by Virgilio Martínez (Octopus Publishing Group Limited, a Hachette Livre UK Company, 2013). All rights reserved. | Pan-fried Squid with Broad Beans & Chorizo from *The Agrarian Kitchen* by Rodney Dunn (Penguin Books Australia, Penguin Random House Australia Pty Ltd, 2013). | Octopus Fairground-style (Pulpo a la Feria) from *Fish & Shellfish* by Rick Stein (BBC Books, The Random House Group Ltd, 2014). | Lobster Thermidor from *Great British Feast* by Marco Pierre White (Orion Books, an imprint of Orion Publishing Group Ltd, a Hachette Livre UK Company, 2008). All rights reserved. **FISH:** Tuna Tataki Salad from *Everyday Harumi: Simple Japanese Food for Family & Friends* by Harumi Kurihara (Octopus Publishing Group Limited, a Hachette Livre UK Company, 2009). All rights reserved. | Fish Congee from *The Songs of Sapa: Stories and Recipes from Vietnam* by Luke Nguyen (Murdoch Books, 2009). All rights reserved. | Pacific-Island-style Cured Fish from *Monica's Kitchen* by Monica Galetti (Quadrille Publishing Ltd, 2012). | Confit of Ocean Trout with Fennel Salad from *Tetsuya* by Tetsuya Wakuda (Harper Collins, 2000). | Black Cod with Miso from *Nobu: The Cookbook* by Nobuyuki Matsuhisa (Quadrille Publishing Ltd, 2001). | Steamed Whole Fish with Ginger, Scallions & Soy from *Vietnamese Home Cooking* by Charles Phan (Ten Speed Press, an imprint of the Crown Publishing Group, a division of Penguin Random House LLC, 2012). All rights reserved. | Basque Fish Stew (Marmitako) from *SABOR* by Nieves Barragán Mohacho (Penguin Books, 2017). | Spanish Mackerel with Artichokes & Prunes from *Four Kitchens* by Colin Fassnidge (Ebury Press, published by Random House, 2014). All rights reserved.

POULTRY: Chicken in Wine (Coq au Vin) from *CUT* by Josh Emett (Random House NZ, The Random House Group Ltd, 2013). | Fried Chicken & Gravy from *Heritage* by Sean Brock (Artisan, a division of Workman Publishing Co., Inc., New York, 2014). All rights reserved. | Fried Baby Chicken with Kimchi Mayonnaise, and Spicy Salt from *Mr Hong* by Dan Hong and Melissa Leong (Murdoch Books, an imprint of

Allen & Unwin, 2014). | Roast Grouse with Game Chips & Bread Sauce from *Tom Kitchin's Meat & Game* by Tom Kitchin (Bloomsbury Publishing Plc, 2017). | Rosemary Roast Chicken with Baked Fennel and Potatoes from *New Classics* by Marcus Wareing (Harper Collins Publishers, 2017). | Perfect Roast Turkey, and Giblet Stock from *The Martha Stewart Living Christmas Cookbook* by Martha Stewart (Martha Stewart Living Omimedia, 2003).

MEAT & OFFAL – MEAT: Ham Croquettes (Jamón Croquetas) from *Seasonal Spanish Food* by José Pizarro (Kyle Books, an imprint of Kyle Cathie Ltd, 2010). | Game Terrine Glazed in Port Jelly with Cranberry Compote from *Tom Kerridge's Proper Pub Food* by Tom Kerridge (Bloomsbury Publishing Plc, 2013). | Pork Rillettes (Rillettes de Cochon) from *French Feasts* by Stéphane Reynaud (Marabout Publishing, an imprint of Hachette Livre, 2012); and (Murdoch Books, an imprint of Allen & Unwin, 2008). | Pot-au-feu with Sharp Horseradish Cream from *Scook – The Complete Cookery Guide* by Anne-Sophie Pic (Jacqui Small, Quarto Group, 2013); and (Hachette Pratique, 2013). | Beef Carpaccio with Caponata from *The Agrarian Kitchen* by Rodney Dunn (Penguin Books Australia, Penguin Random House Australia Pty Ltd, 2013). | Perak Beef Rendang from *Amazing Malaysian* (Square Peg, The Random House Group Ltd, 2016). | Beef Tartare Bistro-style (Tartare de Boeuf Bistrot) from *French Feasts* by Stéphane Reynaud (Marabout Publishing, an imprint of Hachette Livre, 2012); and (Murdoch Books, an imprint of Allen & Unwin, 2008). | Steak & Kidney Pudding from *Nathan Outlaw's Home Kitchen* by Nathan Outlaw (Quadrille Publishing Limited, 2017). | Lancashire Hotpot from *Great British Feast* by Marco Pierre White (Orion Books, an imprint of Orion Publishing Group Ltd, a Hachette Livre UK Company, 2008). All rights reserved; copyright © Marco Pierre White, 2008. | Beef Burgundy (Boeuf Bourguignon) © Diane Holuigue of The French Cooking School, Melbourne. | Veal Shoulder Goulash from *Braise* by Daniel Boulud and Melissa Clark (Harper Collins Publishers, 2006). | Veal with Prosciutto & Sage, Roman-style (Veal Saltimbocca alla Romana) from *Inside the Test Kitchen: 120 New Recipes, Perfected* by Tyler Florence (Clarkson Potter Publishers, an imprint of the Crown Publishing Group, a division of Penguin Random House LLC, 2014). All rights reserved. | Honey Glazed Ham from *Christmas with Gordon* by Gordon Ramsay (Quadrille Publishing Ltd, 2010). | Roasted Pork Belly with Homemade Apple Sauce from *Good Food, Good Life: 130 Recipes You'll Love to Make and Eat* by Curtis Stone (Ballantine Books, an imprint of Random House, a division of Penguin Random House LLC, 2015). All rights reserved; and (Penguin Books Australia, Penguin Random House Australia Pty Ltd, 2015). | Slow-braised Pig Cheek with Celeriac Cream & Mushrooms, and Reduced Veal Stock from *QUAY: Food Inspired by Nature* by Peter Gilmore (Murdoch Books, an imprint of Allen & Unwin, 2010). | Roasted Rib of Beef with Yorkshire Puddings & Horseradish Cream from *Kitchin Suppers* by Tom Kitchin (Quadrille Publishing Ltd, 2012). | Corned Beef & Pickled Tongue from *River Cottage Meat Book* by Hugh Fearnley-Whittingstall (Hodder and Stoughton Limited, 2004, 2007). **OFFAL:** Bone Marrow with Sea Urchin & Purslane from *Finding Fire* by Lennox Hastie (Hardie Grant Books, 2018). | Chicken Livers with Capers,

Parsley & Guanciale from *The Mozza Cookbook: Recipes from Los Angeles's Favorite Italian Restaurant and Pizzeria* by Nancy Silverton (Alfred A. Knopf, an imprint of the Knopf Doubleday Publishing Group, a division of Penguin Random House LLC, 2011). All rights reserved. | Devilled Kidneys from *New British Classics* by Gary Rhodes (BBC Books, The Random House Group Ltd, 1999). | Crumbed Tripe (Tablier de Sapeur) from *Book of Tripe* by Stéphane Reynaud (Marabout Publishing, an imprint of Hachette Livre, 2012); and (Murdoch Books, an imprint of Allen & Unwin, 2014). | Tante Claire Stuffed Pig's Trotter (Pied de Cochon Tante Claire) from *Classic Koffmann – 50 Years a Chef* by Pierre Koffmann (Jacqui Small, part of The Quarto Group, 2016).

BAKING – SAVOURY: Tomato Tart with Goat's Cheese (Tarte Fine à la Tomate, Fromage de Chèvre) from *Classic Koffmann – 50 Years a Chef* by Pierre Koffmann (Jacqui Small, part of The Quarto Group, 2016). | Pizza Pomodoro from *Gjelina: Cooking from Venice, California* by Travis Lett (Chronicle Books LLC, 2015). All rights reserved. SWEET: Almond Biscotti from *BAKING: From My Home to Yours* by Dorie Greenspan (Houghton Mifflin Harcourt Publishing Company, 2006). All rights reserved. | Mogador Macaron from *Pierre Hermé Macarons* by Pierre Hermé (Grub Street, 2011). | King Cake (Galette des Rois) from *My Little French Kitchen* by Rachel Khoo (Penguin Group, 2013). All rights reserved. | Portuguese Custard Tarts (Pastéis de Nata) from *My Lisbon: A Cookbook from Portugal's City of Light* by Nuno Mendes (Ten Speed Press, an imprint of the Crown Publishing Group, a division of Penguin Random House LLC, 2018). All rights reserved. | Dominique's Kouign Amann (DKAs) excerpted from *Dominique Ansel: The Secret Recipes* by Dominique Ansel (Simon & Schuster, 2014). | Traditional Christmas Cake adapted from *The Complete Asian Cookbook* by Charmaine Solomon (Hardie Grant Books, 2011). | Tall & Creamy Cheesecake from *BAKING: From My Home to Yours* by Dorie Greenspan (Houghton Mifflin Harcourt Publishing Company, 2006). All rights reserved. | Banoffee Pie from *Relaxed Cooking with Curtis Stone: Recipes to Put You in My Favorite Mood* by Curtis Stone (Clarkson Potter Publishers, an imprint of the Crown Publishing Group, a division of Penguin Random House LLC, 2009). All rights reserved; and (Ebury Press, Random House Australia Pty Ltd, 2009). | Quintessential Apple Pie from *Art of the Pie: A Practical Guide to Homemade Crusts, Fillings, and Life* by Kate McDermott and Andrew Scrivani (W. W. Norton & Company, Inc., 2016).

DESSERTS & SWEETS: Chocolate Mousse from *Scook – The Complete Cookery Guide* by Anne-Sophie Pic (Jacqui Small, Quarto Group, 2013); and (Hachette Pratique, 2013). | Chocolate & Orange Soufflé from *Mange Tout* by Bruno Loubet (Ebury Press, a division of The Random House Group Ltd, 2013). | Peach Melba from *Maggie's Recipe for Life* by Maggie Beer with Professor Ralph Martins (Simon & Schuster Australia, 2017). | Sherry Trifle from *Nathan Outlaw's Home Kitchen* by Nathan Outlaw (Quadrille Publishing Limited, 2017). | Traditional Tiramisu from *Rustic Italian Food* by Marc Vetri (Ten Speed Press, an imprint of the Crown Publishing Group, a division of Penguin Random House LLC, 2011). All rights reserved. | Italian Meringue from *Michael Caines at Home* by Michael Caines (Preface Publishing, The Random House Group Ltd, 2013). | Pavlova with Strawberries & Rhubarb from *Good Food, Good Life: 130 Recipes You'll Love to Make and Eat* by Curtis Stone (Ballantine Books, an imprint of Random House, a division of Penguin Random House LLC, 2015). All rights reserved; and (Penguin Books Australia, Penguin Random House Australia Pty Ltd, 2015). | Crumble with Poached Rhubarb from *Four Kitchens* by Colin Fassnidge (Ebury Press, published by Random House, 2014). All rights reserved. | Plum Clafoutis from *New Classics* by Marcus Wareing (Harper Collins Publishers, 2017). | Sticky Toffee Pudding from *Perfect* by Felicity Cloake (Penguin Books, 2011). | Bread & Butter Pudding from *Ultimate Cookery Course* by Gordon Ramsay (Hodder and Stoughton Limited, 2012). | Chocolate Profiteroles © Diane Holuigue of The French Cooking School, Melbourne. | Caramelized Pineapple Crêpes with Crème Fraîche excerpted from *A Return to Cooking* by Eric Ripert (Artisan, a division of Workman Publishing Co., Inc., New York, 2002). All rights reserved. | Crêpes Suzette from *Essential Pépin* by Jacques Pépin (Houghton Mifflin Harcourt Publishing Company, 2011). All rights reserved.

BASICS – SIDES & CONDIMENTS: Baba Ghanoush from *New Middle Eastern Food* by Greg & Lucy Malouf (Hardie Grant Books, 2012). | Olive Tapenade from *Marc Forgione: Recipes and Stores from the Acclaimed Chef and Restaurant* by Marc Forgione (Houghton Mifflin Harcourt Publishing Company, 2014). All rights reserved. | Chimichurri from *Ben's BBQ Bible* by Ben O'Donoghue (Hardie Grant Books, 2009). | Salsa Verde from *The Enchilada Queen Cookbook: Enchiladas, Fajitas, Tamales, and More Classic Recipes from Texas Mexico Border Kitchens* by Sylvia Casares (St. Martin's Press, 2016). All rights reserved. | Classic Skordalia with Bread from *Ikaria – Lessons on Food, Life, and Longevity from the Greek Island where People Forget to Die* by Diane Kochilas (Rodale Inc., 2014). | Caramelized Onions from *Marc Forgione: Recipes and Stores from the Acclaimed Chef and Restaurant* by Marc Forgione (Houghton Mifflin Harcourt Publishing Company, 2014). All rights reserved. | Horseradish Gremolata from *Gjelina: Cooking from Venice, California* by Travis Lett (Chronicle Books LLC, 2015). All rights reserved. | Classic Turkey Stuffing from *The Martha Stewart Living Christmas Cookbook* by Martha Stewart (Omnimedia, 2003). PICKLES & PRESERVES: Sauerkraut from *Spring* by Skye Gyngell (Quadrille Publishing Ltd, 2015). | Pickled Vegetables from *Four Kitchens* by Colin Fassnidge (Ebury Press, published by Random House, 2014). All rights reserved. | Fermented Cucumbers from *Finding Fire* by Lennox Hastie (Hardie Grant Books, 2018). | Preserved Lemons from *Mange Tout* by Bruno Loubet (Ebury Press, a division of The Random House Group Ltd, 2013). | Confit Tomatoes from *Gjelina: Cooking from Venice, California* by Travis Lett (Chronicle Books LLC, 2015). All rights reserved. SAUCES: Basic Barbecue Sauce from *Ben's BBQ Bible* by Ben O'Donoghue (Hardie Grant Books, 2009). | Peanut Sauce from *How to Cook Everything Vegetarian* by Mark Bittman (Double B Publishing, Inc., Houghton Mifflin Harcourt Publishing Company, 2017). All rights reserved. | Fermented Chilli Paste from *Finding Fire* by Lennox Hastie (Hardie Grant Books, 2018). | Pomodoro Sauce from *Gjelina: Cooking from Venice, California* by Travis Lett (Chronicle Books LLC, 2015). All rights reserved. | Butter & Sage Sauce

Acknowledgements

I'm grateful to everyone who contributed to making *The Recipe* a reality. I would especially like to thank the suppliers who generously provided many of the ingredients to enable me to recreate the dishes in this book: Kay Gray, Glenn Smith, and Damien Rakich from Bidfood bidfood.co.nz; Martin Bosley; Eastherbrook Farm yellow.co.nz/y/eastherbrook-farm; Havoc Farm Pork havocfarmpork.co.nz; Rodney Alexander and Joyce Lloyd from Manurau manurau.co.nz; William Eriksen, Tim Eriksen, and Simon Eriksen from Neat Meat neatmeat.com; Bridgette Karetai from New Zealand Game Birds nzgamebirds.co.nz; Phil Matheson from Out of the Dark Mushrooms facebook.com/outofthedarkmushrooms; and Justine Powell and Jo Cooper from Sanford Limited sanford.co.nz and Auckland Fish Market afm.co.nz. Thanks also to Felicity and Beverley from Cook the Books for providing access to their wonderful collection of recipe books, cookthebooks.co.nz.

To the team at Blackwell & Ruth: Geoff Blackwell, Ruth Hobday, Karin Reinink, Cameron Gibb, Olivia Hopkinson, and Nikki Addison; their colleagues Teresa McIntyre, Anna King Shahab, Helen Greenwood, and Jason Marshall for their wise editorial words; and photographer Kieran Scott, whose beautiful images have illuminated these dishes beyond compare, my profound thanks.

Deepest gratitude to the many friends, family, and colleagues who have helped and supported me throughout the creation of the book: Margot Kynoch; Susanna Lyles; Christie Stewart, who spent endless early mornings and late nights in my kitchen making sure everything was perfectly prepped; Nomvula Sikhakhane Venter; the Duder and Poole families (for eating most of our leftovers); and my dear family Helen Emett, Finn Emett, and Louis Emett.

Lastly, to all the chefs and cooks who entrusted me with their recipes, thank you. I hope together, we inspire home cooks now and for generations, to create and enjoy the great classic dishes of the world.

– Josh Emett

The photographer would additionally like to thank: Peter Baigent from Factory Ceramics who kindly supplied all the beautiful plates on which the recipes were plated and photographed Instagram.com/factoryceramics; Greg Bramwell, my technical go-to guru for his ever-present advice and support; my trusty and dependable photo assistant Josef Scott for his mind reading and all round super skills; Tamara West for being generally awesome in all things, as well as sourcing and compiling the ceramics; and my devoted canine sidekick Smokey for making us all smile, especially when we needed it.

– Kieran E. Scott